# Food Combining

lets your digestive system process the food you eat with maximum trouble-free benefit to you. It doesn't have to strain to handle two or more incompatible types of food at the same time—as we ask it to when we eat a hamburger, for example, with the bread and the meat digesting under different conditions and at different rates. Our national plague of digestive upsets can be traced in great part to just this unreasonable and constant demand on our systems.

Based on the pioneering food combining research of William Howard Hay, M.D., these more than 1500 recipes for dishes of every kind and sample menus for every occasion open up a new world of maximum nutrition—it's time to put aside the burgers, batter-fried chicken and pepperoni pizza and learn just how delicious healthful eating can be.

# Other Keats Titles of Related Interest

1500
Recipes and Meals...
The Food Combining Way to Eat
Better for Less Money

# EATING FOR HEALTH AND HAPPINESS

ESTHER L. SMITH

Keats Publishing, Inc.　　New Canaan, Connecticut

EATING FOR HEALTH AND HAPPINESS
(Previously published as *Good Foods that Go Together*)

Library of Congress Catalog Card Number: 75-817

Printed in the United States of America

Keats Health Books are published by
Keats Publishing, Inc.
27 Pine Street (PO Box 876)
New Canaan, Connecticut 06840

# Foreword

RECOGNIZED essentials of living are air, water, food, rest, exercise, recreation, sunshine. Except in extreme cases fresh air and sunshine are available everywhere; rest, recreation and exercise are regarded as personal problems; the water supply is protected in all organized communities. But the great question of food remains a mystery so complicated by manufacturing and advertising methods that the housewife, lost in a maze of quasi-authentic statements, is involuntarily led to buy and use denatured and devitalized products because some radio voice or printed article recommends them.

Food—real food—is that which being taken into the body, builds and nourishes it. In providing adequate food three factors are to be considered:—the specific chemical elements to provide growth, replacement and energy requirements; an abundance of essential vitamins to protect against infection and to supply the motive power for dynamic body functioning; and sufficient liquid to keep the food in correct solution for digestion, absorption and elimination processes.

Natural foods, i.e., fruits, whole grain cereals, nuts, vegetables and milk furnish all the requisite elements in wholesome form. At least 75% of all food should be selected from these direct products of nature. To build health, over-refined foods such as white sugar and bleached white flour should be kept to small amounts on special occasions; or, better still, discarded entirely along with fiery condiments, concentrated acid in the form of vinegar, the decayed protein of "ripened" cheeses and inorganic mineral salt (the usual table salt). Replace these denatured and useless items with honey, maple sugar, brown (cane) sugar, molasses, whole grain flours (whole wheat, water ground corn meal, rye), paprika or powdered vegetable leaves and herbs for flavoring, lemon or other fruit juices for tartness, cottage or fresh cream cheese, and vegetable salt.

There is a new thrill in store for those who habitually drown every food with showers of inorganic salt, when first they discover the delicacy of natural flavors. The oft-repeated charge that American cooks lack imagination and ingenuity need no longer apply, if the following suggestions are noted.

Grated lemon or orange rind lends magic to sauces, meat dishes, cooked fruits, salads and custards. The lowly ground-berry or tea-berry is the source of unusual aromatic flavor that is excellent with fruits and vegetables. Natural savories such as parsley, thyme, sage, summer savory, sweet marjoram, mace, celery leaves or mint may be added to any prepared mild vegetable, salad or soup, bringing new gastronomical joy. Coriander gives a special elegancy to dressings and fillings for fowl or vegetables. Lemon juice takes on a tantalizing vivacity when flavored with dill, bay leaves or berries of different kinds. Careful blending of these natural seasonings will change the attitude of any family toward vegetables previously condemned as insipid. Any herb may be purchased fresh and green during Spring and Summer, for the rest of the year the dried leaves or seeds give equally pleasing results.

Grated onion, radish, celery root, carrot, horseradish and other less well-known roots bring out the fine flavors of meat and vegetables. Do not overlook the possibilities of chives, garlic, leeks, sweet peppers and horseradish tops.

Raisins (or raisin syrup) and Tupelo honey combine with any type of food, adding sweetness and distinctive flavor. But to achieve the ultimate in delicacy add rose leaves, fresh violets or rose-geranium petals to custards and other desserts and sauces.

Plain omelettes and roasts assume interesting individuality when served with mushrooms, a dash of curry, truffles, capers or a sprinkling of nutmeg.

Pure spices used in moderation bring excellence of flavor to plain puddings, vegetables and protein foods.

Use butter in cubes, melted or slightly browned to develop natural flavors, keeping in mind that it is a fuel food.

In order to preserve the natural alkalinity of the body, foods that are alkaline, or base forming must predominate in the diet. The ideal proportion is 80% alkaline- to 20% acid-forming varieties. The classification as to alkaline or acid may be simplified by merely stating that animal proteins and concentrated carbohydrate foods except honey are acid forming,—all others are alkaline in ultimate effect.

It must be understood that some acid-forming elements are essential to proper functioning of the body. Active adults, as well as growing children, need carbohydrates and proteins to supply energy, growth and replacement requirements. The chief care in serving these two classes of concentrated foods so different in character, is to keep them entirely separated from each other. The digestion of proteins requires an acid condition in the stomach where this type of food is digested, while digestion of carbohydrate foods can proceed satisfactorily only in an alkaline medium. The presence of both types in the stomach at one time precludes the possibility of complete digestion of either kind. The only sensible plan then is to separate these opposite groups.

The subject of gastro-chemistry may be barely touched upon here. It will be enough to remember that the digestion of starchy food begins in the mouth where such foods are attacked by an enzyme called ptyalin in the saliva. Hence, thorough mastication of all starchy foods is advisable. Very little change takes place in this type of food while it remains in the stomach with other compatible varieties. It is passed on into the duodenum where the process of digestion is again taken up, still in an alkaline medium. To trace the digestion of proteins to this point—no change takes place except the breaking up of the fibre, through mastication; but upon protein entering the stomach, this organ secretes gastric juice containing pepsin and hydrochloric acid. Now if both protein and carbohydrates are present, it is obvious that acid attacking the starchy food will start fermentation, while the presence of the starch will interfere greatly with the protein digestion. The result is chaos—fermentation, gas.

Adherence to the laws of chemistry in choosing and grouping foods, results in following the rules for compatible combinations. Proteins include meats, all sea food, cheese, egg whites. These foods may be cooked and served with all vegetables, fats, acid fruits or gelatin. Carbohydrate foods include starches, i.e., all cereals and cereal products, potatoes, yams, sweet potatoes; all sugars and molasses, honey, Jerusalem artichokes,

# FOREWORD

pumpkins, winter-squash, sweet fruits such as dates, raisins, figs and bananas. These may be combined with fats and all vegetables.

To make compatible eating easier and life less complex, recipes are grouped with reference to correct combinations. Complete compatible menus may be selected from any of the three main sections.

Extensive study of foods with regard to their vitamin potency has shown that natural foods abound in these essential factors. Fruits, vegetables, milk, whole grains and their products,—with plenty of sunshine, these are the best sources. It will be recognized that a plan of eating which is built upon the 80-20 ratio of alkaline, or base-forming foods to concentrated or acid-forming types will supply all the necessary vitamins when a sufficient variety is included. For further information consult the vitamin chart, Section Four.

ESTHER L. SMITH

# INTRODUCTION

*T*HE making of cook books dates far back into antiquity, even as far as our literature extends, and expresses woman's desire to pass on to others the good things she has discovered in her culinary art.

There are cook books of every sort, each seeking to set out more delectable dishes than others have done.

The object has always been to formulate combinations of food ingredients that will tickle the palate and furnish entertainment for the ubiquitous guest, or to instruct the novice in the preparation of meals.

The average housewife has little knowledge of the relative value of the various foods generally employed in building a meal, but assumes that all the foods ordinarily eaten are permissible in any arrangement that appeals to the eye and the palate.

A very large part of the foods ordinarily eaten are not food in any sense of the word, as food is replenishment material for the body.

Any so-called food that does not furnish what the body requires and can use is not to be considered as food at all, and many of these are positively harmful to the body.

There are so many foods that do represent body needs that it is not necessary to introduce anything but these, yet not detract in the slightest degree from the perfection of any meal, from either the utility or the aesthetic pleasures of the table.

It is not only possible to construct dishes and menus wholly of the real foods, but easily so, without the use of any deficient foods whatever.

It is but recently that science has discovered why certain foods nourish and others do not, even though both may contain the food materials on which we have always been taught to depend.

The discovery of the vitamins has thrown a new light on feeding, and we now know that foods that do not contain these vitamins are dead foods, while those containing the vitamins are vital foods; the one does not nourish while the other does.

# INTRODUCTION

Foods are of vastly different sorts, also, as regards their digestive requirements, some being digested largely in one part of the tract, while others digest in a different part, and the body modifies the digestive juices to suit the task on hand at the time.

Two diametrically opposite types of food, as regards their digestion, are the carbohydrate foods and the proteins.

The former comprise all the starchy and sweet foods of concentrated character, such as grain foods and the more concentrated vegetable starches, as potato and winter squash, and also the sugars.

This class of foods will not digest unless first the ptyalin of the saliva splits them into dextroses, or sugars, an act begun in the mouth and continued in the stomach, IF the medium can be kept alkalin, not otherwise.

Nature provides a rather strong alkalinity of the saliva for the purpose of activating the ptyalin.

The protein group of foods comprises meats, eggs, fish and cheese, all of which are quite concentrated sources of protein, or body building material.

Now protein begins its digestion in the stomach, IF the gastric juice is sufficiently acid, and to insure this the stomach secretes a hydrochloric acid for the one purpose of activating the pepsin, or the ferment that alone is able to split the proteins into lower forms.

If the carbohydrates are split into dextroses by the ptyalin, and if the proteins are split into lower forms by the pepsin, then the whole mass enters the small intestine, where both types of digestion go on concurrently in an alkalin medium.

You will readily understand, then, that the medium must be kept alkalin for a considerable time if the ptyalin is given time to convert the starches to dextrose, at least a half to three-quarters of an hour being the time usually required for this process.

Acid fruit taken with starches or sugars will interfere with this splitting process, because it takes away the necessary alkalinity; hence, starches and sugars must be kept away from acids of all kinds.

# INTRODUCTION

Proteins require and early produce in the stomach a hydrochloric acid, to start the peptic digestion of the meats, eggs, fish, or whatever, not allowing enough time for the completion of the splitting of the starches by the ptyalin; hence, proteins of concentrated character should not be taken together with the carbohydrates—the starches and the sugars in other words.

Never before has a cook book comprised the facts necessary to completely separate these diverse foods from each other, and this separation has been made here because the author, being a chemist who understands digestive chemistry, has kept this requirement firmly in mind in compiling every dish. It is of little use to separate these incompatible foods from each other if at the same time composite dishes are eaten in which the various ingredients are not combined in accordance with this same requirement.

It is easy enough to eat your meats at one meal and your breads at another; but if your breads contain much egg, or if your meats are rolled in flour or cornstarch or starchy cracker crumbs, you have violated the very rule you are trying to follow in separating these concentrated foods of such opposite digestive requirements.

The author has been meticulous in her care to make each composite formula compatible in all its own internal chemistry, which is something new under the sun.

Delectable meals can be constructed for every day, with variety as wide as ever graced a less correct cook book, for the foods of the world are at one's disposal.

The fine art of cookery has had more to do with the degeneration of civilized nations than all other causes combined, simply because the usual cook violates every canon of digestive law.

It is not surprising that the usual type of meal generates discomfort, when one knows the chemical requirements of digestion of vastly dissimilar foods, and when these are found mixed in heterogeneous conglomeration whose ultimate would defy the most accomplished chemist.

The physical salvation of this suffering world is dependent on a better understanding of foods and how to prepare and use them.

# INTRODUCTION

Surely medical science has done about all it can to improve health conditions, yet we are as a nation growing weaker with each generation; we have the same diseases as when medicine was in its dark ages; we die from the same causes as our forefathers; the diseases of age or degeneration are constantly on the increase, and the conditions that we regard as due to the ravages of time are appearing earlier in life with each succeeding generation.

All this because we have not known how to administer the most fundamental function of eating.

When time has shown us the truth of the foregoing statement, as it must do, then the author of this work will be hailed as a pioneer. Her work will then be appreciated and correctly evaluated, whereas it will no doubt be thought imaginative by many at the present time, who do not yet realize that the body is made or unmade at the table, and that as we eat so are we.

The world is growing rapidly food-conscious; seeming to realize—after all these generations of failure to arrest the decline of the race through medical science—that therefore we must have been overlooking some material fact or facts that have kept us from realizing the place in nature that we, as the highest creation, should occupy.

If you would put this thing to the test, then live by this book, following its combinations implicitly, and making the meals largely of the natural vegetables, salads, fruits, with milk or buttermilk; and when the concentrated starches, sugars and proteins are used, then make sure that the rules of combination are respected at every meal, each taken in its proper relation.

The concentrated starches and sugars must be separated from both acids and concentrated protein, in order to maintain the alkalinity instituted by the saliva.

When the proteins are used, as meats, eggs, fish and cheese, then admit the acid fruits freely, but exclude all the concentrated starches and sugars.

If you are tired, cross, blue, pessimistic; if you have already developed disease; if you are growing prematurely old, then follow this work meticulously.

During the process of adjustment to the changes in feeding habit, you may lose weight; perhaps at first some strength also; but be assured that this is merely incident to changes in the body chemistry that are preliminary to a more normal state.

The world owes Esther L. Smith a very great debt, and here's hoping it will not long delay recognition of this obligation!

*William Howard Hay, M.D.*

## ACKNOWLEDGMENT

The author desires to express her gratitude to William Howard Hay, M.D., for his kindly guidance and candid criticism.

And to the many friends who so generously gave treasured recipes for adaptation to compatible formulae.

# HOW TO USE THIS BOOK

*T*HERE are two objectives in this book: One is to guide in the preparation of compatible foods, and the other to assist in planning compatible meals, according to the system of food combination as taught by Dr. William Howard Hay. In his system there are three types of food, classified according to their chemical requirements and reactions in the processes of digestion and assimilation.

The three types are: first, the alkaline, or base-forming foods, consisting largely of fruits and vegetables; second, the protein, or body-building foods, chiefly of animal origin, such as eggs, meat, fish and cheese; and third, the carbohydrate, or heat and energy producing foods, consisting of starches and sugars. The protein and carbohydrate types are acid-forming in their chemical reactions, but they require directly opposite conditions for their digestion, and should never be combined.

All the recipes in this book are classified according to these requirements, first in the recipes themselves; and second, in their proper placing in the planning of the meals. For example, if an alkaline meal is desired, turn to Section One, and every recipe in that section is compatible with an alkaline meal. If a protein meal is decided upon, then turn to Section Two, where all the recipes are compatible with a protein meal. The same is true of the carbohydrate type, which will be found in Section Three.

Not only are these recipes classified in their respective sections, but within the sections they are grouped in menu order, making it easy to plan any kind of meal desired. All the recipes that are compatible with any type of meal are found in their respective sections and are grouped according to their proper course in the menu. The meal may be as simple or elaborate as desired, from one, to seven or eight courses, and of unlimited variety.

The alkaline variety of foods and menus should predominate, therefore make large use of Section One. Protein meals should be limited to three or four per week. The same is true of the carbohydrate type, except in the case of young children and very active adults, who will burn up more fuel and energy than inactive persons.

The chief thing to remember, in using this book, is to confine the selection of food for any one meal to those listed in a single section. While some are listed in all three sections it is because they combine with all types.

# GENERAL CONTENTS

# SECTION ONE
# Alkaline Foods

*I*N THIS CHAPTER are grouped recipes for dishes comprised only of alkaline, or base-forming foods. Persons engaged in sedentary occupations will do well to choose at least one meal every day from this group, in addition to breakfast of milk and acid fruit, or fruit juices. Let the menus for at least one entire day each week be selected from alkaline foods.

# INDEX --- SECTION I

## BEVERAGES AND COCKTAILS

## RELISHES

## SOUPS

## FRUIT SALADS

## VEGETABLE SALADS

## SALAD DRESSINGS

# MAIN COURSE

# VEGETABLES

# SAUCES

# DESSERTS

# BEVERAGES AND COCKTAILS

## ALMOND MILK

2 tablespoonfuls almond butter          1 teaspoonful Tupelo honey

Add 1 cup hot water, a little at a time, to make a smooth mixture.

## CABBAGE COCKTAIL

2 parts juice of young green cabbage
1 part grapefruit juice

## CELERY AND LEMON COCKTAIL

1½ cups celery juice          ½ cup lemon juice

## CHILLED HONEY CHOCOLATE

2 tablespoonfuls cocoa or grated chocolate
3 tablespoonfuls Tupelo honey

1½ cups water          ½ cup cream

½ teaspoonful vanilla

Heat 1 cup water to boiling point, add cocoa and honey. Stir and cook until blended. Chill and add remaining water and cream with vanilla. Serve very cold. May be topped with whipped cream.

## CHERRY COCKTAIL

2 cups crushed, frozen lemonade          1 cup pitted black cherries
1 cup pitted white cherries

Freeze lemonade in ice-cube trays. Crush into small irregular pieces, and place in bottom of cocktail glasses. Arrange cherries on ice in geometrical patterns.

## CHERRY SQUASH

1 cup pitted sour cherries          ¼ cup Tupelo honey
1 quart water

Place in liquifier at low speed for 3 minutes, then at high speed for 1 minute.

## CITRUS COCKTAIL

2 large oranges          ½ grapefruit

Remove pulp from oranges and grapefruit in sections.  Cut into uniform dice.  Save all juice and add to pulp.  Put seeds and rind through food chopper and add to pulp and juice.  Chill.  A few drops sherry flavor may be added. If rind is exceptionally thick, use from one-half to one-fourth the amount.

## CITRUS JUICE COCKTAIL

1 cup grapefruit juice                    ½ cup orange juice
2 tablespoonfuls lemon juice
¼ cup Tupelo honey or raisin syrup

Shake all ingredients together to blend. Serve with cracked ice, garnish with red cherry or sprigs of mint.

## CITRUS-PINEAPPLE COCKTAIL

6 oranges                              1 grapefruit
2 lemons                               ¼ pint pineapple juice
                    ¼ pint water

Shake well.

## CLABBER MILK

One quart fresh whole milk.  Put in a bowl in a warm room for 24 hours; when thick, beat vigorously with an egg beater. Place on ice and serve cold. Clabber milk will keep fresh three or four days on ice.

## COCONUT BISQUE

1 quart coconut milk               1 pint raw tomato juice
Shake together; serve cold.

## COCONUT MILK (*natural*)

Puncture fresh coconut and drain off milk from center. Grate coconut. Place in glass bowl or jar and cover with cold water. Let stand three or four hours, then press through cheesecloth. Add strained liquid to natural coconut milk.

## COCONUT MILK (*prepared*)

Grate one fresh coconut very finely. Add to an equal measure of cool water. Let stand two or three hours, press through double cheesecloth or linen. The liquid from the coconut may be substituted for part of the water. Chill before serving. This may be added to any fruit or vegetable beverage.

## CUCUMBER COCKTAIL

Equal parts Cucumber juice and
Grapefruit juice

## EGGNOG

1 cup rich milk

2 egg yolks

1 tablespoonful Tupelo honey

Few grains nutmeg

1 teaspoonful Sherry flavoring

½ cup whipped cream

Beat egg yolks until as light as possible. Add honey, flavoring and milk. Shake in cocktail shaker or beat well. Fold in whipped cream. Pour into glasses and sprinkle with a few grains of nutmeg. All ingredients very cold.

## FRUIT COCKTAILS

Any acid fruits may be combined in making a cocktail; all ingredients must be cold.

1. Grapefruit and Orange Sections.
2. Fresh Pineapple Wedges and Orange Sections.
3. White seeded Grapes and Cherries.
4. Diced Peach, Sliced Strawberries.
5. Diced Grapefruit and Avocado Balls.
6. Pineapple Wedges and Red Raspberries.
7. Grapefruit Sections and Strawberries in Grapefruit Shell.

Garnish Fruit Cocktails with fresh Mint leaves or fruit of contrasting color.

## FRUITADE

1 cup raspberry juice

1 cup strawberry juice

1 cup red currant juice

1 cup cherry juice

½ cup juice of fresh limes

4 cups ice cubes

6 cups carbonated water

Combine chilled fruit juices. Pour over ice cubes. When very cold, add carbonated water. Garnish with cherry rings. This amount will serve twenty persons. Sweeten to taste with Tupelo honey.

## FRUITED MILKSHAKE

¾ cup crushed drained pineapple          3 cups rich milk

4 tablespoonfuls whipped cream

Combine ice cold milk and pineapple. Shake until foamy. Serve with one tablespoonful of whipped cream in each glass. Must be served immediately to avoid curdling.

## FRUIT PUNCH

1 cup orange juice
½ cup pineapple juice

¼ cup grapefruit juice
¾ cup frozen white grape juice

Freeze white grape juice in ice-cube trays. Combine chilled fruit juices with cracked grape juice cubes. Shake well.

## GRAPE CLABBER

Combine equal parts unsweetened grape juice and sweet milk. Shake until thoroughly blended.

## GRAPEFRUIT AND RAW TOMATO JUICE

1 pint grapefruit juice
1 pint raw tomato juice

Add 1 cup of bruised mint leaves and one cup chopped parsley. Let stand two or three hours, strain and chill to serve.

## GREEN COCKTAIL

Equal parts Spinach juice, Parsley juice,
Orange juice.

## HONEY MILK SHAKE

1 quart cold milk          4 tablespoonfuls Tupelo honey
4 tablespoonfuls whipped cream

All ingredients must be cold. Shake honey and milk together until well blended. Pour into tall glasses, top with whipped cream.

## HONEY MINT SYRUP

¼ cup Tupelo honey          2 tablespoonfuls lemon juice
3 tablespoonfuls bruised mint leaves

Combine honey and lemon juice, add mint leaves. Place in glass jar and keep cold for several hours. Add to water or fruit juices in amounts to suit taste. May be strained to remove mint leaves.

## HONEY STRAWBERRY COCKTAIL

1½ cups strawberries          4 tablespoonfuls Tupelo honey
2 cups water          ½ teaspoonful grated lemon rind

Place in liquifier. Run at low speed for 2 minutes, then at high speed for 1 minute.

## ICED POSTUM

Prepare Instant Postum by dissolving in boiling water. Proportion: one tea-spoonful of Postum for each cup of water. Serve with cracked ice. Top with whipped cream, sweetened with Tupelo honey.

*Note*: Co-Veg or other coffee substitutes may be used in place of Postum.

## IRON COCKTAIL

Equal parts watercress and parsley or spinach. Combine the juice of these vegetables with orange juice to taste.

## LEMON FRUIT COCKTAIL

| | |
|---|---|
| ½ cup peach balls | ¾ cup pineapple, finely shredded |
| ¼ cup orange cubes | 2 cups lemon ice |

Arrange chilled fruits in iced cocktail glasses. Top with lemon ice.

## LEMONADE

| | |
|---|---|
| 2 cups water | ½ cup lemon juice |
| | ¼ cup Tupelo honey |

Shake well to combine. Garnish with sprigs of mint or cherries.

## LIME COCKTAIL

| | |
|---|---|
| 2 tablespoonfuls lime juice | ⅓ cup grape syrup |
| 2 tablespoonfuls orange juice | ½ cup ice water |

Place 2 tablespoonfuls cracked ice in cocktail glasses. Pour combined ingredients over.

## LIMEADE

| | |
|---|---|
| ¾ cup fresh lime juice | 4 cups ice water |
| 1 cup orange juice | 2 cups lemon ice |

Combine chilled fruit juices, ice water and lemon ice. Shake vigorously. Add Tupelo honey as desired.

## MILK AND FRUIT JUICE COMBINATIONS

1. Equal parts milk and orange juice
2. 1 quart milk
   Add juice of 2 or 3 lemons
3. 2 parts milk
   1 part grapefruit juice
4. 3 parts milk
   1 part grape juice

## MINTED CITRUS BEVERAGE

1 quart grapefruit or orange juice
½ cup chopped mint

Add mint to juice while chilling, strain before serving.

## MORNING GLORY

1 quart raw tomato juice        ½ cup lemon juice

Shake to combine juices. A little vegetable salt may be added.

## ORANGE CREAM

3½ cups orange juice        ½ cup cream

Stir cream into orange juice just before serving.  Serve cold.

## ORANGE SQUASH

2 cups orange juice        1 cup grapefruit juice
2 cups orange sherbert

Combine ingredients, and shake well.  Garnish with mint or orange slices.

## PEAR AND GRAPE COCKTAIL

4 ripe pears        1 cup white seedless grapes
1 teaspoonful grated orange rind

Pare and core chilled pears. Cut lengthwise in eight pieces and arrange to simulate lily petals. Pile grapes in center and sprinkle with grated orange rind.

## PINEAPPLE COCKTAIL

1½ cups pineapple juice      ¾ cup cracked green ice cubes
1 tablespoonful lemon juice

Strain pineapple juice through double thickness of linen. Chill. Add one tablespoonful of chopped mint, and a trace of green vegetable coloring to water when freezing ice cubes. Combine pineapple and lemon juice with cracked ice cubes. Shake well.

## PINEAPPLE-MINT COCKTAIL

Crush fresh mint leaves. Add ¼ cup of these to 1 quart pineapple. Allow to stand for three hours or until the juice has become well flavored. Strain.

## PINEAPPLE ORANGE SQUASH

1 quart cold tea          ½ cup apricot juice
1 pint pineapple juice     1 quart orange ice

All ingredients must be cold. Place all together in punch bowl. Let stand 10 minutes before serving.

## PINK LADY COCKTAIL

Equal parts strawberry and pineapple juice. Add two tablespoonfuls cream for each cupful of juice. Serve with cherry for garnish.

## POMEGRANATE COCKTAIL

Add ¼ lemon, thinly sliced, to 1 large, peeled pomegranate. Add 1½ pints cold water. Boil together for a few minutes or until color and flavor have been extracted. Strain and add ⅓ cup Tupelo honey. Chill. Add a few drops lemon juice.

## POCONO VEGETABLE JUICE

Equal parts Beets and tops, Carrots, Celery

Combine the juice from these vegetables, serve two or three ounces twice daily. Vegetable juice may be poured into glass and glass filled with tomato juice or fruit juice.

## RADISH AND CELERY COCKTAIL

Equal parts Celery juice and Radish juice combined with fresh fruit juice to serve.

## RAINBOW PUNCH

Freeze in separate trays the following mixtures:
1. Grapejuice; or red raspberry juice sweetened with Tupelo honey
2. Lemonade, sweetened with Tupelo honey and colored green—using pure vegetable coloring.

Fill glasses with cubes of frozen juice. Pour orange juice over cubes. Must be served at once for best effect.

## RASPBERRY COCKTAIL

1¼ cups raspberries          ½ cup crushed raspberries

Use either red or black raspberries. Chill thoroughly. Place whole raspberries in cocktail glasses, and cover with crushed berries. Garnish with sprigs of fresh mint.

## RASPBERRY SHRUB

1 cup red raspberries          ¼ cup Tupelo honey
1 cup water                    2 tablespoonfuls lemon juice

Place in liquifier. Run at low speed for 2 minutes, at high speed for 1 minute. Strain. Serve cold. Sliced lemon garnish.

## RAW TOMATO JUICE

Select perfectly ripe red tomatoes. Cut into thin slices and press through sieve. May be seasoned with a little vegetable salt if desired. Should be used while fresh.

## RUM COCKTAIL

1½ cups orange juice               2 egg yolks
¼ cup lemon juice               A dash of rum flavor
          ¼ cup Tupelo honey
          Ice cubes

Shake for three minutes in a cocktail shaker. Strain into cold glasses. Add ¼ teaspoonful grated orange rind to each glass.

## SAUERKRAUT COCKTAIL

2 cups chopped sauerkraut     2 tablespoonfuls pimiento stars

Arrange sauerkraut in chilled cocktail glasses. Garnish with pimiento stars.

## SOY BEAN MILK

½ pint warm water          1 tablespoonful Soy Bean Milk Powder
1 teaspoonful Tupelo honey
2 tablespoonfuls cream or 1 tablespoonful vegetable oil

Combine milk powder with honey and a little water to make a smooth paste. Add remaining water and cream.

## SPICY PUNCH

| | |
|---|---|
| 1 cup water | 1 cup grapefruit juice |
| 6 whole cloves | ⅓ cup pineapple juice |
| 3 inches stick cinnamon | ¾ cup lemon juice |
| 2 cups orange juice | ½ cup Tupelo honey |

Boil water and spices for ten minutes. Strain, and blend honey with fruit juices. Shake well. Pour over ice cubes, and let stand until ice is partially melted. Will serve eight or ten persons.

## SPRING COCKTAIL

Equal parts dandelion and parsley juice. Add a few drops of onion juice and a little grated lemon rind.

## STRAWBERRY COCKTAIL

3 cups perfectly formed, ripe strawberries     1 cup heavy sweet cream

Wash, drain and chill berries. Do not remove caps or stems. Arrange on glass around tiny sauce pots filled with cream.

## TOMATO COCKTAIL

| | |
|---|---|
| 1 cup diced firm tomato | 2 tablespoonfuls grated carrot |
| ¼ cup shredded cucumber | 1 tablespoonful onion juice |

Combine ingredients lightly. Serve in cold cocktail glasses, with or without sauce.

## TOMATO COCKTAIL WITH HONEY

| | |
|---|---|
| 2 cups tomato juice | 3 tablespoonfuls lemon juice |
| 1 tablespoonful Tupelo honey | ½ teaspoonful vegetable salt |

Combine ingredients thoroughly by shaking together. Chill.

## TOMATO AND FRUIT COCKTAIL

¾ cup balls cut from firm tomato    1 teaspoonful minced green pepper
½ cup shredded orange               1 tablespoonful olive oil
½ cup shredded pineapple            1 teaspoonful lemon juice

Combine fruits; blend lemon juice and oil; add to fruit with minced pepper. Serve in cocktail glasses surrounded with cracked ice.

## WHEY

Heat soured milk keeping at very moderate temperature until the milk solids (curd) separate from the liquids. Strain through double cheesecloth or linen and chill. Whey may be combined with any fruit or vegetable juice.

## YELLOW COCKTAIL

Equal parts Carrot juice and Orange juice.

# RELISHES

ALMONDS, chopped, in balls of minced celery and mayonnaise rolled in paprika.

AVOCADO SLICES, marinated and drained.

BALLS OF FINOCCHIO ROOT, hollowed out and filled with pimento.

BALLS cut from ripe tomato.

CARROT MATCHES, raw with dots of pimento for heads.

CARROT SPLINTERS, marinated and drained.

CAULIFLOWER flowerettes, raw, marinated.

CELERY CURLS, small.

CELERY ROOT, slices, wafers.

CELERY SPIKES, (preferably green or unbleached).

CHERRIES, red, firm, pitted with tip of cress inserted in cavity.

COCONUT wedges.

CRESS, three or four spears tied with thin strips of pimento.

CUCUMBER CUBES, marinated.

GREEN BEANS, cooked, drained, marinated. Tie three together with pimento strips.

KUMQUATS, ripe.

MUSHROOM BUTTONS, tiny raw, marinated in French dressing containing minced chives.

NUT MEATS.

OLIVES, ripe.

PINEAPPLE, ripe, small wedges.

RADISH ROSES, tiny.

ROBIN HOODS, tiny bundles of dandelion leaves. Stalk ends dipped in French dressing and slipped thru small rings of carrot, olive and radish.

SCALLIONS.

TEA BERRIES, on celery spikes.

WALNUTS, marinated in lemon juice.

## APPETIZER

Crisp brussels sprouts. Remove outer leaves, leaving small solid green ball. Cut out center to form small cup. Fill with cream cheese mixed with a little vegetable paste.

## CANAPE BUTTERS

To prepare butters for canapes or sandwiches, keep at room temperature until soft enough to spread easily. Or work with fork until creamy.

## CHIVE BUTTER

Add 1 tablespoonful minced chives to each ½ cup butter.

## CHOPPED NUT BUTTER

Add 2 tablespoonfuls finely chopped nut meats to each ½ cup butter.

## EGG BUTTER

Add 2 hard boiled egg yolks (sieved) and ½ teaspoonful grated lemon rind to each ½ cup butter. Season with vegetable salt.

## LEMON BUTTER

Add grated lemon rind to softened butter; 1 teaspoonful rind to each ½ cup butter.

## MINT BUTTER

Add 2 tablespoonfuls minced mint to each ½ cup butter.

## OLIVE BUTTER

Add 2 mashed ripe olives and ¼ teaspoonful grated lemon rind to each ½ cup butter.

## ONION BUTTER

Add 1 teaspoonful onion juice to each ½ cup butter.

## ORANGE BUTTER

Add 1 teaspoonful grated orange rind to each ½ cup butter.

## PARSLEY BUTTER

Add 2 tablespoonfuls minced parsley to each ½ cup butter.

## PIMIENTO BUTTER

Add 2 tablespoonfuls minced pimiento and ½ teaspoonful grated lemon rind to each ½ cup butter.

## VEGETABLE APPETIZER BASES

Sliced Tomato.

Sliced Mild Onions.

Broiled Mushroom Caps.

Sliced Cooked Carrot.

Cups cut from Ground Cherries, Radishes or Brussels Sprouts: filled with Cream Cheese or chopped vegetables mixed with Mayonnaise.

French Endive: fill with Cream Cheese or Deviled Egg Yolk.

Prunes or Cherries stuffed with Almonds.

Cheese-Celery Balls: combine Cream Cheese with minced Celery. Roll into small balls. Coat with minced Parsley.

## WATERCRESS BUTTER

Add 2 tablespoonfuls minced watercress to each ½ cup butter.

# SOUPS

## ALMOND SOUP

¼ cup minced onion
½ cup ground almonds
3 tablespoonfuls butter

2 cups water
1 cup cream
½ cup steamed small cubes of cucumber

Cook onion, almonds and butter until browned slightly. Add water and simmer 15 minutes. Add warmed cream. Garnish with cucumber cubes.

## ASPARAGUS SOUP

1 lb. green asparagus        4 tablespoonfuls chopped bacon
¼ cup chopped onion tops

Cut tender heads (about one inch) from asparagus. Slice remaining stalks, add to four cups water with bacon and onion tops. Simmer until asparagus is soft. Rub thru fine sieve. Add cooking liquid and asparagus tips with thyme and summer savory to season. Simmer until tips are tender.

## BEET SOUP

2 tablespoonfuls butter
2 tablespoonfuls minced onion
2 tablespoonfuls minced celery
1 cup shredded red cabbage

1 cup sliced raw beet
4 cups water
1 tablespoonful lemon juice
½ cup tiny dice of beet (cooked)

½ cup heavy sweet cream

Cook onion, celery and butter until yellow. Add cabbage and beet slices. Cook until soft. Add water and lemon juice. Simmer for half an hour. Add beet dice and cream. Heat thoroughly.

## BEET TOP SOUP

6 cups chopped beet tops        Simmer in 2 cups water until tender

Force through sieve. Add 1 cup thin cream and vegetable seasoning if desired; or (2) add a dash of lemon juice and 1 tablespoonful butter.

## CARROT SOUP

2 cups mashed, steamed carrots        ½ cup cream — 1½ cups milk
2 tablespoonfuls butter

Combine carrots and butter and beat well, adding cream and milk, a little at a time. Serve hot.

## CARROT BALL SOUP

| | |
|---|---|
| 1 cup carrot balls (very small) | ½ cup chopped celery |
| 2 cups chopped carrot | 2 tablespoonfuls minced chives |
| 1 tablespoonful chopped parsley | 4 cups water |

Cook all ingredients except carrot balls in water until soft. Strain. Season clear broth with pinch of salt, and paprika. Add steamed carrot balls.

## CELERY SOUP

| | |
|---|---|
| 2 cups steamed celery | 1 tablespoonful butter |
| 1 tablespoonful onion juice | 1 cup cream |
| 1 cup milk | |

Put celery through sieve. Heat cream and milk, add celery pulp, butter and onion juice.

## CELERY-ALMOND SOUP

| | |
|---|---|
| 2 cups pureed celery | 1 cup water |
| 1 cup cream | ½ cup shredded almonds |
| ¼ cup whipping cream | |

Combine celery and water, add minced parsley or other herbs to season. Simmer for a few minutes. Add warmed cream. Serve in cups, garnished with whipped cream topped with shredded almonds.

## CELERY CARROT SOUP

| | |
|---|---|
| 1 cup sliced celery | 1 cup diced carrot |
| ¼ cup minced celery tops | ¼ cup minced chives |

Boil vegetables together until quite soft and water is cooked away. Add one quart rich milk. Heat thoroughly. Dust with powdered dried parsley before serving.

## CORN SOUP

2 cups green corn, freshly cut and scraped from cob    4 cups boiling water
2 tablespoonfuls minced root from turnip-rooted parsley

Simmer ingredients together until corn is well cooked. Add one cup of cream and vegetable salt to season. Place one-half teaspoonful minced fresh sage leaves in each soup plate before pouring soup.

## CREAM OF MUSHROOM SOUP

1 lb. mushrooms
2 tablespoonfuls butter

3 cups water
1 cup thin cream

Cook mushrooms in butter for five minutes. Add water. Simmer until mushrooms are tender. Rub through coarse sieve and add hot cream. Dust lightly with paprika.

## CREAM OF TOMATO SOUP

1½ cups water
2 tablespoonfuls minced onion
1 tablespoonful minced parsley
½ bay leaf

2 whole cloves
1 teaspoonful celery salt
2 cups ripe tomatoes sliced
2 cups thin cream

4 tablespoonfuls whipped cream

Place all ingredients except cream in sauce pan and simmer for twenty minutes. Strain. Heat to boiling point. Heat cream, separately, to boiling point. When ready to serve, beat hot cream slightly and stir into it slowly, the tomato purée. Garnish each serving with one tablespoonful whipped cream, dust over lightly with paprika.

## CUCUMBER SOUP

3 cups chopped cucumber (no seeds)
4 tablespoonfuls butter

2 cups celery broth
2 egg yolks

¼ cup heavy cream

Simmer cucumber in butter until slightly browned. Add celery broth and cook until vegetable is soft. Put through fine sieve. Beat cream and egg yolks very light. Add to cucumber purée, cook all over hot water until smooth, stirring constantly. Season very lightly with salt. Dust over with paprika.

## GARDEN SOUP

4 young carrots, sliced
½ cup thinly sliced celery
2 cups chopped spinach

¼ cup minced parsley
2 quarts water
½ cup sliced okra pods

1 tablespoonful minced onion

Add carrots, onion and celery to water. Simmer for 15 minutes. Add remaining vegetables and cook until flavors are well blended. Season with vegetable salt.

## JELLIED VEGETABLE MADRILENE

1 tablespoonful granulated gelatin     1 cup boiling water
1 cup strained tomato juice     1 tablespoonful vegetable paste
½ teaspoonful vegetable salt

Soften gelatin by soaking in ¼ cup strained tomato juice for 5 minutes. Add to boiling water with the vegetable paste; stir until dissolved. Strain and add to tomato juice. Add salt. Chill.

## LETTUCE OR ENDIVE SOUP

6 cups chopped lettuce or endive     1 cup cream
3 cups celery broth     ½ teaspoonful celery salt

Simmer chopped greens in celery broth until soft. Put through sieve. Reduce to 3 cups by cooking gently. Add celery salt and hot cream.

## LUNCHEON SOUP

4 cups chopped tomato     2 tablespoonfuls bacon fat
¾ cup chopped onion     ½ teaspoonful celery salt
1 cup chopped cabbage     4 cups boiling water

Simmer onion in bacon fat until slightly colored. Add cabbage and cook for ten minutes. Add tomato, celery salt and water. Cook gently over low heat until well blended. Before serving, skim off any fat that may come to top of soup.

## MADRILENE

1 quart water     1 quart chopped carrots
1 quart chopped tomatoes     Small bunch parsley
½ cup chopped onion     Sprig of fresh thyme.

Cook all together slowly until flavor is drawn from carrot and onion. Strain through double cheesecloth. Reheat and season with vegetable salt; add 1 tablespoonful vegetable paste. Stir until completely dissolved.

## MALAY PURÉE

1 cup thick purée of young, green lima beans
1 cup boiling water     ¼ cup Julienne strips steamed carrot
1 cup cream     ¼ cup thinly sliced celery, steamed
1 tablespoonful onion juice

Combine all ingredients except cream. Heat to boiling point. Season with vegetable salt. Add warmed cream.

## MINTED VEGETABLE SOUP

| | |
|---|---|
| 2 cups purée of fresh green peas | ¼ cup ground carrot |
| 1½ cups cold water | 1 tablespoonful crushed mint, |
| ½ cup ground celery | finely chopped |
| ½ cup chopped celery tops | ½ teaspoonful celery salt |
| 2 tablespoonfuls minced onion | 1½ cups cream |

Simmer together, for thirty minutes, all ingredients except cream. Add heated cream. Beat for a minute or two with rotary beater before serving.

## MUSHROOM PURÉE SOUP

| | |
|---|---|
| 1 cup finely chopped raw mushrooms | 1 tablespoonful minced parsley |
| 1 tablespoonful butter or vegetable oil | 2 cups cream |
| 2 cups water | |

Cook mushrooms in fat until lightly browned. Add remaining ingredients, except cream. Simmer until flavor of mushrooms is well distributed. Add warmed cream.

## ONION SOUP

| | |
|---|---|
| 1 cup onion rings | 2 tablespoonfuls butter |
| 3 cups boiling water | |

Cook onion in butter until tender, add hot water and ¼ teaspoonful thyme, and simmer for five minutes. Serve with protein toast rounds or protein crackers.

## OYSTER PLANT SOUP

| | |
|---|---|
| 1 cup mashed, steamed oyster plant | ½ teaspoonful vegetable salt |
| 1½ cup thin cream | Paprika |
| 1 cup boiling water | |

Heat cream, add water and oyster plant; season with salt and paprika.

## PARSLEY SOUP

| | |
|---|---|
| 3 bunches parsley | 1 bunch of celery |
| 1 bunch of carrots and tops | 1 pound onions |

Wash all of the vegetables thoroughly, cut in small pieces and place in a large vessel. Cover with water and simmer for 5 hours. When finished, this soup may be strained and served with cream or the vegetables may be puréed and put back in the broth.

## PARSNIP AND CAULIFLOWER SOUP

1½ cups shredded parsnips      1 tablespoonful minced parsley
1½ cups thinly sliced cauliflower   6 cups water

Simmer all ingredients together until vegetables are soft. Add 1 cup milk and vegetable salt to taste.

## PEPPER POT SOUP

1 tablespoonful minced onion     2 tablespoonfuls butter or melted
1 tablespoonful minced green pepper    chicken fat
1 tablespoonful minced parsley     3 cups tomato purée
¼ cup minced celery        ½ cup steamed carrot rings or
                          turnip dice

Cook onion, pepper, parsley and celery with butter for a few minutes. Add tomato purée and carrot or turnip. Simmer to blend for a few minutes. Just before serving add one tablespoonful grated fresh horse-radish and one teaspoonful lemon juice, with sufficient vegetable salt to season.

## POTASSIUM BROTH

1 pound celery and tops      1 pound carrots
¼ pound spinach          Small bunch parsley
1 pound kale             1 head lettuce
1 large onion            3 red beets

Chop the vegetables finely, add water to cover. Simmer slowly for about 2 hours. Strain, season with vegetable salt. Vegetable paste may be added for additional flavor.

## PUREED OKRA SOUP

1 cup sliced okra pods      ¼ cup minced green pepper
¼ cup sliced spring onions   2 tablespoonfuls butter
2 cups chopped ripe tomato   2 cups water
              1 cup cream

Boil together all ingredients except cream until vegetables are soft. Rub thru sieve. Season with vegetable salt and any desired herb. Heat. Add warmed cream.

## SPANISH SOUP

1½ cups cooked or canned tomatoes   1 quart water
¾ cup pearl corn           1 tablespoonful chopped parsley
1 cup green beans, cut into tiny dice  1½ teaspoonful vegetable salt
1 thin slice onion          ½ teaspoonful paprika
        1 tablespoonful Tupelo honey

Simmer all ingredients together until vegetables are soft. Thyme or bay leaf may be added for additional seasoning. Just before serving add 1 level tablespoonful vegetable paste and stir until completely dissolved.

## TOMATO AND OKRA SOUP

3 cups tomato juice
1 cup sliced okra pods

2 tablespoonfuls minced onion
¼ cup minced celery leaves

Simmer until okra is tender. May be seasoned with vegetable salt or vegetable paste.


## VEGETABLE BOUILLON

3 cups vegetable (finely chopped or ground)          3 cups water

Any desired vegetable may be used, or any combination. Cook gently until flavor is extracted. Strain thru linen. Season with vegetable salt and any desired herb. One teaspoonful vegetable paste may be added if desired.


## VEGETABLE BOUILLON JULIENNE

1 cup celery
1 cup carrots
½ cup turnips
½ cup string beans

1 onion
1 teaspoonful chopped parsley
6 cups water
4 tablespoonfuls butter or substitute

Cut vegetables with julienne knife or in thin pieces about the length of a match and twice as thick. Melt butter, add all vegetables and cook over a low fire for 15 minutes. Add water and simmer until vegetables are tender. Add 2 tablespoonfuls vegetable paste before serving.


## VEGETABLE CREAM SOUP

⅓ puréed vegetable          ⅓ cream
⅓ water

Add a little vegetable paste.


## VEGETABLE SOUP

½ cup diced carrot
1 cup sliced tomato
¼ cup diced turnip
⅓ cup sliced celery

2 tablespoonfuls minced onion
4 cups water
4 tablespoonfuls butter
1 teaspoonful minced parsley

Combine ingredients and simmer until all vegetables are tender. Add one teaspoonful vegetable paste.

### VEGETABLE SOUP STOCK

| | |
|---|---|
| 2 large carrots | 1 dozen tomatoes |
| ¼ lb. spinach | 1 beet |
| 3 stalks celery | 1 quart fresh green or wax beans |
| 3 green peppers | 1 onion |
| 1 bunch asparagus | 1 parsnip |

1 small bunch each of parsley, radishes, mustard greens, broccoli and the outside leaves of any green vegetable.

Any or all of the above-mentioned vegetables may be used. Cover well with cold water. Simmer over slow fire until flavor of vegetables is extracted. Strain. Cool. Place in ice box. Reheat as needed.

### VEGETABLE SOUP WITH OKRA

| | |
|---|---|
| ½ cup chopped celery tops | ¼ cup ground carrot |
| 1 cup sliced green okra pods | ¼ cup minced onion tops (green) |
| ¼ cup green peas | ¼ cup ripe tomato |

Boil okra and celery tops in one quart water until soft. Strain. Add remaining vegetables and simmer until blended. Season with vegetable salt and thyme or parsley.

### WATERCRESS SOUP

| | |
|---|---|
| 2 large bunches watercress | ½ teaspoonful celery salt |
| 4 cups water | 3 tablespoonfuls butter |
| | 2 cups thin cream |

Wash cress carefully and cut into short pieces. Melt butter in heavy pan. Add water, celery salt, and cress. A slice of onion or a tiny point of garlic, may also be used if desired. Cook until cress is soft. Rub through coarse strainer and add warmed cream. Sprinkle with paprika and serve.

# FRUIT SALADS

### APPLE AND CELERY SALAD

2 cups sliced tart apples                    1 cup finely sliced celery
English walnut halves

Marinate apple and celery in four tablespoonfuls orange juice, one table-spoonful lemon juice and two tablespoonfuls olive oil for one hour. Drain and place on lettuce. Garnish with halves of English walnuts.

### APPLE AND GRAPEFRUIT SALAD

2 cups diced grapefruit          2 cups diced apple
Endive

Toss apple and grapefruit dice together. Sprinkle lightly with salt. Serve on crisp chopped endive.

### APRICOT SALAD

1½ cups sliced fresh apricots          Sections from one grapefruit
1 cup shredded fresh coconut          Shredded lettuce

Arrange a layer of apricot slices on lettuce, cover with shredded coconut, and arrange grapefruit sections over coconut.

### AVOCADO SALAD

2 Alligator pears                    ¼ cup lemon juice
¼ cup orange juice                   Lettuce or romaine

Pare, core and cut pears in halves. Marinate in fruit juices for at least one hour, keeping very cold. Just before serving drain and arrange on lettuce.

### AVOCADO AND ORANGE SALAD, JELLIED

1 pint prepared lemon gelatin          2 oranges, diced
1 avocado, diced                      ½ cup raisins

Stir fruit into gelatin. Chill in mold.

### AVOCADO AND PERSIMMON SALAD

Arrange sections of avocado and persimmon alternately on bed of salad greens.

## BARTLETT SALAD

4 Bartlett pears
½ cup sliced celery
½ cup broken walnuts

¼ cup chopped ripe olives
3 tablespoonfuls French dressing
Endive

Cut tops from pears. Remove from the skins most of the fruit pulp, without crushing. Dice pears, combine with celery, nuts, olives and French dressing. Place salad in pear cups. Serve on curly endive.

## BLACK WALNUT SALAD

1 cup chopped black walnuts
1 cup tart apple cubes

1 cup sliced celery
Endive

Combine chilled salad ingredients. Serve on endive.

## BLOSSOM SALAD

Place a large slice of pineapple on bed of lettuce. Cover with sliced strawberries arranged in petal fashion. Make center of tablespoonful of mayonnaise garnished with chopped ripe olive.

## BRAZIL SALAD

1 cup sliced brazil nuts
1 cup pineapple cubes

1 cup balls cut from peach or pear
Lettuce

Combine chilled salad ingredients. Serve on lettuce. Sections cut from small, whole oranges, make an effective garnish.

## CANOE SALAD

½ cup diced grapefruit
½ cup diced apple
½ cup diced unsweetened pineapple

4 medium cucumbers
Shredded lettuce
French dressing

Cut cucumbers lengthwise in halves. Remove as much as possible of pulp, leaving shell intact. Cut ends to shape of canoe. Combine grapefruit, apple and pineapple, and toss together with French dressing. Drain. Fill cucumber shells with mixture and arrange on lettuce.

## CELERY, RAISIN AND NUT SALAD

1 cup sliced celery
1 cup chopped raisins
1 teaspoonful lime juice

1 cup chopped nuts
2 tablespoonfuls orange juice

Combine celery, raisins and nuts with orange and lime juice. Marinate for half an hour. Drain and arrange on lettuce.

## CHERRY SALAD

1 cup Oxheart cherries          Blanched almonds
1 cup black Spanish cherries    Lettuce

Remove pits from cherries. Insert an almond in each cherry. Arrange in any pattern on lettuce.

## CHERRY AND PEAR SALAD

6 halves fresh or canned pears      1 cup red cherries
Lettuce

Place pears on lettuce. Fill centers with cherries.

## CHERRY SPRINKLE SALAD

1 cup drained crushed unsweet-     ¼ lb. cottage cheese
   ened pineapple                  ½ cup whipped cream
1 cup fruit of choice              Lettuce
              4 tablespoonfuls chopped cherries

Beat cream and cheese together until well blended. Mix fruit and arrange in lettuce cups. Cover with cheese mixture and sprinkle with cherries.

## CHEESE BALL SALAD

4 slices unsweetened pineapple     4 red cherries
4 tablespoonfuls cream cheese      Lettuce
2 tablespoonfuls chopped nuts      Mayonnaise

Place pineapple rings on lettuce. Fill centers with cream cheese made into balls and rolled in nuts. Press a cherry into each cheese ball.

## CITRUS SALAD

2 cups orange dice        2 tablespoonfuls white grape juice
1 cup grapefruit dice     3 tablespoonfuls olive oil
              Chopped endive

Shake grape juice and oil together until blended. Pour over fruit and mix lightly. Drain. Serve on crisp chopped endive.

## COCONUT FRUIT SALAD

½ cup shredded coconut        ½ cup diced celery
2 cups tart apple (diced)     1 tablespoonful orange juice
              1 tablespoonful fresh lime juice

Dice apple and sprinkle with lime and orange juice; combine with celery and coconut. Serve on lettuce. Decorate with rings of cherries.

## FROZEN CANNED FRUIT SALAD

1 large can unsweetened fruit of choice     Lettuce
¼ cup red cherries

Freeze fruit in can. Remove from can without crushing. Slice, and serve on crisp lettuce. Garnish with sliced cherries.

## GRAPE SALAD

2 cups large white grapes     Lettuce
¾ cup pecans or almonds     6 kumquats

Wash and drain grapes. Remove seeds and press a nut meat into each grape. Pile in lettuce cups. Slice kumquats for garnishing.

## GRAPE AND ENDIVE SALAD

2 cups chopped endive     2 cups seeded Tokay grapes
French dressing

Combine grapes and chopped endive with French dressing. Serve on lettuce.

## GRAPE, APPLE AND CELERY SALAD

2 cups Malaga grapes, seeded and     ½ cup diced tart apple
    sliced     ½ cup sliced celery

Combine salad ingredients. Serve on endive or cress.

## GRAPEFRUIT AND AVOCADO SALAD

1 grapefruit     Romaine
2 avocados     6 red cherries

Separate grapefruit into sections. Pare, core, and cut avocados into sections lengthwise. Marinate for a few minutes in four tablespoonfuls French dressing. Drain. Arrange fruit on romaine. Garnish with sliced red cherries.

## GRAPEFRUIT, ORANGE AND APPLE SALAD

1 red apple     1 large orange
1 small grapefruit

Peel orange and grapefruit and cut in sections. Cut the apple in sections about the same size as orange and remove the core. On individual plates of lettuce arrange the sections of fruit alternately to look like one half a colored ball. Serve with mayonnaise.

## GRAPEFRUIT, ORANGE AND AVOCADO SALAD

2 avocados                3 oranges
1 grapefruit              ¼ cup lemon juice
                Lettuce

Pare and core pears, cover with lemon juice. Arrange sections of grapefruit and orange on lettuce. Drain pears and add to salad. Serve immediately without dressing.

## GRAPEFRUIT, ORANGE AND KUMQUAT SALAD

1 large grapefruit (sections)    4 kumquats
3 oranges (sections)             Romaine
                                 Mayonnaise

Arrange salad greens on individual plates. Build a nest of grapefruit and orange sections, and place nuts in center. Top with mayonnaise and garnish with sliced kumquats.

## GRAPEFRUIT, TOMATO AND AVOCADO SALAD

Arrange sections of grapefruit, avocado and tomato alternately in pinwheel fashion on bed of salad greens.

## LIME GELATIN SALAD

1¼ cups orange juice         6 tablespoonfuls Tupelo honey
2 tablespoonfuls lime juice  1 tablespoonful granulated gelatin
            ¼ cup shredded apple

Soften gelatin by soaking in half of the orange juice. Heat over boiling water until dissolved. Add Tupelo honey, then remaining juices. Add apple when gelatin is ready to congeal. Chill in individual molds. Serve on curly endive (chicory).

## MALAGA SALAD

2 cups Malaga grapes        4 apple cups
  (seeded and halved)       4 tablespoonfuls whipped cream

Combine grapes and cream. Serve in red apple cups.

## MARTHA'S FRUIT SALAD

Arrange on serving platter with crisp lettuce the following fruits:

Peach halves filled with cottage cheese.

Pear halves, convex side spread thinly with mayonnaise or whipped cream and covered with halves of seeded white grapes.

Pineapple slices spread with cream cheese and garnished with sliced almonds.

Marinated apple slices made into sandwiches with cottage cheese.

For garnishing, place a small sprig of mint in each peach half. Add a grape leaf to each pear. Place red cherry in center of pineapple slices. Arrange sliced black olives petal fashion on apple sandwiches.

## MINTED PEACH SALAD

Fill halves of peaches, either fresh or canned, with sliced almonds. Pipe mint flavored whipped cream around the edge of the peach. Serve on cress or lettuce.

## NEAPOLITAN SALAD

½ cup diced grapefruit
½ cup apples, sliced in thin strips
½ cup diced orange
½ cup shredded almonds

¼ cup sliced red cherries
   or strawberries
½ cup diced unsweetened pineapple
½ cup cream mayonnaise

Combine ingredients, pack in square mold and freeze. Slice and serve on lettuce. Garnish with fresh fruit.

## ORANGE CUP SALAD

1 cup diced orange        ½ cup shredded pineapple
½ cup sliced seeded Tokay grapes

Combine salad ingredients. Serve in orange cups.

## ORANGE FLOWER SALAD

4 large, sweet oranges
4 steamed prunes

Fruit dressing
4 ½-inch slices of firm head lettuce

Place lettuce slices on salad plates. Arrange orange sections as flower petals and use prune for center. Serve with fruit salad dressing or mayonnaise.

## ORANGE, PRUNE AND NUT SALAD

1½ cups orange dice       ½ cup chopped nuts
1 cup sliced cooked Santa Clara prunes

Combine fruit and nuts. Arrange on lettuce.

## PARTY SALAD

Amount given is for individual service.

2 large sections grapefruit
2 large sections orange
1 large slice unsweetened pineapple
1 strip preserved ginger

1 teaspoonful chopped red
cherries
½ teaspoonful chopped ripe olives

Color pineapple pale green, using vegetable color. Set on white lettuce. In center of slice place strip of preserved ginger. On each side of ginger use one grapefruit section, (convex side in) next orange sections. Dot with cherries and olives.

## PEAR AND GELATIN SALAD

Arrange halves of canned or fresh pear on salad greens; pipe whipped cream around edge of pear. Fill centers with tiny dice of colored gelatin.

## PEAR AND GRAPE SALAD

8 halves of pears
½ cup chopped red grapes

½ cup ground blanched almonds
½ cup cream mayonnaise

Color pear halves delicately with vegetable color. Arrange white crisp lettuce on four individual salad plates. Place mayonnaise on lettuce. Set pear halves on mayonnaise. Fill centers with grapes. Sprinkle with almonds.

## PEAR AND ORANGE SALAD

3 cups diced pear
¼ cup chopped red cherries

1 cup orange sections

Combine pear and cherries. Pile in mounds on lettuce. Set orange sections on end about the mounds. Top with whole cherry.

## PEAR AND WATERCRESS SALAD

2 cups chopped watercress
2 tablespoonfuls French dressing

4 large halves of pear
Mayonnaise

Combine chilled cress and French dressing. Drain. Arrange on salad plates. Place halves of pears on cress, cut side up, and fill cavities with mayonnaise. Dust with paprika or 1 tablespoonful finely chopped cress.

## PEPPER CUP SALAD

1½ cups grapefruit dice
4 green pepper cups

2 cups sliced celery

Combine salad ingredients with mayonnaise. Serve in pepper cups.

## PINEAPPLE AND CITRUS FRUIT SALAD

4 large slices pineapple          2 tangerines
1 grapefruit                      4 green dessert cherries
2 oranges                         Lettuce

Place on each salad plate one pineapple slice (on lettuce). Build a dome of grapefruit sections, orange sections and tangerine sections. Dressing may be filled in center space as dome is built up. Top with green cherry or kumquat.

## PINEAPPLE AND CHERRY SALAD

4 slices unsweetened pineapple          4 ¾-inch slices from large apple
                    1 cup red cherries

Either fresh or canned pineapple may be used. Slices of baked or steamed apple, chilled, are placed upon pineapple. Set a circle of cherries over apple ring, fill center of ring with salad dressing.

## PINEAPPLE AND PEAR SALAD

1½ cups diced pineapple          1 cup diced pear
½ cup sliced celery              3 tablespoonfuls French dressing

Pour French dressing over salad ingredients and chill thoroughly. Drain and serve on beds of endive.

## PINEAPPLE AND NUT SALAD

1 cup shredded unsweetened pine-          1 cup broken nut meats
    apple                                 4 tomatoes

Scald and skin tomatoes. Chill and cut into baskets with handles. Sprinkle inside of tomato baskets lightly with salt and fill with salad mixture.

## PINEAPPLE SALAD WITH ALMONDS

For individual salad spread slice of pineapple with mayonnaise, sprinkle thickly with chopped almonds. Place large red cherry or strawberry in center. Serve on endive.

## PRUNE SALAD

1½ cups sliced steamed Santa Clara          ½ cup blanched almonds
    prunes                                  1 cup chopped celery
                    ¼ cup tart dressing of choice

Combine salad ingredients with dressing. Drain. Serve on lettuce.

## PRUNE AND BLACKBERRY SALAD

1 cup sliced Italian prunes          1 cup orange dice
1 cup blackberries                   2 tablespoonfuls grapefruit juice
            1 tablespoonful olive oil

Combine fruits with oil and grapefruit juice. Chill thoroughly and serve on lettuce.


## SPECIAL FRUIT SALAD COMBINATIONS

Grapefruit, oranges and pineapple.
Sauerkraut, pineapple and oranges.
Peaches, pears, grapefruit and pineapple.
Shredded cabbage, apples and raisins.
Shredded cabbage and diced pineapple.
Shredded cabbage, celery, apples and parsnips.
Shredded apples, celery and raisins.
Pineapple, oranges, celery.
Shredded pineapple, cabbage and nuts.
Shredded spinach leaves, celery, apples, carrots and raisins.
Diced fresh peaches, pineapple wedges, sliced celery.
Grapefruit sections, pineapple wedges, diced fresh apricots.
Diced fresh pineapple, sliced white grapes.
Shredded pineapple, sliced strawberries.
Orange dice, sliced strawberries.
Apricot halves filled with raisins.
Prunes stuffed with nuts or cream cheese.


## SPRING FRUIT SALAD

Line salad bowl with endive, divide bowl into quarters with half slices of pineapple. Fill first section with alternating sections of grapefruit and apple; second section filled with strawberries. Fill third section with orange slices and the fourth with seedless white grapes. Garnish with mint.


## STRAWBERRY SALAD

1 cup strawberries, (halves)          ½ cup diced pineapple
            ½ cup diced orange

Combine berries and other fruit. Serve on lettuce. Garnish with a few whole berries.

### STRAWBERRY AND CHEESE SALAD

1 cup sliced strawberries      ¾ cup cream cheese
½ cup whipped cream      Fruit salad dressing
<br>Crisp lettuce

Mash cheese with fork and work to a smooth paste with whipped cream. Add the sliced berries and shape into a loaf. Chill thoroughly, slice, and serve on lettuce.

### STRAWBERRY AND GRAPEFRUIT SALAD

2 cups sliced strawberries      2 cups diced grapefruit
<br>Lettuce

Combine fruit. Serve on lettuce. Garnish with fresh whole strawberries (caps and stems NOT removed). Interesting when served in grapefruit cups.

### STRAWBERRY AND GRAPE SALAD

1½ cups seeded and halved white      1½ cups halved strawberries
    grapes

Combine grapes and strawberries. Serve on lettuce.

### STUFFED APPLE SALAD

Remove the tops from red apples, scoop out inside pulp, leaving just enough adhering to the skin to keep apples in shape. Using the apple pulp which has been removed, refill the shells with a mixture made by adding chopped celery, chopped walnuts and mayonnaise. Place on crisp lettuce on individual plate and serve.

### SUNNYSIDE SALAD

4 halves canned unsweetened      4 slices unsweetened pineapple
    peaches

Arrange lettuce on four salad plates. Place a slice of pineapple on each. Cover pineapple with whipped cream. Now fill cavities of peaches with mayonnaise, invert and place in the center of each salad.

### TANGERINE SALAD

2 cups diced tangerine      ½ cup diced apple
<br>½ cup diced unsweetened pineapple

Combine ingredients and serve on romaine.

## TANGERINE AND PINEAPPLE SALAD

Peel the tangerines, separate in sections and remove the membrane, leaving the pulp unbroken. Place tangerine sections in the form of a star on lettuce on individual plates. Pile pineapple cubes in the center.

## TART AVOCADO SALAD

Peel avocados, cut in halves. Fill center with lemon gelatin combined with crushed drained pineapple. Chill until gelatin is firm, cut each half into quarters, serve on bed of crisp salad greens.

## TART PEACH SALAD

4 peaches                         Lettuce
Special dressing

Peel peaches. Remove stone from stem end. Do not break peach. Serve on lettuce with French dressing made with one tablespoonful of lime juice; one tablespoonful of lemon juice; four tablespoonfuls oil.

## TOWER SALAD

Place a slice of lettuce on a bed of greens. Combine a ring of pineapple and a ring of orange to resemble a tower. Top with a mound of sour cherries.

## WALDORF SALAD

1 cup finely cut celery              ¼ cup chopped nuts
1 cup diced apple                    ¼ cup pecan halves
Cress

Combine celery, apple and chopped nuts. Serve on crisp watercress and garnish with pecan halves.

## YELLOW DAISY SALAD

On individual salad plates arrange orange sections to form petals. In center place cream cheese ball covered with chopped ripe olives.

# VEGETABLE SALADS

### APPLE, CELERY AND RAISIN SALAD

1½ cups sliced apple (do not pare)     ¼ cup raisins
1½ cups sliced celery                  Lettuce

Arrange sliced celery on lettuce. Dip apple rings into French dressing and place on celery. Distribute chopped raisins over apple.

### APPLE AND CELERY ROOT SALAD

2 cups diced tart apple          2 tablespoonfuls grapefruit juice
1 cup diced celery root          Mayonnaise
½ cup chopped ripe olives        Lettuce

Pour grapefruit juice over apple as soon as it is pared and diced. Mix lightly with celery root, olives and walnuts. Serve with mayonnaise on lettuce. Green dessert cherries for garnish.

### APPLE AND CARROT SALAD

1½ cups cubes of tart apple       2 tablespoonfuls lemon juice
1½ cups thinly sliced carrots     Endive

Scrub carrots, wipe dry. Cut into quarters lengthwise. Now slice very thinly. Add apple cubes which have been sprinkled with lemon juice, to prevent discoloration. Arrange on endive.

### APPLE, PEA AND CELERY SALAD

1 cup steamed small peas          1 cup diced apple
            1 cup sliced celery

Marinate each vegetable separately for half an hour in French dressing. Drain and mix lightly. Serve on lettuce.

### APPLE SANDWICH SALAD

Core large red apples. Cut into slices about ¼ inch in thickness. Spread half the slices with a combination of mayonnaise and chopped nuts. Top with plain slices. Serve on generous beds of lettuce or other greens.

*Note*: Apple slices should be dipped in lemon juice to prevent discoloration.

### ASPARAGUS SALAD

4 bundles cooked asparagus        2 teaspoonfuls lemon juice
            1 cup chilled thick sweet cream

Sprinkle asparagus with lemon juice and chill thoroughly. Serve with cream.

## ASPARAGUS, CABBAGE AND BEET SALAD

2 cups raw asparagus tips           1 cup shredded raw beets
1 cup shredded cabbage              Green lettuce leaves

Arrange cabbage on beds of lettuce. Form a star of asparagus points on cabbage. Pile beet in center.

## ASPARAGUS TIP SALAD

1 lb. cooked asparagus tips     6 tablespoonfuls French dressing
Lettuce

Marinate asparagus in French dressing for one hour. Drain and serve on lettuce. Pimiento strips for garnish.

## AVOCADO AND ONION SALAD

2 large avocados        ½ cup minced onion
½ cup minced celery

Pare and dice avocados. Combine with celery and onion. Serve on chicory.

## BEAN AND CELERY SALAD

1 cup steamed small green beans,    1 cup sliced celery
    2-inch lengths                 2 tablespoonfuls grated onion
½ cup shredded green pepper        French dressing

Toss together salad ingredients and dressing and serve on lettuce.

## BEAN AND ONION SALAD

4 cups steamed green beans      4 medium size mild onions
2 tablespoonfuls minced chives  Lettuce
Mayonnaise

Remove as much of center of onions as possible to leave firm shell. Fill these with mayonnaise. Cut beans into one-inch lengths, and marinate in French dressing for fifteen minutes. Combine minced chives with drained beans and arrange on lettuce. Place one onion on each salad plate.

## BEET SALAD

8 medium sized cold boiled beets     Small lettuce leaves
4 tablespoonfuls French dressing     4 tablespoonfuls chopped olives

Cut beets in halves crosswise and marinate in French dressing for one hour. At serving time place ½ beet on each lettuce leaf and sprinkle finely chopped olives over salad.

## BEET AND APPLE SALAD

2 cups sliced steamed beets, marinated     2 cups sliced apple
Endive

Arrange sliced beets and apple in circles on endive.

## BEET CUP SALAD

4 large steamed beets     1½ cups diced cooked carrot (marinated)
Lettuce

Remove centers from cooked beets, leaving cups. Marinate in French dressing. Drain. Fill with carrot. Serve on lettuce.

## BEET AND CELERY SALAD

2 cups diced cooked beets     1½ cups sliced celery

Marinate diced beets in French dressing for one hour. Drain. Combine with celery. Serve on lettuce.

## BEET AND ONION SALAD

1 cup diced cooked beets     French dressing
1 cup chopped sweet onion     4 cucumber cups or boats
Boiled dressing

Marinate beets in French dressing for one hour. Drain, and mix lightly with onion. Fill into cucumber shells. Serve on lettuce with boiled dressing.

## BERMUDA SALAD

1 cup finely chopped Bermuda onion     ¼ cup French dressing
1 cup crushed (drained) pineapple     4 tomato cups
Lettuce

Toss onion and pineapple together with dressing. Drain. Fill tomato cups with mixture and set on lettuce.

## CABBAGE AND PECAN SALAD

1 cup chopped pecans     4 whole pecan meats
2 cups shredded white cabbage     Lettuce

Combine cabbage and nuts with mayonnaise. Serve on lettuce. One-half pecan to top each salad.

## CABBAGE AND PINEAPPLE SALAD

1½ cups shredded cabbage     6 tablespoonfuls salad dressing
½ cup shredded unsweetened     4 apple cups
    pineapple

Combine cabbage, pineapple and dressing. Mix lightly. Place in apple cups. For variation substitute orange dice, peach balls or apple cubes for pineapple.

## CABBAGE AND CELERY SALAD

1½ cups shredded white cabbage           4 stuffed olives
1½ cups chopped celery                   Curly lettuce (green)

Combine cabbage, and celery.  Arrange on lettuce and slice olives over salad to garnish.

## CABBAGE AND ONION SALAD

2 cups shredded white cabbage            1 tablespoonful minced green
½ cup onion rings                          pepper
                          Romaine

Combine salad ingredients.  Serve on Romaine.

## CABBAGE, CRESS AND CELERY SALAD

1 cup shredded cabbage                   1 cup sliced celery
1 cup chopped cress                      4 lettuce cups
                    French dressing

Combine salad ingredients and dressing; pile into lettuce cups.  Garnish with pimiento strips.

## CABBAGE, COCONUT AND ALMOND SALAD

½ medium sized head of cabbage                    1 cup almonds
                1 cup fresh shredded coconut

Shave cabbage as thin as possible.  Slice the almonds, and combine all ingredients.

## CABBAGE BOWL SALAD

1 large red cabbage                      ½ cup chopped carrots
1 cup shredded celery                    2 tablespoonfuls grated onion

Cut a slice from top of cabbage.  Remove center of head, leaving firm outer shell.  Chill.  Chop enough of the cabbage to make one cup, mix with celery, carrots, onion and dressing; and pile into cabbage bowl.

## CABBAGE AND CARROT SALAD

2 cups chopped cabbage                   2 tablespoonfuls minced onion
1 cup grated or chopped carrots          ¼ cup diced cucumber

Combine ingredients.  Toss together with a little French dressing.

## CABBAGE, TURNIP AND CARROT SALAD

2 cups chopped cabbage
1 cup shredded raw turnip

1 cup grated carrot
¼ cup French dressing

Combine chilled ingredients. Serve on lettuce.

## CABBAGE, CRESS AND RADISH SALAD

2 cups shredded cabbage
2 cups chopped cress
½ cup thinly sliced radishes

¼ cup thinly sliced green onion
French dressing
4 hard boiled egg yolks

Toss first four ingredients with enough French dressing to moisten. Place in salad bowl which has been lined with lettuce. Force egg yolks through fine sieve and sprinkle over salad.

## CABBAGE, APPLE AND CELERY SALAD

2 cups shredded cabbage
¾ cup diced apple

¾ cup sliced celery
¼ cup French dressing

Combine cabbage with French dressing and form into nests. Fill these with apple and celery tossed together.

## CARROT AND WALNUT SALAD

2 cups ground raw carrots
½ cup chopped walnuts

½ cup small cubes of tart apple
2 tablespoonfuls lemon juice

Romaine or endive

Mix apple and lemon juice, add carrot and nuts, toss together lightly. Arrange on romaine or endive.

## CARROT AND RADISH SALAD

1½ cups grated raw carrots
1 cup sliced tiny red radishes

2 tablespoonfuls minced onion
4 lettuce cups

Combine salad ingredients and fill into lettuce cups.

## CARROT RING SALAD

3 cups cooked carrot rings      1 cup chopped Bermuda onion
Lettuce

To prepare carrot rings, slice cooked carrot ¼ inch thick. Remove centers with apple corer. Make a border of overlapping carrot rings on lettuce. Pile onion in center.

## CARROT AND CRESS SALAD

2 cups ground carrots            2 cups chopped cress
¼ cup French dressing

Toss cress with half the given quantity of French dressing. Combine carrots with remaining dressing and arrange on cress.

## CARROT, LETTUCE AND CELERY SALAD

1 cup shredded carrots            ½ cup chopped celery
1½ cups shredded lettuce            2 tablespoonfuls lemon juice

Mix lightly together celery, lettuce, carrots and lemon juice. Combine with mayonnaise. Serve on lettuce.

## CARROT AND PEA SALAD

1 cup cold steamed peas            2 cups shredded lettuce
1 cup grated raw carrot            ¼ cup French dressing

Mix peas and carrots with French dressing. Make nests of shredded lettuce and fill with carrots and peas. Dust with paprika.

## CARROT AND LETTUCE SALAD

1 cup chopped raw carrots            2 cups shredded lettuce
Thousand Island dressing

Combine carrot and lettuce with dressing. Serve on endive.

## CAULIFLOWER SALAD

Place large steamed cauliflowerette in center of individual salad plate. Surround with ring of steamed peas, then a ring of diced beet and finally a ring of sliced carrot.

## CAULIFLOWER AND TOMATO SALAD

1 pint firm tomatoes cut in quarters            ¼ cup French dressing
1 pint steamed cauliflower flowerettes            Lettuce
Chopped parsley

Marinate cauliflower in French dressing for one hour. Drain. Combine with tomato and arrange on lettuce. Sprinkle with chopped parsley.

## CAULIFLOWER AND BRUSSELS SPROUTS SALAD

2 cups Brussels sprouts            1 cup cauliflower flowerettes

Chill steamed vegetables. Marinate separately. Drain. Combine and serve on lettuce.

## CAULIFLOWER AND SLICED TOMATO SALAD

Cut out center of thick slice of peeled tomato. Place cauliflowererette in this opening. Surround with Frenched green beans, pipe a border around tomato of cream cheese combined with cream.

## CELERY AND PEA SALAD

1 can small peas
1½ cups chopped celery

1 onion
Celery tops for garnishing

Drain liquid from peas. Combine peas, grated onion, celery and salad dressing. Serve from salad bowl garnished with celery tops.

## CELERY AND TOMATO CUP SALAD

4 tomato cups
¼ cup shredded green pepper
2 cups sliced celery

Combine celery and pepper. Fill tomato cups with mixture.

## CELERY, CUCUMBER AND RADISH SALAD

½ cup diced radishes
1½ cups sliced celery

½ cup diced cucumbers
¼ cup minced onion

Combine vegetables. Place on lettuce and cover with mayonnaise. Garnish with crossed strips of pimiento.

## CELERY AND TOMATO SALAD

1½ cups diced tomato
1 tablespoonful onion juice
1½ cups crisp sliced celery

Combine celery, tomato and onion juice. Serve on lettuce with mayonnaise.

## CELERY ROOT SALAD

3 cups steamed celery root
Pimiento strips

Marinate sliced celery root for half an hour in French dressing. Drain. Serve on lettuce. Garnish with pimiento strips.

## CHOP SUEY SALAD

2 cups thinly sliced cabbage
1 green pepper and 1 pimiento minced
½ cup thinly sliced onion
1 cup bean sprouts
1 cup thinly sliced celery
4 carrots shredded
½ cucumber diced

Sprinkle the ingredients with olive oil; combine as lightly as possible.

## COLD SLAW

| | |
|---|---|
| ¼ cup boiling water | 1 tablespoonful olive oil |
| ¼ cup lemon juice | 3 egg yolks |
| Pinch of salt | ½ cup cream |
| Dash of paprika | 6 cups shredded cabbage |

4 tablespoonfuls pimiento stars, for garnishing

Combine first five ingredients. Heat to boiling point and pour over well-beaten egg yolks. Cook in double boiler until thick. Add cream and beat well. Pour hot over cabbage. Chill thoroughly before serving.

## COOKED VEGETABLE SALAD

Stand cauliflowerette in center of salad plate. Surround with cooked carrot rings, diced beets, sliced asparagus. Place diamond cut green beans as a border around vegetables.

## CRESS SALAD

4 cups cress                    1 onion
Lettuce cups

Break cress into two-inch lengths. Arrange in lettuce cups. Sprinkle finely chopped onion over cress.

## CRESS, CABBAGE AND CARROT SALAD

1 cup chopped cress          1 cup shredded cabbage
1 cup ground carrot

Mix each vegetable separately with jellied mayonnaise. Pack in layers in brick mold. Chill. Slice and serve on endive.

## CRESS AND NUT SALAD

2 small firm heads of iceberg          2 cups chopped cress
lettuce                                1 cup ground nuts

Cut through lettuce heads from top to bottom. Cut out centers, and turn on sides to form cups. Fill with shredded cress and nuts combined with French dressing.

## CRESS AND TOMATO SALAD

4 ripe tomatoes                  1 cup water cress
2 cups marinated water cress

Prepare tomatoes by removing centers. Chill. Invert on beds of marinated cress. Cut slits evenly in tomato and insert sprigs of cress in these.

### CRESS, CABBAGE AND CUCUMBER SALAD

1 cup watercress cut in one-inch        1 cup shredded cabbage
   lengths                              1 cup diced cucumber
                ½ cup diced radishes (white)

Combine salad ingredients. Serve on crisp lettuce. Garnish with olive rings.

### CRESS AND CUCUMBER SALAD

2 cups chopped cress                    ½ cup shredded radishes
1 cup diced cucumber                    French dressing
¼ cup minced scallions                  Lettuce cups

Mix together lightly, cucumber, cress, scallions. Place in lettuce cups. Top
with shredded radishes.

### CUCUMBER SALAD

2 cups sliced cucumbers             ¼ cup French dressing
                Lettuce

Slice cucumbers paper thin. Arrange on lettuce and serve with French dressing.

### CUCUMBER AND APPLE SALAD

1 cup diced crisp cucumber        1 cup diced tart apple
                2 cups chopped endive

Arrange endive in nests on individual plates. Fill with cucumber and apple
combined.

### CUCUMBER BASKET SALAD

1½ cups chopped crisp radish        4 baskets cut from large cucumbers
1½ tablespoonfuls French dressing   Lettuce

Combine radish and dressing. Place in cucumber baskets and serve on
lettuce.

### CUCUMBER AND TOMATO SALAD

3 cups ½-inch slices cucumber       1 cup balls cut from firm tomato

Remove seeds from cucumbers, place a ball of tomato in center of each ring.
Serve on lettuce with mayonnaise.

## DANDELION SALAD

3 cups chopped dandelion
French dressing

1 tablespoonful chopped chives
4 lettuce cups

Combine dandelion with chives and dressing. Drain. Serve in lettuce cups.

## ENDIVE AND CUCUMBER SALAD

2 cups diced crisp cucumber          2 cups chopped endive
French dressing

Combine vegetables and moisten with dressing. Serve on lettuce or greens of choice.

## FILLED CUCUMBER SALAD

Select small, crisp cucumbers. Remove seeds with apple corer. Fill with cream cheese seasoned with minced pimiento and onion juice. Chill. Slice to serve.

## FROZEN TOMATO SALAD

2 cups stewed tomato          ⅛ teaspoonful celery salt
Lettuce

Rub tomato through strainer. Add celery salt. Pour into individual molds and freeze. Unmold on lettuce. Garnish with small crisp cucumber.

## GRAPEFRUIT AND ENDIVE SALAD

1½ cups diced grapefruit          1½ cups shredded endive

Combine endive and grapefruit. Arrange in grapefruit cups. Serve on lettuce.

## GREEN BEAN AND CELERY SALAD

1 cup marinated string beans
1 cup sliced celery
½ cup chopped onion

½ cup diced radishes
Pimiento strips
Endive

Watercress

Combine first four ingredients with French dressing. Drain. Arrange on endive. Garnish with small bunches of cress tied with pimiento strips.

## GREEN LIMA SALAD

2 cups steamed baby limas
¾ cup diced celery

¼ cup minced green pepper
Pimiento strips

Marinate limas and celery, separately, for half an hour. Drain. Mix lightly together beans, celery, and pepper. Garnish with pimiento strips.

## HAY SALAD

On individual salad plates stand short stocks of marinated giant asparagus. Surround with shredded mixed salad greens.

## HEAD LETTUCE SALAD

1 large tender head lettuce
¾ cup salad dressing

¼ cup shredded almonds
¼ cup sliced ripe olives

Select a perfect head of lettuce. Immerse in ice water for half an hour. Hold under water and pull leaves apart (open) without breaking. Drain in ice box. When ready to serve set upright in salad bowl. Insert dressing between leaves. Garnish with olives and almonds. To serve cut into quarters.

## JELLIED TOMATO VEGETABLE SALAD

1 cup tomato juice
1½ teaspoonfuls granulated gelatin
½ cup chopped celery

¼ cup string beans
¼ cup diced cauliflower
¼ cup diced carrots

Soften gelatin by soaking in 1 tablespoonful of cold water. Heat the tomato juice and combine with gelatin. Stir until gelatin is dissolved. Put the vegetables in four molds, cover with the gelatin mixture and let stand in a cold place to set. Serve on chicory with mayonnaise.

## JELLIED SAUERKRAUT SALAD

1 tablespoonful granulated gelatin

¼ cup cold sauerkraut juice
1 cup boiling sauerkraut juice
1 teaspoonful lemon juice

1 cup shaved cabbage
¼ cup thinly sliced celery
¼ cup Julienne strips of pimiento

Soften gelatin by soaking in cold sauerkraut juice about 5 minutes. Add to hot sauerkraut juice, and stir until dissolved. Add lemon juice and strain. Chill until ready to congeal, fold in vegetables, chill in individual molds. Serve on bed of lettuce.

## LETTUCE, CRESS AND ENDIVE SALAD

1 cup chopped cress
1 cup shredded lettuce

1 cup chopped endive
½ cup radish rings

French dressing

Cut centers from crisp radishes and slice remaining shells to make rings. Combine all ingredients with dressing. Serve in lettuce cups.

## LETTUCE AND ONION SALAD

2 cups shredded lettuce          2 finely sliced sweet onions
2 small solid red tomatoes

Arrange lettuce and onion in layers on salad plates.  Garnish with quarters of tomatoes.

## LOG CABIN SALAD

¾ cup unsweetened canned cherries          ¾ cup diced grapefruit
¾ cup diced unsweetened canned          Celery
peaches          Lettuce          Mayonnaise

On lettuce covered plates build individual "log cabins" of celery.  Mix salad ingredients and fill cabins.  Place a spoonful of mayonnaise on each.  Arrange lettuce leaves for thatched roofs.

## MIXED GREENS SALAD

1 cup shredded lettuce          1 cup chopped chicory
1 cup chopped watercress

Toss together with three tablespoonfuls of French dressing.

## NOEL SALAD

2 medium sized tomatoes          1 head of lettuce
1 large avocado          1 hard boiled egg yolk

Wash and chill lettuce and tomatoes.  Just before serving, remove stone and skin from pear.  Cut pear in thin strips.  Cut tomatoes in small sections.  Place lettuce on salad plates and arrange tomato and pear alternately in a circle.  Fill center with mayonnaise and sprinkle mayonnaise with hard boiled egg yolk that has been put through a sieve.

## ONION SALAD

3 Bermuda or Spanish onions          2 cups shredded lettuce
Paprika

Slice onions wafer thin, and arrange on lettuce.  Dust with paprika and serve at once.

## ONION AND BEAN SALAD

2 large Bermuda onions
1 green pepper
½ cup grated carrot

1 cup string beans 2 inch lengths,
  steamed
Shredded lettuce

Place shredded lettuce on individual salad plates. For each service allow three slices onion, rub with olive oil and pile in center of lettuce. One green pepper ring on each salad, fill with marinated carrot. Make a border of green beans.

## ONION AND ORANGE SALAD

8 slices orange, ½-inch thick          8 slices Bermuda onion
                    Endive

Set orange slices on beds of endive. Arrange one onion slice on each slice of orange.

## ORANGE AND WATERCRESS SALAD

4 oranges
4 cups chopped watercress

2 tablespoonfuls French dressing
Lettuce

Toss cress in dressing and arrange on lettuce. Slice or separate oranges in sections.

## PEAR, CELERY AND SAUERKRAUT SALAD

1 cup diced pear                    1 cup sliced celery
                1 cup chopped sauerkraut

Combine ingredients. Serve on lettuce.

## PEPPER AND BEET SALAD

2 cups finely shredded sweet green
  peppers

2 cups diced cooked beets
1 tablespoonful minced chives

1 tablespoonful minced parsley

Toss salad ingredients in French dressing and serve on lettuce.

## PIMIENTO AND PEA SALAD

4 pimiento cups
2 cups steamed tiny green peas
Celery hearts

¼ cup mayonnaise
1 teaspoonful minced onion

Fill pimiento cups with peas, mayonnaise and onion combined. Place on lettuce leaves and garnish with small celery hearts.

## PIMIENTO CUP SALAD

4 pimiento cups
½ cup chopped nuts
A few cold cooked asparagus tips
Endive

¼ cup chopped celery
1 cup chopped cucumber
1 teaspoonful minced chives

Carefully combine nuts, celery, cucumber, chives, and fill pimiento cups with mixture. Stand asparagus tips about the edge (inside) of cups. Pour over each cup a generous amount of French dressing. Arrange on endive.

## PINEAPPLE AND CABBAGE SALAD

4 slices unsweetened pineapple
1 cup shredded coconut
½ cup shredded white cabbage
½ cup shredded red cabbage

¼ cup French dressing
½ teaspoonful lime juice
Lettuce
Bamboo sprouts, marinated

Place slices of pineapple on lettuce. Combine cabbage, lime juice, coconut and French dressing. Drain. Place on pineapple. Garnish with bamboo sprouts.

## PINEAPPLE AND BEET SALAD

2 cups shredded, drained, unsweetened pineapple
12 slices cooked beets

2 cups chopped endive
2 tablespoonfuls grapefruit juice
French dressing

Marinate beets in French dressing. Sprinkle grapefruit juice over endive, mix well and form circles on salad plates. Fill these with pineapple. Use a vegetable cutter to cut beets into uniform shapes and arrange on pineapple.

## PINEAPPLE AND CELERY SALAD

2 cups sliced celery
1 cup shredded unsweetened pineapple

Combine celery and pineapple. Serve on romaine.

## POINSETTIA SALAD

4 tomatoes                                     Ripe olives

Scald, peel and chill tomatoes. Cut (almost through) tomato into eight sections. Pull back sections to resemble flower petals. Make stamens of pieces of ripe olives. Arrange on lettuce. Serve with French dressing.

## PORCUPINE SALAD

4 yellow tomatoes                    1 cup celery in match-like strips
½ cup shredded almonds

Scald, peel and chill tomatoes. Remove hard center and invert on lettuce. Stick full of celery strips and almonds.

## PRUNE SLAW

2 cups sliced cabbage              ½ cup sliced raw prunes
1 cup shredded apple              1 large orange, diced

Combine ingredients with mayonnaise. Serve on bed of salad greens.

## RADISH AND BEAN SALAD

¾ cup thinly sliced radishes      ¾ cup diced cucumber
¾ cup shredded string beans      4 pepper cups

Marinate vegetables for salad in French dressing. When ready to serve, drain and place in pepper cups. Arrange on lettuce.

## RADISH AND PEPPER SALAD

1 cup red radishes, thinly sliced      Lettuce
1 cup shredded green pepper      4 tomato cups
1 tablespoonful onion juice      Salad dressing

Prepare and chill tomato cups. Combine radish, pepper and onion juice. Place in tomato cups, cover with dressing and serve on curly lettuce.

## RED AND YELLOW TOMATO SALAD

4 small red tomatoes              ¾ cup crushed pineapple
4 small yellow tomatoes          Jellied green mayonnaise

Scald, peel and chill tomatoes. Remove core and cut almost through in three evenly-spaced slices. Pull back sections to form petals. Set on flat leaves of lettuce. Use pineapple for centers of flowers, and cut leaves from jellied green mayonnaise.

## ROMAINE AND ESCAROLE SALAD

1½ cups chopped romaine                    1½ cups escarole

Serve with French dressing seasoned with garlic.


## SALAD BOWL WITH WATERCRESS

Line salad bowl with crisp lettuce. Fill with layers of chopped watercress, diced tomatoes, sliced cucumbers and shredded radishes. Garnish with chopped hard boiled egg yolk.


## SALAD SUGGESTIONS

Chopped Cress on shredded Lettuce, sprinkled with chopped Mint.
Circle of Avocado slices filled with sliced Kumquats and Celery.
Diced Orange, Avocado and Pineapple.
Diced Pineapple, sliced Strawberries, diced Orange.
Diced Pineapple, sliced Strawberries, Pear balls.
Chopped Watercress and Julienne Mushrooms served on Endive.
Shredded Beets, diced Cucumber and sliced Celery.
Thick slice Yellow Tomato garnished with minced Green Pepper.
Shredded Pineapple, sliced Celery and sliced Almonds.
Shredded Cabbage garnished with crisp Bacon and hard boiled Egg Yolk.
Shredded Cabbage; add minced Chives and Pimiento to season.
Chopped Dandelion and Cress with sliced Chives or Leeks.
Tomato cups filled with steamed Peas and sliced raw Cauliflower.
Sliced marinated Beets garnished with minced Mint.
Diced Grapefruit, sliced Celery and halved seeded Grapes.
Bean Sprouts, sliced Celery, shredded Radishes and diced Tomato.
Diced Apple, sliced Celery and sliced seeded Grapes.
Celery and Sauerkraut.
Pineapple, Cherries, Almonds.
Julienne Celery and Beets.
Green Peppers stuffed with Celery, Apple and Cabbage.
Mound of steamed Green Limas bordered with sliced cooked Beets.
Tomato filled with shaved Onion and Julienne Celery.
Julienne Cucumber and Apple with sliced Avocado.

## SALAD SUGGESTIONS

Shredded Red Cabbage and minced Green Pepper.

Diced Pear and red Raspberries.

Avocado sections and diced Persimmon.

Diced Avocado, sliced Celery, steamed Green Limas and shaved Leeks.

Avocado slices, Red Cherries, diced Orange.

Apples stuffed with Celery, Cherries and Raisins.

Celery, Cucumber, Endive and chopped hard boiled Egg Yolk.

Tomato and Avocado.

Celery, Grapefruit, Almonds and chopped Black Olives.

Diced Orange and Pineapple.

Shredded Beet, Julienne Eggplant and shaved Cabbage.

Thick slice of Tomato surrounded with Julienne Apple and sliced Celery.

Alternate sections of Orange and Grapefruit, mound of sliced dark Grapes in center.

Alternate sections of Mango, Avocado and Orange.

Diced Artichoke bottoms, sliced Celery and minced Green Peppers.

Center of steamed Cauliflowerettes surrounded with Julienne Green Beans.

Steamed Peas, diced Carrot, sliced Asparagus, shredded Turnip.

Thick slice of Tomato topped with balls cut from ripe Pear.

Seeded White Cherries, diced Bamboo Shoots, minced Pimiento.

Layers of chopped Cabbage, shredded Carrot and chopped Watercress.

Avocado slices and chopped Walnuts on Lettuce slice.

Marinated Cauliflowerettes and Julienne Mushrooms garnished with Green Pepper ring.

Circle of sliced cooked Beets, diced Pear in center.

Julienne Cucumbers and Mushrooms, sliced Celery.

Circle of alternate slices Beet and Cucumber, center of diced Tomato.

Sliced Asparagus tips, sliced Celery and Julienne Apple.

Half of Avocado, filled with Waldorf Salad.

Shredded Cabbage, sliced Celery and minced Pimiento.

Diced Orange and diced Tomato.

Diced Celery Root, Green Limas, garnished with minced Green Pepper and Pimiento.

Circle of sliced baby Beets; fill center with sliced Celery and minced Green Pepper.

Tomato sections on sliced Pineapple.

Marinated Carrots, sliced paper thin; garnish with minced Parsley.

Thick slice of Chinese Cabbage garnished with shredded Radishes or Beet.

Tomato cups filled with Corn, minced Green Pepper and Onion.

Sliced cooked Asparagus tips and diced baked Beets.

## SAUERKRAUT AND CARROT SALAD

1½ cups sauerkraut                    1 cup grated carrot

Combine carrots and sauerkraut. Arrange in lettuce cups.

## SAUERKRAUT AND TOMATO SALAD

3 slices of tomato          ¼ cup raw sauerkraut
(Sufficient for individual salad)

Place the three slices of tomato in the center of lettuce arranged on salad plate. Heap the sauerkraut in the center and garnish with parsley. Serve with sour cream.

## SHREDDED TURNIP AND PINEAPPLE SALAD

⅓ cup shredded white turnips              1 slice of pineapple
(Makes one portion)

Place a slice of pineapple on lettuce arranged on salad plate, cover the center of pineapple with a mound of shredded turnip and garnish with pimiento.

## SHREDDED VEGETABLE SALAD

1½ cups each, shredded raw beet, carrot and cucumber. Arrange in small mounds on bed of lettuce or endive.

## SPECIAL SALAD COMBINATIONS

Shredded cabbage and celery
Celery, cabbage and carrots, shredded
Shredded parsnips, celery, beets and cabbage
Shredded carrots and raisins
Green beans, green peas, tomatoes and celery
Shredded beets and carrots
Cabbage, green peppers and pimiento.

## SPINACH AND LETTUCE SALAD WITH BACON DRESSING

2 quarts tender young spinach leaves      6 tablespoonfuls lemon juice
2 quarts spring lettuce                   3 slices fat bacon
1 small onion minced                      ½ teaspoonful vegetable salt
Dash of paprika

Fry bacon until crisp. Reserve fat, to which add lemon, salt and paprika. Heat until steaming. Pour over salad greens and onion and mix over heat until leaves are well coated with dressing. Serve in warm (not too hot) dish. Garnish with chopped bacon slices.

## SPROUT SALAD

2 cups Brussels sprouts          1 cup asparagus tips

Marinate steamed vegetables, separately. Drain. Combine and serve on lettuce.


## STEAMED VEGETABLE SALAD

½ cup steamed carrots                    ½ cup diced steamed beets
½ cup steamed cauliflower flowerettes    ½ cup steamed asparagus tips
                    French dressing

Marinate vegetables separately in dressing. Drain. Arrange asparagus tips on lettuce, top with mixed vegetables.


## STRING BEAN SALAD

1 lb. cooked string beans                    Lettuce

Arrange cooked beans on lettuce. Serve with

### DRESSING

¼ cup minced celery      2 tablespoonfuls minced pimiento
            ⅓ cup French dressing

Shake ingredients together.

### STUFFED TOMATO SALAD

4 tomatoes                          1 tablespoonful onion juice
2 cups string beans, 1-inch lengths    ½ cup mayonnaise

Scald, peel and chill tomatoes. Cut slice from top and remove centers. Sprinkle with celery salt and invert while chilling again. Marinate beans in French dressing for half an hour. Drain and add onion juice and mayonnaise. Place in tomato cups.


## TOMATO ASPIC SALAD

2 cups canned tomatoes            2 whole cloves
¾ cup water                      1 teaspoonful paprika
1 stalk celery, chopped          Blade of mace
2 carrots, sliced                ½ teaspoonful vegetable salt
½ small onion, chopped           1½ tablespoonful gelatin
½ small green pepper, chopped    1 tablespoonful lemon juice

Place tomatoes and ½ cup water in saucepan with vegetables and seasoning. Simmer 15 minutes. Soften gelatin by soaking in the remaining ¼ cup cold water about 5 minutes. Add to strained tomato mixture (hot). Chill in flat pan and cut in star shapes to serve. (Serves 6.)

## TOMATO CABBAGE SALAD

Fill tomato cups with thinly shaved cabbage and sliced almonds.

## TOMATO CUP SALAD

| | |
|---|---|
| 4 tomato cups | ½ cup chopped celery |
| ½ cup diced cucumber | ½ cup diced tart apples |

Fill tomato cups with salad mixture and arrange on endive or lettuce. Garnish with finely chopped olives.

## TOMATO, CUCUMBER AND ONION SALAD

| | |
|---|---|
| 4 cucumber cups | ½ cup diced cucumber |
| ½ cup diced tomato | ½ cup diced mild onion |
| ¼ cup French dressing | |

Mix dressing with salad ingredients and place in cucumber cups. Serve on beds of lettuce.

## TOMATO, CUCUMBER AND RADISH SALAD

| | |
|---|---|
| 4 medium sized tomatoes | 4 radishes |
| 2 cucumbers | ½ sweet green pepper (minced) |
| Lettuce | |

Scald, peel and chill tomatoes. Pare cucumbers. Slice both. Arrange lettuce on salad plates, place vegetables in layers on lettuce; first a slice of tomato, then cucumber and last a slice of radish. Sprinkle with green pepper and serve.

## TOMATO AND PEPPER SALAD

| | |
|---|---|
| 2 tablespoonfuls minced green peppers | 3 cups balls cut from firm tomatoes |
| | 2 tablespoonfuls French dressing. |

Combine tomatoes, pepper and dressing. Serve on lettuce.

## TOMATO PUFF SALAD

| | |
|---|---|
| 1 cup tomato purée | 1 cup whipped cream |
| Lettuce | |

Mix tomato puree with whipped cream. Pack in individual molds and freeze. Turn out on lettuce.

## TURNIP AND CELERY SALAD

2 cups steamed turnip balls          4 tablespoonfuls finely chopped
1 cup diced celery                            parsley

Marinate turnip balls in French dressing for half an hour.  Drain.  Combine
with celery and parsley. Serve on lettuce. Garnish with pimiento.

## VARIETY SALAD

1 cup shredded cabbage          ½ cup sliced celery
½ cup diced, steamed beets          ¼ cup minced pimiento
½ cup steamed carrot rings          Endive or lettuce
          1 tablespoonful onion juice (optional)

Toss salad ingredients together lightly and serve on endive or lettuce.

## VEGETABLE AND NUT SALAD

1 cup grated carrots          ½ cup finely shredded green peppers
1 cup shredded cabbage          4 tablespoonfuls French dressing
½ cup chopped pecans or walnuts          Romaine

Combine carrots, cabbage, nuts, pepper and French dressing.  Serve on beds
of romaine.

# SALAD DRESSINGS

### ALMOND DRESSING

½ cup water
3 egg yolks
Pinch of salt

2 tablespoonfuls lemon juice
½ cup shredded, blanched almonds
1 cup whipped cream

Beat egg yolks with salt until thick. Add lemon juice and hot water. Cook over hot water until thick and smooth, stirring constantly. Chill. When ready to use add whipped cream and almonds.

### AVOCADO SALAD DRESSING

Rub avocado through fine sieve, beat until as light as possible. Combine with an equal amount of mayonnaise.

### BEET AND CHIVE DRESSING

2 tablespoonfuls minced chives
2 tablespoonfuls chopped cooked beet
6 tablespoonfuls oil

2 tablespoonfuls lemon juice
Few grains paprika
1 tablespoonful beet juice

½ teaspoonful vegetable salt

Shake until well blended. Keep cold.

### BOILED DRESSING

4 egg yolks
2 tablespoonfuls olive oil

1½ tablespoonfuls lemon juice
½ cup boiling water

¼ teaspoonful vegetable salt

Beat egg yolks until very light. Add salt, lemon juice, oil and water. Cook over hot water until thick, stirring constantly.

### BUTTERMILK DRESSING

½ cup rich buttermilk                    1 teaspoonful lemon juice
Pinch of salt

Combine ingredients. Beat with rotary beater until very light. Should be used immediately. Excellent with cucumbers.

## CANNED MILK DRESSING

2 tablespoonfuls lemon juice                    1 cup evaporated milk

Have milk and lemon juice very cold. Beat with rotary beater until thick and light.

A satisfactory substitute for real sour cream dressing. For best results immerse can of milk in boiling water and boil for one hour. Chill thoroughly before beating.

## CELERY AND NUT MAYONNAISE DRESSING

1 cup mayonnaise                    ½ cup finely minced celery hearts
½ cup chopped nuts

Combine ingredients. Keep cold.

## CHIFFONADE DRESSING

1 tablespoonful chopped green pepper     ½ tablespoonful chopped onion
1 tablespoonful chopped pimiento         ¼ teaspoonful paprika
½ tablespoonful chopped parsley          ⅔ cup French dressing

Prepare French dressing and add other ingredients.

## COOKED FRUIT SALAD DRESSING

½ cup Tupelo honey          2 teaspoonfuls lemon juice
½ cup grapejuice            2 egg yolks

Beat egg yolks until very light, add juices and honey heated together. Cook in double boiler until of a creamy consistency.

## CREAM FRUIT DRESSING

1 cup whipped cream               3 tablespoonfuls tart fruit juice
½ teaspoonful grated orange rind

Combine ingredients and serve at once.

## CREAM MAYONNAISE DRESSING

½ cup whipped cream               ½ cup mayonnaise

Stir together until well blended. Keep as cold as possible without freezing.

## CREAM OF TOMATO DRESSING

½ cup heavy cream (sweet or sour)     2 tablespoonfuls olive oil
½ cup tomato purée     1 tablespoonful lemon juice
½ teaspoonful vegetable salt

Mix oil, salt, and lemon juice. Beat in tomato purée, finally add cream, beating until smooth and well blended. Keep cold.

## EGG DRESSING

6 tablespoonfuls olive oil     2 hard boiled egg yolks
2 tablespoonfuls lemon juice     1 tablespoonful minced chives

Shake oil, lemon juice and minced chives together. Press egg yolk through fine sieve, add to oil mixture with a few grains salt and a pinch of paprika.

## FAVORITE CREAM DRESSING

3 egg yolks (hard boiled)     2 tablespoonfuls lemon juice
1 raw egg yolk     ½ cup cream
6 tablespoonfuls olive oil     ½ teaspoonful salt
Dash of paprika

Rub hard boiled yolks through fine sieve. Rub with raw yolk to a smooth paste. Add cream and oil and beat hard. When light and evenly mixed add lemon juice, salt and paprika.

## FRENCH DRESSING

6 tablespoonfuls olive oil     2 tablespoonfuls lemon juice

Shake until well blended. This is the basis of all French dressings. Use for marinade for fish, meat or vegetables. Vary this dressing to suit the taste of your family, by the addition of a clove of garlic, a few chopped chives, two tablespoonfuls sweet cream, or minced parsley, carrot, etc. Lemon juice may be heated with berries, cooled and strained, to add distinctive flavor.

## FROZEN SALAD DRESSINGS

Use orange ice, pineapple, lemon or raspberry sherbet on any fruit salad, in place of usual dressing.

## GARLIC DRESSING

1 cup mayonnaise     ½ cup chopped olives
¼ teaspoonful paprika     ¼ cup chopped sweet peppers
1 clove garlic

Rub bowl with bruised garlic. Mix all ingredients lightly together  Keep cold.

## LIME DRESSING

1 tablespoonful fresh lime juice      6 tablespoonfuls olive oil
1 tablespoonful lemon juice      ⅛ teaspoonful vegetable salt

Pour cold ingredients into bottle and shake until blended.

## MAYONNAISE DRESSING

2 cups olive oil      1 tablespoonful Tupelo honey
3 tablespoonfuls lemon juice      2 egg yolks
½ teaspoonful vegetable salt

Beat egg yolks for a few minutes. Continue beating and add lemon juice a few drops at a time, alternately with oil, one tablespoonful at a time. Add honey and salt; beat for several minutes more. Pack in glass and keep cold.

## MAYONNAISE WITH FRUIT JUICE

2 egg yolks      3 tablespoonfuls fruit juice (half lemon
2 cups salad oil      and half pineapple or grapefruit,
1 teaspoonful vegetable salt      orange and lime may be used)
¼ teaspoonful paprika      1 tablespoonful Tupelo honey

Beat egg yolks, salt and paprika for a few minutes. Continue beating and add fruit juice a few drops at a time, alternately with oil, one tablespoonful at a time. Add honey. When all ingredients have been incorporated, beat for several minutes more. Pack in glass and keep cold.

## MINT DRESSING

6 tablespoonfuls olive oil      2 tablespoonfuls lemon juice
1 tablespoonful bruised mint leaves

Combine cold ingredients. Shake well. Let stand at least one hour. Strain.

## RADISH CREAM DRESSING

½ cup mayonnaise      2 tablespoonfuls minced radishes
¼ cup sour cream      1 teaspoonful lemon juice
1 tablespoonful minced parsley      ½ teaspoonful vegetable salt

Beat all ingredients together until well blended.

## RIPE OLIVE DRESSING

½ cup French dressing      ¼ teaspoonful grated onion
12 ripe olives (chopped fine)

Blend one-half hour before using. Keep cold.

## RUSSIAN DRESSING

⅔ cup mayonnaise
⅓ cup tomato juice or purée

1 hard boiled egg yolk chopped fine
1 tablespoonful chopped pimiento

Add ingredients to mayonnaise and mix well.

## SOUR CREAM DRESSING

1 cup whipped cream
2 tablespoonfuls lemon juice

½ teaspoonful vegetable salt
Pinch of paprika if desired

Blend ingredients and keep cold.
If using soured cream, add only one tablespoonful lemon juice.

## SPANISH DRESSING

½ cup French dressing
¼ cup chopped olives

1 teaspoonful onion chopped fine
1 teaspoonful radish chopped fine

1 teaspoonful green pepper chopped fine

Prepare French dressing, add remaining ingredients, and let stand a few minutes before serving.

## STRAWBERRY DRESSING

3 egg yolks, beaten light
¼ cup orange juice
¼ cup strawberry juice

2 tablespoonfuls olive oil
½ cup whipped cream
¼ cup sliced strawberries

Beat egg yolks and fruit juice together over hot water until smooth and thick. Add oil and beat again.
When cold, fold in whipped cream and sliced berries.  Serve at once.

## TART FRUIT DRESSING

¼ cup strained strawberry juice
1 teaspoonful lemon juice

1 tablespoonful orange juice
2 tablespoonfuls olive oil

Combine chilled ingredients and shake until well blended.

## THOUSAND ISLAND DRESSING

½ cup mayonnaise
2 tablespoonfuls tomato purée

2 tablespoonfuls chopped ripe olives
1 tablespoonful chopped pimiento

1 tablespoonful lemon juice

All ingredients   mixed together until well blended.

# MAIN COURSE

### APPLE AND LIMA BEAN CASSEROLE

2 cups steamed baby limas                    2 cups apple sauce
3 tablespoonfuls butter

Use apple sauce made from red apples if possible. Arrange alternate layers of beans and apple sauce in buttered casserole. Dot top with butter. Bake in moderate oven.

### APRICOT OMELETTE

4 egg yolks                    4 tablespoonfuls cream
½ cup purée of apricots

Beat egg yolks as light as possible. Season lightly with salt. Add cream. Pour into oiled or buttered pan and cook over slow heat or in moderate oven until set. Turn out on heated platter, spread with apricot purée, fold over and serve immediately.

### ASPARAGUS IN GOLDEN SAUCE

1¼ lbs. crisp asparagus tips                    3 egg yolks
1½ cups celery broth                    10 drops lemon juice

Cook asparagus (standing upright in pan) in celery broth until tender. Arrange in hot dish, handling carefully to prevent breaking. Beat egg yolks until very light. Pour one cup of liquid from asparagus (hot) over yolks, beating constantly, add lemon juice and cook over hot water until smooth. Pour over asparagus. Sprinkle over top, two tablespoonfuls ground walnuts, browned in hot oven. Serve hot.

### BAKED BEETS

Scrub beets. Do not cut tops away until after beets are cooked. Bake in casserole in moderate oven until tender. Small young beets are most satisfactory for baking.

### BAKED CARROTS

Scrub carrots. Discard tops. Bake in covered casserole in moderate oven until tender.

### BAKED CELERIAC

4 cups sliced celeriac                    Cream

Arrange vegetable in casserole. Add cream to keep moist, sprinkle with vegetable salt and bake until tender.

## BAKED CORN ON COB

Open husk on each ear of corn. Cut away any bad spots. Remove silk and outer husks leaving two thicknesses next to the ear. Place in hot oven and bake for 8 to 10 minutes. Remove remaining husks before serving.

## BAKED EGGPLANT

| | |
|---|---|
| 1 large eggplant | ½ cup chopped onion |
| 4 tablespoonfuls butter | 3 tablespoonfuls minced green |
| 1½ cups tomato dice | pepper |
| ½ cup sauted mushrooms | |

Cut slice from top of eggplant, remove enough of center to make room for filling. Pare. Rub outside and inside with butter (melted) and fill eggplant with remaining ingredients. Set top on, secure with small skewers if necessary. Place in buttered casserole and bake in moderate oven. Baste occasionally with water or vegetable broth.

## BAKED KOHL-RABI

Scrub kohl-rabi. Bake in casserole until tender.

## BAKED MANGEL-WURZELS

2 lb. mangel-wurzel

Slice or cut into large dice and bake in covered glass casserole in moderate oven.

## BAKED SAUERKRAUT

4 cups sauerkraut                    4 slices bacon

Place sauerkraut in casserole and cover top with sliced bacon. Bake in hot oven until bacon is crisp. Use same recipe, substituting two cups sliced apple for half given amount of sauerkraut. Or fill red apples with sauerkraut, cover with chopped bacon.

## BAKED TOMATO

4 large ripe tomatoes                4 tablespoonfuls butter

Select firm, ripe tomatoes. Wash and wipe dry. Rub with olive oil. Remove stem and make cavity large enough to hold one tablespoonful butter. Bake in hot oven.

## BAKED TOMATOES FILLED WITH OKRA AND CORN

4 smooth ripe tomatoes      2 cups steamed okra and grated fresh corn combined

Stuff tomatoes with vegetables and bake on glass.

## BAKED TOMATO, MUSHROOM FILLING

4 smooth ripe tomatoes      2 cups blanched button mushrooms
4 tablespoonfuls melted butter

Remove center from tomatoes. Fill with mushrooms. Pour over each one tablespoonful melted butter. Bake on glass until tender.

## BAKED VEGETABLE CROQUETTES

½ cup thin cream      ½ teaspoonful celery salt
3 egg yolks, beaten      1 teaspoonful onion juice
2 hard-cooked egg yolks, sieved      1 cup any cooked, diced, vegetable

Heat cream, beat into egg yolks, cook over hot water until thickened. Add sieved yolks, celery salt, onion juice and mix well. Stir in vegetables. Chill. Shape into croquettes. Dip in beaten egg yolk, then in protein flour. Bake in hot oven until browned.

## BLANCHED BUTTON MUSHROOMS

3 cups button mushrooms      3 tablespoonfuls melted butter

Cook mushrooms in boiling water until tender. Drain thoroughly. Serve in hot dish with melted or browned butter. Save liquid for flavoring vegetable or meat dishes.

## BRAISED CELERY AND CARROTS

2 cups sliced celery      3 tablespoonfuls butter
2 cups diced carrots      ¼ cup water

Cook celery and carrots in butter for five minutes. Remove to casserole, add a bit of onion salt if desired and water. Cook in moderate oven until tender.

## BRAISED CELERY HEARTS

8 celery hearts      ¼ cup butter
¼ cup vegetable broth

Cook whole celery hearts in butter for ten minutes. Place in casserole, add vegetable broth. Bake in moderate oven until tender.

## BRAISED KALE

½ peck kale      4 tablespoonfuls butter

Melt butter in heavy pan. Add drained small heads of kale. Steam until tender. Serve with strips of broiled fat bacon.

## BRAISED LETTUCE

| | |
|---|---|
| 4 small heads iceberg lettuce | ¼ cup water or celery broth |
| 2 tablespoonfuls butter | ½ teaspoonful celery salt |

Melt butter and cook lettuce heads in it for five minutes, turning frequently. Remove to small buttered casserole and pour liquid around lettuce. Cook until tender, and liquid is evaporated or absorbed.

## BROILED BACON

Lay thin slices of fat bacon on rack in broiling pan and broil at moderate temperature until lightly browned and crisp. Turn once. May be baked in very hot oven.

## BROILED MUSHROOM CAPS

| | |
|---|---|
| 1 lb. large solid mushrooms | 4 tablespoonfuls olive oil |
| 1 bead of garlic | |

Peel mushroom caps. Discard stems. Rub a small bowl with bruised garlic. Place mushrooms in bowl, add oil. Shake about until each cap is covered with oil. Let stand for half an hour. Drain. Broil under hot flame. Place small piece of butter in each cap.

## BUTTERED CARROTS AND PARSLEY ROOT

| | |
|---|---|
| 2 cups carrot rings | 2 cups diced parsley root |

Steam together until tender. Serve with butter or desired sauce.

## BUTTERED TURNIPS AND PEAS

| | |
|---|---|
| 2 cups steamed fresh green peas | 2 cups steamed diced turnips |
| 2 tablespoonfuls melted butter | |

Arrange vegetables in layers in serving dish. Pour butter over.

## BUTTERED VEGETABLES

| | |
|---|---|
| ½ cup carrot cubes, steamed | ½ cup turnip balls, steamed |
| ½ cup string beans, steamed, 2 inch lengths | ½ cup cauliflower, steamed |
| | ½ cup peas, steamed |

Add 1 tablespoonful melted butter to each vegetable. Arrange in separate mounds on hot dish. Any combination of vegetables may be used. A good way to use left overs.

## CABBAGE CASSEROLE

| | |
|---|---|
| 3 cups cabbage, white or red | 1 cup sour apple, sliced |
| 1 cup seeded white grapes | ¼ cup chopped onion |

Combine apple, grapes and onion. Arrange with cabbage in alternate layers in casserole, sprinkle each layer lightly with vegetable salt. Dot top with butter and bake at moderate temperature until flavors are well blended.

## CABBAGE AND EGGPLANT CASSEROLE

Place equal parts sliced cabbage and diced eggplant alternately in casserole. Bake until tender.

## CABBAGE AND ONION CASSEROLE

1 firm head cabbage
3 tablespoonfuls bacon drippings
3 tablespoonfuls chopped onion
3 tablespoonfuls shredded carrot
1 cup vegetable broth

Quarter cabbage, remove heart. Steam for fifteen minutes. Set in bacon drippings in small casserole. Add onion, carrot and vegetable broth. Bake in moderate oven until tender.

## CARROT AND LIMA CASSEROLE

2 cups tiny green limas
2 cups shredded carrot
1 cup sliced onion

Arrange ingredients in layers in casserole. Bake until tender in moderate oven.

## CASSEROLE OF LEEKS AND ASPARAGUS BEANS

Cut French asparagus beans into four inch pieces. Arrange in buttered glass casserole with one-fourth their weight in leek tips. Sprinkle with vegetable salt, add cream to moisten and bake in moderate oven.

## CASSEROLE OF RED CABBAGE AND APPLE

3 cups red cabbage, shredded
¼ cup chopped raw fat bacon
1 tablespoonful minced onion
1 teaspoonful celery salt
4 tart apples

Cook bacon and onion for a few minutes. Place cabbage and seasoning in casserole. Pare apples and cut into quarters. Press these into cabbage to cover. Bake in moderate oven until apples are tender.

## CASSEROLE OF EGGPLANT WITH VEGETABLES

1 large eggplant
1 large onion
¼ pound mushrooms
2 green peppers
3 tomatoes
Grated rind of ½ lemon
3 tablespoonfuls butter or vegetable oil

Dice eggplant, shred peppers, slice onion, cut tomatoes into sections. Cook mushrooms with butter for a few minutes, until lightly browned. Combine eggplant, onion, peppers, and mushrooms. Place tomato sections around casserole, fill with eggplant mixture. Arrange any remaining tomato sections over top. Bake at moderate temperature.

## CASSEROLE OF PARSNIP AND TOMATO

1 quart steamed, mashed parsnip

| | |
|---|---|
| 6 tomatoes | 1 tablespoonful minced parsley |
| ¼ cup chopped onion | 3 tablespoonfuls cream |

3 tablespoonfuls butter or vegetable oil

Beat parsnips with cream and butter, adding vegetable salt to taste. Slice skinned tomatoes. Line bottom and sides of casserole with sliced tomatoes, sprinkle with onion and parsley. Add parsnips. Top with remaining tomato slices, sprinkle with onion, parsley and vegetable salt. Bake in moderate oven.

## CASSEROLE OF VEGETABLES POLONNAISE

½ cup cooked green peas
½ cup cooked baby green lima beans
½ small head of cooked cauliflower
8 stalks cooked asparagus
1 stalk of celery, cut in small pieces and cooked
1 tablespoonful chopped parsley
¼ cup chopped bacon
2 hard boiled egg yolks, chopped

Place all the vegetables in a casserole. Heat the bacon in a pan and cook until crisp. Add chopped egg yolks and parsley. Pour this mixture over the vegetables. Cover the casserole and bake in a moderate oven.

## CAULIFLOWER WITH PUNGENT SAUCE

| | |
|---|---|
| 1 head cauliflower, steamed | ½ teaspoonful celery salt |
| 3 tablespoonfuls butter | 2 tablespoonfuls minced pepper |
| 2 tablespoonfuls lemon juice | 2 tablespoonfuls minced pimiento |

Set steamed cauliflower in hot serving dish. Pour sauce over.

*Sauce*: Melt butter, add lemon juice, salt, pepper and pimiento. Blend well and heat.

## CELERIAC AND PEA ROAST

| | |
|---|---|
| 1 quart mashed, steamed celeriac | 1 cup steamed small green peas |
| | ½ cup cream or ⅓ cup vegetable broth |
| 3 egg yolks | Pinch of grated nutmeg, if desired |

Beat egg yolks as light as possible. Add remaining ingredients except peas and beat light. Fold in peas. Bake in casserole in moderate oven.

## CHARD RING

1½ pounds Swiss Chard

Strip leaves from stems. Steam and chop leaves. Season with a little vegetable salt and butter. Pack into ring mold and keep hot. Cut stems into 1½ inch pieces. Steam until tender, add a little cream. Season with vegetable salt if desired. Turn out green ring onto serving plate. Fill center with creamed stalks.

## CORN CHOWDER

¼ cup chopped bacon
1 cup thinly sliced onion
½ cup shredded sweet pepper
2 cups tomato purée
4 cups freshly cut sweet corn

Cook bacon until slightly browned. Remove cooked particles and keep hot. Pour off all but two tablespoonfuls fat. Cook onion and pepper in fat until slightly browned. Add tomato purée and corn. Simmer until corn is tender. Season with vegetable salt, parsley and any desired herb. Sprinkle bacon particles on top.

## CORN PUDDING

2 cups corn, young and tender
½ teaspoonful vegetable salt
1 cup milk
2 tablespoonfuls butter
4 egg yolks
1 tablespoonful Tupelo honey

Beat egg yolks until as light as possible. Add all other ingredients. Poach in casserole at moderate temperature about 1 hour, or until set.

## CREAMED CARROTS AND MUSHROOMS

1½ cups steamed diced carrot
1½ cups blanched button mushrooms
¼ cup cream
½ teaspoonful celery salt

Combine ingredients and serve hot.

## CURRIED CABBAGE

2 tablespoonfuls butter
2 tablespoonfuls onion or chives, minced
1 teaspoonful minced parsley
3 cups chopped cabbage
1 teaspoonful curry powder
Coconut milk

Cook onion, parsley, and cabbage in butter over direct heat until browned. More butter should be added as needed. Add sufficient coconut milk to moisten well. Simmer until tender. Five minutes before serving add curry.

## EGG YOLKS CODDLED

4 egg yolks                    4 tablespoonfuls thin cream

Stir cream into egg yolks. Pour into oiled or buttered pan and stir constantly over moderate heat until of the desired consistency.

## EGG YOLKS HARD BOILED

Place eggs in cold water to cover. Heat slowly to boiling point. Simmer for 30 minutes. Yolks may be removed either hot or cold.

## EGG YOLK SOUFFLÉ

1 cup milk                                4 egg yolks
1 cup puréed vegetables

Season with vegetable salt, minced parsley, or chopped pimiento. Poach in individual casseroles.

## EGG YOLKS POACHED

To poach the egg yolk, the entire egg must be placed carefully in boiling water. Break the egg into a saucer, then slide into boiling water in shallow pan. Place cover on pan, reduce heat below the boiling point. Let stand until as firm as desired. White must be cut away, taking care not to break yolk. A small round cookie cutter is best for this purpose.

## EGGPLANT ALAMO

Slice raw eggplant (unpeeled) about ½ inch thick. Spread each slice with a paste made by combining nut meal and cream. Place one whole nut meat in the center of each slice. Bake in moderate oven until eggplant is tender and the crust is crisp and lightly browned.

## EGGPLANT, ONION AND PIMIENTO CASSEROLE

Cut eggplant into small dice. Place in casserole in layers, sprinkling each layer with minced onion and chopped pimiento. Bake until tender.

## EGGPLANT AND TOMATO CASSEROLE

1 eggplant                                ½ cup cream
3 large tomatoes                          ¼ cup chopped crisp fat bacon

Pare eggplant and cut into thick slices. Skin tomatoes and slice. In buttered baking dish place a layer of eggplant. Sprinkle over this a little chopped bacon. Add a layer of tomatoes and more bacon. When vegetables are arranged, pour cream over all and bake in moderate oven.

## GREEN BEANS IN TOMATO SAUCE

1 pound green beans                    ½ cup chopped onions
2 cups cooked or canned tomatoes
2 tablespoonfuls bacon or drippings

Cook onion in fat until lightly browned. Add tomatoes and beans. Simmer until beans are tender and sauce is thickened. Season with vegetable salt.

## LYONAISE VEGETABLES

2 cups onion slices                    1 cup carrots cut in fine strips
1 cup Frenched green beans

Bake onions in oiled dish until golden brown and tender. Steam carrots and beans until tender but firm. Toss all vegetables together until thoroughly mixed.

## MASHED PARSNIPS

4 cups steamed parsnips                4 tablespoonfuls butter
4 tablespoonfuls cream

Mash parsnips as soon as tender; beat butter and cream into the vegetable and reheat in glass baking dish. (Either butter or cream may be omitted).

## MINTED PEAS

2 tablespoonfuls butter          1 tablespoonful chopped parsley
2 tablespoonfuls minced onion    Pods from peas
1 tablespoonful chopped mint     3 cups green peas

Cook all ingredients except shelled peas together with 1½ cups water, until pods are soft. Put through sieve. Add peas to purée and cook until tender. Do not attempt this recipe unless peas are very young and tender.

## MOLDED CHARD, HOLLANDAISE SAUCE

3 cups steamed tender chard          Hollandaise sauce

Form four molds of hot steamed chard. Serve with Hollandaise sauce. Pimiento for garnishing.

## MUSHROOM OMELETTE

8 egg yolks                      4 tablespoonfuls cream
2 tablespoonfuls melted butter   1 cup broken mushrooms
  or vegetable oil               ⅛ teaspoonful vegetable salt

Cook mushrooms in fat for 5 minutes. Beat egg yolks slightly, add cream and salt. Pour over mushrooms. Cook over low heat. As soon as mixture begins to set, slip a spatula under to prevent sticking or burning. Cook until firm.

## MUSHROOM TIMBÁLES

2 cups mushroom purée          4 tablespoonfuls cream
4 egg yolks, well beaten        ½ teaspoonful celery salt

Combine ingredients. Pour into buttered timbale molds and poach until firm. (Moderate oven). Serve with tomato sauce

## MUSHROOM AND TOMATO CASSEROLE

1 pound mushrooms                        4 tomatoes
2 Spanish or other large, sweet onions

Steam sliced onions until tender. Arrange ingredients in layers in casserole. Bake in moderate oven.

## ONION, APPLE AND TOMATO CASSEROLE

3 Spanish or other large, sweet onions
3 apples                      1½ cups tomato purée

Slice onions and steam until tender. Arrange in casserole in alternate layers with cored, sliced apples. Sprinkle each layer with vegetable salt if desired. Pour tomato purée over. Bake at moderate temperature until apples are tender and the tomato purée well blended with other ingredients.

## ONIONS IN CREAM

4 large mild onions                  ½ cup thin cream
½ teaspoonful celery salt

Slice onions thinly, arrange in layer in buttered casserole. Pour cream, mixed with celery salt, over onions and bake until tender.

## ONIONS, BAKED IN TOMATO SAUCE

12 white onions                    2 tablespoonfuls shredded green
2 cups tomato purée (thick)           pepper
2 tablespoonfuls butter           ½ teaspoonful celery salt
Dash of paprika

Steam onions until tender. Place in buttered casserole and pour over the tomato purée which has been mixed with butter, green pepper and seasonings. Bake in moderate oven.

## OYSTER PLANT PATTIES

3 cups cooked, mashed oyster plant (salsify)
2 egg yolks, beaten                ½ teaspoonful vegetable salt
1 tablespoonful cream or melted butter

Combine ingredients. Shape into small patties. Dot with butter and bake in moderate oven until lightly browned.

## PAN BROILED BACON AND EGG YOLKS

Cook two strips fat bacon for each serving, in heavy pan until crisp. Keep hot. Drain fat from pan and cook egg yolks in same pan, stirring until cooked as much as desired. Place yolks on heated platter and surround with bacon.

## PARSNIP CROQUETTES

Combine steamed mashed parsnips with a little minced onion, minced parsley and pimiento. Shape into croquettes, bake in moderate oven. Baste with a little butter.

## PEPPER BASKETS

Steam green peppers and shape into baskets. Fill with steamed fresh corn, combined with a little heavy cream. Garnish with pimiento stars.

## POTTED BEANS

3 cups tender green beans cut in 1 inch lengths
1 teaspoonful summer savory

Follow directions for Potted Peas.

## POTTED PEAS

3 cups tiny green peas                6 lettuce leaves

Place three large lettuce leaves in bottom of small stone jar. Add peas. Top with lettuce leaves. Cover tightly. Set in pan of boiling water in moderate oven and cook until peas are tender. One teaspoonful chopped mint may be added to peas.

## PUFFED EGG YOLKS IN NESTS

Pan broil 4 strips of fat bacon until clear, not crisp or browned. Beat 4 egg yolks as light as possible, add 4 tablespoonfuls heavy cream, ½ teaspoonful minced parsley, pinch vegetable salt. Line muffin tins with the partially cooked bacon, place a small piece of bacon in the bottom of tins and fill three-quarters full with egg mixture. Bake in moderate oven until the eggs are firm and the bacon slightly browned.

## SAVORY CARROTS

4 cups carrot rings or balls      ¼ cup minced onion
2 tablespoonfuls butter     1 cup vegetable broth
2 egg yolks

Cook onion and carrot in butter until browned a little. Add vegetable broth and simmer until tender. Remove carrot and beat two egg yolks into liquid. Cook until smooth and pour over carrot. Garnish with chopped parsley.

## SHIRRED EGG YOLKS

Place 1 tablespoonful cream in small individual baking cup. Add 1 egg yolk and a little minced parsley to each cup, sprinkle with vegetable salt. Cook in moderate oven until yolks are set.

## SOUR CUCUMBERS IN TOMATOES

2 cucumbers     ¼ cup minced onion
4 large tomatoes     ½ cup sour cream
1 tablespoonful butter or vegetable oil

Cook onion in butter until lightly browned. Add cucumbers cut into cubes (not pared) and sour cream. Simmer until cucumbers are tender and liquid has been evaporated. Place in tomato cups. Bake in hot oven until tomato is tender.

## SPANISH OMELETTE

Prepared omelette     1 tablespoonful shredded green pepper
1 onion, thinly sliced     4 minced ripe olives
1 tablespoonful vegetable shortening     1 cup tomatoes
Vegetable salt to taste

Heat fat in a pan, add onion and cook until golden brown, add tomato, green pepper and olives; simmer gently until onions are cooked and mixture thickened. Before folding omelette, add one or two tablespoonfuls of this mixture, then fold and pour remainder of mixture around the omelette. Serve at once.

## SPINACH TIMBALES

2 cups chopped, drained, steamed     3 well beaten egg yolks
spinach     ½ teaspoonful celery salt
½ cup thin cream, hot     4 large broiled mushrooms
2 tablespoonfuls browned butter

Beat cream and salt into egg yolks. Add spinach and place in buttered individual molds. Set in pan of hot water and poach in moderate oven until firm. Turn out on hot plates. Set a mushroom on each timbale of spinach and distribute browned butter over mushrooms.

## SPINACH EGG YOLKS

Follow recipe for coddled egg yolks. Add ½ cup chopped, cooked, drained spinach to mixture; season with vegetable salt and proceed as in original recipe.

## SPINACH RING WITH BEETS

3 cups steamed chopped spinach
1 tablespoonful lemon juice

2 tablespoonfuls butter
2 cups buttered beet cubes or balls

Add butter and lemon juice to spinach and press into ring mold. Keep hot. Turn out on hot platter and fill center with buttered beets. Serve with Hollandaise sauce if desired.

## SPINACH RING WITH MUSHROOMS

3 cups steamed, chopped spinach
2 cups sauted button mushrooms
¼ cup heavy cream

3 tablespoonfuls lemon juice
Pinch of salt

Mix spinach, lemon juice and salt. Press into ring mold. Keep hot while preparing mushrooms. When mushrooms are sauted in butter, add cream. Heat well. Turn spinach out on hot platter. Fill center with creamed mushrooms.

## SPINACH WITH COCONUT CREAMED

3 cups cooked, chopped spinach
½ cup finely grated coconut

½ cup heavy cream

Combine ingredients. Heat thoroughly. If freshly grated coconut is used, only ¼ cup cream will be required.

## STEAMED BROCCOLI, HOLLANDAISE SAUCE

4 servings steamed broccoli
Hollandaise sauce

8 slices broiled bacon

Lay two strips of bacon over each serving of broccoli. Serve with Hollandaise sauce. When buying broccoli select dark green variety with tightly closed buds.

## STEAMED BRUSSELS SPROUTS, ORANGE SAUCE

3 cups steamed Brussels sprouts
*Orange Sauce:*
⅓ cup butter    3 tablespoonfuls water and lemon juice (equal parts)
1 tablespoonful grated orange rind

Cook above ingredients together for two minutes. Add ¼ cup orange juice, pour over one beaten egg yolk and cook over hot water until smooth and thick. Pour over hot Brussels sprouts.

## STEAMED CARROTS AND TURNIPS

2 cups yellow turnip balls        2 cups carrot rings

Place vegetable in steamer and cook until tender. Dress with melted butter. (Equal amount of peas may be added.)

## STEAMED CAULIFLOWER

1 large cauliflower        1 cup tomato sauce

Separate cauliflower into flowerettes. Tie in four even bundles. Steam until tender. Serve with tomato sauce.

## STEAMED CELERY AND PEAS

2 cups celery cut in 1 inch lengths        2 cups small green peas

Place celery and peas in pan together and steam until tender. Serve in hot dish with melted butter.

## STEAMED LETTUCE AND PEAS

3 cups tiny green peas                1 tablespoonful grated onion
2 tablespoonfuls butter              1 large heart of lettuce

Melt butter and mix with onion. Cut lettuce heart into four sections and lay in buttered dish. Distribute peas evenly in dish and pour butter over. Steam until lettuce is tender. Cook in dish that will be used for serving.

## STEAMED PEAS

4 cups peas

Steam peas until tender. Serve with melted butter in covered hot dish. Small peas contain so little starch that they may be combined with all foods, whereas large peas must not be combined with acid food or protein.

## SUCCOTASH

2 cups fresh, young corn        2 cups tiny, green lima beans
2 tablespoonfuls butter or vegetable oil
¼ cup cream

Melt butter in saucepan. Add vegetables. Simmer until tender. Season with vegetable salt, add cream. Continue cooking for 10 minutes.

## SUMMER HASH

2 tablespoonfuls chopped fat bacon
1 cup sliced sweet onion
1 cup tomato dice

¼ cup minced green pepper
4 cups summer squash (diced)
Minced parsley

Prepare squash by removing seeds and cutting into dice. Do not pare if skin is tender. Saute bacon, remove cooked particles from fat. Add onion to fat and cook until lightly browned. Add tomato, pepper and squash. Season with vegetable salt. Cook gently until squash is tender. Remove from pan leaving fat. Add bacon particles and sprinkle with parsley.

## TURNIP OR CARROT CUPS WITH PEAS

Large carrots that appear in the markets during the winter months should be used for cups. Steam the carrots until tender. Shape into cups and fill with hot buttered peas. Baked or steamed turnips are interesting when cut into cups and filled with peas.

## VEGETABLE CASSEROLE

Fill casserole with layers of green baby limas and sauted mushrooms, add sufficient tomato juice to keep moist. Bake in moderate oven.

## VEGETABLE PIES

1½ cups thinly sliced onion          3 tablespoonfuls butter
2 medium sized tomatoes, cut into dice and drained
¼ cup minced mushrooms      ⅓ teaspoonful vegetable thickening
½ teaspoonful minced parsley      ½ teaspoonful vegetable salt
¼ teaspoonful paprika

Cook onion in butter for a few minutes until golden color. Remove from pan and cook mushrooms for 5 minutes in same pan. Combine vegetable thickening with mushrooms and onions while hot. Add tomatoes, parsley, salt and paprika. Place in individual glass baking cups. Top with protein pastry. Bake in hot oven.

## VEGETABLE PLATTER COMBINATIONS

Buttered peas, steamed carrot strips, steamed cauliflowerettes.
Broiled mushroom caps, steamed string beans, diced beets.
Buttered string beans, steamed onions, grilled tomatoes.
Buttered cauliflower, diced carrots, spinach molds.
Stuffed green peppers, diced celeriac, baked tomatoes.
Steamed asparagus, diced baked beets, steamed small green limas.
Grilled onion rings, mashed yellow turnips, steamed peas.
Eggplant Almano, steamed Brussels sprouts, baked tomato.
Creamed corn in peppers, mashed parsnips, shredded beets.
Stuffed mushroom caps, steamed asparagus, diced carrots.

## VEGETABLE RING

2 cups purée of mixed vegetables          6 egg yolks (beaten)
1 cup thin cream

Mix ingredients and poach in buttered ring mold. Turn out on hot platter.

## VEGETABLE TIMBALES

1 cup puréed baby lima beans          2 tablespoonfuls chopped parsley
1 cup puréed carrots                  2 tablespoonfuls chopped onions
½ cup chopped nuts                    ½ cup chopped celery
2 egg yolks                           2 teaspoonfuls vegetable paste

Mix in order given, put in buttered individual timbale molds or in muffin tins, set in hot water and bake approximately 30 minutes or until they are set.

## WAX BEANS WITH ONION AND CELERY

3 cups yellow wax beans               1 cup rings of mild onions
1 cup sliced celery                   2 tablespoonfuls chopped fat bacon

Arrange ingredients in casserole. Bake at moderate temperature.

## WINTER STRING BEANS

1 can green beans          2 tablespoonfuls chopped fat bacon
2 tablespoonfuls minced onions

Heat beans in their own liquid. Cook bacon and onion together until light brown and add drained beans. Serve hot. Use liquid from beans in making vegetable broth.

# VEGETABLES

## ASPARAGUS MOLDS

1 cup asparagus purée (hot)          4 hard-boiled egg yolks
3 egg yolks beaten light             1 cup asparagus tips
               4 large mushroom caps, broiled

Combine hot purée and egg yolks. Place one hard-boiled egg yolk in each of four individual buttered molds. Pour purée over and poach until firm. Turn out and garnish with hot asparagus tips. Set one broiled mushroom cap on each mold.

## ASPARAGUS SOUFFLÉ

1 cup milk          1 cup asparagus purée
          6 egg yolks, well beaten

Pour hot milk over egg yolks. Beat well. Stir in asparagus purée. Bake in individual buttered molds until firm. Turn out on warm plates, and surround with steamed asparagus tips.

## BAKED BEETS AND GREENS

Bake medium sized beets until tender. Steam beet tops, chop and season with vegetable salt, butter, and a little lemon juice. Slip skins from baked beets. Scoop out centers and fill with prepared greens.

## BAKED CELERIAC

Place diced raw celeriac in casserole with a little butter or vegetable oil. Bake until tender.

## BAKED ENDIVE

4 small heads endive          4 tablespoonfuls melted butter

Set endive in well-buttered casserole. Pour butter over. Cover and bake until tender. Turn each head over when half done. Oven heat must be moderate. Sprinkle with celery salt before serving.

## BAKED OKRA AND TOMATO

3 cups sliced okra          4 sliced ripe tomatoes

Arrange in layers in casserole adding a little chopped onion if desired. Bake in moderate oven until okra is tender and there is no excess liquid.

## BEET TOPS AND LETTUCE

2 quarts chopped beet tops          2 tablespoonfuls butter
2 quarts chopped green lettuce      2 tablespoonfuls lemon juice

Steam beet tops and lettuce together until tender. Melt butter and add lemon juice. Blend with greens. Serve hot.

## BOILED COLLARDS

4 small heads collard          ¼ lb. bacon in piece

Score bacon deeply and boil in a little water for three hours. Add the center parts of four heads of collard. Simmer until tender and water is boiled away. Discard bacon.

## BOILED CORN ON THE COB

Corn when picked very young and tender in full milk may be used as a vegetable; but should be eaten within twenty four hours of the time of picking, otherwise it should be treated as a starch. Immerse in boiling water, set over direct heat. When water reaches boiling point again the corn is sufficiently cooked. Serve on cob or cut off and dress with melted butter or cream.

## BOILED WHITE ONIONS

8 medium size onions          2 cups water
2 cups milk                   ½ teaspoonful celery salt

Peel onions under running water. Combine milk and water and heat to boiling point. Drop onions into this and simmer until tender. Drain, add celery salt and serve immediately.

## BRAISED CHICORY

Substitute chicory for endive in recipe for Braised Endive.

*Note*: 2 cups steamed cabbage may be dressed and served as in recipe for Braised Endive.

## BRAISED ENDIVE

1 lb. endive          2 tablespoonfuls butter

Cut in two-inch lengths. Melt butter in heavy pan, add endive. Cover and cook slowly for fifteen minutes.

## BRAISED LEEKS

Melt a little butter in heavy pan, add leeks (green tops removed) and cook quickly until lightly browned. Cover pan and steam vegetables until tender. Sprinkle with vegetable salt before serving.

## BROILED APPLE RINGS

8 rings cut from large apples (skin not removed)
¼ cup chopped raw fat bacon

Rub apple rings with oil on one side. Place oiled side down on baking sheet. Distribute chopped bacon over rings and broil.

## BROILED TOMATO SLICES

Thick slices ripe, firm tomato      Thin slices sweet large onion
Chopped raw fat bacon

Butter large broiling sheet. Set tomato slices on sheet, one onion slice on each. Top with chopped bacon. Broil under medium heat.

## BROILED TOMATOES

1½ lbs. firm tomatoes

Do not peel. Cut into one-inch slices, discarding uneven top. Dip each slice in oil and broil under hot flame.

## BROWNED MUSHROOMS IN CREAM

1 pound button mushrooms or sliced mushrooms
1 cup cream

Place mushrooms in heavy pan with ¼ cup of cream. Cook at high temperature until cream is evaporated, stirring constantly. A brown residue will be formed in the pan. Add 1 tablespoonful of cream at a time, stirring to distribute the brown part evenly.

## BUTTERED BEEFSTEAK LETTUCE

4 heads tender beefsteak lettuce

Steam until tender. Serve with melted butter.

## BUTTERED BEETS

4 cups baby beets          4 tablespoonfuls butter

Steam beets until tender. Remove skins. Shake in melted butter and serve hot. One tablespoonful of lemon juice may be added.

## BUTTERED CARROTS

3 cups steamed carrots     2 tablespoonfuls green pepper  } Optional
2 tablespoonfuls butter    1 tablespoonful pimiento

Melt butter and pour over carrots. If using pimiento and green pepper, cook in butter for five minutes before adding to carrots, being careful not to brown.

## BUTTERED FRENCH ASPARAGUS BEANS

1½ lbs. beans

Break or cut the beans into two or three inch lengths. Steam until tender. Serve with melted butter.

## BUTTERED KOHL-RABI

1½ lbs. kohl-rabi          4 tablespoonfuls butter

Pare vegetables (thinly) and cut into dice or wedge-shaped pieces. Steam until tender. Pour butter over and serve hot.

## BUTTERED RADISHES

Steam small red radishes whole or sliced, until tender. Serve with melted butter. For creamed radishes, add a little cream in place of butter.

## BUTTERED STRING BEANS

4 cups steamed green beans     4 tablespoonfuls melted butter

Combine and serve hot.

## CARROT AND LIMA CASSEROLE

2 cups tiny green limas        2 cups shredded carrot
1 cup shredded apple

Arrange ingredients in layers in casserole. Bake until tender in moderate oven.

## CASSEROLE OF SUMMER VEGETABLES

Place in alternate layers in casserole the following vegetables:

| | |
|---|---|
| Sliced tomato | Peas |
| Marble onions | Celery |
| Green beans | |

Sprinkle with vegetable salt. Add sufficient vegetable broth to keep moist while baking. Bake in moderate oven.

## CAULIFLOWER HOLLANDAISE

Serve steamed cauliflower flowerettes masked with Hollandaise sauce. Garnish with pimiento stars.

## CAULIFLOWER MOLDS

Using recipe for Asparagus Molds, substitute cauliflower for asparagus.

## CELERY AND BRUSSELS SPROUTS

1½ cup sliced celery                2½ cups steamed sprouts
                    ½ cup cream

Cook celery in 2 tablespoonfuls butter for five minutes. Add cream. Simmer until tender, add sprouts. Heat thoroughly and serve.

## CELERY AND CABBAGE IN CREAM

2 cups celery, sliced and steamed        ¼ cup cream
2 cups steamed shredded cabbage          Pinch of salt

Combine ingredients. Serve hot.

## CELERY BROTH

4 cups chopped celery            4 cups water

Simmer until celery is soft. Strain through double thickness of linen. Add a pinch of salt.

## CELERY CUSTARD

3 cups sliced celery (steamed)        ½ cup blanched button mushrooms
½ cup shredded green pepper           1½ cups milk
  (sauted)                           6 egg yolks
            1 tablespoonful chopped pimiento

Beat egg yolks. Add hot milk slowly. Fold into mixture the prepared vegetables. Poach in moderate oven until firm.

## CELERY ROOT

4 cups sliced celery root

Steam until tender. Serve with melted butter.

## CELERY WITH PARSLEY BUTTER

8 small celery hearts

Place celery in buttered pan. Cook gently until tender. Remove to hot platter. Spread top (side) of each stalk with parsley butter.

## CHICORY, HOLLANDAISE SAUCE

Steam chicory until tender and serve with Hollandaise sauce.

## CHINESE CABBAGE

4 cups chopped Chinese cabbage      ½ cup tomato purée
2 tablespoonfuls minced onion

Steam cabbage until tender. Add tomato purée and onion cooked for five minutes in olive oil. Mix thoroughly and simmer for a few minutes to blend.

## COMPOTE OF VEGETABLES

6 small carrots                2 cups steamed peas
2 bunches scallions            4 cups new cabbage, steamed

Cut carrots into 1 inch sticks. Slice the scallions, and steam these together. Combine peas and cabbage, place in center of serving dish, arrange a border of carrots and scallions.

## CREAMED ASPARAGUS

1½ lbs. asparagus        1 cup cream

Cook asparagus in steamer until tender. Heat cream until steaming and pour over asparagus.

## CREAMED CABBAGE

1 solid head white cabbage        ½ cup cream

Cut cabbage into quarters. Remove heart. Steam until tender. Cook away all water. Add cream and simmer for five minutes.

## CREAMED CABBAGE AND PEPPERS

3 cups steamed chopped cabbage        ¼ cup sauted sliced pepper
½ cup cream

Combine ingredients and serve.

## CREAMED OKRA

1 quart okra pods          ½ cup heavy cream (heated)

Small green okra pods may be steamed whole. Larger pods should be sliced. Steam until tender and serve with cream.

## CREAMED ONIONS

12 small steamed onions          ½ cup cream
¼ teaspoonful celery salt

Heat onions in cream with celery salt. Serve hot.

## CREAMED ONIONS AND TURNIPS

Cook onions in milk until tender. Drain. Chill. Slice 1½ cupfuls. Simmer turnips in celery broth until well done. Drain and chill. Dice 2 cupfuls. Combine vegetables with ½ cup cream. Season with celery salt. Heat thoroughly.

## CREAMED PEAS

4 cups tiny green peas          1 cup sweet cream

Steam peas until tender. Add cream. Heat until steaming.

## CREAMED SPINACH

2 cups chopped, cooked spinach          ¼ cup cream
1 egg yolk

Combine all ingredients. Place in double boiler. Cook until no raw egg taste remains.

## CREAMED STRING BEANS

4 cups steamed green beans          ½ cup cream

Combine and serve hot.

## CREAMED TURNIPS

3 cups steamed turnip balls          ¼ cup heavy cream, hot

Combine turnips and cream, heat together.

## EMERALD CAULIFLOWER

1 head steamed cauliflower          3 tablespoonfuls melted butter
2 tablespoonfuls finely minced parsley

Heat parsley in butter. Pour over hot cauliflower.

## GIANT DANDELION

Cultivated dandelion is tender and may be purchased either green or bleached. Green variety is excellent steamed as spinach or other greens, or as a salad. Bleached dandelion is more delicate in flavor and is especially delicious served raw with plain oil dressing.

## GREEN CURLY CABBAGE

1 head green curly cabbage          1½ tablespoonfuls butter

Place cabbage head in pan with small amount of boiling water. Keep cooking rapidly until water is all absorbed or evaporated, and vegetable is tender. Add butter and serve hot.

## GREENS

POLK — cook like asparagus.

NETTLE — (gathered when 3 - 4 inches long).

SWISS CHARD; PLANTAIN; MILKWEED; LAMB'S QUARTER; MUSTARD GREENS; DANDELION; SWEET POTATO TOPS; BEET TOPS; RADISH TOPS; TURNIP TOPS; LEAVES FROM KOHL-RABI; all may be steamed and served like spinach.

MILKWEED, DANDELION, and PLANTAIN should be used raw for salads frequently.

## GRILLED ONION SLICES

Slice mild onions ¼ inch thick. Place in baking pan. Keep each slice unbroken. Add a little water and bake at moderate temperature until tender. All water should have evaporated. Dip each slice in oil, broil under direct heat until lightly browned.

## GRILLED TOMATO SLICES

Slice tomatoes ½ inch thick. Coat with oil. Broil until lightly browned. Sprinkle with vegetable salt.

## GROUND CHERRIES AND OKRA

2 cups yellow or red ground cherries     3 cups okra pods (sliced if large)
2 tablespoonfuls butter

Melt butter and brown slightly. Add ground cherries and okra. Simmer together until well blended. Vegetable salt or an herb may be added for flavor.

## LETTUCE IN CREAM

2 heads lettuce                          1 tablespoonful minced onion
½ teaspoonful celery salt                2 tablespoonfuls butter
                        ½ cup cream

Cut each head in two and lay cut side up, in pan. Sprinkle with onion and celery salt. Steam for fifteen minutes. Add butter and cream and continue cooking until tender. Serve on hot dishes and sprinkle thickly with finely shredded carrots.

## MASHED TURNIPS

4 cups steamed turnips

Put through potato ricer and drain. Serve hot. Two tablespoonfuls butter if desired.

## ORANGE FLAVORED BEETS

3 cups diced cook beets       ½ cup orange juice
        1 tablespoonful grated orange rind

Simmer beets in orange juice for ten minutes. Sprinkle with grated orange rind.

## PARSLEY CARROTS

3 cups steamed carrot balls            1 teaspoonful minced chives
1 tablespoonful minced parsley         (optional)
                    ½ cup cream
Combine ingredients and serve hot.

## PEAS WITH BACON

2 slices fat bacon                2 tablespoonfuls sliced onion

Cook bacon and onion together until browned. Pour off all fat. Add 3 cups small green peas and ¼ cup water. Simmer until peas are tender, and water is evaporated. Sprinkle with vegetable salt and a little grated lemon rind.

## PEPPERED CORN

3 cups young corn            2 tablespoonfuls shredded green pepper
            3 tablespoonfuls butter or vegetable oil
2 tablespoonfuls minced onion        1 tablespoonful minced pimiento
                ½ teaspoonful vegetable salt
½ teaspoonful paprika                              ½ cup milk

Cook onion and green pepper in butter until golden color. Add remaining ingredients. Simmer until corn is tender and mixture is thickened.

## SAUERKRAUT ROSES

4 smooth ripe tomatoes          2 cups sauerkraut
4 tablespoonfuls butter

Remove centers from tomatoes.  Fill with sauerkraut, top with one tablespoonful butter, and bake in moderate oven.

## SAUTEED OYSTER PLANT

3 cups diced oyster plant        3 tablespoonfuls butter
2 tablespoonfuls minced parsley

Melt butter, add vegetable and a little celery salt if desired.  Cook gently until tender.  Sprinkle with minced parsley.

## SHREDDED BEETS

4 cups shredded raw beets        2 tablespoonfuls butter

Melt butter in heavy pan.  Add beets and cook quickly until tender, stirring occasionally.

## SHREDDED PARSNIPS

Melt 1 tablespoonful butter in heavy pan.  Add 1 cup shredded parsnips for each serving.  Stir often, cook over moderate heat until tender.  If vegetable is too dry add a little cream.  Season with minced parsley.

## SOUR CABBAGE

Steam shredded cabbage until tender.  Add Tupelo honey and lemon juice combined.  Serve with melted butter.  Use 1 teaspoonful of honey for each tablespoonful of lemon juice.

## STEAMED BRUSSELS SPROUTS

Always soak in salt water for one hour to remove any insects.  Must be handled carefully to keep intact.  Steam until tender.  Serve with (1) melted butter, (2) lemon juice, (3) Hollandaise sauce.

## STEAMED BRUSSELS SPROUTS, ORANGE SAUCE

3 cups steamed Brussels sprouts
*Orange Sauce*:

⅓ cup butter      3 tablespoonfuls water and lemon juice (equal parts)
1 tablespoonful grated orange rind

Cook above ingredients together for two minutes.  Add ¼ cup orange juice, pour over one beaten egg yolk and cook over hot water until smooth and thick.  Pour over hot Brussels sprouts.

## STEAMED CABBAGE

4 cups shredded cabbage

Steam until tender.

## STEAMED CELERY-ASPARAGUS

1½ lb. celery asparagus

Steam until tender and serve with butter or desired sauce.

## STEAMED CHARD

½ peck chard          2 tablespoonfuls butter

Young tender chard will be steamed, chopped and served like spinach. Melt butter and pour over chard. Older leaves must be treated differently, the green leaf should be stripped from its thick stem, then treated as the young leaf. Stems may be steamed separately and served in the manner of asparagus.

## STEAMED CHICORY

Steam chicory until tender and serve with butter or sauce of choice.

## STEAMED COLLARDS

½ peck selected collards

Chop finely and steam until tender. May be served with melted butter or desired dressing.

## STEAMED COS LETTUCE (ROMAINE)

4 heads cos lettuce          4 tablespoonfuls butter
½ teaspoonful onion juice

Steam cos lettuce until tender. Serve with melted butter combined with onion juice.

## STEAMED FINOCCHIO

4 cups diced stalks and root of finocchio

Steam until tender. Serve with butter, cream or desired dressing.

## STEAMED JAPANESE TURNIP LEAVES

½ peck leaves from Japanese foliage turnip

Steam until tender. Pack into individual molds, and serve with melted butter.

## STEAMED LEEK TIPS

Use small tender leeks. Cut to about five inches in length. Tie in individual bundles. Steam until tender. Serve plain, with butter or cream as desired.

## STEAMED MANGEL-WURZEL TOPS

Young tender tops may be steamed as kale or other greens.

## STEAMED OKRA

1 qt. okra pods

Small green okra pods may be steamed whole. Larger pods should be sliced. Steam until tender and serve with melted butter.

## STEAMED ONIONS

3 cups steamed pearl onions     3 tablespoonfuls melted butter

Pour butter over onions and serve.

## STEAMED PARSLEY ROOT

Roots of turnip-rooted parsley may be sliced or diced and steamed. Serve with butter.

## STEAMED ROMAINE

Large head of romaine     3 tablespoonfuls butter
1 small onion sliced thinly

Clean romaine carefully and cut leaves into two-inch pieces. Melt butter in small sauce-pan, add onion. Cook for five minutes, being careful not to brown onion. Stir into the romaine and place in steamer. No water is required. Cook until tender.

## STEAMED SAUERKRAUT

3 cups sauerkraut     ¼ teaspoonful caraway seeds

Place sauerkraut mixed with caraway seed in buttered casserole. Add sufficient sauerkraut juice to keep moist and steam until tender.

## STEAMED SEA KALE GREENS

½ peck sea kale leaves

Steam until tender. Serve with butter or sauce of choice.

## STEAMED WHITE CUCUMBER RINGS

1½ lbs. fresh white cucumbers

Cut into thick slices, remove seeds making rings of the vegetables. Steam until tender. Serve with Hollandaise sauce or marinate in French dressing and serve cold.

## STEAMED WHITE GUMBO

1 qt. white pods

Slice gumbo pods. Steam until tender. Serve with cream or butter.

## STEWED CABBAGE

1 solid head cabbage
1 tablespoonful parsley, minced

1 tablespoonful minced onion
1 cup celery broth

Cut cabbage into quarters, remove hard center. Place in saucepan and cook until about half done. Remove to buttered au gratin dish. Pour over hot celery broth with onion and parsley. Simmer until tender.

## STEWED CORN

4 cups corn freshly cut from the cob
½ cup cream

1 tablespoonful minced onion
½ tablespoonful minced parsley

1 tablespoonful butter

Cook butter and onion together until the onion is soft, add the corn and stir constantly for ten minutes over a moderately hot fire. Add cream a little at a time and cook slowly so as to evaporate moisture. Add a little vegetable salt. Serve in a bowl with minced parsley as garnish.

## STEWED CUCUMBERS

4 cups 1½ inch slices of cucumber          2 tablespoonfuls butter

Cut cucumber slices in quarters and remove seeds. Simmer in milk until tender. Drain. Melt butter in flat heavy pan. Shake cucumbers in butter over medium heat to expel moisture. Do not brown. Serve immediately.

## STEWED ONIONS, EGG SAUCE

4 large mild onions
Milk to cover onions

4 egg yolks
2 tablespoonfuls chopped parsley

Simmer onions in milk until tender. Remove from pan. Beat egg yolks and add to milk, cook over hot water until smooth. Season with a pinch of celery salt. Pour over onions and serve hot, garnish with chopped parsley.

## STEWED TOMATOES

5 ripe tomatoes, peeled and in sections
3 tablespoonfuls butter or olive oil
¼ teaspoonful celery salt

1 teaspoonful onion juice
1 tablespoonful minced green pepper

Melt butter. Add remaining ingredients. Cook until tomatoes are tender.

## STEWED TURNIPS

3 cups turnip balls      3 tablespoonfuls minced onion
3 tablespoonfuls butter

Cook onion and turnips in butter until browned lightly. Add ½ cup milk. Simmer until tender, cooking away all moisture.

## STEWED TOMATOES AND CELERY

1 pound tomatoes, cut into quarters
*or*
3 cups drained canned tomatoes      2 cups sliced celery
2 tablespoonfuls olive oil

Cook celery in olive oil for about 10 minutes. Add tomatoes. Simmer until celery is tender and the vegetable flavors are blended. Season to taste with vegetable salt.

## STRING BEANS, HOLLANDAISE SAUCE

4 cups steamed string beans

Arrange beans to form nest. Sauce in center.

## SUCCOTASH

2 cups fresh, young corn      2 cups tiny, green lima beans
2 tablespoonfuls butter or vegetable oil
¼ cup cream

Melt butter in saucepan. Add vegetables. Simmer until tender. Season with vegetable salt, add cream. Continue cooking for 10 minutes.

## SUMMER SQUASH

Cut squash in quarters, remove seeds and fibre. Steam until tender. Serve with melted butter.

## SUMMER SQUASH IN CREAM

Steam diced squash until tender. Add a light sprinkle of salt and one tablespoonful cream for each cup of cooked squash.

## TOMATO GUMBO

1 pint tomatoes, raw or cooked      2 green peppers, shredded
1½ pints tiny okra pods      1 cup sliced onion
2 cups young corn      3 tablespoonfuls bacon drippings

Cook onion and pepper in fat until lightly browned. Add remaining ingredients. Simmer until okra is tender and mixture thickened. Season with vegetable salt.

## TURNIPS, LEMON SAUCE

3 cups steamed diced turnips

While hot, serve with Boiled dressing freshly made, and hot.

## VEGETABLES AU GRATIN

3 cups steamed green beans, carrots, or a combination of vegetables
⅓ cup cream          ⅔ cup fresh cottage cheese

Arrange vegetables and cheese in layers in baking dish. Pour cream over. Bake in moderate oven.

## VEGETABLE BROTH

4 cups mixed vegetables          4 cups water

Simmer vegetables in water until soft. Strain. Add a pinch of celery salt. Keep this vegetable broth on hand at all times. It will add flavor and interest to many plain dishes. If tomatoes are used this becomes an acid broth, since cooking develops acid in tomatoes. Keep this in mind in combining the broth with other foods.

## VEGETABLE PURÉE

Steam any desired vegetable or combination of vegetables, until tender. Press through sieve. If a thick purée is desired, simmer over moderate heat until desired consistency is reached.

## VEGETABLE SOUFFLÉ

Use any desired vegetable. Follow recipe for Spinach Timbales.

# SAUCES

### AGAR JELLY, FRUIT OR VEGETABLE

1 pint fruit or vegetable juice          1 tablespoonful agar
½ teaspoonful lemon juice

Soften agar in ½ cup of measured liquid; heat and simmer for a few minutes until completely dissolved. Add remaining juice. Tupelo honey may be added to fruit juice.

### APPLESAUCE

Select richly flavored fruit, not over ripe. Wash apples, cut in small pieces. Do not remove skin or seeds. Steam until tender. Press through sieve. Sweeten to taste with Tupelo honey.

### BEET RELISH

4 cups chopped raw beets          1 cup lemon juice
½ cup Tupelo honey               1 tablespoonful whole mixed spices

Tie spices in cheesecloth bag. Cook all ingredients together slowly until thinly and cut into fancy shapes.

### BEET SAUCE

½ cup grated cooked beets     1 tablespoonful lemon juice
Combine ingredients and serve hot.

### CHEESE SAUCE

½ cup cream                    ½ cup cream cheese
Dash of paprika

### CUSTARD FOR DECORATING

2 egg yolks                    2 tablespoonfuls cream
Small pinch of salt

Mix ingredients, poach in buttered ramekin in hot water. When cold slice thick. Remove spices.

### CUSTARD SAUCE

1 cup thin cream               ¼ teaspoonful vanilla
2 egg yolks, well beaten       ¼ cup Tupelo honey

Pour hot cream over egg yolks, beating constantly. Add honey. Cook over hot water until thick and smooth. When cool stir in flavoring. Chill.

## FROZEN APPLESAUCE

2 cups applesauce                                    Red cherries

Color applesauce delicately with vegetable color and freeze in individual molds. Turn out and top with cherries.

## GOLDEN SAUCE

2 egg yolks                                    1 tablespoonful lemon juice
½ cup celery broth                             Pinch of salt
                        Paprika

Heat celery broth to boiling point. Pour over well beaten egg yolks, and cook over hot water until smooth. Add lemon juice, and one tablespoonful butter. Season with paprika, onion juice, or other vegetable seasoning.

## HOLLANDAISE SAUCE

½ cup butter                                    3 egg yolks
1 tablespoonful lemon juice                     ¼ cup hot water
                        Pinch of salt

Cream butter, add egg yolks one at a time, beating constantly. Add salt and lemon juice. Add hot water and cook in top of double boiler until smooth and thickened, stirring constantly.

## HORSERADISH SAUCE

¼ cup grated celery root                        2 tablespoonfuls grated horseradish
¼ cup grated white radish                       Lemon juice

Combine grated vegetables and mix with enough lemon juice to give desired consistency.

## LEMON BUTTER

Combine melted butter and lemon juice in proportion of one tablespoonful lemon juice to each half cup of butter. Add minced parsley or paprika if desired. Shake together. One tablespoonful grated lemon rind may be added to each cup butter.

## LEMON CREAM SAUCE

1 cup heavy sweet cream     1 tablespoonful grated lemon rind

Heat over boiling water and serve with vegetables or plain puddings.

## ONION SAUCE

1½ cup onion rings

Cook in a little butter until golden color. Steam until very soft. Put through sieve. Add to ¾ cup cream. Add 1 teaspoonful minced parsley. Season with vegetable salt.

## ORANGE MARMALADE

2 cups orange pulp and juice of 2 large California oranges
Pulp and juice of 1 lemon                    1 cup Tupelo honey

Slice unpeeled fruit very thin. Add Tupelo honey and boil 15 minutes or until syrupy and clear. Pour into sterilized glasses. Cover with parafine when cold.

## ORANGE SAUCE

1 cup orange juice                    4 egg yolks, beaten
1 tablespoonful lemon juice           1 cup orange dice

Heat orange and lemon juice. Pour over beaten eggs and cook over hot water until thick and smooth. Add orange dice and serve hot. Tupelo honey may be added as desired.

## PARSLEY SAUCE

¼ cup chopped parsley           1 tablespoonful butter

Add parsley and butter to "Golden Sauce."

## PICKLED GRAPES AND CHERRIES

1½ cups Tupelo honey            3 cups large dessert cherries
1 cup lemon juice              3 cups seedless grapes

Boil honey and lemon juice together for about 20 minutes or until slightly thickened. Pour over the fruit and heat to boiling point.

## PIMIENTO SAUCE

1 cup cream                 ¼ cup minced pimiento
¼ cup minced ripe olives

## RAISIN SAUCE

¼ cup Tupelo honey            1 cup boiling water
¼ cup lemon juice             ¼ cup seedless raisins
1 tablespoonful butter

Simmer all ingredients except butter until somewhat thickened. Add butter.

## RAISIN SYRUP

1 package seedless raisins (15 oz.)  3 cupfuls water

Cook raisins in water fifteen minutes. There should be 1⅓ cupfuls thin syrup, equal to ⅜ cupful brown sugar for sweetening purposes.

The raisins need not be discarded, as they may be used in cooking foods, in salads, as a breakfast dish, or a dessert (with or without cream), for any type lunch or dinner.

## SPANISH SAUCE

2 cups cooked tomatoes  1 tablespoonful chopped onion
1 tablespoonful minced pepper  2 tablespoonfuls butter or vegetable oil

Cook onion and pepper in fat until golden color. Add tomatoes. Simmer until thick. Strain. Season with vegetable salt.

## TOMATO SAUCE

2 tablespoonfuls butter  1 teaspoonful onion juice
1 cup tomato puree  1 tablespoonful minced parsley
1 cup mushrooms, broken in small  1 tablespoonful minced green pepper
   pieces  ¼ teaspoonful vegetable salt

Cook mushrooms, onion, parsley, pepper in butter. Add tomato and vegetable salt. Cook for five minutes. Mushrooms may be omitted.

# DESSERTS

## AMBROSIA

Sliced orange sections
Shredded fresh pineapple

Sliced strawberries
Shredded or grated fresh coconut

Arrange fruits and coconut in layers, using equal parts of each fruit and about one-third as much coconut as combined fruit. Serve in crystal sherbets. Garnish with fresh cherries.

## APPLE ICE

1 quart apple juice
¾ cup Tupelo honey

1 cup orange juice

Combine ingredients and freeze in rotary freezer.

## APPLE PIE—NUTMEAL CRUST

Slice tart apples without removing skin. Bake with Tupelo honey until tender. Place in individual baking cups, add a few raisins if desired or a little grated nutmeg, cinnamon or grated lemon rind. Cover with a thick paste made by combining nut meal with cream. Bake until the crust is crisp and lightly browned. Any acid fruit may be substituted for the apples.

## APPLE PUDDING

4 cups sliced apples
½ cup chopped pecans

¾ cup seedless raisins

Place apples in baking dish in layers. Sprinkle with a few raisins and nuts over each layer. Bake in moderate oven.

## APPLE SOUFFLE

1 cup diced apple
2 cups milk

5 egg yolks
½ cup ground raisins

Cinnamon

Combine heated milk with raisins and egg yolks. Stir apple thru custard. Pour into buttered glass dish. Dust with cinnamon. Poach in moderate oven until firm. Serve cold.

## APPLE WHIP

4 medium sized apples
1 cup nut meal

½ cup chopped raisins
1 cup whipped cream

Few grains grated nutmeg

Grate apples and add nut meal and raisins. Combine with cream and nutmeg. Place in individual serving dishes and chill.

## APRICOT BAVARIAN CREAM

2 teaspoonfuls granulated gelatin          ¼ cup cold water
¼ cup fruit juice                          ¼ cup Tupelo honey
1½ cups apricot purée, fresh or canned     1½ cups whipping cream

Soak gelatin in cold water. Heat honey and fruit juice to boiling point and add gelatin, stirring until completely dissolved. Add to purée. Chill until mixture begins to thicken. Fold in cream which has been whipped. Turn into mold and chill until firm. Garnish with fresh fruit. Any variety of fruit or berries may be used in place of apricots.

## APRICOT CRUSH

2 cups apricot purée          ½ cup Tupelo honey
1 cup orange juice            3 tablespoonfuls lemon juice
3 pints cold water            2 cups crushed ice

Beat orange juice, honey and apricot purée as light as possible or place in liquifier and run at low speed for a few minutes. Add remaining ingredients. Garnish with cherry rings.

## BAKED APPLES

Core baking apples. Do not remove skins. Fill with Tupelo honey, apricots, prunes or raisins. Top with ½ teaspoonful butter. Place in baking dish with a little water in bottom to prevent browning or burning. Bake in moderate oven until tender.

## BAKED APPLES, ORANGE SAUCE

4 baking apples               2 tablespoonfuls butter
1 cup orange juice            ⅓ cup chopped raisins
2 tablespoonfuls lemon juice  6 egg yolks, beaten light

Prepare apples for baking, stuff with raisins and butter, mixed. Pour ½ fruit juices over apples and bake until tender. Remove apples from baking dish. To juice remaining in dish add enough boiling water to make ½ cup. Add to ½ cup fresh orange juice, and remaining lemon juice and heat to boiling point. Combine with egg and stir over hot water until thick. Pour over apples and serve when cold.

## BAKED CUSTARD

4 egg yolks                        2 cups milk
4 tablespoonfuls Tupelo honey

Beat egg yolks slightly, add honey and cream, strain and pour into custard cups. Set in a pan of hot water and place in moderate oven. Bake until firm in center, determining firmness by inserting a knife through the center. If the knife comes out clean, the custard is baked.

## BAKED FRUIT PUDDING

Layer pitted soaked prunes          Layer chopped soaked raisins
Layer pitted soaked apricots        Layer grated raw carrots

Make an uncooked custard of milk and egg yolks (no sweetening), pour over above, sprinkle with coconut and bake until custard is set.

## BAKED GRAPEFRUIT

Cut in half and core as many grapefruit as needed. Sprinkle with cinnamon, two teaspoonfuls of Tupelo honey and a square of butter to each half of grapefruit. Bake for 30 minutes in a moderate oven and serve hot.

## BAKED ORANGES

4 large seedless oranges

Stand in ice water for three hours. Wipe dry. Cut out stem end. Fill with butter. Set in small shallow casserole. Keep moist with water or orange juice, and Tupelo honey, equal parts. Bake at moderate heat until tender. Cool in juice in casserole. Top with whipped cream.

## BAKED PEACHES

4 extra large ripe peaches          4 tablespoonfuls Tupelo honey

Scald and peel peaches. Set in buttered baking dish. Add honey. Cover closely and bake slowly until fruit is clear. Chill and serve with whipped cream.

## BAKED PEARS

4 large ripe pears        1 teaspoonful lemon juice

Cut slice from top of pears. Remove cores. Sprinkle with lemon juice. Add Tupelo honey and bake slowly until tender.

## BAKED QUINCES

Select ripe, deep yellow quinces. Pare and core. Boil skin and core in a little water—enough to cover—for 25 minutes. Cut pared quinces in halves. Place in baking dish, fill cavities with Tupelo honey adding a little grated lemon rind if desired. Pour water from paring in bottom of dish. Bake slowly until tender and a clear red color. May require 3 hours.

## BAKED STUFFED APPLES

4 large baking apples                    ½ cup English walnuts
4 tablespoonfuls chopped, dried apricots, soaked until tender
4 tablespoonfuls Tupelo honey

Prepare apples for baking. Fill centers with nuts and apricots mixed. Add honey. Bake in moderate oven.

## BAKED STUFFED ORANGES

4 large seedless oranges     About ½ cup shredded fresh coconut
¼ cup chopped seeded raisins

Cut thick slices from top of oranges. Remove all pulp carefully to prevent crushing. Discard all membrane, cut pulp into even-sized pieces. Combine with raisins and coconut and fill orange shells. (Quantity of coconut will vary with size of oranges.) Set in shallow glass dish, surround with equal parts water and Tupelo honey, and bake in moderate oven. Keep enough liquid in dish to prevent browning or drying of orange rind.

## BUTTERMILK ICE CREAM

3 cups rich buttermilk          ¼ cup Tupelo honey
1 cup cream (whipped)           1 tablespoonful vanilla
1 cup chopped nut meats

Freeze in electric unit or rotary freezer.

## BUTTERMILK SHERBET

2 cups buttermilk          6 tablespoonfuls Tupelo honey
1 cup crushed pineapple heated to boiling point, then chilled
1 teaspoonful liquid rennet

Warm buttermilk. Do not heat above lukewarm. Add rennet, honey, pineapple. Stir only enough to mix thoroughly. Place in freezing tray and freeze to a mush. Remove from tray and beat until as light as possible. Return to complete freezing.

## CANNED APRICOT SHERBET

1 can unsweetened apricots          1 cup cold water
¼ cup Tupelo honey

Press apricots through colander. Add honey and water. Freeze and serve with pieces of apricot for garnish.

## CHERRY CUSTARD

Follow recipe for Apple Soufflé, substituting 1 cup drained canned cherries for apple.

## CHOCOLATE ICE CREAM

Add two ounces melted chocolate to recipe for vanilla ice cream.

## COCONUT APPLES

½ cup chopped raisins          ½ cup shredded coconut
2 tablespoonfuls coconut milk          4 large baking apples

Core apples and pare half way to bottom. Dip pared halves in orange juice, and set apples upright in buttered au gratin dish. Fill with raisins mixed with coconut milk. Bake until tender.

## COCONUT ICE CREAM

2 cups thin cream
1 cup grated coconut

1 cup double cream (whipped)
½ cup Tupelo honey

Combine ingredients and freeze, stirring often. If prepared in electric unit, remove from pan when partially frozen, beat thoroughly and return to freeze.

## EMERGENCY DESSERT

2 cups whipped cream
½ teaspoonful grated orange rind

2 cups diced chilled fruit
¼ cup Tupelo honey

Combine and chill in frappe glasses. Top with cherries or orange cubes.

## FRUIT BOMB

2 or 3 cups whipped cream (flavored)
2 cups thick fruit purée or chopped fruit, sweeten to taste with Tupelo honey.

Line mold with whipped cream. Set in electric refrigerator and freeze. Fill center with fruit and cover with balance of whipped cream. Freeze thoroughly. Turn out on cold plate and cover with shredded almonds.

## FRUIT CUP

½ cup sliced orange sections
½ cup shredded apple

½ cup fresh pineapple (finely diced)
1 cup sliced strawberries or other fruit

Combine chilled fruit lightly. Serve cold. Garnish with mint.

*Note*: Any combination of 3 or more fresh or canned unsweetened fruits may be served as a fruit cup.

## FRUIT ICE CREAM

Add ¾ cup crushed fruit sweetened with Tupelo honey to recipe for vanilla ice cream.

## FRUIT MOUSSÉ

2 cups fruit purée      2 cups whipped cream
¼ cup Tupelo honey

If fruit purée is not thick add one teaspoonful plain gelatin (softened and melted over hot water). Fold chilled purée, honey and whipped cream together and freeze.

## FROZEN FRUIT

1 cup sliced strawberries
1 cup diced canned peaches
  (unsweetened)

1 cup shredded orange
1 cup juice from canned peaches
A little non-alcoholic brandy flavor

Place all ingredients in freezing tray. Stir two or three times while freezing, always from edges toward center of pan. Do not allow to become too hard.

## FROZEN FRUIT PURÉE

Put cooked or canned unsweetened fruits through fine sieve. Arrange in layers in freezing tray in any combination desired. Suggestions:

Pear purée and shredded pineapple.

Apricot purée and cherry purée.

## FROZEN ORANGE CREAM

1 quart mold orange sherbet

Turn out on cold platter. Cover top with whipped cream piled unevenly. Garnish platter with sections of whole orange.

## GELATINS

Granulated gelatin is always used in making compatible gelatin desserts. Pure fruit juice is sweetened to taste with Tupelo honey; one tablespoonful granulated gelatin will make a jelly of the right consistency when combined with one pint of sweetened juice. Lemon and lime gelatins are the only exception to this rule, as these juices are too acid to be used full strength; they are combined with water to give the desired tartness without too much acidity. Gelatin must be softened by soaking in ¼ cup water or juice for about five minutes. Boiling water is added or the soaked gelatin is stirred over boiling water until entirely dissolved. Remaining juice is added and the gelatin cooled then poured into a mold rinsed with cold water. To unmold, dip quickly into a pan of warm water. Place a cold plate over top of mold and invert. Lift mold from gelatin.

## GELATIN WITH FRUIT

Fresh or unsweetened canned fruits will rise to top of gelatin if added while gelatin is liquid. A little gelatin should be poured into mold, about ¼ inch thick, and allowed to set. Then fruit may be placed on gelatin and enough gelatin added to anchor fruit. If this is chilled, another or several layers of fruit may be added in the same way. To secure the even distribution of fruit or berries throughout gelatin, chill gelatin until it begins to set. Stir chilled fruit through and place in mold to set.

## GELATIN, LAYER

A. Prepare gelatin as usual. When it begins to congeal, beat one half until light and fluffy. Pile into mold and chill until firm. Keep remaining plain gelatin at room temperature until whipped gelatin is set. Pour plain gelatin into top of mold and chill again until set.

B. Two flavors of gelatin may be colored with pure vegetable coloring. Chill each separately until ready to congeal. Pour half of one flavor into mold and chill until firm. Add half of second flavor and chill again until firm. Repeat until all gelatin has been used.

## GLAZED APPLES

Cut blossom end from baking apples. Pare about ⅓ of apple from blossom end. Remove core. Fill with Tupelo honey. Baste with honey while baking. When tender, there should be a smooth glaze over the apples. Finish under broiler if necessary to produce glaze.

## GRAPE PUFF

1 cup grape juice          2 cups rich cream

Beat together and freeze in electric tray or ice cream freezer.

## HONEY PARFAIT

½ cup Tupelo honey                    ½ cup water
4 egg yolks                          2 teaspoonfuls vanilla
                2 cups whipped cream

Heat honey and water to boiling point. Beat egg yolks as light as possible. Pour hot liquid over yolks, stirring constantly. Cook over low heat until light and fluffy. Chill. Add cream and vanilla. Freeze in tray. Do not stir.

## IRISH MOSS BLANC MANGE

2 cups milk                    4 tablespoonfuls Irish moss
          3 tablespoonfuls Tupelo honey

Wash the moss in several waters. Place in double boiler with milk and honey. Heat until it thickens when dropped on a cold plate. Add ¼ teaspoonful vanilla. Pour into custard cups that have been rinsed in cold water. Chill, and serve with whipped cream or fresh fruit.

## JUNKET

2 cups milk                    2 teaspoonfuls warm water
1 junket tablet                ¼ cup Tupelo honey

Dissolve junket tablet in warm water; add to honey and milk heated slightly. Mix thoroughly and pour into serving dish. When chilled it is ready to serve. Sprinkle thickly with coconut and garnish with one cup sliced or cubed fresh fruit. A few drops vanilla extract may be added if desired.

## LEMON GELATIN

1 tablespoonful gelatin, granulated          1 cup cold water
⅜ cup Tupelo honey                               ⅜ cup lemon juice
½ cup boiling water     ½ teaspoonful grated lemon rind, if desired

Soften gelatin by soaking in ½ cup cold water for a few minutes. Add boiling water and stir until gelatin is dissolved. Add remaining ingredients, stir until thoroughly blended. Chill in mold.

## LEMON VELVET

3 cups milk                              ½ cup Tupelo honey
1 cup 40% cream                       1 cup orange juice
                  ½ cup lemon juice

Freeze in rotary freezer. The mixture will curdle at first, but will smooth out in the freezing process.

## LIME GELATIN

Substituting lime juice for lemon juice, follow directions for lemon gelatin.

## MINCE-MEAT APPLES

4 large baking apples                    1 cup mince-meat

Prepare apples for baking. Fill cavities with mince-meat. Bake in moderate oven until tender. When cold, serve with whipped cream flavored delicately with sherry or rum flavoring.

## MOCHA MOUSSÉ

          ¾ cup strong prepared coffee or substitute
6 tablespoonfuls Tupelo honey        2 teaspoonfuls vanilla
1½ cups heavy cream (40%)            1 teaspoonful gelatin

Soften gelatin in ¼ cup beverage. Heat ½ cup beverage to boiling point and add softened gelatin. Stir until gelatin is dissolved. Add honey. Cool until mixture begins to congeal then beat as light as possible. Add cream, whipped, and vanilla. Freeze in tray without stirring.

## ORANGE APPLES

6 red apples          1½ cups diced orange

Prepare apples for baking. Fill centers with orange dice. (A few raisins may be added.) Bake until apple is tender.

## ORANGE CUSTARD

2 cups orange juice
8 egg yolks, well beaten

1 cup whipped cream
¼ cup Tupelo honey

Heat orange juice to boiling point. Pour over well beaten egg yolks, stirring constantly. Add honey. Cook over hot water until thick and smooth. Cool and fold in whipped cream. Chill or freeze and serve in sherbet glasses, garnished with sliced kumquats or cherry rings. Raspberry juice may be substituted for orange juice for variation.

## ORANGE GELATIN

1 tablespoonful granulated gelatin
1 tablespoonful lemon juice
½ teaspoonful grated orange rind, if desired

1¾ cup orange juice
¼ cup Tupelo honey

Proceed as for lemon gelatin.

## ORANGE ICE

1 quart orange juice
1 tablespoonful granulated gelatin

½ cup Tupelo honey

Soak gelatin in ½ cup juice. Heat over boiling water until completely dissolved. Add to remaining juice and honey. Freeze in rotary freezer for best results. If done in tray, the mixture must be beaten at least twice during the freezing process. Any fruit juice may be substituted for orange.

## ORANGE ICE CREAM

1 cup orange juice
1 tablespoonful grated orange rind

1 cup Tupelo honey
2 egg yolks, well beaten
1 teaspoonful gelatin

2 cups whipped cream

Cook orange juice and rind with honey, heating to boiling point. Pour over beaten egg yolks, and cook for 5 minutes in double boiler. Soften gelatin by soaking in 3 tablespoonfuls orange juice for 5 minutes; add to hot orange mixture and stir until gelatin is dissolved. Chill. Beat with rotary beater, and fold into whipped cream. Freeze in tray.

## ORANGE SHERBET

Ingredients for orange ice

1 pint rich milk

Follow directions for orange ice. When frozen to a mush, add milk and continue freezing.

## ORANGE VELVET

1 cup orange juice

2 cups milk and cream combined

1 tablespoonful grated lemon rind

¼ cup Tupelo honey

Combine and freeze in ice cream freezer. May curdle at first but will smooth out.

## PEACH CUSTARD

2 cups rich milk

5 egg yolks, well beaten

2 tablespoonfuls melted butter

¼ cup Tupelo honey

1 teaspoonful tartaric acid baking powder

2 cups sliced peaches

Arrange sliced peaches in buttered casserole. Pour over these the remaining ingredients beaten together. Bake in moderate oven until custard is firm. Serve with cream slightly flavored with almond.

## PEACH GRANITE

1 cup chopped ripe peaches

1 cup white grape juice

1 cup orange juice

Freeze combined ingredients in rotary freezer.

## PEACH MOUSSE

1 cup crushed peaches

1 cup heavy cream

5 drops almond flavor

¼ cup Tupelo honey

Beat cream, add flavor. Freeze to mush. Stir, add peaches and honey. Return to freezing unit to finish.

## PEACH SHERBET

2 cups purée of peaches, ice cold

1 cup cold milk

1 cup whipped cream

¼ cup Tupelo honey

Combine ingredients and freeze.

## PEAR COMPOTE

Cut fresh ripe pears into cubes. Arrange in serving dish, pour hot grape juice over. Serve hot or cold.

## PECAN MOUSSE

2 cups cream

1 teaspoonful vanilla

1 cup ground pecans

¼ cup Tupelo honey

Whip cream, add nuts, honey and vanilla. Freeze in tray or mold.

## PINEAPPLE BETTY

1 cup crushed, drained pineapple     1 cup shredded coconut
½ cup shredded carrot

Arrange in layers in baking dish. Pour a little pineapple juice over to keep moist. Bake in moderate oven.

## PINEAPPLE CUSTARD

1½ cups pineapple juice        4 egg yolks
Pinch of nutmeg

Beat egg yolks as light as possible. Stir into juice, add nutmeg. Poach in individual baking cups. Serve with fresh fruit or whipped cream sweetened with Tupelo honey.

## PINEAPPLE ISLAND

8 slices fresh pineapple     1 cup orange juice

Cover pineapple with orange juice and set in refrigerator for an hour or more. Serve two slices for each person. Top with whipped cream if desired.

## PINEAPPLE MINT SHERBET

2 cups milk        6 tablespoonfuls Tupelo honey
1 cup crushed pineapple heated    Small bunch fresh mint
to boiling point, then chilled    1 teaspoonful liquid rennet

Crush mint and add to milk 1 hour before needed. Heat milk to lukewarm, remove mint. Add remaining ingredients. Place in tray and freeze to a mush. Remove from tray and beat until light as possible. Return to complete freezing.

## PRUNE WHIP

½ pound prunes, steamed and pitted     1 pint whipping cream

Rub prunes through fine sieve. Whip cream until light. Combine fruit with cream. Chill in individual serving dishes. Top with pieces of fruit. Apricots, raisins or other dried fruits may be substituted for prunes.

## QUINCE MOUSSÉ

1 cup quinces stewed over slow heat until red
2 cups whipped cream    Almond flavor

Press quinces thru colander. Add ¼ cup Tupelo honey. Add to cream with flavoring. Freeze in electric unit.

## RAISIN CUP

Soak raisins in orange juice for several hours. Arrange drained raisins in sherbet glasses with a little grated coconut distributed through. Top with an orange section.

## RASPBERRY ORCHIDS

2 cups prepared black raspberry gelatin     1 cup whole black raspberries
1 cup whipped cream, sweetened with Tupelo honey

Chill gelatin in shallow dish. Shred finely with fork. Fold in whipped cream, mixing until of an even lavender color. Chill until ready to serve. To serve, place whole berries in bottom of parfait glasses, add gelatin mixture and top with whipped cream.

## REFRIGERATOR ICE CREAM

2 cups light cream (20%)     ½ cup Tupelo honey
2 teaspoonfuls vanilla     ½ cup cold water
2 teaspoonfuls granulated gelatin     ¾ cup heavy cream (40%)

Soften gelatin by soaking in cold water. Dissolve over boiling water. Combine with honey and light cream. Place in freezing tray and allow to remain until slightly thickened. Remove from tray and beat until as light as possible. Beat heavy cream, add to gelatin mixture and vanilla. Return to tray to continue freezing.

## RICED GELATIN

1 cup each, three flavors gelatin, each colored differently. Chill gelatin until firm. Force through potato ricer and pile in layers into serving dishes or glass bowl.

## RUM BISQUE ICE CREAM

1 pint heavy cream     2 tablespoonfuls rum flavoring
1 cup shredded almonds     6 tablespoonfuls Tupelo honey

Combine ingredients, beat until very light and freeze.

## SLICED ORANGE DESSERT

Combine orange sections with grated fresh coconut. Arrange in sherbet glasses, cover with thin custard and garnish with a bit of whipped cream.

## SOAKED DRIED FRUIT

Wash unsulphured, dried fruit. Add only enough water to cover, so that all water will be absorbed. When fruit is plump, or has resumed its original shape it is ready for use.

## STEAMED APPLES

Core apples. Fill with raisins or a mixture of raisins and nuts. Steam until tender.

## STEAMED CUSTARD

| | |
|---|---|
| 3 cups milk | 4 egg yolks, beaten until light |
| 4 tablespoonfuls Tupelo honey | ½ teaspoonful vanilla |

Pinch of nutmeg

Combine ingredients. Pour into custard cups, and cook in steamer until set.

## STEAMED RAISINS

Steam one pound seedless raisins until plump and tender. Serve cool with cream.

## STEWED BLUEBERRIES

| | |
|---|---|
| 1 quart blueberries | 1 teaspoonful grated lemon rind |

5 tablespoonfuls Tupelo honey

Place berries, honey and lemon rind in double boiler. Cook about 10 minutes or until tender. Serve cold.

## STEWED DRIED FRUITS

Wash unsulphured, dried fruit. Cover with cold water. Soak until fruit has regained its original shape. Use only as much water as is necessary. Steam until tender. Tupelo honey may be added during steaming if desired. A little lemon juice or rind will add flavor to prunes, raisins and pears.

## TOMATO SWEET

| | |
|---|---|
| ½ cup sliced raisins | 1 cup whipping cream |

1 cup drained diced ripe tomatoes

Grated rind of 1 lemon

Whip the cream, fold in remaining ingredients, place in sherbet glasses and chill thoroughly.

## VANILLA ICE CREAM

| | |
|---|---|
| 3 cups 20% cream | 6 tablespoonfuls Tupelo honey |
| 1 cup 40% cream | 1 teaspoonful vanilla |

Combine ingredients and freeze in rotary freezer.

## VANILLA MOUSSÉ

1 pint heavy cream (40%)          1 teaspoonful vanilla
6 tablespoonfuls Tupelo honey

Beat cream light. Add honey and vanilla. Freeze in tray without stirring.


## VINE PEACH PUDDING

Follow recipe for Apple Soufflé, substituting one cup diced vine peach for apple and 2 cups thin cream for milk.


## WHIPPED GELATIN

Prepare any fruit gelatin and cool until it begins to congeal. Beat with rotary beater until light and fluffy. Pile into mold and chill.

# SECTION TWO
## Protein Foods

$\mathcal{S}$ ECTION TWO (2) contains compatible recipes for protein meals. Since meat is one of the most popular foods the question of limiting amounts eaten is a real problem, especially when two ounces of concentrated protein foods per day is all that is required for repair of body tissues. One successful plan is the serving of protein foods three times weekly. Then if properly combined with the right vegetables and fruits, larger amounts will cause no trouble to healthy persons. All meats, sea-foods cheese and egg (whites) are included in protein group. Milk contains proteins to the extent that it is not compatible with carbohydrates, and because of the difference in structure of proteins the digestion of milk is not carried on satisfactorily when taken with meats or other concentrated proteins. Egg white contains a type of protein very difficult to digest; they are not included in recipes in this book. All protein foods may be used with acid fruits, vegetables, fats. Recommended fats are cream, butter, olive oil, oily nuts and egg yolk.

Recipes frequently specify rather large amounts of meat. This does not mean that any person may take a pound of roast at one time. To preserve texture, flavor and food value it is not advisable to attempt to roast small pieces of meat. Any left-over meats may be kept for two or three days in the refrigerator without deterioration.

Philadelphia cream cheese and cottage cheese only, are recommended for use. The former is classified as a fat; the latter is a concentrated Protein. Cottage cheese is a good substitute for meat, being a neutral food.

Select all foods to be included in protein menu from recipes contained in this section.

# INDEX---SECTION 2

## BEVERAGES AND COCKTAILS

## PROTEIN   RELISHES

# SOUPS

# FRUIT  SALADS

# PROTEIN   SALADS

# VEGETABLE SALADS

## ACID SALAD DRESSINGS

## PROTEINS

# INDEX (*continued*)

# SAUCES

# VEGETABLES

# DESSERTS

# BEVERAGES AND COCKTAILS

### ALMOND MILK

2 tablespoonfuls almond butter        1 teaspoonful Tupelo honey

Add 1 cup hot water, a little at a time, to make a smooth mixture.

### CABBAGE COCKTAIL

2 parts juice of young green cabbage        1 part grapefruit juice

### CHERRY COCKTAIL

2 cups crushed, frozen lemonade        1 cup pitted black cherries
1 cup pitted white cherries

Freeze lemonade in ice cube trays. Crush into small irregular pieces, and place in bottom of cocktail glasses. Arrange cherries on ice in geometrical patterns.

### CHERRY SQUASH

1 cup pitted sour cherries        ¼ cup Tupelo honey
1 quart water

Place in liquifier at low speed for 3 minutes, then at high speed for 1 minute.

### CHILLED HONEY CHOCOLATE

3 tablespoonfuls Tupelo honey        ½ teaspoonful vanilla
1½ cup water                         ½ cup cream
2 tablespoonfuls cocoa or grated chocolate

Heat 1 cup water to boiling point, add cocoa and honey. Stir and cook until well blended. Chill and add remaining water and cream with vanilla. Serve very cold. May be topped with whipped cream.

### CITRUS COCKTAIL

2 large oranges        ½ grapefruit

Remove pulp from oranges and grapefruit in sections. Cut into uniform dice. Save all juice and add to pulp. Add 1 tablespoonful grated orange rind. Chill. Garnish with mint or cherry.

### CLAM COCKTAIL

Arrange clams on half shells on beds of cracked ice. Serve with Cocktail Sauce.

## CRAB FLAKE COCKTAIL

¾ cup crab flakes                    ¼ cup diced cucumber
½ cup diced celery                   ½ cup mayonnaise
               ¼ cup minced ripe olives

Combine crab flakes, celery, cucumber, and one-half given amount of mayonnaise. Pile in cocktail glasses, top with mayonnaise and garnish with olives.

## COCONUT BISQUE

1 quart coconut milk                 1 pint raw tomato juice

Shake together; serve cold.

## COCONUT MILK (*Natural*)

Puncture fresh coconut and drain off milk from center. Grate coconut. Place in glass bowl or jar and cover with cold water. Let stand three or four hours, then press through cheesecloth. Add strained liquid to natural coconut milk.

## COCONUT MILK (*Prepared*)

Grate one fresh coconut very finely. Add to an equal measure of cool water. Let stand two or three hours, press through double cheesecloth or linen. The liquid from the coconut may be substituted for part of the water. Chill before serving. This may be added to any fruit or vegetable beverage.

## CUCUMBER COCKTAIL

Equal parts Cucumber juice and
Grapefruit juice

## FRUIT COCKTAILS

Any acid fruits may be combined in making a cocktail; all ingredients must be cold.

1. Grapefruit and Orange Sections.
2. Fresh Pineapple Wedges and Orange Sections.
3. White seeded Grapes and Cherries.
4. Diced Peach, Sliced Strawberries.
5. Diced Grapefruit and Avocado Balls.
6. Pineapple Wedges and Red Raspberries.
7. Grapefruit Sections and Strawberries in Grapefruit Shell.

Garnish Fruit Cocktails with fresh Mint leaves or fruit of contrasting color.

## FRUIT PUNCH

1 cup orange juice                    ¼ cup grapefruit juice
½ cup pineapple juice              ¾ cup frozen white grape juice

Freeze white grape juice in ice cube trays. Combine chilled fruit juices with cracked grape juice cubes. Shake well.

## FRUITADE

1 cup raspberry juice              1 cup cherry juice
1 cup strawberry juice            ½ cup juice of fresh limes
1 cup red currant juice           4 cups ice cubes

6 cups cold water

Combine chilled fruit juices. Pour over ice cubes. Add water. Garnish with cherry rings. This amount will serve twenty persons.

## GRAPEFRUIT AND RAW TOMATO JUICE

1 pint grapefruit juice                    1 pint raw tomato juice

Add 1 cup of bruised mint leaves and one cup chopped parsley. Let stand two or three hours, strain and chill to serve.

## GREEN COCKTAIL

Equal parts Spinach juice, Parsley juice,
Orange juice.

## HONEY MINT SYRUP

¼ cup Tupelo honey               2 tablespoonfuls lemon juice
3 tablesponfuls bruised mint leaves

Combine honey and lemon juice, add mint leaves. Place in glass jar and keep cold for several hours. Add to water or fruit juices in amounts to suit taste. May be strained to remove mint leaves.

## HONEY STRAWBERRY COCKTAIL

1½ cups strawberries               4 tablespoonfuls Tupelo honey
2 cups water                             ½ teaspoonful grated lemon rind

Place in liquifier. Run at low speed for 2 minutes, then at high speed for 1 minute.

## ICED POSTUM

Prepare Instant Postum by dissolving in boiling water. Proportion: one teaspoonful of Postum for each cup of water. Serve with cracked ice. Top with whipped cream, sweetened with Tupelo honey.

*Note*: Co-Veg or other coffee substitutes may be used in place of Postum.

## IRON COCKTAIL

Equal parts watercress and parsley or spinach. Combine the juice of these vegetables with orange juice to taste.

## LEMON FRUIT COCKTAIL

½ cup peach balls       ¼ cup pineapple, finely shredded
¼ cup orange cubes       2 cups lemon ice

Arrange chilled fruit in iced cocktail glasses. Top with lemon ice.

## LIME COCKTAIL

2 tablespoonfuls lime juice       ⅓ cup grape syrup
2 tablespoonfuls orange juice       ½ cup ice water

Place 2 tablespoonfuls cracked ice in cocktail glasses. Pour combined ingredients over.

## LIMEADE

¼ cup fresh lime juice       4 cups ice water
1 cup orange juice       2 cups lemon ice

Combine chilled fruit juices, ice water and lemon ice. Add Tupelo honey as desired. Shake vigorously.

## LOBSTER COCKTAIL

Chill cooked or canned lobster cut into suitable pieces for serving. Serve with Cocktail Sauce combined with an equal amount of Mayonnaise.

## MINTED CITRUS BEVERAGE

1 quart grapefruit or orange juice       ½ cup chopped mint

Add mint to juice while chilling, strain before serving.

## MORNING GLORY

1 quart raw tomato juice       ½ cup lemon juice

Shake to combine juices. A little vegetable salt may be added.

## ORANGE CREAM

3½ cups orange juice          ½ cup cream

Mix just before serving and serve cold.


## ORANGE SQUASH

2 cups orange juice          1 cup grapefruit juice
2 cups orange sherbet

Combine ingredients, and shake well. Garnish with mint or orange slices.


## OYSTER COCKTAIL

2 dozen Blue Point Oysters on half shell

Serve cold with
*Sauce*:
½ cup minced celery heart or root     ½ cup thick sweet cream
2 tablespoonfuls lemon juice

Combine ingredients and chill.


## PEAR AND GRAPE COCKTAIL

4 ripe pears          1 cup white seedless grapes
1 teaspoonful grated orange rind

Pare and core chilled pears. Cut lengthwise in eight pieces and arrange to simulate lily petals. Pile grapes in center and sprinkle with grated orange rind.


## PINEAPPLE COCKTAIL

1½ cups pineapple juice          ¾ cup cracked green ice cubes
1 tablespoonful lemon juice

Strain pineapple juice through double thickness of linen. Chill. Add one tablespoonful chopped mint, and a trace of green vegetable coloring to water when freezing ice cubes. Combine pineapple and lemon juice with cracked ice cubes. Shake well.


## PINEAPPLE-MINT COCKTAIL

Crush fresh mint leaves. Add ¼ cup of these to 1 quart pineapple juice. Allow to stand for three hours or until the juice has become well flavored. Strain.

## PINEAPPLE-ORANGE SQUASH

1 quart cold tea                  ½ cup apricot juice
1 pint pineapple juice            1 quart orange ice

All ingredients must be cold. Place all together in punch bowl. Let stand
10 minutes before serving.

## PINK LADY COCKTAIL

Equal parts strawberry and pineapple juice. Add two tablespoonfuls cream
for each cupful of juice. Serve with cherry for garnish.

## POCONO VEGETABLE JUICE

Equal parts Beets and tops, Carrots, Celery

Combine the juice from these vegetables, serve two or three ounces twice
daily. Vegetable juice may be poured into glass and glass filled with tomato
juice or fruit juice.

## POMEGRANATE COCKTAIL

Add ¼ lemon, thinly sliced, to 1 large, peeled pomegranate. Add 1½ pints
cold water. Boil together for a few minutes or until color and flavor have been
extracted. Strain and add ⅓ cup Tupelo honey. Chill. Add a few drops lemon
juice.

## RADISH AND CELERY COCKTAIL

Equal parts Celery juice and Radish juice combined with fresh fruit juice to
serve.

## RAINBOW PUNCH

Freeze in separate trays the following mixtures:

1. Grapejuice; or red raspberry juice sweetened with Tupelo honey.
2. Lemonade, sweetened with Tupelo honey and colored green—
   using pure vegetable coloring.

Fill glasses with cubes of frozen juice. Pour orange juice over cubes. Must
be served at once for best effect.

## RASPBERRY SHRUB

1 cup red raspberries           2 tablespoonfuls lemon juice
1 cup water                     ¼ cup Tupelo honey

Place in liquifier. Run at low speed for 2 minutes, at high speed for 1 minute.
Strain. Serve cold. Sliced lemon garnish.

## RASPBERRY COCKTAIL

1½ cups raspberries      ½ cup crushed raspberries

Use either red or black raspberries.  Chill thoroughly.  Pile whole raspberries in cocktail glasses, and cover with crushed berries.  Garnish with sprigs of fresh mint.

## RAW TOMATO JUICE

Select perfectly ripe red tomatoes.  Cut into thin slices and press through sieve. May be seasoned with a little vegetable salt if desired.  Should b͗ used while fresh.

## RUM COCKTAIL

1½ cups orange juice            ¼ cup Tupelo honey
¼ cup lemon juice               Ice cubes
2 egg yolks                     A dash of rum flavor

Shake for three minutes in cocktail shaker.  Strain into cold glasses.  Add ¼ teaspoonful grated orange rind to each glass.

## SAUERKRAUT COCKTAIL

2 cups chopped sauerkraut        2 tablespoonfuls of pimiento stars

Arrange sauerkraut in chilled cocktail glasses.  Garnish with pimiento stars.

## SEAFOOD COCKTAIL

Allow ¼ cup flaked crabmeat, cubed lobster, or broken shrimp for each serving.  Sprinkle with a little lemon juice.  Serve cold with tomato or other cocktail sauce.

## SHRIMP COCKTAIL

2 cups chilled shrimp             2 tablespoonfuls fresh tomato pulp
6 tablespoonfuls grapefruit juice   1 tablespoonful minced parsley

Arrange shrimp on glass.  Combine ingredients for sauce; chill and pour over shrimp.

## SOY BEAN MILK

½ pint warm water        1 tablespoonful Soy Bean Milk Powder
1 teaspoonful Tupelo honey
2 tablespoonfuls cream or 1 tablespoonful vegetable oil

Combine milk powder with honey and a little water to make a smooth paste. Add remaining water and cream.

## SPICY PUNCH

| | |
|---|---|
| 1 cup water | 1 cup grapefruit juice |
| 6 whole cloves | 1 cup pineapple juice |
| 3 inches stick cinnamon | ¾ cup lemon juice |
| 2 cups orange juice | ½ cup Tupelo honey |

Boil water and spices for ten minutes. Strain, and blend with honey, then fruit juices. Shake well. Pour over ice cubes, and let stand until ice is partially melted. Will serve eight or ten persons.

## SPRING COCKTAIL

Equal parts dandelion and parsley juice. Add a few drops of onion juice and a little grated lemon rind.

## STRAWBERRY COCKTAIL

3 cups perfectly formed, ripe strawberries    1 cup heavy sweet cream

Wash, drain and chill berries. Do not remove caps or stems. Arrange on glass, around tiny sauce pots filled with cream.

## TOMATO AND FRUIT COCKTAIL

| | |
|---|---|
| ¾ cup balls cut from firm tomato | 1 teaspoonful minced green pepper |
| ½ cup shredded orange | 1 tablespoonful olive oil |
| ½ cup shredded pineapple | 1 teaspoonful lemon juice |

Combine fruits, blend lemon juice and oil; add to fruit with minced pepper. Serve in cocktail glasses surrounded by cracked ice.

## TOMATO COCKTAIL WITH HONEY

| | |
|---|---|
| 2 cups tomato juice | 3 tablespoonfuls lemon juice |
| 1 tablespoonful Tupelo honey | ½ teaspoonful vegetable salt |

Combine ingredients thoroughly by shaking together. Chill.

## WHEY

Heat soured milk keeping at very moderate temperature until the milk solids (curd) separate from the liquids. Strain through double cheesecloth or linen and chill. Whey may be combined with any fruit or vegetable juice.

## YELLOW COCKTAIL

Equal parts Carrot juice and Orange juice.

## PROTEIN RELISHES

ALMONDS, chopped, in balls of minced celery and mayonnaise rolled in paprika.

ANCHOVIES, on Cucumber Slices.

AVOCADO CUBES.

BALLS OF FINOCCHIO ROOT, hollowed out and filled with pimiento.

BALLS cut from ripe tomato.

BUTTON MUSHROOMS, marinated.

CARROT MATCHES, raw with dots of pimiento for heads.

CARROT SPLINTERS, marinated and drained.

CAULIFLOWER flowerettes, raw, marinated.

CAVIAR in small celery stalks.

CELERY-ASPARAGUS STALKS, filled with minced ham and mayonnaise.

CELERY CURLS, small.

CELERY HEARTS.

CELERY SPIKES, (preferably green or unbleached).

CELERY SPIKES, holding cooked, marinated dice of beets, circles of carrot, triangles of marinated raw apple, topped with cube of steamed marinated chicken.

CELERY ROOT, latticed wafers.

CELERY STUFFED.

CHERRIES, red, firm, pitted, with tip of cress inserted in cavity.

CHERRIES, firm red, filled with bits of cream cheese, nuts or chicken breast.

COCONUT wedges.

CHICKEN LIVER, steamed and diced on cucumber spikes.

CREAM CHEESE BALLS

CRABMEAT - SHRIMPS, steamed and marinated.

CUCUMBER CUBES, marinated.

CUCUMBER SLICES, thin and topped with thin round of sliced turkey breast. Ball of lime gelatin on each.

DEVILED EGG YOLKS.

FRUIT GELATIN, dice three or four varieties.

GRAPES, red, firm, seeded and stuffed with tiny pieces of drained tuna fish.

GREEN BEANS, cooked, drained, marinated. Tie three together with pimiento strips.

HAM, baked, small thin squares bearing one-half teaspoonful ground raisins mixed with mayonnaise.

KUMQUATS, ripe.

LOBSTER CLAWS.

MUSHROOM BUTTONS, tiny raw, marinated in French dressing containing minced chives.

MUSHROOM CAPS, small steamed and filled with ground chicken and mayonnaise.

NUT MEATS, coated with gelatin.

OLIVES, ripe; either green or black.

ORANGE DICE, gelatin coated.

OYSTER - CRABS, marinated, (raw or steamed).

OYSTER HEARTS, raw dipped in horseradish sauce.

PATE DE FOIE GRAS.

PINEAPPLE, ripe, small wedges.

PRUNES, stuffed with nuts or cream cheese.

RADISH ROSES, tiny.

RASPBERRIES, red or black coated with gelatin.

ROBIN HOODS. Tiny bundles of dandelion leaves. Stalk ends dipped in French dressing and slipped thru small rings of carrot, olive and radish.

SARDINE PASTE, on cucumber slices.

SCALLIONS.

SHRIMP, steamed, dipped in French dressing, then in minced parsley.

SMOKED TONGUE, rounds of tongue bordered with mayonnaise put thru rose tube.

STRAWBERRIES, fresh, in thin coating of gelatin.

TANGERINE SECTIONS, gelatin coated.

TONGUE ROLLS, paper thin slices smoked tongue, spread with tart dressing and rolled.

TEA BERRIES on celery spikes.

WALNUTS, marinated in lemon juice.


## SAVORIES


DEVILED HAM—chop cooked ham finely, mix with a little mayonnaise and finely chopped dill pickle. Spread on cucumber slices.

CHICKEN LIVER—cook ½ lb. chicken livers in a little water with chopped celery, vegetable salt and onion. When tender, remove from liquid and cool. Cut into small pieces when ready to serve. Wrap each piece in bacon prepared as directed below, and broil until bacon is crisp.

(Bacon to be cooked slowly until clear and some fat drained away, but not crisp or browned.)

After cooking, place a party pick in each.

ANCHOVY—prepare ½ cup anchovy paste by mashing anchovies and combining with 1 hard-boiled egg yolk and enough mayonnaise to hold together well. Spread on protein crackers or thin slices of apple which have been dipped in lemon juice to prevent discoloration.


## OYSTER APPETIZER


Allow 3 or 4 oysters for each serving. Heat oysters in shallow pan in their own liquor. When edges begin to curl, remove from heat; cut away the tough muscles, marinate the remaining soft portions in French dressing. Chill. Serve with any desired cocktail sauce.

## Spreads for Protein Appetizer

### CHICKEN LIVER SPREAD

Add ½ cup mashed, cooked chicken livers and 1 teaspoonful minced parsley to sufficient mayonnaise to give desired consistency.

### COTTAGE CHEESE SPREAD

Combine cottage cheese with sufficient whipped cream to give a good consistency. Add lemon juice for flavor.

### CRABMEAT OR SHRIMP SPREAD

Combine 1 cup mashed, steamed crabmeat or shrimp with ½ cup mayonnaise. Add a little lemon juice if desired.

### DEVILED HAM SPREAD

Combine chopped, cooked ham with sufficient mayonnaise to give desired consistency. Add a little grated onion and one mashed hard boiled egg yolk for each ½ cup ham.

### LIVER SPREAD FOR APPETIZERS

| | |
|---|---|
| 1 steamed goose liver | 1 tablespoonful butter |
| 2 hard boiled egg yolks | Few drops onion juice |

Mash liver and egg yolks and put through sieve. Add butter. Season with onion juice, vegetable salt, paprika to taste. Use to fill short pieces of celery, or to spread cucumber slices.

### LOBSTER PASTE

2 tablespoonfuls mashed, sieved lobster meat; combine with 1 teaspoonful lemon juice and a few drops onion juice. Add to ¼ cup mayonnaise.

### PATE DE FOIE GRAS

Steam a goose liver until tender. Mash and force through fine wire sieve. Add creamed butter in proportion of 1 tablespoonful butter to 6 tablespoonfuls liver. Beat until light, adding onion juice and vegetable salt to taste. Serve on cucumber slices or use as filling for celery.

## SHRIMP PASTE

1 pound cleaned cooked shrimp    1 teaspoonful vegetable salt
½ cup butter    ½ teaspoonful paprika

Pound shrimp in a mortar or chop fine and then mash to a paste. Cream the butter and combine with shrimp, add seasoning and beat until as light as possible. Keep cold. Use for filling celery or other appetizers; or paste may be heated and served over other fish.

## TUNA FISH SPREAD

Combine ½ cup shredded tuna with ¼ cup mayonnaise. Add 1 teaspoonful lemon juice and a little grated lemon rind.

*Note:* Small protein crackers may be used as base for protein appetizers.

# SOUPS

### ALMOND SOUP

| | |
|---|---|
| ¼ cup minced onion | 2 cups water |
| ½ cup ground almonds | 1 cup cream |
| 3 tablespoonfuls butter | ½ cup steamed small cubes of cucumber |

Cook onion, almonds and butter until browned slightly. Add water and cream. Simmer 15 minutes. One teaspoonful vegetable paste may be added if desired. Garnish with cucumber cubes.

### ASPARAGUS SOUP

1 lbs. green asparagus     4 tablespoonfuls chopped bacon
¼ cup chopped onion tops

Cut tender heads (about one inch) from asparagus. Slice remaining stalks, add to four cups water with bacon and onion tops. Simmer until asparagus is soft. Rub through fine sieve. Add cooking liquid and asparagus tips with thyme and summer savory to season. Simmer until tips are tender.

### BEET SOUP

| | |
|---|---|
| 2 tablespoonfuls butter | 1 cup sliced raw beet |
| 2 tablespoonfuls minced onion | 4 cups water |
| 2 tablespoonfuls minced celery | 1 tablespoonful lemon juice |
| 1 cup shredded red cabbage | ½ cup tiny dice of beet (cooked) |
| ½ cup heavy sweet cream | |

Cook onion, celery and butter until yellow. Add cabbage and beet slices Cook until soft. Add water and lemon juice. Simmer for half an hour. Strain. Add beet dice and cream. Heat thoroughly.

### BEET TOP SOUP

6 cups chopped beet tops.

Simmer in 2 cups water until tender. Force through sieve. Add 1 cup thin cream and vegetable seasoning if desired; or (2) add a dash of lemon juice and 1 tablespoonful butter.

## CARROT SOUP

| | |
|---|---|
| 1 cup carrot balls (very small) | ½ cup chopped celery |
| 2 cups chopped carrot | 2 tablespoonfuls minced chives |
| 1 tablespoonful chopped parsley | 4 cups water |

Cook all ingredients except carrot balls in water until soft. Strain. Season clear broth with pinch of salt, and paprika. Add carrot balls, steamed until tender. Add 1 teaspoonful vegetable paste.

## CELERY SOUP

| | |
|---|---|
| 2 cups steamed celery | 1 tablespoonful butter |
| 1 tablespoonful onion juice | 1 cup cream |
| 2 cups water | |

Put celery through sieve. Heat cream and water, add celery pulp, butter and onion juice.

## CLAM BISQUE

| | |
|---|---|
| 1 quart clams | 2 cups thin cream |
| 2 tablespoonfuls minced onion | 2 tablespoonfuls butter |

Drain clams, be sure they are free from shell particles and grit. Reserve juice. Cut soft part of clams in small pieces. Chop hard part of clams. Add water to clam juice to make one cup, place clams in this and cook for twenty minutes. Melt butter, brown onion in it. Add butter to clams and when ready to serve stir in the cream which has been heated and slightly beaten.

## CLAM BROTH

| | |
|---|---|
| 12 large clams in shells | 4 cups cold water |

Scrub clams carefully. Place in pan. Cover with 2 cups of water. Heat until shells open. Strain the broth. Can be served hot or cold.

## CLAM CHOWDER

2 cups clams
2 cups tomatoes, diced
1½ cups carrots, diced
2 cups water
1½ cups celery, diced
1½ cups onions, diced

1 cup cream
4 slices bacon, chopped
2 tablespoonfuls butter
2 tablespoonfuls minced parsley
½ teaspoonful thyme
Clam liquor

### Paprika

Wash clams carefully before opening. Save liquor. Separate hard and soft parts of clams. Chop hard parts finely; cup soft parts into medium sized pieces. Broil bacon until crisp. Cook onion in a little oil until clear, but not browned. Combine tomatoes, celery, carrots and parsley with 1 cup water and steam until tender. Add hard parts of clams and let boil 2 minutes. Combine clam liquor, butter and soft parts of clams and let come to boil. Add thyme and bacon. Blend all cooked ingredients and boil for 5 minutes. Heat cream with 1 cup water. Just before serving add heated cream and paprika. Serve hot. This recipe is sufficient for about 15 servings.

## CORN SOUP

2 cups green corn, freshly cut and scraped from cob
4 cups boiling water
2 tablespoonfuls minced root from turnip-rooted parsley

Simmer ingredients together until corn is well cooked. Add one cup cream and vegetable salt to season. Place one-half teaspoonful minced fresh sage leaves in each soup plate before pouring soup.

## CRAB SOUP

3 cups well seasoned vegetable soup          1 cup steamed crab claw meat

Heat crab meat in vegetable soup. Serve immediately.

## CREAM OF TOMATO SOUP

½ cup water
2 tablespoonfuls minced onion
1 tablespoonful minced parsley
½ bay leaf

2 whole cloves
1 teaspoonful celery salt
2 cups ripe tomatoes sliced
2 cups thin cream

4 tablespoonfuls whipped cream

Place all ingredients except cream in sauce pan and simmer for twenty minutes. Rub through sieve. Heat to boiling point. Heat cream, separately, to boiling point. When ready to serve, beat hot cream slightly and stir into it slowly, the tomato purée. Garnish each serving with one tablespoonful whipped cream, dust over lightly with paprika.

## CUCUMBER SOUP

3 cups chopped cucumber (no seeds)
4 tablespoonfuls butter

2 cups celery broth
2 egg yolks
¼ cup heavy cream

Simmer cucumber in butter until slightly browned. Add celery broth and cook until vegetable is soft. Put through fine sieve. Beat cream and egg yolks very light. Add to cucumber purée, cook all over hot water until smooth, stirring constantly  Season very lightly with salt. Dust over with paprika.

## GAME SOUP

3 cups well seasoned vegetable soup
1 cup finely shredded, cooked game meat (rabbit, pheasant, venison or squirrel)
2 egg yolks

Heat soup. Form balls from meat and egg yolk, seasoned with vegetable salt. Drop into hot soup and simmer for twenty minutes.

## JELLIED BOUILLON

4 cups clear tomato juice     2 tablespoonfuls granulated gelatin

Soften gelatin in ¼ cup cold tomato juice. Dissolve over boiling water. Add to remaining liquid. Chill in bouillon cups. Break slightly with fork before serving.

## JELLIED CLAM BOUILLON

1½ tablespoonfuls granulated gelatin     3 tablespoonfuls cold water
3 cups hot clam bouillon

Soak gelatin in cold water, dissolve in hot clam bouillon, cool and chill in refrigerator. Serve plain or put through potato ricer into bouillon cups, garnish with whipped cream seasoned to taste with vegetable salt.

## LETTUCE OR ENDIVE SOUP

6 cups chopped lettuce or endive
3 cups celery broth

1 cup cream
½ teaspoonful celery salt

Simmer chopped greens in celery broth until soft. Put through sieve. Reduce to 3 cups by cooking gently. Add celery salt and hot cream.

## LUNCHEON SOUP

4 cups chopped tomato
¾ cup chopped onion
1 cup chopped cabbage

2 tablespoonfuls bacon fat
½ teaspoonful celery salt
4 cups boiling water

Simmer onion in bacon fat until slightly colored. Add cabbage and cook for ten minutes. Add tomato, celery salt and water. Cook gently over low heat until well blended. Before serving, skim off any fat that may come to top of soup.

## MINTED VEGETABLE SOUP

2 cups purée of fresh green peas
1½ cups cold water
½ cup ground celery
½ cup chopped celery tops
2 tablespoonfuls minced onion

¼ cup ground carrot
1 tablespoonful crushed mint
finely chopped
½ teaspoonful celery salt
1½ cups cream

Simmer together, for thirty minutes, all ingredients except cream. Add heated cream. Beat for a minute or two with rotary beater before serving.

## MINUTE SOUP

2 cups vegetable extract broth
¼ cup minced onion

1 tablespoonful butter
2 tablespoonfuls cream cheese

Cook onion in butter. Add broth. Simmer to blend flavors. Serve with ½ tablespoonful cheese in each cup.

## ONION SOUP

1 cup onion rings          2 tablespoonfuls butter
3 cups boiling water

Cook onion in butter until tender, add water and simmer for five minutes. Serve with protein toast rounds or protein crackers.

## OYSTER-PLANT SOUP

1 cup boiling water
1 cup mashed, steamed oysterplant
Paprika

1½ cup thin cream
½ teaspoonful vegetable salt

Heat cream, add water and oyster-plant; season with salt and paprika.

## PARSNIP AND CAULIFLOWER SOUP

1½ cups shredded parsnips      1½ cups thinly sliced cauliflower
1 tablespoonful minced parsley
6 cups water

Simmer all ingredients together until vegetables are soft. Add 1 cup cream and vegetable salt to taste.

## PEPPER POT SOUP

1 tablespoonful minced onion          2 tablespoonfuls butter or melted
1 tablespoonful minced green              chicken fat
    pepper                            3 cups tomato purée
1 tablespoonful minced parsley        ½ cup steamed carrot rings or
¼ cup minced celery                       turnip dice

Cook onion, pepper, parsley and celery with butter for a few minutes. Add tomato purée and carrot or turnip. Simmer to blend for a few minutes. Just before serving add one tablespoonful grated fresh horseradish and one teaspoonful lemon juice, with sufficient vegetable salt to season.

## PUREED OKRA SOUP

1 cup sliced okra pods               ¼ cup minced green pepper
¼ cup sliced spring onions           2 tablespoonfuls butter
2 cups chopped ripe tomato           2 cups water
                1 cup cream

Boil together all ingredients except cream until vegetables are soft. Rub thru sieve. Season with vegetable salt and any desired herb. Heat. Add warmed cream.

## SALMON SOUP

3 cups ripe tomatoes          1 cup chopped celery and tops
                2 cups boiling water

Cook tomato and celery until soft. Rub thru sieve. Season with vegetable salt, parsley, etc. Heat. Combine ½ cup shredded red salmon with 1 egg yolk. Shape into small balls, simmer in soup for twenty minutes.

## SAVORY VEGETABLE SOUP

½ cup chopped celery tops            ¼ cup green peas
1 cup sliced green okra pods         ¼ cup ground carrot
                ¼ cup ripe tomato

Boil okra and celery tops in one quart water until soft. Strain. Add remaining vegetables and simmer until blended. Season with vegetable salt and thyme or parsley.

## SOY BEAN SOUP

| | |
|---|---|
| 1 cup soy beans | 1 quart water |
| ¼ cup sliced onion | ¼ cup sliced celery |

2 tablespoonfuls butter or vegetable oil
1 teaspoonful grated lemon rind

Soak soy beans for 6 to 8 hours. Place in water and add onion and celery which have been cooked for a few minutes in fat, until golden brown. Simmer until beans are soft. Rub through sieve. Add lemon rind and vegetable salt to season.

## VEGETABLE ASPIC

| | |
|---|---|
| 2 tablespoonfuls vegetable paste | 1 tablespoonful granulated gelatin |
| ½ cup cold water | 1½ cups boiling water |

Soak gelatin in cold water for five minutes. Add to boiling water with vegetable paste. Stir until liquid is clear. Strain. May be chilled in bouillon cups to be served in place of soup. Break lightly with a fork and garnish with a slice of lemon or a bit of parsley.

If vegetable aspic is to be used as a base for salads, cool until it is ready to congeal before adding an equal amount of shredded or diced vegetables. Chill in individual molds.

## VEGETABLE BOUILLON

3 cups vegetable (finely chopped or ground)    3 cups water

Any desired vegetable may be used, or any combination. Cook gently until flavor is extracted. Strain thru linen. Season with vegetable salt and any desired herb. One teaspoonful vegetable paste may be added if desired.

## VEGETABLE CREAM SOUP

⅓ pureed vegetable    ⅓ cream
⅓ water

Add a little vegetable paste.

## VEGETABLE SOUP STOCK

2 large carrots
¼ lb. spinach
3 stalks celery
3 green peppers
1 bunch asparagus

1 dozen tomatoes
1 beet
1 quart fresh green or wax beans
1 onion
1 parsnip

1 small bunch each of parsley, radishes, mustard greens, broccoli
and the outside leaves of any green vegetable.

Any or all of the above-mentioned vegetables may be used. Cover well with cold water. Simmer over slow fire until flavor of vegetables is extracted. Strain. Cool. Place in ice box. Reheat as needed.

## WATERCRESS SOUP

2 large bunches watercress
4 cups water

½ teaspoonful celery salt
3 tablespoonfuls butter

2 cups thin cream

Wash cress carefully and cut into short pieces. Melt butter in heavy pan. Add water, celery salt, and cress. A slice of onion or a tiny point of garlic, may also be used if desired. Cook until cress is soft. Rub through coarse strainer and add warmed cream. Sprinkle with paprika and serve.

# FRUIT SALADS

### APPLE AND CELERY SALAD

2 cups diced tart apples           Lettuce
1 cup finely sliced celery         English walnut halves

Marinate apple and celery in four tablespoonfuls orange juice, one tablespoonful lemon juice and two tablespoonfuls olive oil for one hour. Drain and
place on lettuce. Garnish with halves of English walnuts.

### APPLE AND GRAPEFRUIT SALAD

1½ cups diced grapefruit           2 cups diced apple
                    Endive

Toss apple and grapefruit dice together. Serve on crisp chopped endive.

### APRICOT SALAD

1½ cups sliced fresh apricots      Sections from one grapefuit
1 cup shredded fresh coconut       Shredded lettuce

Arrange a layer of apricot slices on lettuce, cover with shredded coconut and
arrange grapefruit sections over coconut.

### APRIL SALAD

2 cups lemon gelatin               1 cup diced pear
1 cup tart apple cut in strips     ¼ cup sliced Royal Anne cherries

Combine cooled gelatin with fruit. Pour into rather tall mold. Chill. When
firm, turn out on lettuce.

### BARTLETT SALAD

4 Bartlett pears                   ¼ cup chopped ripe olives
½ cup sliced celery                3 tablespoonfuls French dressing
½ cup broken walnuts               Endive

Cut tops from pears. Remove from skins most of the fruit pulp, without
crushing. Dice pear, combine with celery, nuts, olives and French dressing. Pile
salad into pear cups. Serve on curly endive.

## BERRY SALAD

4 3-inch squares raspberry gelatin
2 cups whole red raspberries

Cream Mayonnaise
Lettuce

Set gelatin squares on lettuce. Mask with cream mayonnaise. Arrange berries over dressing.

## BLACK WALNUT SALAD

1 cup chopped black walnuts
1 cup tart apple cubes

1 cup sliced celery
Endive

Combine chilled salad ingredients and serve on endive.

## BRAZIL SALAD

1 cup sliced brazil nuts
1 cup pineapple cubes

1 cup balls cut from peach or pear
Lettuce

Combine chilled salad ingredients. Serve on lettuce. Sections cut from small, whole oranges, make an effective garnish.

## BRIDGE SALAD

Amount given is for individual service

2 large sections grapefruit
2 large sections orange
1 teaspoonful chopped red cherries

1 large slice unsweetened pineapple
½ teaspoonful chopped ripe olives
1 strip preserved ginger

Color pineapple pale green, using vegetable color. Place on lettuce. In center of slice place a strip of preserved ginger. On each side of ginger use one grapefruit section (convex side in), next orange sections. Dot with cherries and olives.

## CANOE SALAD

½ cup diced grapefruit
½ cup diced apple
½ cup diced unsweetened pineapple

4 medium cucumbers
Shredded lettuce
French dressing

Cut cucumbers lengthwise in halves. Remove as much as possible of pulp, leaving shell intact. Cut ends to shape of canoe. Mix grapefruit, apple and pineapple, and toss together with French dressing. Drain. Fill cucumber shells with mixture and arrange on lettuce.

## CELERY, RAISIN AND NUT SALAD

1 cup sliced celery
1 cup chopped raisins
1 cup chopped nuts
2 tablespoonfuls orange juice
1 teaspoonful lime juice

Combine celery, raisins and nuts with orange and lime juice. Marinate for half an hour. Drain and arrange on lettuce.

## CHEESE BALL SALAD

4 slices unsweetened pineapple
4 tablespoonfuls cream cheese
2 tablespoonfuls chopped nuts
4 red cherries
Lettuce

Place pineapple rings on lettuce, fill centers with cheese made into balls and rolled into nuts. Press a cherry into each cheese ball.

## CHERRY SALAD

1 cup Oxheart Cherries
1 cup black Spanish cherries
Almonds

Remove pits from cherries. Insert an almond in each cherry. Arrange in any pattern on lettuce.

## CHERRY AND PEACH SALAD

¾ cup unsweetened canned cherries    ¾ cup diced grapefruit
¾ cup chopped unsweetened canned peaches

Combine ingredients. Serve on lettuce.

## CHERRY AND PEAR SALAD

6 halves fresh or canned pears
1 cup red cherries

Place pears on lettuce. Fill centers with cherries.

## CHERRY SPRINKLE SALAD

1 cup drained crushed unsweetened
  pineapple
1 cup fruit of choice
¼ lb. Philadelphia cream cheese
½ cup whipped cream
Lettuce cups
4 tablespoonfuls chopped cherries

Beat cream and cheese together until well blended. Mix fruit and arrange in lettuce cups. Cover with cheese mixture and sprinkle with cherries.

## CHERRY AND STRAWBERRY SALAD

1½ cups pitted white cherries (halves)
1½ cups sliced strawberries

Combine ingredients and serve on crisp lettuce.

## CITRUS SALAD

2 cups orange dice
1 cup grapefruit dice

2 tablespoonfuls white grape juice
3 tablespoonfuls olive oil

Chopped endive

Shake grape juice and oil together until blended. Pour over fruit and mix lightly. Drain and serve on crisp chopped endive.

## COCONUT FRUIT SALAD

½ cup shredded coconut
2 cups tart apples, diced

½ cup diced celery
1 tablespoonful orange juice

1 tablespoonful fresh lime juice

Dice apple and sprinkle with lime and orange juice; combine with celery and coconut. Serve on lettuce. Garnish with rings of red cherries.

## COUNTRY CLUB SALAD

2 cups white grape juice
1 tablespoonful granulated gelatin

1 cup chopped mixed fruit
½ cup thinly sliced celery

Soften gelatin in ¼ cup cold water. Dissolve over boiling water. Add to grape juice. When ready to congeal add fruit and celery. Cool in flat pans. Serve in three-inch squares on crisp lettuce. Garnish with tiny gold-sticks cut from firm apple (marinated) or horseshoes cut from ripe olives.

## EASTER BUNNY SALAD

4 halves of pear
8 whole blanched almonds
4 marshmallows

A few pink candies
4 tablespoonfuls cream mayonnaise
dressing

Baskets woven of endive

On a large green lettuce leaf set a low basket woven from endive. Place one tablespoonful dressing in center of each piece of pear and invert in basket. Make ears of almonds, nose and eyes of pink candies, and tail of marshmallow.

## FROZEN CANNED FRUIT SALAD

1 large can unsweetened fruit of choice                Lettuce
        ¼ cup red cherries

Freeze fruit in can. Remove from can without crushing. Slice, and serve on crisp lettuce. Garnish with sliced cherries.

## FROZEN FRUIT SALAD

½ pint heavy cream                 1 teaspoonful granulated gelatin
1½ cups fruit, finely cut          2 tablespoonfuls cold water
¼ cup mayonnaise                   Lettuce

Soak gelatin in cold water. Melt it over steam. Beat cream and stir mayonnaise and gelatin into it. Add fruit and mix well. Pack in mold and freeze. Slice to serve.

## FROZEN GRAPEFRUIT SALAD

1 large can grapefruit             2 cups shredded lettuce
2 tablespoonfuls French dressing   Paprika

Pack grapefruit (in the can) in salt and ice, and freeze. Or place in electric freezing unit. When ready to serve, cut top from can, slice the frozen fruit and place slices on shredded lettuce. Dust with paprika.

## GELATIN SALAD

1½ cups firm Tokay grapes       1½ cups cubes of raspberry gelatin

Use plain raspberry gelatin that has set in flat pan. Cut in ½ inch cubes. Combine with grapes (seeded and cut in halves.)

## GRAPE SALAD

2 cups large white grapes          ¾ cup pecans or almonds
        6 kumquats

Wash and drain grapes. Remove seeds and press a nut meat into each grape. Serve on lettuce. Garnish with sliced kumquats.

## GRAPE, APPLE AND CELERY SALAD

2 cups Malaga grapes, seeded       ½ cup diced tart apple
    and sliced                     ½ cup sliced celery

Combine salad ingredients. Serve on endive or cress.

## GRAPE AND APPLESAUCE SALAD

2 cups lime gelatin                          1 cup sliced firm white grapes
                    1 cup apple sauce

When gelatin has begun to congeal, stir apple sauce and grapes into it, without thoroughly mixing. This will leave uneven streaks of apple sauce through gelatin. Cool in flat pan. Cut into small cubes.

## GRAPE AND ENDIVE SALAD

2 cups chopped endive        2 cups seeded Tokay grapes

Combine grapes and chopped endive. Serve on lettuce.

## GRAPEFRUIT AND AVOCADO SALAD

1 grapefruit                          French dressing
2 avocados                            Romaine
                    6 red cherries

Separate grapefruit into sections. Pare, core and cut avocados into sections lengthwise. Marinate for a few minutes in four tablespoonfuls French dressing. Drain. Arrange fruit on Romaine. Garnish with sliced red cherries.

## GRAPEFRUIT, ORANGE AND AVOCADO SALAD

2 avocados                            3 oranges
1 grapefruit                          ¼ cup lemon juice
                    Lettuce

Peel and core avocados, cover with lemon juice. Let stand a few minutes. Drain. Arrange sections of grapefruit, avocados and orange on lettuce.

## GRAPEFRUIT, ORANGE AND KUMQUAT SALAD

1 grapefruit (sections)        4 kumquats
3 oranges, diced               Romaine
                    Mayonnaise

Arrange salad greens on individual plates. Build a nest of grapefruit sections, and place orange dice in center. Top with mayonnaise and garnish with sliced kumquats.

## JELLIED APPLE AND ORANGE SALAD

2 cups orange gelatin (ready to congeal)        1 cup apple, cut in strips
                    1 cup orange dice

Combine gelatin with fruit. Cool in flat pan. Cut into four squares and serve on lettuce. Put mayonnaise through pastry tube to garnish.

## JELLIED AVOCADO AND GRAPEFRUIT SALAD

2 cups lemon gelatin                    1 cup diced avocado
                 1 cup diced grapefruit

When gelatin is ready to congeal add diced fruit. Pour into mold to congeal.
Serve on cress.

## JELLIED GRAPEFRUIT SALAD

2 cups lemon gelatin                    2 cups grapefruit sections

Pour gelatin into a flat pan. When ready to congeal, press grapefruit sections
into it. Be sure each is entirely coated. When cool and firm cut into crescent
shaped pieces, with a section of grapefruit in each.

## JELLIED ORANGE SALAD

4 oranges                    2 cups standard orange gelatin

Separate the peeled oranges into sections. Lay these in cooling orange gelatin.
When almost firm, take up sections and tie together in original orange shape.
Set on cold plate and pour a few drops orange gelatin over at a time, returning
to refrigerator at once to become firm. Each orange must be entirely coated.
Serve on chilled plates, on lime gelatin leaves. Make orange blossoms of whipped
cream forced through pastry tube; use bits of orange gelatin for centers.

## JELLIED PEACH AND PINEAPPLE SALAD

1 can sliced unsweetened          ¼ cup shredded unsweetened
   peaches                           pineapple
1 tablespoonful granulated gelatin    ¼ cup orange dice
                 Orange juice

Drain peaches, strain juice. Add enough orange juice to make two cups
liquid. Soften gelatin in ¼ cup fruit juice. Dissolve over boiling water. Add
to remaining fruit juice. When ready to congeal add fruit.

## JELLIED PINEAPPLE AND CARROT SALAD

1 cup orange gelatin              ½ cup shredded unsweetened
1 cup lemon gelatin                  pineapple
                 ½ cup raw grated carrot

Pour orange gelatin into bowl surrounded by cracked ice. Beat until very
light. Have lemon gelatin ready to congeal. Combine plain and beaten gelatin
with pineapple and carrot, stirring a little. Do not mix entirely. Chill in round
molds. Serve on lettuce. Garnish with sliced almonds.

*Important*: Always heat raw pineapple to boiling point, then cool, before
combining with a gelatin mixture.

## LIME RING SALAD

2 cups lime gelatin  
⅔ cup diced, marinated, apple

⅔ cup chopped pecans  
½ cup diced orange

Chill gelatin in individual ring molds. When firm, turn out on lettuce and fill centers with fruit and nuts, combined.

## MALAGA SALAD

2 cups Malaga grapes  
  (seeded and halved)

4 apple cups  
4 tablespoonfuls whipped cream

Combine grapes and cream. Serve in red apple cups.

## MINTED ORANGE SALAD

1½ cups orange cubes  
1½ cups lemon or lime gelatin

¼ cup mint leaves  
Lettuce

Add bruised mint leaves to gelatin mixture while hot. When cool, strain and pour into flat pan to become firm. To serve, cut mint gelatin into cubes and combine with orange cubes. Garnish with sprigs of mint.

## MOLDED FRUIT SALAD

2 cups chopped fruit of choice  
1 cup lemon gelatin (ready to congeal)  
6 halves of canned unsweetened peaches

Combine chopped fruit and gelatin. Pour fruit-gelatin mixture into mold. When firm turn out on bed of crisp salad greens. Fill center of peaches with salad dressing and arrange around gelatin.

## NEAPOLITAN SALAD

½ cup diced grapefruit  
½ cup Julienne strips of apples  
¼ cup sliced strawberries

½ cup diced orange  
½ cup shredded almonds  
½ cup diced unsweetened pineapple

½ cup cream mayonnaise

Combine ingredients, pack in square mold and freeze. Slice and serve on lettuce. Garnish with fresh fruit.

## ORANGE SALAD

4 large oranges

1 tablespoonful granulated gelatin

Cut oranges in halves. Extract juice without breaking rind. Strain 1½ cups juice, and combine with one tablespoonful gelatin that has been soaked in ½ cup water and softened over boiling water. Scrape out rind to make as thin as possible. Fill with orange gelatin and chill. When firm cut each piece in quarters. and arrange on endive.

## ORANGE CUP SALAD

½ lb. Malaga grapes                    ¼ cup English walnuts
1 orange, diced                        2 slices pineapple, diced

Combine all salad ingredients. Serve in orange cups on lettuce.


## ORANGE FLOWER SALAD

4 large, sweet oranges        4 steamed prunes
4 ½ inch slices of firm head lettuce

Place lettuce slices on salad plates. Arrange orange sections as flower petals and use prune for center.


## ORANGE, PRUNE AND NUT SALAD

1½ cups orange dice                    1 cup sliced cooked Santa Clara
½ cup chopped nuts                        prunes

Combine fruit and nuts. Arrange on lettuce.


## PEACH SALAD

8 halves of canned peaches        ½ cup minced celery root
1 cup cottage cheese              ½ cup shredded, blanched almonds
        2 tablespoonfuls minced ripe olives

Drain peaches and wipe quite dry. Chill. Arrange crisp lettuce on individual salad plates. Spread convex side of peaches with cheese. Dip in celery, nuts and olives combined. Set on lettuce.


## PEACH SNOWBALL SALAD

8 halves canned unsweetened peaches        3 tablespoonfuls mayonnaise
½ pint heavy cream                         1 cup lemon gelatin
2 tablespoonfuls chopped nuts              1½ cups freshly grated coconut

Drain peach halves and wipe as dry as possible with linen. Fill cavities with nuts and mayonnaise mixed together. Now fasten two halves together (with a stick of cinnamon) to simulate a whole peach. When all the peaches are so prepared, roll them in the gelatin which should be almost firm, then in coconut. Place in refrigerator for at least one hour. At serving time, beat cream very light. Arrange lettuce on salad plates. Allow a generous portion of cream next, sprinkle with any coconut that may have been left, and place a "snow-ball" on each.

### PEAR AND GRAPE SALAD

8 halves of pears                    ½ cup chopped red grapes
                    ½ cup shredded almonds

Color pear halves delicately with vegetable colors. Arrange white crisp lettuce on four individual salad plates. Set pear halves on lettuce. Fill centers with grapes. Sprinkle with almonds.

### PEAR AND ORANGE SALAD

3 cups diced pear                    ¼ cup chopped cherries
1 cup orange sections                3 tablespoonfuls mayonnaise

Combine pear, cherries, and mayonnaise. Pile in mounds on lettuce. Set orange sections on end about the mound. Top with whole cherry.

### PEAR AND WATERCRESS SALAD

2 cups chopped watercress            4 large halves of pear
2 tablespoonfuls French dressing     Mayonnaise

Combine chilled cress and French dressing. Drain. Arrange on salad plates. Place halves of pears on cress, cut side up, and fill cavities with mayonnaise. Dust with paprika or 1 tablespoonful finely minced cress.

### PEPPER CUP SALAD

1½ cups grapefruit dice              2 cups sliced celery
                    4 green pepper cups

Combine salad ingredients with mayonnaise. Serve in pepper cups.

### PINEAPPLE AND CHERRY SALAD

4 slices unsweetened pineapple       4 ¾-inch slices from large apple
                    1 cup red cherries

Either fresh or canned pineapple may be used. Slices of baked or steamed apple, chilled, are placed upon pineapple. Set a circle of cherries over apple ring, fill center of ring with salad dressing.

## PINEAPPLE AND CITRUS FRUIT SALAD

4 large slices pineapple
1 grapefruit
2 oranges

2 tangerines
4 dessert cherries
Lettuce

Place on each salad plate one pineapple slice (on lettuce). Build a dome of grapefruit sections, orange sections, and tangerine sections. Dressing may be filled in center space as dome is built up. Top with cherry.

## PINEAPPLE AND PEAR SALAD

1½ cups diced pineapple
½ cup sliced celery
1 cup diced pear

3 tablespoonfuls French dressing
Cream-mayonnaise
Endive

Pour French dressing over salad ingredients and chill thoroughly. Drain, and serve on beds of endive.

## PINEAPPLE AND NUT SALAD

1 cup shredded unsweetened pineapple
1 cup broken nut meats

4 tomatoes
2 tablespoonfuls French dressing

Marinate pineapple in French dressing. Scald and skin tomatoes. Chill until firm, and cut into baskets with handles. Fill with salad mixture.

## PINEAPPLE SALAD

4 slices pineapple
4 tablespoonfuls red fruit gelatin

½ cup finely chopped Malaga grapes
Shredded lettuce

Skin, then seed and chop the grapes. Set pineapple slices on shredded lettuce. A ball of gelatin in center of each slice. Sprinkle grapes about the edge of pineapple.

## PINWHEEL SALAD

4 oranges
4 ripe peaches

2 tablespoonfuls strawberry gelatin
Shredded lettuce

Separate oranges, being careful not to break sections. Peel and slice peaches. Chill separately. Arrange fruit on lettuce in form of pin-wheel. Use ½ tablespoonful strawberry gelatin in center of each salad.

## PRUNE SALAD

1½ cups sliced steamed Santa
    Clara prunes
    3 tablespoonfuls tart dressing of choice

1 cup chopped celery
½ cup blanched almonds

Combine salad ingredients with dressing. Serve on lettuce.

## PRUNE AND BLACKBERRY SALAD

1 cup sliced Italian prunes        1 cup orange dice
1 cup blackberries        2 tablespoonfuls grapefruit juice
1 tablespoonful olive oil

Combine fruits with oil and grapefruit juice. Chill thoroughly, drain and serve on lettuce.

## PRUNE AND CHEESE SALAD

2 cups steamed pitted prunes        ½ cup cottage cheese
1 teaspoonful grated lemon rind

Combine cottage cheese and lemon rind. Stuff prunes with cheese. Serve on endive with boiled dressing.

## SALAD COMBINATIONS

Diced fresh peaches, pineapple wedges, sliced celery.
Grapefruit sections, pineapple wedges, diced fresh apricots.
Diced fresh pineapple, sliced white grapes.
Shredded pineapple, sliced strawberries.
Orange dice, sliced strawberries.
Apricot halves filled with raisins.
Prunes stuffed with nuts or cream cheese.

## STRAWBERRY SALAD

1 cup strawberries (halves)        ½ cup diced pineapple
½ cup diced orange

Combine fruit and berries. Serve on lettuce. Garnish with whole strawberries.

## STRAWBERRY AND CHEESE SALAD

1 cup sliced strawberries        ¾ cup cream cheese
½ cup whipped cream        Fruit salad dressing
Crisp lettuce

Mash cheese with silver fork and work to a smooth paste, with whipped cream. Add the sliced berries and shape into a loaf. Chill thoroughly, slice and serve on lettuce.

## STRAWBERRY AND GRAPE SALAD

1½ cups seeded and halved white grapes
1½ cups halved strawberries

Arrange grapes and strawberries on lettuce. Garnish with mayonnaise put through pastry tube.

## STRAWBERRY AND GRAPEFRUIT SALAD

2 cups sliced strawberries          2 cups diced grapefruit
Lettuce

Combine fruit and berries. Serve on lettuce. Garnish with whole fresh strawberries.

## SUNBURST SALAD

2 oranges (sections whole)          Lettuce or cress
4 cheese balls                      2 Pimientos

Arrange salad greens on individual plates. Place on one side of each plate a cheese ball dusted with paprika and a touch of curry. Arrange orange sections in sunburst style. Slice pimiento as finely as possible and place one strip beside each orange section.

## SUNNYSIDE SALAD

4 slices unsweetened pineapple          4 halves, canned unsweetened peaches

Arrange lettuce on four salad plates. Place a slice of pineapple on each. Cover pineapple with whipped cream. Now fill cavities of peaches with mayonnaise, invert, and place in the center of salads.

## TANGERINE SALAD

2 cups diced tangerine          ½ cup diced apple
½ cup diced unsweetened pineapple

Combine ingredients. Serve on lettuce.

## TART PEACH SALAD

4 peaches                      Lettuce
Special dressing

Peel peaches. Remove stone from stem end. Do not break peach. Serve on lettuce with French dressing made with one tablespoonful lime juice; one tablespoonful lemon juice; four tablespoonfuls oil.

## VIOLET SALAD

1 cup purple grape juice
1 cup white grape juice
½ cup fine strips apple, colored pale green with vegetable coloring

1½ tablespoonfuls granulated gelatin
1 cup whipped cream
¼ cup green maraschino cherries, chopped

2 tablespoonfuls chopped raisins

Soften gelatin in ½ cup cold water. Dissolve over boiling water. Add to grape juice. Divide into two equal parts. Set first part in bowl in large pan of cracked ice. When ready to set, whip with rotary beater until very light. Fold in green cherries and one cup whipped cream. Fill bottom of mold with this mixture. When second part is ready to congeal, add apple strips and ground raisins. Pour into mold when first half has become firm. Chill thoroughly. Turn out on crisp lettuce. Garnish with fresh violets.

## WALDORF SALAD

1 cup finely cut celery
1 cup diced apples

¾ cup chopped nuts
¼ cup pecan halves

Cress

Combine celery, apple and chopped nuts. Serve on crisp watercress, and garnish with pecan halves.

# PROTEIN SALADS

### ANCHOVY SALAD

1 cup shredded celery
1 cup shredded anchovies
2 hard boiled egg yolks, chopped

1 tablespoonful minced chives
4 tablespoonfuls French dressing
Lettuce

Combine all salad ingredients with French dressing. Serve on lettuce.

### BAMBOO SHOOT SALAD

1 lb. marinated bamboo shoots      4 hard boiled egg yolks
Lettuce

Arrange bamboo shoots and sections of hard boiled egg on lettuce.

### BEET AND EGG SALAD

6 hard boiled egg yolks
6 small boiled beets

French dressing
Mayonnaise

Cress

Slice beets and marinate in French dressing. Slice egg yolks. Arrange cress on salad plates; on this make circles of alternate slices of beets and egg yolks. Place mayonnaise in center.

### BOILED TONGUE SALAD

1 calf's tongue            2 cups lemon gelatin
Lettuce

Set calf's tongue (boiled until tender) in lemon gelatin, in small round pan. Chill. Turn out on lettuce. Slice to serve.

### BREAST OF CHICKEN SALAD

4 chicken breasts, uniform size
2 cups lemon gelatin

Sliced, pitted ripe olives
4 celery hearts

Simmer chicken in celery broth until tender. Be careful not to break meat. Set on platter. Pour cooling gelatin over chicken, a few drops at a time, until well covered. Keep cold. Now place a row of rings from olives down center of each breast. Pour over a little more gelatin. When set, serve on crisp lettuce, garnish with hearts of celery, quartered.

## CELERY AND CARROT SALAD

1½ cups sliced celery  
½ cup grated carrot  
½ cup cottage cheese  

2 tablespoonfuls French dressing  
½ cup walnut halves  
Cress  

On beds of cress distribute carrot and cheese mixed with French dressing. Cover with sliced celery and garnish with walnut halves.


## CELERY AND TRUFFLE SALAD

1½ cups sliced celery     1½ cups sliced canned truffle

Combine ingredients and serve on lettuce. Garnish with pimiento stars.


## CELERY CURL SALAD

2 cups celery curls  
1½ cups shredded lettuce  

¼ cup French dressing with onion  
2 hard boiled egg yolks  

Cut celery in two-inch lengths. Slash each end four times and place in ice water for one hour. Mix lettuce with French dressing, drain and pile in center of salad plate. Drain celery curls and shake dry. Arrange in circle around lettuce. Garnish with hard boiled egg yolks.


## CHEESE AND FRUIT SALAD

1 cup white grapes, seeded  
1 cup cottage cheese  

1 cup tiny balls cut from peaches  
¼ cup blanched almonds  

Stuff grapes with almonds. Form cheese into balls size of grapes and roll in finely grated coconut. Marinate peach balls in French dressing. Combine and serve on lettuce.


## CHEESE AND TOMATO SALAD

4 tomato cups  
1 cup cottage cheese  
1 tablespoonful grated onion  

2 tablespoonfuls minced sweet pepper  
Mayonnaise, ¼ cup  
Lettuce  

Beat together cheese, dressing, onion and pepper. Fill tomato cups with cheese mixture and serve on lettuce.

## CHEESE AND VEGETABLE SALAD

1 cup cottage cheese
Dash of paprika
¾ cup grated raw carrot

2 cups cooked, drained spinach
3 tablespoonfuls French dressing
Romaine

Arrange romaine on salad plates. Mix spinach (chopped) with French dressing, press into four molds and turn out on romaine. Chill. Mix cottage cheese with sufficient paprika to season well, shape into small balls and roll in grated carrot. Place cheese balls around spinach mounds and serve.

## CHICKEN SALAD

1 cup marinated breast of chicken, diced
½ cup sliced celery
½ cup tiny green peas (steamed)

¼ teaspoonful vegetable salt
¼ cup shredded almonds
Olives to garnish
Lettuce cups

Have all salad ingredients very cold. Toss together lightly, and pile into lettuce cups. Garnish with olives, sliced or whole.

## CHICKEN AND PINEAPPLE SALAD

1½ cups diced white chicken meat
1 cup finely sliced celery
2 tablespoonfuls French dressing
¼ cup mayonnaise

4 large slices unsweetened pineapple
16 cold, steamed asparagus tips
Shredded lettuce

Marinate chicken in French dressing for half an hour. Drain. Add to celery and mayonnaise. On shredded lettuce beds, place slices of pineapple. Arrange chicken mixture on pineapple, and garnish with asparagus tips. Dust with paprika.

## CHICKEN LIVER SALAD

2 cups diced chicken liver (cooked)
¼ cup diced mild onion

1 cup sliced celery
Lettuce

Combine all ingredients. Serve on lettuce. Garnish with whole olives.

## CHICKEN AND OYSTER SALAD

1 cup diced steamed chicken
1 cup chopped oysters
1 cup sliced celery

1 cup tomato juice
1 tablespoonful granulated gelatin
1 cup jellied mayonnaise

Soften gelatin in two tablespoonfuls cold water, add to boiling tomato juice and stir until dissolved. Cool. When ready to congeal, line individual molds with this jelly. (Molds set in flat pan filled with cracked ice.) Almost fill with chicken, oyster, celery, jellied mayonnaise mixture. Chill. Top with tomato jelly. Chill thoroughly. Turn out on beds of cress.

## CHICKEN-CUCUMBER SALAD

1 cup cucumber cubes            1 cup diced chicken
1 cup English walnuts           Lettuce or cress

Marinate chicken and cucumber separately. Drain. Combine with nuts and serve on lettuce.

## COLD MEAT SALAD

1 cup diced cold meat           2 cups shredded lettuce
1 cup chopped cress             ¼ cup mayonnaise
½ cup steamed carrot balls      1 tablespoonful parsley

Marinate cold meat in French dressing. Add cress and carrot. Mix lettuce with ¼ cup French dressing. Rub the salad bowl with a clove of garlic. Arrange lettuce in bowl, on this place meat, cress and carrot mixture. Stir parsley into mayonnaise, and spread over salad. Garnish with tiny cubes of marinated beet or carrot.

## COTTAGE CHEESE SALAD (*molded*)

1 cup unsweetened pineapple, diced    1½ cups cottage cheese
½ cup carrots, grated                 ½ cup cream, whipped
¼ cup green peppers, minced           1 tablespoonful granulated gelatin
                    ¼ cup cold water

Combine pineapple, carrots, peppers and cheese. Soak gelatin in cold water, melt over hot water and add to mixture. Fold in whipped cream. Pour into moistened mold and chill until firm. Serve on crisp lettuce with mayonnaise.

## CREAM CHEESE SALAD

¾ lb. cream cheese              Paprika
Shredded lettuce                Curry powder or turmeric
Minced parsley                  ¼ cup mayonnaise
                French dressing

Mash cheese and mix with mayonnaise until smooth. Shape into small balls. Roll half of these in parsley, a few in paprika, the remainder in curry or turmerick. Toss lettuce in French dressing and arrange on salad plates. Place cheese balls on lettuce.

### CRAB SALAD

1½ cups white lump crab meat  
1 cup chopped celery  
3 tablespoonfuls French dressing  
4 hard boiled egg yolk, chopped  
Parsley  

¾ cup mayonnaise  
Tiny celery hearts  
Crab claws  
Lettuce or endive  
4 crab shells  

Marinate crab meat in French dressing for one hour. Drain and combine with celery, egg yolks and mayonnaise. Place salad in cleaned crab shells. Set on lettuce. Garnish with crab claws, celery hearts, and sprigs of parsley.

### CRAB FLAKE SALAD

3 cups crab flakes      Lettuce cups

*Special Dressing:*

½ cup mayonnaise  
4 tablespoonfuls fresh tomato pulp, drained  
1 tablespoonful minced chives  
4 tablespoonfuls minced celery hearts (or root)  
1 tablespoonful minced parsley  

Combine all ingredients for dressing and add to crab flakes. Serve in lettuce cups. Garnish with tiny bunches of watercress.

### CRAB MEAT AND GRAPEFRUIT SALAD

2 cups marinated crab meat (lump meat preferred)  
2 cups diced grapefruit  

Serve on crisp endive with mayonnaise or cream of tomato dressing.

### CURLIQUE SALAD

16 shrimp  
16 thick slices cucumber (do not pare)  
French dressing  
2 cups shredded green lettuce  
1 tablespoonful onion juice  

Marinate cucumber slices in French dressing for 15 minutes. Drain. Toss lettuce in French dressing and one tablespoonful onion juice, and arrange on four salad plates. Place on each plate 4 slices cucumber, with a shrimp on each slice.

### EGG AND CABBAGE SALAD

6 hard-boiled egg yolks  
2 cups shredded cabbage  
½ cup French dressing  
4 firm red tomatoes  

Toss cabbage with French dressing and arrange on salad plates. Cut tomatoes in quarters and arrange on cabbage with sliced egg yolks.

## EGG SALAD WITH HAM DRESSING

4 hard-boiled egg yolks
2 cups lemon gelatin
2 bunches crisp cress

8 pimiento strips
½ cup mayonnaise
4 tablespoonfuls minced boiled ham

Lettuce

When gelatin is ready to set pour small amount into individual molds to become firm. Place a hard boiled egg yolk in each mold and fill with gelatin When firm turn out on lettuce. Divide cress into 4 bunches. Tie each bunch with 2 strips pimiento. Place one with each mold. Serve with mayonnaise into which minced ham has been stirred.

## FILLET SALAD

1 large fillet of any firm white fish
½ cup French dressing
Cress
Lemon cups

Cucumber relish
6 large steamed beets
Shredded cabbage
Mayonnaise

Steam fish until tender. Place whole upon glass and cover with French dressing. Let stand one hour on ice. Remove to bed of chopped cress. Fill lemon cups with cucumber relish. Remove centers from beets and fill with cabbage mixed with mayonnaise. Use filled beet and lemon cups for garnishing.

## FROZEN CHEESE SALAD

½ lb. cottage cheese
½ cup whipped cream
¼ cup mayonnaise

½ cup walnuts or almonds, chopped
Endive or cress
Grated carrots

Mash cheese and beat with mayonnaise until smooth. Fold in whipped cream. Add nuts and mix well. Pack into individual molds and freeze. Make beds of cress or endive on salad plates. Cover thickly with grated carrot and turn out cheese molds on this. Garnish with a few nut meats.

## FROZEN CHEESE AND PINEAPPLE SALAD

2 cups cottage cheese
1 cup drained crushed un-
 sweetened pineapple

½ cup mayonnaise
¼ cup chopped red cherries
Watercress or endive

Mix cottage cheese, mayonnaise, pineapple and cherries until well blended. Freeze. To serve cut in cubes and arrange on salad greens.

## FRUITED CHICKEN SALAD

| | |
|---|---|
| 1 cup diced breast of chicken | ½ cup sliced celery |
| ½ cup pitted red cherries | ½ cup shredded almonds |
| ¼ cup seeded Malaga grapes | Lettuce cups |

Toss salad ingredients lightly together. Serve in lettuce cups.


## GRAPEFRUIT AND SHRIMP SALAD

| | |
|---|---|
| 1½ cups shrimp | French dressing |
| 1 cup diced grapefruit | 1 tablespoonful chopped pimiento |
| ½ cup diced celery | 1 tablespoonful chopped green pepper |

Radish roses

Marinate shrimp in French dressing for one hour. Drain. Combine with grapefruit dice and celery. Arrange on lettuce. Sprinkle with pimiento and pepper. Garnish with radish roses.


## HALIBUT SALAD

| | |
|---|---|
| 1 cup flaked halibut | ·3 tablespoonfuls French dressing |
| ½ cup sliced celery | Cress |
| ½ cup diced cucumber | Green mayonnaise |
| 1 tablespoonful onion juice | Mayonnaise |

2 hard boiled egg yolks, chopped

Toss together halibut, celery, cucumber, onion juice and French dressing. Serve on chopped cress with mayonnaise. Garnish with marinated beet slices and chopped egg yolks.


## HAM 'N' EGG SALAD

| | |
|---|---|
| 1 cup tiny cubes of boiled ham | ½ cup cubes of pineapple |
| 1 cup diced hard boiled egg yolks | Curly lettuce |
| 4 tablespoonfuls French dressing | Mayonnaise |

Paprika

Sprinkle ham and egg with French dressing. Add pineapple cubes. Toss lightly together and arrange on lettuce. Cover with mayonnaise and dust with paprika.

## JELLIED CHICKEN SALAD

⅔ cup diced chicken (white meat)  ⅛ teaspoonful powdered parsley
⅓ cup shredded almonds            1 cup whipped cream
 1 cup lemon gelatin              Lettuce
 2 egg yolks                      Mayonnaise
⅛ teaspoonful paprika             6 steamed carrots (whole)

Beat egg yolks and gradually add hot gelatin. Stir over hot water until thickened. When cool stir into this, chicken, almonds, paprika, parsley, whipped cream. Pour into an oblong mold to become firm. At serving time, trim the cold carrots into canoe shapes, and hollow out as much as possible. Fill cavities with mayonnaise and set around the chicken mixture which has been unmolded on lettuce.

## JELLIED HAM SALAD

2 cups  strained tomato juice       1 bay leaf
1 tablespoonful granulated gelatin  2 cups diced boiled ham
1 tablespoonful onion juice         Cress
½ teaspoonful vegetable salt        Boiled dressing

Soften gelatin in ½ cup tomato juice. Add to remaining juice heated to boiling, with bay leaf. Stir until gelatin is dissolved. Remove bay leaf, add onion juice, and salt. When ready to congeal add ham and pour into wet mold. Chill. Turn out on crisp cress and serve with boiled dressing.

## LETTUCE ROLLS SALAD

8 large lettuce leaves       8 tablespoonfuls cottage cheese
        8 teaspoonfuls mayonnaise

Combine cheese and mayonnaise. Spread on lettuce. Roll each leaf and tie with a spear of endive.

## LOBSTER SALAD

1½ cups lobster              1 cup mayonnaise
 1 cup diced celery          ½ cup oyster crabs
        Lettuce cups

Marinate lobster in French dressing for half an hour. Drain, and mix lightly with celery and mayonnaise. Serve in lettuce cups. Garnish with oyster crabs (raw). The tiny crabs may be immersed in boiling water for three minutes, if preferred. Drain and sprinkle with lemon juice.

## MASKED HALIBUT SALAD

4 rounds steamed halibut 1-inch thick    1 cup mayonnaise
1 tablespoonful granulated gelatin    ¼ cup olive rings
1 tablespoonful water    ¼ cup shredded almonds
¼ cup cubed beets marinated in lemon juice

Soften gelatin in water. Heat until melted. Stir into mayonnaise. Mask slices of fish with mayonnaise mixture, and decorate with nuts, olives, and beets. Chill and serve on cress.

## MAYONNAISE OF CHICKEN BREAST SALAD

2 cups diced cold breast of chicken    1 cup almonds (shredded)
¼ cup French dressing    1 cup jellied mayonnaise (freshly
Paprika                                  made)
¼ teaspoonful celery salt    Sliced olives
1 cup finely sliced celery    Tiny celery hearts

Dust chicken with paprika (or powdered parsley) and marinate in French dressing for one hour. Drain and combine with salt, celery, almonds and mayonnaise. Rinse mold with ice water. Pack chicken mixture in mold. Thoroughly chill, and turn out on lettuce. Garnish with olive rings and celery hearts.

## MEAT ROLL SALAD

8 thin slices boiled ham    2 tablespoonfuls French dressing
2 cups crisp dandelion    ½ cup mayonnaise

Spread mayonnaise on ham. Roll each slice and tie with spear of dandelion. Combine dandelion with French dressing and arrange on salad plates. Place two meat rolls on each plate.

## MEAT SALAD IN CUPS

1 cup diced meat (chicken    ½ cup mayonnaise
    or lamb)                         3 sweet red peppers
1 cup thinly sliced celery    3 sweet green peppers
½ cup chopped nuts    Lettuce

Remove stems and seeds from peppers. Cut into even sized cups, chill. Toss together lightly, chicken, celery and nuts. Mix with mayonnaise, and fill peppers with salad mixture. Serve on lettuce.

## MOLDED CRABMEAT SALAD

| | |
|---|---|
| 1 cup tomato juice | ½ cup water |
| 4 ounces Philadelphia cream cheese | 1 pound crabmeat |
| 1 tablespoonful granulated gelatin | 1 cup thinly sliced celery |

Soften gelatin by soaking in water for a few minutes. Add cream cheese to hot tomato juice with soaked gelatin. Cool until slightly thickened. Add vegetable salt to taste, then fold in the crabmeat and celery. Chill in mold.

## MOLDED SALMON SALAD

| | |
|---|---|
| 2 cups lemon gelatin | Dash of paprika |
| 1½ cups flaked red salmon | 4 hard-boiled egg yolks |
| ¼ cup chopped celery | 1 lemon |
| 1 tablespoonful lime juice | Lettuce |

When gelatin is ready to congeal, add lime juice, paprika, celery and salmon to ½ quantity. Pour the plain gelatin in bottom of mold; chill, then arrange on it sliced hard-boiled egg yolks. Cover with salmon-gelatin mixture. Set in refrigerator to become firm. Turn out on lettuce; and garnish with slices of lemon.

## MUSHROOM SALAD

| | |
|---|---|
| 1 cup chopped celery | 2 tablespoonfuls olive oil |
| 1 cup tiny green peas, steamed | Mayonnaise |
| 1 cup button mushrooms | Lettuce cups |

Stuffed olives

Break mushrooms in small pieces and place in pan with olive oil. Shake over heat for five minutes. Cool, sprinkle with celery salt. Add peas and celery and combine with mayonnaise. Chill. Place in lettuce cups and garnish with slices of olives.

## OYSTER SALAD

| | |
|---|---|
| 1 pint small oysters | 1 cup chopped walnuts |
| 4 tablespoonfuls lemon juice | Mayonnaise |
| 1 cup chopped celery | Lettuce |

Heat oysters until edges begin to curl. Drain, add lemon juice and chill. Combine with celery and nuts, add mayonnaise. Serve on crisp lettuce. Garnish with pimiento stars.

## OYSTER AND GRAPEFRUIT SALAD

4 grapefruit cups
1½ cups diced, drained grapefruit

1½ cups chopped oysters, raw or
steamed

⅓ cup tomato purée

Combine all ingredients and serve on lettuce, in grapefruit cups. Garnish with sections of grapefruit.

## PARTY CHICKEN SALAD

2 cups cubed chicken (white meat only)
½ cup shredded almonds
½ cup chopped pecans

1 cup seedless white grapes
1 cup thinly sliced celery
2 tablespoonfuls minced parsley
2 cups lemon gelatin

When gelatin is ready to congeal, combine all ingredients and chill in molds. When firm, turn out on crisp cress.

## PEACHES AND CREAM SALAD

2 cups whipped cream
1 cup cottage cheese
1 cup shredded peaches
1 cup lemon gelatin

2 tablespoonfuls pimiento stars
Lettuce
Mayonnaise
Peach halves

Beat cool gelatin with rotary beater until very light, add cream, cheese, peaches and pimiento. Blend all together smoothly. Mold in attractive shape. Turn out on lettuce. Garnish with peach halves filled with mayonnaise.

## PINEAPPLE, CHEESE AND TOMATO SALAD

¼ cup cottage cheese
¼ cup mayonnaise
2 tablespoonfuls chopped nuts

1 tablespoonful grated carrot
Lettuce
4 slices from firm ripe tomato

4 slices fresh unsweetened pineapple

Beat cheese and mayonnaise until smooth and light. Add nuts and carrot. Chill. Marinate slices of tomato in olive oil for fifteen minutes. Drain. Set a slice of pineapple on lettuce-covered plate. Arrange tomato slice next. Force cheese mixture through pastry tube to form border around tomato slice.

## PLAIN CHICKEN SALAD

2 cups diced chicken
1 cup diced celery

Lettuce cups
2 hard-boiled egg yolks

2 tablespoonfuls minced onion

Marinate chicken in French dressing for one hour. Drain and combine with onion and celery. Pile in lettuce cups. Garnish with sections of hard boiled egg yolk.

## ROAST BEEF SALAD

| | |
|---|---|
| 1 cup cold, diced roast beef | French dressing |
| 1 cup chopped celery | ¼ teaspoonful paprika |
| ½ cup minced onion | Lettuce |
| 2 tablespoonfuls minced parsley | Mayonnaise |

Marinate diced meat in French dressing. Add celery, parsley, onion. Cover with mayonnaise, and dust with paprika. Serve on lettuce.

## ROE SALAD

| | |
|---|---|
| 2 cups broken steamed shad roe | ½ cup French dressing |
| Endive | |

Marinate roe in French dressing. Let stand one hour. Make a nest of endive and fill with drained roe.

## SALMON SALAD

| | |
|---|---|
| 1 cup flaked salmon (red) | 2 hard-boiled egg yolks |
| 1 cup diced celery | ½ cup mayonnaise |
| 1 cup diced cucumber | Lettuce |

Toss lightly together salmon, celery, cucumber, chopped eggs and mayonnaise. Serve on lettuce. Garnish with slices of lemon.

## SARDINE SALAD

| | |
|---|---|
| ½ cup small carrot dice (cooked) | 4 tablespoonfuls French dressing |
| ½ cup steamed green beans 1-inch lengths | 12 sardines |
| | Parsley |
| ½ cup shredded lettuce | 2 hard-boiled egg yolks |
| 4 tablespoonfuls tiny diced beets | |

Combine carrots, beans and lettuce with French dressing. Form into shallow nests. Place three sardines in each nest, and garnish with sliced egg yolks, diced beets and sprigs of parsley.

## SCALLOP SALAD

Follow instructions for Crab Salad, substituting steamed diced sacllops for crab meat.

## SHRIMP SALAD

| | |
|---|---|
| 1 cup broken shrimp | 6 thinly sliced radishes |
| 1 cup diced cucumber | 2 tablespoonfuls minced chives |
| 2 hard-boiled egg yolks, chopped | Lettuce |

2 tablespoonfuls lemon juice — lemon slices

Combine shrimp, cucumber, egg yolks, radishes and lemon juice. Add chives. Serve on lettuce. Garnish with slices of lemon.

## SHRIMP AND CELERY SALAD

| | |
|---|---|
| 1 cup shrimp | 1 tablespoonful minced pimiento |
| 1 cup finely sliced celery | ¼ teaspoonful vegetable salt |
| 1 hard boiled egg yolk | Pinch of paprika |
| 2 tablespoonfuls minced sweet pepper | Lettuce |

Combine salad ingredients with mayonnaise. Serve on lettuce.

## SHRIMP AND ORANGE SALAD

| | |
|---|---|
| 1 cup shrimp | 2 tablespoonfuls grapefruit juice |
| 1½ cups orange sections | 2 cups lemon gelatin |

Cress

Combine gelatin and grapefruit juice. Pour a thin layer in fish mold and let harden on ice. Arrange shrimp and orange sections on gelatin and cover with remaining cool gelatin. Chill. Turn out on crisp watercress.

## SHRIMP AND PINEAPPLE SALAD

| | |
|---|---|
| 1½ cups cleaned shrimp | 1½ cups cubes of unsweetened pineapple |
| ½ cup sliced ripe olives | |

Lettuce or endive

On beds of salad greens, place mounds of pineapple. Arrange cooked, chilled shrimp around these. Distribute sliced olives over salads.

## SOY BEAN SALAD

| | |
|---|---|
| 2 cups cooked soy beans | ¼ cup shredded green pepper |
| 1 cup sliced celery | 2 tomatoes |
| ½ cup shaved onion | Mayonnaise |

Combine all ingredients except tomatoes using enough mayonnaise to give right consistency. Place in nest of greens in salad bowl. Garnish with sections of tomato.

## STUFFED CELERY SALAD

2 cups tender celery cut in one
    inch lengths
½ cup cream cheese

⅛ teaspoonful prepared mustard
2 tablespoonfuls mayonnaise
Cress

Combine cheese, mayonnaise, and mustard, and fill celery with this mixture. Arrange on beds of cress.

## SWEETBREAD SALAD

1 pair sweetbreads
1 tablespoonful lemon juice
½ tablespoonful olive oil
½ teaspoonful celery salt

⅛ teaspoonful paprika
Lettuce
1 cup celery (sliced)
1 cup mayonnaise

Sweetbreads must be plunged into cold water as soon as received and soaked for one hour. Remove from cold water, place in boiling acidulated water (1 teaspoonful salt; 1 teaspoonful lemon juice; 1 quart water) and continue boiling for twenty minutes. Now immerse in ice water until firm. Remove all membrane. Cut into cubes. Add oil, salt and paprika, and chill for one hour. Mix with diced celery and ½ cup mayonnaise. Top with remaining dressing.

## TOMATO AND SOY BEAN SALAD

Fill tomato cups with tender cooked soy beans combined with minced chives and pimiento.

## TOMATO SURPRISE SALAD

4 tomatoes
¾ cup diced cucumber
½ cup diced cold chicken
¼ cup chopped nuts

¼ cup mayonnaise
Lettuce or romaine
Truffles
French dressing

Scald, peel and chill tomatoes. Cut slice from top and trim edge of tomato with fluted cutter. Remove seeds and sprinkle inside of tomato with vegetable salt. Invert and stand in refrigerator for an hour. Marinate cucumber, chicken and nuts in four tablespoonfuls French dressing. Fill tomato cups and arrange on lettuce. For garnishing use truffles.

## TOMATO AND SHRIMP SALAD

4 medium sized tomatoes
1½ cups shrimp (marinated)

½ cup boiled dressing
Shredded lettuce

4 whole shrimp, steamed (in shell)

Scald, peel and chill tomatoes. Form into cups. Fill with shrimp combined with dressing. Serve on lettuce. Set one whole shrimp on each salad.

## TUNA SALAD

1 cup flaked tuna
½ cup diced tomato, drained
½ cup cucumber dice

3 tablespoonfuls French dressing
Cress
Mayonnaise

Marinate tuna in French dressing. Combine with tomato and cucumber. Arrange on cress and serve with mayonnaise.

## TUNA AND APPLE SALAD

1 cup flaked tuna
1 cup diced tart apples
Crisp lettuce

½ cup sliced celery
¼ cup French dressing

Combine salad ingredients with dressing very carefully, to prevent breaking fish. Serve on crisp lettuce leaves.

## TUNA CABBAGE SALAD

Combine 3 cups finely shredded cabbage, 2 green peppers, chopped, 1½ cups cucumber, 1 cup tuna fish. Mix with mayonnaise. Serve on crisp lettuce.

## TUNA AND WATERCRESS SALAD

1 cup shredded tuna
1 cup sliced celery
1 tablespoonful lemon juice

¾ cup mayonnaise
2 cups watercress

Pour lemon juice over tuna. Combine with celery and mayonnaise. Make a ring of watercress (tossed in French dressing) around the salad plate. Pile tuna mixture in center. Garnish with pimiento stars.

## TUNA AND VEGETABLE SALAD

1 cup diced celery
½ cup chopped cabbage
1 cup flaked tuna

½ cup cucumber, diced
¼ cup olive rings
Lettuce or cress

Combine tuna, celery, cabbage, cucumber. Garnish with olive rings. Serve on lettuce or cress.

## TURKEY SALAD

2 cups diced white turkey meat       1 cup sliced celery
1 cup mayonnaise

Garnish with celery hearts.

## VEGETABLE-FISH SALAD

1 cup flaked fish                       1 tablespoonful minced onion
1 cup tiny green peas               ½ cup chopped celery
(Carrots, green beans, diced beets may be substituted for peas.)

Marinate fish in French dressing for half an hour. Prepare one cup vegetables. Combine with fish, celery and onion.

## WALNUT SQUARE SALAD

2 cups walnut halves               2 cups lemon gelatin
2 tablespoonfuls sherry flavoring

Stir flavoring into gelatin. Pour a very thin layer of cool gelatin into a flat square pan. Set walnuts on gelatin in regular rows. Chill. Add remaining gelatin. When firm cut into blocks with a nut in each. Serve on lettuce.

## WHITE FISH SALAD

2 cups flaked white fish           1 cup tiny diced beets (marinated)
4 hard-boiled egg yolks            Lettuce

Toss fish and beets together with two tablespoonfuls French dressing. Arrange on lettuce. Garnish with wedges of hard boiled egg yolk.

## YELLOW ROSE SALAD

For each salad place slice of lettuce on bed of endive. Turn out mold of egg yolk souffle on lettuce. Surround with leaves cut from green pepper. Serve with French dressing containing chopped raw mushrooms.

# VEGETABLE SALADS

### APPLE AND CARROT SALAD

1½ cups cubes of tart apple
1½ cups thinly sliced carrots

2 tablespoonfuls lemon juice
Cream-mayonnaise dressing

Endive

Scrub carrots and wipe dry. Cut into quarters lengthwise. Now slice very thinly. Add apple cubes which have been sprinkled with lemon juice (to prevent discoloration). Arrange on endive and serve with cream-mayonnaise dressing.

### APPLE, CELERY, RAISIN SALAD

1½ cups sliced apple (do not pare)
1½ cups sliced celery

¼ cup raisins
Lettuce

Mayonnaise

Arrange sliced celery on lettuce. Dip apple rings into French dressing and place on celery. Distribute chopped raisins over apple. Serve with mayonnaise.

### APPLE AND CELERY ROOT SALAD

2 cups diced tart apple
1 cup sliced celery root
½ cup chopped walnuts

2 tablespoonfuls grapefruit juice
Mayonnaise
Lettuce

Pour grapefruit juice over apple as soon as it is pared and diced. Combine with celery root and walnuts. Serve with mayonnaise, on lettuce.

### APPLE, PEA AND CELERY SALAD

1 cup steamed small peas
1 cup sliced celery

1 cup diced apple

Marinate each vegetable separately for half an hour in French dressing. Drain and mix lightly.

### ASPARAGUS SALAD

4 bundles cold cooked asparagus
1 cup chilled thick sweet cream

2 teaspoonfuls lemon juice

Sprinkle asparagus with lemon juice and chill thoroughly. Serve with cream.

## ASPARAGUS TIP SALAD

1 lb. cooked asparagus tips         6 tablespoonfuls French dressing
Lettuce

Marinate asparagus in French dressing for one hour. Serve on lettuce. Garnish with pimiento strips.


## ASPARAGUS, CABBAGE AND BEET SALAD

1 cup raw asparagus tips, sliced lengthwise     1 cup shredded cabbage
1 cup shredded raw beets

Arrange cabbage on beds of lettuce. Form a star of asparagus points on cabbage. Pile beet in center.


## ASPARAGUS AND YELLOW TOMATO SALAD

1¼ lbs. steamed asparagus         4 small ripe yellow tomatoes
Endive

Arrange beds of endive on individual salad plates. Cut tomatoes into quarters, and arrange with asparagus on the greens.


## AVOCADO CELERY AND BEET SALAD

Arrange sections of avocado on bed of salad greens to form rings. Fill with equal parts chopped, marinated, cooked beet and sliced celery.


## AVOCADO, KUMQUAT AND CELERY SALAD

Form ring of avocado sections on bed of salad greens. Fill with thinly sliced kumquats (or orange dice) and sliced celery.


## BEAN AND ONION SALAD

4 cups steamed green beans         4 medium sized mild onions
2 tablespoonfuls minced chives     Lettuce
Mayonnaise

Remove as much of center of onions as possible to leave firm shell. Fill these with mayonnaise. Cut beans into one inch lengths, and marinate in French dressing for fifteen minutes. Combine minced chives with beans and arrange on lettuce. Place one onion cup on each salad plate.

## BEAN, PEPPER AND CELERY SALAD

1 cup steamed small green beans,    1 cup sliced celery
  2-inch lengths                    2 tablespoonful grated onion
½ cup shredded green pepper    French dressing

Toss together salad ingredients and dressing, and serve on lettuce.

## BEET SALAD

8 medium sized cold cooked beets    Small lettuce leaves
4 tablespoonfuls French dressing    4 tablespoonfuls chopped olives

Cut beets in halves crosswise and marinate in French dressing for one hour. At serving time place ½ beet on each lettuce leaf and sprinkle finely chopped olives over salad.

## BEET AND APPLE SALAD

2 cups sliced steamed beets, marinated    2 cups sliced apple
Endive

Arrange sliced beets and apple in circles on endive.

## BEET AND CELERY SALAD

1½ cups diced, steamed beets    1½ cups sliced celery

Marinate diced beets in French dressing for one hour. Drain. Combine with celery. Serve on lettuce or endive.

## BEET CUP SALAD

4 large steamed beets    1¼ cups diced cooked carrot (marinated)
Lettuce

Remove centers from cooked beets, leaving cup. Marinate in French dressings. Fill with carrot. Serve on lettuce.

## BEET AND ONION SALAD

1 cup diced cooked beets    French dressing
1 cup chopped sweet onion    4 cucumber cups or boats
Boiled dressing

Marinate beets in French dressing, for one hour. Drain, and mix lightly with onion. Fill into cucumber shells. Serve on lettuce with boiled dressing.

## BEET, ORANGE AND ONION SALAD

1½ cups diced, cooked beets     1½ cups diced orange
½ cup shaved onion

Combine all ingredients.

## BERMUDA SALAD

1 cup finely chopped Bermuda     ¼ cup French dressing
 onion                          4 tomato cups
1 cup crushed (drained) pineapple    Lettuce

Toss onion and pineapple together with dressing. Drain. Fill tomato cups with mixture and set on lettuce.

## CABBAGE AND APPLE SALAD

Equal parts sliced cabbage and diced apple.

## CABBAGE, APPLE AND CELERY SALAD

2 cups shredded cabbage     ¾ cup sliced celery
¾ diced apple              ¼ cup French dressing

Combine cabbage with French dressing and form into nests. Fill these with apple and celery tossed together.

## CABBAGE BOWL

1 large red cabbage        ½ cup chopped carrots
1 cup shredded celery      2 tablespoonfuls grated onion

Cut a slice from top of cabbage. Remove center of head, leaving firm outer shell. Chill. Chop enough of the Cabbage to make one cup, combine with celery, carrots, onion and dressing; and pile into cabbage bowl.

## CABBAGE AND CARROT SALAD

2 cups chopped cabbage        2 tablespoonfuls minced onion
1 cup grated or chopped carrots    ¼ cup diced cucumber

Combine ingredients and serve on lettuce or cress.

## CABBAGE CARROT AND PRUNE SALAD

2 cups thinly sliced cabbage    1 cup thinly sliced celery
½ cup grated carrot            ½ cup sliced prunes

Combine ingredients lightly. Serve on bed of salad greens.

## CABBAGE AND CELERY SALAD

1½ cups shredded white cabbage    1½ cups chopped celery
French dressing

Combine cabbage, celery and dressing. Arrange on lettuce and garnish with overlapping circles of sliced green peppers.

## CABBAGE, CRESS AND CELERY SALAD

1 cup shredded cabbage    1 cup sliced celery
1 cup chopped cress    French dressing

Combine salad ingredients and dressing and arrange on lettuce. Garnish with pimiento strips.

## CABBAGE, CRESS AND RADISH SALAD

1½ cups shredded cabbage    ¼ cup thinly sliced green onions
1½ cups chopped cress    French dressing
½ cup thinly sliced radishes    4 hard-boiled egg yolks

Toss first four ingredients with enough French dressing to moisten. Place in salad bowl which has been lined with lettuce. Force egg yolks through fine sieve and sprinkle over salad.

## CABBAGE AND ONION SALAD

2 cups shredded white cabbage    1 tablespoonful minced green pepper
½ cup onion rings    ¼ cup French dressing
Romaine

Combine salad ingredients and dressing. Serve on romaine.

## CABBAGE AND PECAN SALAD

1 cup chopped pecans    2 cups shredded white cabbage
Lettuce

Combine cabbage and nuts with mayonnaise. Serve on lettuce.

## CABBAGE AND PINEAPPLE SALAD

1½ cups shredded cabbage    6 tablespoonfuls salad dressing
½ cup shredded unsweetened    4 apple cups
pineapple

Combine cabbage, pineapple and dressing. Place in apple cups. For variation substitute orange dice, peach balls or apple cubes for pineapple.

## CABBAGE, TURNIP AND CARROT SALAD

1½ cups chopped cabbage        1 cup shredded raw turnip
1 cup grated carrot

Combine chilled ingredients. Serve on lettuce or cress.


## CARROT, CABBAGE AND PEPPER SALAD

1 cup grated carrots           ½ cup finely shredded green
1 cup shredded cabbage            peppers
4 tablespoonfuls French dressing

Combine carrots, cabbage, peppers, and French dressing. Serve on beds of Romaine.


## CARROT, CRESS AND WALNUT SALAD

2 cups shredded carrots        2 cups chopped cress
1½ cups chopped English walnuts    ¼ cup French dressing

Toss cress with half the given quantity of French dressing. Mix carrots and nuts with remaining dressing and arrange on cress.


## CARROT AND LETTUCE SALAD

1 cup chopped raw carrots      2 cups shredded lettuce
Thousand Island dressing

Combine carrot and lettuce with dressing and serve on endive.


## CARROT AND PEA SALAD

1½ cups shredded raw carrot    ¾ cup chopped celery
1½ cups cooked peas            6 ripe olives, sliced

Combine ingredients lightly. Serve on lettuce.


## CARROT AND RADISH SALAD

1½ cups shredded raw carrots   2 tablespoonfuls minced onion
1 cup sliced red radishes      4 lettuce cups
¼ cup French dressing

Combine salad ingredients with dressing, and serve on lettuce.

## CARROT AND RAISIN SALAD

2 cups shredded carrot                ¾ cup seedless raisins

Combine ingredients and serve on watercress or endive.


## CARROT RING SALAD

3 cups cooked carrot rings            French dressing
1 cup chopped Bermuda onions          Lettuce

To prepare carrot rings, slice cooked carrot ¼ inch thick.  Remove centers with apple corer.  Make a border of overlapping carrot rings on lettuce.  Pile onion in center.  Serve with French dressing.


## CARROT AND WALNUT SALAD

2 cups shredded raw carrot            ½ cup small cubes of tart apple
½ cup chopped walnuts                 2 tablespoonfuls lemon juice
                    Romaine or endive

Combine apple and lemon juice, add carrot and nuts, toss together lightly.  Arrange on romaine or endive.


## CAULIFLOWER SALAD

1 firm white cauliflower              8 large crisp lettuce leaves

Steam cauliflower until tender.  Chill.  Arrange lettuce leaves in bowl to resemble leaves of cauliflower and set cauliflower in center.


## CAULIFLOWER AND BRUSSEL SPROUTS SALAD

2 cups Brussels sprouts               1 cup cauliflower flowerettes

Chill steamed vegetables.  Marinate separately.  Drain.  Combine and serve on lettuce.


## CAULIFLOWER AND CELERY SALAD

                2 cups thinly sliced raw cauliflower
2 cups sliced celery                  ¼ cup minced pimiento
                2 tablespoonfuls shredded green pepper

Marinate cauliflower in French dressing for ½ hour.  Drain and combine with remaining ingredients.

## CAULIFLOWER AND TOMATO SALAD

1 pint firm tomatoes cut in quarters
1 pint steamed cauliflower flowerettes
¼ cup French dressing

Lettuce
Mayonnaise
Chopped parsley

Marinate cauliflower in French dressing for one hour. Drain. Combine with tomato and arrange on lettuce. Cover with mayonnaise and sprinkle with chopped parsley.

## CELERIAC SALAD

3 cups steamed celery root

2 tablespoonfuls French dressing

Marinate sliced celeriac for half an hour in French dressing. Drain. Serve on lettuce. Garnish with pimiento strips.

## CELERY, CUCUMBER AND RADISH SALAD

½ cup diced radishes
1½ cups sliced celery

½ cup diced cucumbers
¼ cup minced onion

Combine vegetables. Place on lettuce and cover with mayonnaise. Garnish with crossed strips of pimiento.

## CELERY AND PEA SALAD

1 can small peas
1½ cups chopped celery

Cream dressing
1 onion

Drain liquid from peas. Combine peas, grated onion, celery and dressing. Serve from salad bowl.

## CELERY AND TOMATO SALAD

1½ cups diced tomato          1½ cups crisp sliced celery
1 tablespoonful onion juice

Combine celery, tomato and onion juice. Serve on lettuce with mayonnaise.

## CELERY AND TOMATO CUP SALAD

4 tomato cups
2 cups sliced celery

¼ cup shredded green pepper
6 tablespoonfuls French dressing

Combine celery, pepper and French dressing. Fill tomato cups with mixture. Serve on endive.

## COLD SLAW

¼ cup boiling water                  1 tablespoonful olive oil
¼ cup lemon juice                    3 egg yolks
Pinch of salt                        ½ cup cream
Dash of paprika                      6 cups shredded cabbage
            1 tablespoonful Tupelo honey
        4 tablespoonfuls pimiento stars for garnishing

Combine first five ingredients. Heat to boiling point and pour over well-beaten egg yolks. Cook in double boiler until thick. Add cream, and beat well. Pour hot over cabbage. Chill thoroughly before serving.

## COMBINATION SALAD

1 cup chopped cress                  1 cup shredded cabbage
            1 cup ground carrot

Mix each vegetable separately with jellied mayonnaise. Pack in layers in brick mold. Chill. Slice and serve on endive.

## COOKED VEGETABLE IN TOMATO ASPIC

½ cup small peas                     ½ cup carrot rings
½ cup green beans, 1 inch lengths    1 cup boiling water
½ cup cauliflower flowerettes        ½ cup tomato juice
½ cup asparagus tips                 2 tablespoonfuls lemon juice
            1 tablespoonful granulated gelatin.
            1 tablespoonful Tupelo honey

Steam all vegetables together until tender. Chill. Soften gelatin in tomato juice. Dissolve in boiling water. Add lemon juice and honey. When ready to congeal add vegetables. Chill in individual molds. Serve on dandelion greens.

## CREAM OF TOMATO SALAD

1 cup tomato purée                   Lettuce
1 cup whipped cream                  Mayonnaise

Mix tomato purée with whipped cream. Pack in individual molds and freeze. Turn out on lettuce and serve with mayonnaise.

## CRESS AND NUT SALAD

2 small firm heads iceberg lettuce     2 cups shredded cress
1 cup sliced nuts

Cut through lettuce heads from top to bottom. Cut out centers, and turn on side to form cups. Fill with shredded cress and nuts mixed with French dressing.

## CRESS SALAD

4 cups cress                    1 onion

Break cress into two-inch lengths. Arrange on lettuce. Sprinkle finely chopped onion over cress.

## CRESS AND CUCUMBER SALAD

2 cups chopped cress            ¼ cup minced scallions
1 cup diced cucumber            ½ cup shredded radishes
French dressing

Mix together lightly, cucumber, cress, scallions and ¼ cup of French dressing. Drain. Arrange on lettuce. Top with shredded radishes.

## CRESS, CABBAGE AND CUCUMBER SALAD

1 cup watercress cut in 1 inch       1 cup diced cucumber
    lengths                          ½ cup diced radishes
1 cup shredded cabbage               French dressing

Combine salad ingredients and add dressing. Serve on lettuce.

## CRESS AND TOMATO SALAD

4 ripe tomatoes                  1 cup watercress
2 cups marinated watercress

Prepare tomatoes by removing hard center. Chill. Invert on beds of marinated cress. Cut slits evenly in tomatoes and insert sprigs of cress in these.

## CUCUMBER SALAD

2 cups diced cucumbers           ¼ cup French dressing
Lettuce

Add French dressing to cucumbers. Drain. Arrange on lettuce. Garnish with onion rings.

## CUCUMBER AND APPLE SALAD

1 cup diced crisp cucumber      1 cup diced tart apple
2 cups chopped endive

Arrange endive in nests on individual plates. Fill with cucumber and apple, mixed.


## CUCUMBER BASKET SALAD

1½ cups chopped crisp radish       4 baskets cut from large cucumbers
1½ tablespoonfuls French dressing  Lettuce

Combine radish and dressing. Place in cucumber baskets and serve on lettuce.


## CUCUMBER JELLY SALAD

2 cups grated cucumber          ¼ cup cold water
1 tablespoonful granulated gelatin    ¼ cup chopped onion
1 tablespoonful lemon juice

Soften gelatin in cold water. Set over hot water and stir until dissolved. Add to grated cucumber with lemon juice. Add onion. Chill in individual mold. Turn out on cress.


## CUCUMBER ROLL SALAD

4 small cucumbers              2 tablespoonfuls grated onion
½ cup grated carrot            2 cups standard lemon gelatin

Cut cucumber in thin slices lengthwise. Sprinkle lightly with carrot and onion mixed. Roll. Set rolls on edge in small flat dish. Cover with lemon gelatin. When firm cut in cubes, with a roll in each cube. Serve on lettuce. Garnish with tomato balls.


## CUCUMBER AND TOMATO SALAD

3 cups ½-inch slices cucumber            1 cup tomato gelatin
or 1 cup balls cut from firm tomato

Remove seeds from cucumbers, place a ball of tomato in center of each ring. Serve on lettuce.


## DANDELION SALAD

4 cups chopped dandelions       ¼ cup French dressing
1 tablespoonful chopped chives

Combine dandelion with chives and dressing. Serve on lettuce.

## ENDIVE AND CUCUMBER SALAD

2 cups diced crisp cucumber      2 cups chopped endive
French dressing

Combine vegetables and moisten with dressing. Serve on lettuce or greens of choice.

## FOUR LEAF CLOVER SALAD

4 green peppers, uniform size      2 cups lemon gelatin
12 radish roses

Steam peppers until tender but not soft. Drain. Fill with gelatin, colored green. Chill thoroughly. Slice ¼ inch thick. Arrange four slices on each salad plate (on lettuce) to simulate four leaf clover. Garnish with radish roses.

## FROZEN TOMATO SALAD

2 cups stewed tomato      ⅛ teaspoonful celery salt

Rub tomato through strainer. Add celery salt. Pour into individual molds and freeze. Unmold on lettuce.

## GREEN BEAN SALAD

2 cups cooked green beans,      ¼ cup finely chopped onion
2 inch lengths      1 cup pimiento, shredded

Combine beans, pimiento and onion. Serve on lettuce.

## GREEN BEAN AND CELERY SALAD

1 cup marinated string beans      ½ cup diced radishes
1 cup sliced celery      Pimiento strips
½ cup chopped onion      Endive
Watercress

Combine first four ingredients with French dressing. Drain. Arrange on endive. Garnish with small bunches of cress tied with pimiento strips.

## GREEN BEAN-PIMIENTO SALAD

3½ cups steamed green beans      1 pimiento, shredded
2 tablespoonfuls minced onion

If beans are large, cut into narrow strips, lengthwise. Marinate in French dressing if desired. Combine with onion and pimiento.

## GREEN LIMA SALAD

2 cups steamed baby limas                ¼ cup minced green pepper
¾ cup diced celery                       Pimiento strips

Marinate limas and celery, separately, for half and hour.  Drain.  Mix lightly together beans, celery and pepper.  Serve on lettuce.  Garnish with pimiento strips.

## HEAD LETTUCE SALAD

1 head lettuce                           ¼ cup shredded almonds
¾ cup salad dressing                     ¼ cup sliced ripe olives

Select a perfect head of lettuce.  Immerse in ice water for half an hour.  Hold under water and pull leaves apart (open) without breaking.  Drain in ice box. When ready to serve set upright in salad bowl.  Insert dressing between leaves. Garnish with almonds and ripe olives.  To serve cut into quarters.

## JELLIED BEET AND PEA SALAD

### Part 1

1 cup diced steamed beets                1 cup lemon gelatin
              1 tablespoonful beet juice

### Part 2

1 cup tiny steamed peas         1 cup lemon gelatin colored green

### Part 1

Combine beets and juice with gelatin that is ready to congeal.  Chill in flat pan.

### Part 2

When green gelatin is ready to congeal add peas.  Chill in flat pan.

To serve cut gelatin in small cubes and serve on lettuce.  Garnish with sliced lemon.

### JELLIED GRAPEFRUIT AND CUCUMBER SALAD

1 cup diced grapefruit                1 cup diced cucumber
2 cups lemon gelatin

When gelatin is ready to congeal, stir in grapefruit and cucumber. Chill in ring mold. Turn out on crisp lettuce and fill center of ring with preferred dressing.

### JELLIED VEGETABLE SALAD

1½ cups boiling water                1 cup shredded cabbage
¼ cup cold water                     1 tablespoonful onion juice
1½ tablespoonfuls plain granulated   ½ cup shredded raw carrot
    gelatin                          ½ cup sliced celery
         ¼ cup lemon and lime juice, mixed

Soften gelatin in cold water. Add to boiling water. Add lemon and lime juice. When cool add remaining ingredients. Chill in mold. Serve on lettuce.

### LETTUCE, CRESS AND ENDIVE SALAD

1 cup chopped cress                  1 cup chopped endive
1 cup shredded lettuce               ½ cup radish rings
             French dressing

Cut centers from crisp radishes and slice remaining shells to make rings. Combine all ingredients with dressing. Serve on lettuce.

### LETTUCE AND ONION SALAD

2 cups shredded lettuce          2 thinly sliced sweet onions
             2 tomatoes

Arrange lettuce and onions in layers on salad plates. Garnish with quarters of tomato.

### LETTUCE SALAD WITH CAVIAR

4 hearts of lettuce                  ½ cup mayonnaise
          4 tablespoonfuls caviar

Set lettuce hearts upright on salad plates. Pull apart the leaves and insert portions of mayonnaise into which the caviar has been well mixed.

### MIXED GREENS SALAD

1 cup shredded lettuce       1 cup chopped chicory
          1 cup chopped watercress

Toss together with three tablespoonfuls French dressing.

## MOLDED ASPARAGUS SALAD

1 cup steamed asparagus tips    1 tablespoonful granulated gelatin
2 cups strained tomato juice    1 cup marinated asparagus tips
                    Lettuce

Soften gelatin in two tablespoonfuls tomato juice. Dissolve in one cup tomato juice heated to boiling point. Add remaining liquid. When ready to congeal add asparagus tips. Chill in flat pan. Cut into blocks or fancy shapes and serve on lettuce, garnish with marinated asparagus tips.

## NUT AND CELERY SALAD

1 cup chopped nuts              2 cups shredded lettuce
                1 cup sliced celery

Combine salad ingredients. Serve on crisp lettuce. Garnish with halves of English walnuts.

## ONION SALAD

2 Bermuda or Spanish onions     2 cups shredded lettuce
                    Paprika

Slice onions wafer thin, and arrange on lettuce. Dust with paprika.

## ONION AND BEAN SALAD

2 large Bermuda onions          1 cup string beans 2-inch lengths,
1 green pepper                     steamed
½ cup grated carrot (marinated)  Shredded lettuce

Place shredded lettuce on individual salad plates. For each service allow three slices onion, rub with olive oil and pile in center of lettuce. One green pepper ring on each salad, fill with marinated carrot. Make a border of green beans.

## ONION AND ORANGE SALAD

8 slices orange, ½ inch thick       8 slices Bermuda onion
                    Endive

Set orange slices of beds of endive. Arrange one onion slice on each slice of orange.

## ORANGE AND WATERCRESS SALAD

4 oranges                    4 cups chopped watercress
2 tablespoonfuls French dressing

Toss cress in dressing and arrange on lettuce.  Slice or separate oranges in sections, and arrange on cress.

## PEAR, CELERY AND SAUERKRAUT SALAD

1 cup diced pear                    1 cup sliced celery
1 cup chopped sauerkraut

Combine ingredients. Serve on lettuce.

## PEPPER AND BEET SALAD

1½ cups finely shredded sweet green peppers
1½ cups diced cooked beets          1 tablespoonful minced chives
1 tablespoonful minced parsley

Toss salad ingredients in French dressing, and serve on lettuce.

## PERFECTION SALAD

3 tomatoes, diced             1 green pepper, diced
1 cup celery, diced           Juice and grated rind of 1 lemon
1 cup cabbage, shredded       1 tablespoonful granulated gelatin
1 cup boiling water

Soak gelatin in 2 tablespoonfuls cold water a few minutes, then add boiling water; add juice and grated rind of 1 lemon. Just before it sets, add tomato, celery, cabbage and green pepper. Chill in mold. Serve on crisp lettuce leaves with mayonnaise.

## PIMIENTO AND PEA SALAD

4 pimiento cups                    ¼ cup mayonnaise
2 cups steamed tiny green peas     1 teaspoonful minced onion
Celery hearts

Fill pimiento cups with peas, mayonnaise and onion combined. Place on lettuce leaves and garnish with small celery hearts.

## PINEAPPLE AND BEET SALAD

2 cups shredded, drained, unsweetened pineapple
12 slices cooked beets

French dressing
2 cups chopped endive.
2 tablespoonfuls grapefruit juice

Marinate pineapple and beets, separately in French dressing. Sprinkle grapefruit juice over endive, mix well and form circles on salad plates. Fill these with drained pineapple. Use a vegetable cutter to cut beets into uniform shapes and arrange on pineapple.

## PINEAPPLE AND CELERY SALAD

2 cups sliced celery      1 cup shredded unsweetened pineapple

Combine celery and pineapple. Arrange on beds of romaine.

## PINEAPPLE, COCONUT AND CABBAGE SALAD

4 slices unsweetened pineapple
1 cup shredded coconut
½ cup shredded white cabbage
      Bamboo shoots, marinated

½ cup shredded red cabbage
¼ cup French dressing
½ teaspoonful fresh lime juice

Place slices of pineapple on lettuce. Combine cabbage, lime juice, coconut and French dressing. Drain. Pile on pineapple. Garnish with bamboo shoots.

## POINSETTIA SALAD

4 tomatoes      ¼ cup French dressing
      Ripe olives

Scald, peel and chill tomatoes. Cut (almost through) tomato into eight sections. Pull back sections to resemble flower petals. Make stamens of pieces of ripe olives. Arrange on green lettuce. Serve with French dressing.

## PORCUPINE SALAD

4 yellow tomatoes
1 cup celery in match-like strips

½ cup shredded almonds
Mayonnaise

Scald, peel and chill tomatoes. Remove hard center and invert on lettuce. Stick full of celery strips and almonds. Serve with mayonnaise.

## RADISH AND BEAN SALAD

¾ cup thinly sliced radishes      ¾ cup shredded string beans
      ¾ cups diced cucumber

Marinate vegetables for salad in French dressing. Drain and serve on chickory.

## RADISH AND PEPPER SALAD

1 cup red radishes thinly sliced          1 tablespoonful onion juice
1 cup shredded green pepper               4 tomato cups
                          Salad dressing

Prepare and chill tomato cups. Combine radish, pepper and onion juice. Place in tomato cups, cover with dressing and serve on lettuce.

## ROMAINE AND ESCAROLE SALAD

1½ cups chopped romaine          1½ cups chopped escarole

Combine greens. Serve with French dressing seasoned with garlic.

## SAUERKRAUT AND CARROT SALAD

1½ cups sauerkraut          ¼ cup mayonnaise
1 cup grated carrot         ½ cup walnut halves

Combine carrots, sauerkraut and mayonnaise. Arrange on lettuce. Garnish with walnuts.

## SHAMROCK SALAD

For each salad—

Use three rings of green pepper, place the pepper rings in the form of shamrocks or three-leaved clovers on lettuce arranged on individual plate. Heap the centers of the rings with drained crushed pineapple and in the center where the rings come together put a spoonful of mayonnaise. Sprinkle with paprika.

## SHREDDED CARROT, BEET AND PARSNIP SALAD

2 tablespoonfuls shredded raw carrots     2 tablespoonfuls shredded raw parsnips
2 tablespoonfuls shredded raw beets       3 rings of green pepper
Sufficient for individual salad.

Place the three pepper rings in the form of a three leaved clover in the center of lettuce arranged on salad plate. Fill the centers of rings, one with carrot, one with beet and one with parsnips.

## SHREDDED CARROT AND TURNIP SALAD

Combine equal parts shredded carrot and turnip, adding a little grated lemon rind to season. Rub wooden salad spoon with a bud of garlic and use with wooden fork to combine vegetables with French dressing. Serve on crisp lettuce, sprinkle with shredded almonds.

## SPECIAL VEGETABLE SALAD COMBINATIONS

Shredded cabbage and celery
Celery, cabbage, and carrots
Shredded parsnips, celery, beets and cabbage
Shredded carrots and raisins
Green beans, green peas, tomatoes and celery
Shredded beets and carrots
Shredded cabbage, green peppers and pimiento
Grated parsnip and shredded radish
Shredded beet and thinly sliced spring onions
Shredded carrot and diced apple and raisins
Sliced cauliflowerettes, shaved cucumber and sliced spring onions
Sliced cauliflowerettes and shredded radishes
Shredded celeriac and shredded beet
Shredded celeriac, diced apple and chopped walnuts
Sliced celery and shredded beet
Shredded yellow turnip, sliced cabbage and broken pecans
Sliced brussels sprouts, orange sections.

## SPINACH SALAD

1 pint steamed spinach        2 hard-boiled egg yolks

Chop spinach and press into four molds. Turn out on lettuce. Sprinkle with chopped egg yolks.

## SPINACH AND LETTUCE SALAD, BACON DRESSING

2 quarts tender young spinach leaves      6 tablespoonfuls lemon juice
2 quarts spring lettuce      3 slices fat bacon
1 small onion, minced      ¼ teaspoonful vegetable salt
Dash of paprika

Fry bacon until crisp. Reserve fat, to which add lemon, salt and paprika. Heat until steaming. Pour over salad greens and onion and mix over heat until leaves are well coated with dressing. Serve in *warm* (not too hot) dish. Garnish with chopped bacon slices.

## SPROUTS SALAD

2 cups Brussels sprouts      1 cup asparagus tips

Marinate steamed vegetables, separately. Drain. Combine and serve on lettuce.

## STEAMED VEGETABLE SALAD

½ cup steamed carrot rings
½ cup steamed cauliflower
    flowerettes

½ cup diced steamed beets
½ cup steamed asparagus tips

Marinate vegetables separately in dressing. Drain. Arrange asparagus tips on lettuce, top with mixed vegetables.

## STRING BEAN SALAD

1 lb. cooked string beans                Lettuce

Arrange cooked beans on lettuce. Serve with

### *Dressing*:

2 tablespoonfuls minced celery
2 tablespoonfuls minced pimiento

⅓ cup French dressing
Shake ingredients together.

## STUFFED TOMATO SALAD

4 tomatoes                1 cup lemon gelatin
1 cup mixed, steamed vegetables

Scald and peel tomatoes. Remove centers to make cups. Sprinkle with vegetable salt, invert and chill. Combine cooled gelatin and mixed vegetables, and fill tomatoes. Chill until firm. Cut in sections and arrange on crisp salad greens.

## STUFFED TOMATO SALAD WITH GREEN BEANS

4 tomatoes
2 cups string beans, 1 inch lengths
¼ cup mayonnaise

1 tablespoonful onion juice
¼ cup French dressing

Scald, peel and chill tomatoes. Cut slice from top and remove centers. Sprinkle with vegetable salt and invert while chilling again. Marinate beans in French dressing for half an hour. Drain and add onion juice and mayonnaise. Place in tomato cups.

## TOMATO ASPIC

4 cups tomatoes, raw or cooked
1 tablespoonful chopped onion
4 tablespoonfuls minced celery
1 tablespoonful Tupelo honey
½ cup cold water
2 teaspoonfuls lemon juice
2 tablespoonfuls granulated gelatin
1 teaspoonful vegetable salt
½ cup boiling water

Soak gelatin in cold water for five minutes. Add to boiling water and stir over heat until completely dissolved. Cook remaining ingredients together for 20 minutes. Strain and add to gelatin. Chill. May be cut into cubes and combined with vegetables or meat or fish for salad; or riced and served in bouillon cups in place of soup.

When combining tomato aspic with shredded or diced vegetables for salads, allow the aspic to cool until ready to congeal before adding the vegetables.

## TOMATO CUP SALAD

4 tomato cups
½ cup diced cucumbers
¼ cup mayonnaise
½ cup chopped celery
½ cup diced tart apples

Fill tomato cups with salad mixture and arrange on endive or lettuce. Garnish with finely chopped olives.

## TOMATO JELLY SALAD

2 cups strained tomato juice
1 tablespoonful granulated gelatin
½ cup diced unsweetened pineapple
1 tablespoonful onion juice
½ cup diced cucumber

Soften gelatin in two tablespoonfuls tomato juice. Heat one cup tomato juice to boiling point and dissolve gelatin in it. Add remaining tomato juice and onion juice. When ready to congeal, stir in cucumber and pineapple. Chill in individual molds. Serve on lettuce.

## TOMATO, CUCUMBER AND RADISH SALAD

4 medium sized tomatoes
2 cucumbers
4 radishes
½ green pepper
Lettuce

Scald, peel and chill tomatoes. Pare cucumbers. Slice both. Arrange lettuce on salad plates, place vegetables in layers on lettuce. First a slice of tomato, then cucumber and last a slice of radish. Sprinkle with chopped green pepper, and serve with French dressing.

### TOMATO, CUCUMBER AND ONION SALAD

1 cup diced tomato
½ cup diced cucumber

½ cup diced onion
¼ cup French dressing

Combine dressing with salad ingredients. Serve on beds of lettuce.

### TOMATO AND PEPPER SALAD

2 tablespoonfuls minced green
  pepper

3 cups balls cut from firm tomatoes
2 tablespoonfuls French dressing

Combine tomatoes, pepper, and dressing. Serve on lettuce.

### TURNIP AND CELERY SALAD

2 cups steamed turnip balls
1 cup sliced celery

½ cup French dressing
4 tablespoonfuls finely chopped parsley

Marinate turnip balls in French dressing for half an hour. Drain. Combine with celery and parsley. Arrange on lettuce, cover with mayonnaise and garnish with pimiento strips.

### VARIETY SALAD

1 cup shredded cabbage
½ cup diced, steamed beets
½ cup steamed carrot rings
½ cup sliced celery

¼ cup minced pimiento
  Endive or lettuce
¼ cup French dressing
2 tablespoonfuls minced onion

Toss salad ingredients together lightly with dressing, and serve on endive or lettuce.

# SALAD DRESSINGS

### ALMOND DRESSING

½ cup water

3 egg yolks

2 tablespoonfuls lemon juice

½ cup shredded almonds

1 cup whipped cream

Beat egg yolks until thick. Add lemon juice and hot water. Cook over hot water until thick and smooth, stirring constantly. Chill. When ready to use add whipped cream and almonds.

### BEET AND CHIVE DRESSING

2 tablespoonfuls minced chives

2 tablespoonfuls chopped cooked beet

½ teaspoonful vegetable salt

6 tablespoonfuls oil

2 tablespoonfuls lemon juice

Few grains paprika

1 tablespoonful beet juice

Shake until well blended. Keep cold.

### BOILED DRESSING

4 egg yolks

2 tablespoonfuls olive oil

1½ tablespoonfuls lemon juice

¼ teaspoonful vegetable salt

½ cup boiling water

Beat egg yolks until very light. Add salt, lemon juice, oil and wate . Cook over hot water until thick, stirring constantly.

### BUTTERMILK DRESSING

½ cup rich buttermilk          1 teaspoonful lemon juice

Pinch of salt

Combine ingredients. Beat with rotary beater until very light. Should be used immediately. Excellent with cucumbers.

### CELERY AND NUT MAYONNAISE DRESSING

1 cup mayonnaise          ¼ cup finely minced celery hearts

¼ cup chopped nuts

Combine ingredients. Keep cold.

## CHEESE MAYONNAISE

½ cup mayonnaise
3 tablespoonfuls cream cheese

1 tablespoonful whipping cream
½ teaspoonful paprika

Combine cream with cheese; work in paprika. Beat as light as possible, and add mayonnaise.

## CREAM FRUIT DRESSING

1 cup whipped cream          3 tablespoonfuls tart fruit juice
½ teaspoonful grated orange rind

Combine ingredients and serve at once.

## CREAM MAYONNAISE DRESSING

½ cup whipped cream          ½ cup mayonnaise

Stir together until well blended. Keep as cold as possible without freezing.

## CREAM OF TOMATO DRESSING

½ cup heavy cream (sweet or sour)     2 tablespoonfuls olive oil
½ cup tomato purée                    1 tablespoonful lemon juice
½ teaspoonful vegetable salt

Mix oil, salt, and lemon juice. Beat in tomato purée, finally add cream, beating until smooth and well blended. Keep cold.

## EGG DRESSING

6 tablespoonfuls olive oil     2 hard boiled egg yolks
2 tablespoonfuls lemon juice   1 tablespoonful minced chives

Shake oil, lemon juice and minced chives together. Press egg yolks through fine sieve, add to oil mixture with a few grains salt and a pinch of paprika.

## FAVORITE CREAM DRESSING

3 egg yolks (hard boiled)     2 tablespoonfuls lemon juice
1 raw egg yolk                ½ cup cream
6 tablespoonfuls olive oil    ¼ teaspoonful salt
Dash of paprika

Rub hard boiled yolks through fine sieve. Rub with raw yolk to a smooth paste. Add cream and oil and beat hard. When light and evenly mixed add lemon juice, salt and paprika.

## FRENCH DRESSING

6 tablespoonfuls olive oil          2 tablespoonfuls lemon juice

Shake until well blended. This is the basis of all French dressings. Use for marinade for fish, meat or vegetables. Vary this dressing to suit the taste by the addition of a clove of garlic, a few chopped chives, two tablespoonfuls sweet cream, or minced parsley, carrot, etc. Lemon juice may be heated with berries, cooled and strained, to add distinctive flavor.

## FROZEN SALAD DRESSINGS

Serve orange ice, pineapple, lemon or raspberry sherbet on any fruit salad, in place of usual dressing.

## GARLIC DRESSING

1 cup mayonnaise                    ½ cup chopped olives
¼ teaspoonful paprika               ¼ cup chopped sweet peppers
                    1 clove garlic

Rub bowl with bruised garlic. Mix all ingredients lightly together. Keep cold.

## HONEY CHEESE DRESSING

2 egg yolks                         ¼ cup Tupelo honey
¼ cup lemon juice                   3 tablespoonfuls cream
                    1 cup cottage cheese

Cook lemon juice, honey and egg yolks in double boiler until smooth. Cool. Beat cream into cottage cheese, blend mixtures. Chill thoroughly.

## ITALIAN DRESSING

¼ cup olive oil                     ¼ cup tomato paste
                    1 tablespoonful lemon juice

Beat ingredients together until well blended.

## JELLIED MAYONNAISE DRESSING

1 cup mayonnaise      ½ to 1 teaspoonful granulated gelatin
                    2 tablespoonfuls cold water

Soften gelatin in cold water. Heat over boiling water until dissolved. Add to mayonnaise. Pack into mold to become firm. Individual molds are attractive. Amount of gelatin used in this recipe will vary according to manner in which finished product is to be used. The maximum amount will produce jellied mayonnaise firm enough to slice and cut into fancy shapes for garnishing salads or cocktails.

## LEMON JUICE MAYONNAISE

2 cups olive oil
3 tablespoonfuls lemon juice

2 egg yolks
½ teaspoonful vegetable salt
1 tablespoonful Tupelo honey

Beat egg yolks and salt for a few minutes. Continue beating and add lemon juice a few drops at a time, alternately with oil, one tablespoonful at a time. When all ingredients have been incorporated, beat for several minutes more. Pack in glass and keep cold.

Adapt the dressing to the salad. By addition of herbs, or minced vegetables, chopped fruits or cream, it is possible to have a new and interesting salad dressing whenever wanted.

## LIME DRESSING

1 tablespoonful fresh lime juice
1 tablespoonful lemon juice

6 tablespoonfuls olive oil
⅛ teaspoonful vegetable salt

Pour cold ingredients into bottle and shake until blended.

## MINT DRESSING

6 tablespoonfuls olive oil        2 tablespoonfuls lemon juice
1 tablespoonful bruised mint leaves

Combine cold ingredients. Shake well. Let stand at least one hour. Strain.

## PARSLEY DRESSING WITH PEAS

1 cup mayonnaise
½ cup whipped cream

½ cup thick purée of green peas
2 tablespoonfuls minced parsley
2 tablespoonfuls minced ripe olives

Blend ingredients, cover tightly and keep cold until ready to use.

## RADISH CREAM DRESSING

½ cup mayonnaise
¼ cup sour cream
1 tablespoonful minced parsley

2 tablespoonfuls minced radishes
1 teaspoonful lemon juice
½ teaspoonful vegetable salt

Beat ingredients together until well blended.

## RIPE OLIVE DRESSING

½ cup French dressing        ¼ teaspoonful grated onion
12 ripe olives (chopped fine)

Blend one-half hour before using. Keep cold.

## SOUR CREAM DRESSING

1 cup whipped cream
2 tablespoonfuls lemon juice

½ teaspoonful vegetable salt
Pinch of paprika if desired

Blend ingredients and keep cold.  If using sour cream, add only one table-spoonful lemon juice.

## STRAWBERRY DRESSING

3 egg yolks, beaten light
¼ cup orange juice
¼ cup strawberry juice

2 tablespoonfuls olive oil
½ cup whipped cream
¼ cup sliced strawberries

Beat egg yolks and fruit juices together over hot water until smooth and thick.  Add oil and beat again.  When cold, fold in whipped cream and sliced berries.

## TART FRUIT DRESSING

¼ cup strained strawberry juice
1 teaspoonful lemon juice

1 tablespoonful orange juice
2 tablespoonfuls olive oil

Combine chilled ingredients and shake until well blended.

## THOUSAND ISLAND DRESSING

½ cup mayonnaise
2 tablespoonfuls chopped ripe
  olives

2 tablespoonfuls tomato purée
1 tablespoonful chopped pimiento
1 tablespoonful lemon juice

Beat ingredients together until well blended.

# PROTEINS

### ALKALINE CHOPS

1 cup chopped mushrooms, cooked 5 minutes in oiled pan
¾ cup protein spaghetti (3½ ounces)
¾ cup chopped almonds or almond meal

½ cup thick tomato purée | 2 teaspoonfuls vegetable salt
2 tablespoonfuls vegetable paste | 1 tablespoonful paprika
1 teaspoonful powdered sage | Soy bean milk powder

Break spaghetti into small pieces and pack into cup when measuring. Cook in boiling water until tender but not soft. Drain and add to all remaining ingredients except soy bean powder. Place over low heat and stir until well blended. Add soy bean powder to make a rather stiff dough. Spread on platter to chill. Shape into form of chops; coat with beaten egg yolk, then with soy bean milk powder and nut-meal combined. Broil until lightly browned on both sides. Serve with broiled mushroom caps.

### APARTMENT CHICKEN

1 cup sliced sweet onion and peppers combined
3 slices fat bacon, chopped
3 cups diced raw chicken or lamb

Cook bacon, onion and peppers until slightly browned. Remove from fat. Cook chicken in fat until tender, add to cooked bacon and vegetables.

### APPLE AND CHEESE CASSEROLE

1 quart sliced apples          2 cups cottage cheese

Arrange apple and cheese in layers in casserole. Pour a little cream over top to keep moist. Bake in moderate oven until apple is tender.

### ASSORTED FILLED OMELETTES

For individual omelette, use:

2 egg yolks          ¼ cup cream

Beat egg yolks until as light as possible; add cream and pinch of vegetable salt. Turn into hot buttered omelette pan and bake in moderate oven until firm. Make four of these; fill with:

1. Tomato paste
2. Creamed shrimp
3. Well drained crushed pineapple
4. Chopped ham

Cut each into fourths. One portion of each omelette for individual serving.

## BAKED BLUEFISH

1 lb. cleaned bluefish, cut into four equal pieces
2 tablespoonfuls chopped onion
1 teaspoonful lemon juice

Butter baking platter, sprinkle onion over bottom, arrange bluefish on onion and sprinkle lemon juice over fish. Cover and bake in moderate oven. Serve with sauce.

*Sauce:*

| | |
|---|---|
| 1 teaspoonful minced onion | 1 tablespoonful minced parsley |
| ½ cup broken mushroom caps | 2 tablespoonfuls butter or oil |
| 2 tablespoonfuls chopped cooked ham | 3 tablespoonfuls tomato paste |
| | ¼ cup vegetable broth |

Cook mushrooms and onion in butter for five minutes. Add other ingredients and stir over heat until blended.

## BAKED CHICKEN STUFFED WITH OYSTERS

| | |
|---|---|
| 1 roasting chicken (about 4 lbs.) | 1 cup chopped celery |
| 1 pint Blue Point oysters | 2 teaspoonfuls minced parsley |
| 1 cup shredded carrot | 4 tablespoonfuls butter |
| ½ teaspoonful vegetable salt | |

Prepare chicken for roasting. Stuff with oysters, celery, parsley, carrots and salt, combined. Rub with butter and roast in very hot oven for fifteen minutes. Reduce heat to medium and continue cooking until tender and slightly browned. Sprinkle lightly with vegetable salt and paprika when half cooked.

## BAKED CHICKEN AND SAUERKRAUT

Slice all dark meat from a three pound chicken. Reserve breast for use in salads or other dishes. Place sliced chicken in casserole, alternately with layers of sauerkraut (about 3 cups). One cup onion rings may be distributed through casserole. Bake in moderate oven until chicken is tender.

## BAKED CLAMS

### 2 dozen clams

Clams should be scrubbed in salt water. Bake in shell in hot oven. Provide each person served with a hot ramekin half full of melted butter. Serve on beds of heated rock salt.

## BAKED FISH WITH TOMATO SAUCE

1 lb. fillet of white fish  
1 cup tomato puree  
1 tablespoonful minced onion  

1 tablespoonful minced green pepper  
½ teaspoonful vegetable salt  

Place fish on buttered baking platter. Mix onion, pepper and salt into the tomato purée, and pour over fish. Bake in moderate oven.

## BAKED HADDOCK WITH VEGETABLES

Place 2 fillets of Haddock on oiled or buttered baking platter. Cover with sliced mushrooms, then tomato slices. Sprinkle with vegetable salt. Dot with butter. Bake in moderate oven until fish is tender and a sauce has formed from the tomatoes.

## BAKED HALIBUT WITH MUSHROOMS

1 lb. halibut steak  
1 cup broken mushrooms  
2 egg yolks  

1 cup steamed shrimp  
1 cup cream  

Brush halibut with lemon juice. Cook until tender in steamer. Place on hot platter and pour mushroom sauce over. Garnish with parsley.

### Sauce:

Heat cream until steaming. Beat egg yolks until very light, and continue beating while adding hot cream. Cook over hot water until smooth. Add broken shrimp to sauce; sauté mushrooms in butter and add last. Heat.

## BAKED HAM

1 small ham  
1 cup raisins  
Few whole cloves  

2 cups fruit juice, or water and cooking sherry  

Scrub ham and place in roaster with fruit juice or water and sherry, cloves and raisins. Bake slowly, basting often and adding more liquid as necessary. When tender remove skin and place on rack under broiler. Keep heat moderate to brown evenly.

## BAKED HAM, EGG SAUCE

1½ inch slice from center of small ham  
¼ teaspoonful vegetable salt  

1½ cups thin cream  
5 egg yolks, well-beaten  

Simmer ham in a little butter until tender, without browning. Place in buttered casserole. Combine egg yolks, cream and vegetable salt. Pour over ham. Cook in slow oven until egg is set. Garnish with parsley.

## BAKED HAM WITH FRUIT

2 inch slice from center of small ham
1½ cups crushed unsweetened pineapple

Place ham on buttered baking platter. Brush with melted butter or oil, cover with pineapple and bake in moderate oven. Keep closely covered to prevent drying or browning too much. Vary by use of fresh or canned (unsweetened) peaches, apple slices, apricots, cherries, grape juice, cider or orange juice.

## BAKED SHAD ROE

1 lb. shad roe          1 tablespoonful lemon juice
¼ cup butter or oil

Melt butter in casserole. Roll roe in butter until well coated. Sprinkle with lemon juice. Cover and bake in moderate oven.

## BAKED SHAD WITH SPINACH

2½ lb. shad                    1 tablespoonful olive oil
3 cups steamed spinach         1 teaspoonful lemon juice

Bake shad on buttered oven platter. Surround with spinach mixed with oil and lemon pressed into molds. If roe is to be served with shad, cook it for ten minutes in boiling water with a slice of lemon. Drain. Roll in oil and bake with shad.

## BAKED SHAD ROE WITH ORANGE JUICE

1 lb. shad roe
½ cup orange juice with 2 tablespoonfuls sherry flavor

Wash and wipe roe dry. Roll in melted butter or oil. Sprinkle lightly with salt, and add orange juice. Bake until tender in buttered casserole.

## BAKED SLICED HAM WITH NUTS

1 2-inch slice from center of small        1 cup nut meal
        ham                                1 teaspoonful lemon juice
                    Sweet cream

Butter glass baking dish. Brush top of ham with lemon juice. Mix nut meal with sweet cream, beating well together. Use as much cream as possible without making paste thin enough to run. Spread over ham, and bake slowly until tender. Serve on hot platter, with baked apples stuffed with orange.

## BAKED STUFFED HALIBUT

Have halibut steaks cut thin. Remove skin. Place 1 slice on buttered glass platter. Spread with filling. Place second slice on top. Brush with melted butter or bacon drippings. Bake at moderate temperature.

### FILLING

Combine equal parts shredded carrot, celery and oysterplant with a little grated onion. Add vegetable salt and paprika to season.

## BAKED TOMATO, SPINACH AND HAM

3 cups spinach chopped fine    2 cups ham chopped fine (cooked)

Remove center from tomatoes and fill with spinach and ham. Bake in moderate oven.

## BAKED TOMATO AND HAM

4 large firm tomatoes          ¼ cup vegetable broth or cream
1 cup chopped, cooked ham      1 egg yolk, beaten

Without peeling, prepare tomato cups. Combine ham, vegetable broth and egg. Fill tomatoes and bake in moderate oven.

## BAKED VOLCANOS

1 cup "base for croquettes"     1 beaten egg yolk
  (see Sauces)                  ¼ cup cream cheese
2 cups diced cold meat          2 tablespoonfuls heavy cream

Prepare meat and croquette base as croquettes, in cone shape. Roll in beaten egg yolk. Chill. When ready to bake, make cavity in top of each cone, and fill with cheese mixed with cream. Bake in hot oven. Sprinkle with paprika.

## BARBECUED CHICKEN

2 broiling chickens, about 1½ pounds each
6 tablespoonfuls vegetable oil or butter
1½ cups water                  Juice of ½ lemon
6 tablespoonfuls tomato purée  1 tablespoonful minced parsley
Vegetable salt as desired

Split the chickens as for broiling, cook all other ingredients together for 5 minutes to make sauce. Broil the chickens, using the prepared sauce for basting. When chickens are tender, place in a roasting pan, pour remaining sauce over them, simmer for about 50 minutes.

## BEEF HASH

| | |
|---|---|
| 1 pound ground round steak | ½ cup shaved onion |
| ½ cup chopped cooked beets | 3 tablespoonfuls minced dill pickle |
| 1 teaspoonful vegetable salt | ½ teaspoonful paprika |

2 egg yolks, beaten

Saute meat in oiled or buttered pan until lightly browned. Add remaining ingredients, stir to combine. Brown lightly without further stirring.

## BEEF TONGUE EN CASSEROLE

Scrub and scrape beef tongue. Steam until tender. Skin and remove all membranes. Roll up and tie into shape. Place in casserole. Cover with minced onion and strips of bacon. Add 3 tablespoonfuls lemon juice and 1 teaspoonful vegetable salt. Bake in moderate oven for 1 hour. Remove tongue from casserole, strain liquid, add ½ cup orange juice, ½ cup seeded raisins, ½ cup finely shredded almonds. Cook for 10 minutes, and serve with the tongue.

## BELGIAN HARE

2½ lbs. Belgian Hare

After hare is dressed immerse in ice water for half an hour. Drain and keep on ice until ready to use. May be stuffed with shredded vegetables. Baste with melted butter and cherry juice or water. Roast as chicken; hot oven for fifteen minutes; reduce heat and continue cooking until meat is tender.

## BOILED DINNER

| | |
|---|---|
| 2½ lbs. lean beef | 1 rutabaga, cut in pieces the size of onions |
| 6 carrots | 4 medium sized onions |
| 8 baby beets | 4 medium sized turnips |

Cover meat with cold water and cook until almost tender. One hour before serving time add the vegetables. Simmer until meat and vegetables are tender. Serve meat on large platter and arrange vegetables around it. Have nearly all liquid cooked away, so that vegetables will be rich in flavor. Left-over meat will make good croquettes.

## BOILED FISH

Small fish are boiled whole; larger varieties may be sliced. Place fish on wire rack in vessel large enough to permit fish to lie flat. Pour boiling water into pan to cover fish. Add one whole lemon cut in pieces for two pounds of fish. Boil gently until tender. Remove skins and serve on hot platter, garnished with parsley, chervil or cress and lemon points.

## BOILED LAMB

| | |
|---|---|
| 2 lbs. lamb for boiling | 1 slice onion |
| 3 slices carrot | 1 tablespoonful parsley |

Cover lamb with boiling water. Add vegetables and a little vegetable salt. Simmer gently until tender. Allow water to cook away as much as possible. Serve with Hollandaise sauce or mint sauce.

## BONED ROAST CHICKEN

Chicken or any other fowl may be boned easily by splitting straight down the back, and using a sharp narrow-bladed knife cutting the flesh from the bony structure. Turn the flesh back as it is freed from the carcass. When wings and legs are reached, the flesh is pulled back carefully and scraped from the bones, turning the fowl completely inside out. Dust with vegetable salt, turn right side out and stuff with chicken forcemeat. Sew up and roast as usual, allowing additional time to cook raw meat filling. (See Dressings, page 250.)

## BRAISED CALVES HEARTS

| | |
|---|---|
| 2 hearts | ½ cup diced tomato |
| ¾ cup sliced celery | ¼ cup chopped onion |
| ½ cup shredded carrot | 4 tablespoonfuls bacon fat |

Wash hearts, lay in ice water for an hour. Drain. Remove arteries and veins. Fill with vegetables. Sew. Brown lightly in bacon fat. Set in small buttered casserole. Almost cover with vegetable broth and bake slowly. During last half hour of cooking add ½ cup cherry or orange juice.

## BRAISED CALF LIVER AND MUSHROOMS

| | |
|---|---|
| 1½ lb. piece of calf liver | 1 lb. mushrooms |

Brown liver on all sides in butter or bacon fat. Remove to covered casserole, and cook in moderate oven until tender. Add broken mushrooms and ¼ cup cream; sprinkle with vegetable salt and continue cooking until mushrooms are tender.

## BRAISED FLANK STEAK PATTIES

| | |
|---|---|
| 1 flank steak (about 1¼ lbs.) | ½ teaspoonful vegetable salt |
| ½ cup onion rings or mushrooms | ¾ cup vegetable broth |

Roll steak crosswise and secure with oiled skewers, two or three inches apart. Cut roll into slices, with a skewer in each part to hold meat in shape. Brown quickly in butter or oil on both sides. Set in casserole, add liquid, distribute onions and salt over meat. Cover and cook in moderate oven until very tender. If mushrooms are used instead of onion, do not add until 20 minutes before serving.

## BRAISED LIVER

1½ lbs. calf liver (one piece)          3 tablespoonfuls beet suet or oil
2 tablespoonfuls minced onions          1 cup vegetable broth

Chop suet very fine, add to onion and cook for a few minutes. Add vegetable broth. Set liver in buttered casserole, sprinkle with chopped parsley and cover with vegetable broth mixture. Bake in moderate oven. Serve with crisp bacon curls.

## BRAISED PIGEONS

4 pigeons                          2 tablespoonfuls minced carrot
2 cups celery broth                2 tablespoonfuls chopped onion
2 tablespoonfuls butter or oil     ½ cup orange juice
2 tablespoonfuls currant juice or grape juice

Simmer butter, onion and carrot in baking pan for a few minutes. Set pigeons in pan, add celery broth, a little vegetable salt and chopped parsley. Simmer until tender. If birds are old allow four hours. Last half hour set in oven, without cover, baste frequently. Remove birds to hot platter. Add orange and currant juice to pan liquor and heat for sauce.

## BRAISED RUMP OF BEEF

Marinate four or five pounds rump roast in French dressing with onion juice for three or four hours. Lard with strips of fat bacon and brown on all sides in Dutch oven or heavy pan. Sprinkle with vegetable salt. Add to meat one-half cup of lightly sauted vegetables (carrot, onion, celery), one tablespoonful powdered herbs and two tablespoonfuls vegetable broth. Simmer over slow heat until quite tender.

## BREAST OF CHICKEN SOUFFLE

Breast of large chicken          2 egg yolks
1 cup heavy cream

Steam one half chicken breast until very tender. Cut into small even dice. Chop other half of chicken breast and pound to paste, then force through purée strainer. Add strained egg yolks beaten light and cream whipped as light as possible. Season with vegetable salt, add a bit of minced parsley. Now fold in cooked chicken. Turn into individual molds which have been buttered and decorated with sliced truffles, shredded pimiento and sliced ripe olives. Poach in moderate oven until firm. Serve with creamed mushrooms.

## BROILED BASS

Split bass, remove head and tail. Rub all over with soft butter or oil. Sprinkle with vegetable salt. Broil, cut side first; turn over and cook until skin is brown and crisp. Garnish with small tomatoes stuffed with grated cucumbers, small amount grated horseradish and lemon juice.

## BROILED BLUE FISH

Follow directions for broiled bass. Serve with mushroom sauce.

## BROILED BRAINS

Brains from calf, lamb or mutton may be used. All are very delicate and tender. Soak brains in cold water until all blood is removed. Dip in boiling water and remove membranous covering. Coat with lemon juice then with melted butter or oil. Broil under moderate heat. Season with vegetable salt. Handle carefully to prevent breaking.

## BROILED BUTTER FISH

Dip prepared fish in melted butter or oil and broil under moderate heat until until nicely browned. Sprinkle with lemon juice, vegetable salt and paprika before serving.

## BROILED CAPON

Follow instructions for broiled spring chicken. Capon must be small for broiling. Serve on hot platter surrounded by baked peach halves each holding one ripe olive.

## BROILED FILLET OF SOLE

Wipe with damp cloth, dip in melted butter or oil and broil under medium heat. Serve with parsley butter and lemon.

## BROILED FILLET OF TURKEY

Wrap strips of meat from legs or breast of turkey around metal skewer. Dip in melted butter or oil. Broil under moderate heat.

### BROILED FRESH COD

Follow instructions for Broiled Sliced Fish.

### BROILED FILLET STEAKS

4 one inch fillet steaks                          4 strips bacon
4 tablespoonfuls butter or substitute

Wrap each steak in a strip of bacon. Place 1 tablespoonful butter on each. Set on rack in broiling pan, and cook under quick heat. Turn three or four times, each time basting with juice in pan. Serve with sauted mushrooms, or onion rings.

### BROILED HAM

1 slice ham, ¾ inch thick

Wipe ham with damp cloth, brush with melted butter or oil and broil for eight or ten minutes. Turn two or three times. Serve with broiled pineapple slices.

### BROILED KIDNEYS WITH TOMATO SLICES

8 slices tomato          4 lamb or calf kidneys (parboiled)
Sliced bacon

Set tomato slices on buttered pan, one half kidney on each. Cover with bacon. Broil under moderate fire. Slip into hot oven a few minutes before serving.

### BROILED LAMB CHOPS

Select loin chops about 1½ inches thick. Fasten thin end of chop around center loin and secure with small skewer. Brush with cooking oil or melted butter. Broil until tender, turning as necessary to brown on both sides. Sprinkle with vegetable salt.

### BROILED LAMB OR CALF KIDNEYS

Cut kidneys to remove fat and tubes. Cover with cold water for a half hour before cooking. Dry and dip in melted butter. Broil under moderate heat. Season with vegetable salt.

### BROILED LOBSTER

Split live lobster. Place flesh side toward heat and broil for ten minutes. Spread with butter and continue to cook until tender. Serve with melted butter and lemon juice.

### BROILED FRESH MACKEREL

Follow directions for broiled bass. Serve parsley carrots and broiled tomato slices around fish.

## BROILED MEAT CAKES

| | |
|---|---|
| 1 lb. chopped beef | 2 beaten egg yolks |
| 1 tablespoonful minced onion | 2 teaspoonfuls celery broth |
| ½ tablespoonful vegetable salt | 8 strips bacon |

Mix celery broth and beaten egg, add onion and salt. Combine with meat, and form into eight round cakes. Wrap each in a strip of bacon and secure ends with small skewers. Place on broiling rack and cook under steady heat to the desired degree of rareness.

## BROILED OYSTERS

1 pint small oysters        8 metal skewers
8 to 10 slices bacon

Cut sliced bacon in one inch pieces. Arrange oysters and bacon squares alternately on skewers. Broil until oysters are firm. Pour 1 teaspoonful melted butter over each skewer of oysters. Serve on hot plates. The metal skewer acts as heat conductor and assists in cooking. Do not crowd oysters together.

## BROILED PERCH

Follow instructions for broiled butter fish.

## BROILED QUAIL

Prepare quail for broiling by splitting down the back and dressing as broiling chicken. Dip in melted butter. Broil until tender. Garnish with watercress.

## BROILED RUFFED GROUSE

Follow instructions given for Broiled Spring Chicken. Garnish with radish roses and tiny celery hearts.

## BROILED SCALLOPS

1 lb. scallops                     1 beaten egg yolk
1 tablespoonful lemon juice

Steam scallops until tender. If large they may be cut into two to four pieces. Coat with egg and lemon, then roll in protein bread crumbs. Place in buttered shallow pan and brown under broiler. Shake or turn over to brown on all sides. Serve with Hollandaise sauce.

## BROILED SLICED FISH

Steam slices of white fish. When tender spread with Dressing for Broiled Fish. Set under broiler until browned. (See sauce recipes for dressing.)

## BROILED SOFT SHELL CRABS

Clean and dry crabs. Dip in beaten egg yolk. Place on buttered pan, a small lump of butter on top of each crab. Broil, under side first. Serve with lemon.

## BROILED SPRING CHICKEN

Dress chicken and split down the back. Allow one-half chicken for each serving. Wipe dry and coat with melted butter. Place on broiling rack, cut side up first. When seared, turn over. Repeat turning and cooking until thoroughly cooked. Slip into hot oven for five minutes before serving. Sprinkle with vegetable salt.

## BROILED SQUAB

4 squabs

Squab should be just four weeks old for broiling. Dress, split down the back, rub with melted butter and broil until tender. Garnish with bunches of cress.

## BROILED STEAK

1½ lbs. Porterhouse steak          2 tablespoonfuls butter

Rub broiling rack with olive oil. Wipe steak with damp cloth. Place on broiling rack and cook under quick heat. Turn two or three times. Allow eight minutes for rare steak; twelve or fifteen for steak well done. Remove to hot platter. Add butter and ½ teaspoonful horseradish to juice in pan; when butter is melted pour over steak.

## BROILED TRIPE

1 lb. fresh tripe

Wipe tripe as dry as possible. Brush with oil on both sides. Broil under direct heat, first on the smooth side, then on honey-comb side. Arrange on hot platter. Spread with butter. Sprinkle with salt and paprika or chopped parsley. Garnish with lemon points.

## BROILED TROUT

Follow directions for broiled bass.

## BROILED VENISON

Venison steak, 1 inch thick

Rub with butter and broil near intense heat for about eight minutes. Venison is always served rare. Spread with gelatin flavored with currant juice.

## BRUNSWICK STEW

1 fowl, about 3 to 4 pounds
¼ cup chopped onion
1½ cups green baby lima beans

2 cups diced tomatoes or canned
  tomatoes
1½ cups young corn

Steam chicken until tender. Remove meat from bones discarding gristle and skin. Combine with remaining ingredients. Add vegetable salt to taste. Cook until thick.

## CABBAGE ROAST

1 solid cabbage
1 lb. round steak, chopped

1 cup diced carrot
½ cup tomato puree

1 teaspoonful vegetable salt

Scoop out center of cabbage, leaving solid wall. Fill with meat, carrot, salt and tomato purée mixed together. Cover with strips of bacon. Bake in moderate oven. Baste frequently with vegetable broth to prevent browning.

## CALF'S TONGUE

2 calves tongues

*Sauce:*

1 cup celery broth
2 tablespoonfuls butter

1 teaspoonful grated lemon rind
1 teaspoonful lemon juice

½ cup currant gelatin

Wash tongues and cook in boiling water to which has been added one small onion, and one bay leaf. Cook thirty minutes for each pound of meat. Skin and remove any loose membranes. Serve sliced, with currant sauce.

*Currant Sauce:* Mix all ingredients and simmer until gelatin is dissolved.

## CALVES' LIVER CASSEROLE

Cut 1 pound of calves' liver into small cubes, brown lightly in a little butter. Remove from pan. In same pan cook 2 cups of sliced onion rings, 1 cup sliced green pepper until softened and slightly browned. Place all together in a casserole, add sufficient tomato juice to come to top of vegetables, cover and bake at moderate temperature until liver is tender.

## CASSEROLE OF LAMB

4 loin chops of lamb (1 inch thick)
4 tablespoonfuls butter
¼ cup shredded pepper

1 cup diced carrots
1 cup diced rutabagas
1 cup green peas

Melt butter and brown chops in it. Arrange vegetables in layers in buttered casserole, place chops on top, pour butter over. Cover and bake in moderate oven until vegetables are tender. Add a little water or cream to keep vegetables moist.

## CASSEROLE OF SWEETBREADS WITH CHICKEN LIVERS AND MUSHROOMS

2 cups diced, cooked sweetbreads     1 cup raw chicken livers, diced
2 cups mushrooms, broken

Cook chicken livers and mushrooms in a little butter until well browned. Place in casserole with sweetbreads, add vegetable salt and minced parsley to season. Pour cream over to come to top of meats. Bake in moderate oven until livers are tender.

## CASSEROLE OF TONGUE AND MUSHROOMS

1 small tongue, cooked, skinned, diced     2 cups mushrooms
½ cup cream

Cook mushrooms in a little butter until browned. Add tongue. Place in casserole with cream and sufficient vegetable salt to season. Bake at moderate temperature for half an hour.

## CAULIFLOWER WITH BLUE POINTS

1 large head steamed cauliflower

Place in hot dish and cover with hot sauce.

### Sauce:

2 cups chopped Blue Point oysters     1 tablespoonful sauted green pepper
½ cup heavy cream     2 tablespoonfuls sauted mushrooms
½ teaspoonful vegetable salt

Mix all ingredients together and heat thoroughly.

## CHEESE OMELETTE

6 egg yolks     ¼ teaspoonful vegetable salt
⅔ cup cottage cheese     Dash of paprika
¼ cup thin cream     1 teaspoonful minced parsley

Beat egg yolks, add cream, salt, paprika, parsley and all of the cheese but two tablespoonfuls. Pour omelette in buttered pan. Cook slowly until nearly done, then finish under broiler. Sprinkle with remaining cheese, fold and serve.

## CHEESE SOUFFLÉ

2 cups milk     1½ cups cottage cheese
6 well beaten egg yolks     2 tablespoonfuls minced pimiento

Stir milk and cheese into well-beaten egg yolks. Add pimiento. Pour into buttered ring mold, set in pan of hot water and poach in moderate oven until set. Turn out on hot chop plate. Set a custard cup containing hot tomato sauce in center of ring, and serve sauce over portions of soufflé.

## CHICKEN A LA KING

2 cups diced cooked chicken
1 cup mushrooms
2 hard boiled egg yolks
½ green pepper
½ sweet red pepper

1 cup cream
1 tablespoonful vegetable paste
½ teaspoonful vegetable salt
½ teaspoonful paprika
3 egg yolks, beaten

Make a cream sauce in a double boiler of the cream, vegetable paste and beaten egg yolks. Add the seasoning and other ingredients. Serve very hot.

## CHICKEN CASSEROLE WITH PINEAPPLE

2 tablespoonfuls butter
1 cup sliced sweet onion
½ cup carrot rings
½ cup sliced celery

½ cup tiny green peas
½ cup drained bean sprouts
½ cup diced pineapple
2 cups raw chicken (diced)

Brown onion in butter, add remaining ingredients and bake in covered casserole in moderate oven.

## CHICKEN CUTLETS

Substitute chicken for lamb in recipe for lamb cutlets.

## CHICKEN LIVERS IN BLANKETS

1 lb. chicken livers          Sliced bacon

Simmer chicken livers in celery broth until tender. Wrap each in a strip of bacon. Secure with toothpick. Broil until bacon is crisp.

## CHICKEN LOAF

4 cups cooked chicken, free of skin
1 cup steamed mushrooms
1 cup thinly sliced celery
1 teaspoonful onion juice

2 tablespoonfuls shredded pimiento
½ cup sliced green olives
2 cups prepared lemon gelatin

Combine onion juice and lemon gelatin. When cool and ready to congeal, add remaining ingredients. Chill in loaf mold. Turn out on large platter. Garnish with halves of tomato filled with salad dressing.

## CHICKEN AND OKRA CASSEROLE

3 lbs. chicken
½ cup diced raw ham
¼ cup butter
¼ cup diced onion

4 cups okra pods
1 teaspoonful vegetable salt
1 tablespoonful thyme
2 cups tomatoes diced.

Cook ham and chicken (cut in pieces for serving) in butter for five minutes. Remove to casserole. Cook onion and okra in remaining butter in pan, add to casserole with thyme and tomato. Pour one cup boiling water over and cover closely. Bake in moderate oven.

## CHICKEN WITH MUSHROOMS

3 lb. chicken
5 tablespoonfuls melted butter
1 teaspoonful celery salt

1 cup boiling water
1 cup cream
2 cups mushroom caps

Cut chicken in pieces for serving. Dip each piece in melted butter, place in casserole and pour boiling water over. Cover and cook for forty minutes. Add vegetable salt, continue cooking until tender, and water is absorbed. Break mushrooms in pieces, saute lightly in melted butter, add to chicken, with heated cream. Cook twenty-five minutes more.

## CHICKEN AND MUSHROOM SOUFFLÉ

½ cup cream
1½ cups celery broth
6 egg yolks, beaten
2 cups diced cooked chicken

1 cup sauted mushrooms
2 tablespoonfuls minced green
    pepper
½ teaspoonful vegetable salt

Dark meat of chicken may be used for this recipe. Scald cream and celery broth combined; pour over egg yolks, beating constantly. Add remaining ingredients. Pour into a buttered casserole and set in pan of hot water. Poach in moderately hot oven.

## CHICKEN PIE

1 fowl, about 3 to 4 pounds
½ cup sliced celery
½ pound mushrooms

1 small onion, sliced
2 tablespoonfuls minced parsley
2 hard boiled egg yolks

Soy bean or Protein biscuit dough

Steam fowl until tender. Remove meat from bones, discarding gristle and skin. Saute mushrooms in a little butter until browned. Combine all ingredients, adding vegetable salt to season. Place in casserole, add cream to come to top of mixture. Cover with rounds of biscuit dough. Bake in hot oven about one half hour.

## CHOP SUEY

2 cups cubed, raw, breast of chicken
2 teaspoonfuls minced green pepper
1 cup sliced onion
1 cup shredded celery

1 cup broken mushrooms
½ cup water
2 tablespoonfuls of butter
2 cups bean sprouts

Brown meat in butter and fry until outside of each cube is evenly colored. Add green pepper, celery, onion, water, and simmer until vegetables are cooked. Saute mushrooms in 2 tablespoonfuls of butter and add to other ingredients with bean sprouts. Cook gently until the desired consistency is reached. Season lightly with paprika and vegetable salt.

## COCONUT CHICKEN DINNER

4 whole coconuts
1 cup sautéd mushrooms
¼ cup chopped raw bacon
¼ cup sliced celery

2 tablespoonfuls minced green
   pepper
1 tablespoonful minced onion
1 cup tomato dice

2 cups diced raw chicken breast

Saw tops from coconuts. Remove and shred coconut from tops, keeping top of shell intact. Cook bacon until crisp, remove from fat with strainer. Cook onion, green pepper and celery in fat until tender; combine with bacon, mushrooms, tomato, chicken and ¼ cup shredded coconut. Divide evenly and fill coconuts, using sawed-off tops for covers. Seal with a strip of linen covered with flour paste. Set coconuts in baking dish containing a little boiling water. Bake for 2½ hours in hot oven. Keep boiling water in pan.

## COD FISH CAKES

½ lb. shredded cod fish
⅓ lb. shredded carrots

1 tablespoonful butter
3 egg yolks

Soak fish one hour then shred. Mix carrots and fish, cover with hot water and cook until tender. Drain mixture, mash; add egg yolks and butter and beat until light. Mold into small cakes, place in buttered tin and bake until brown, but not dry.

## CORNED BEEF HASH

Mix 3 cups chopped corned beef, 1½ cups finely shredded raw turnip, 1½ cups finely shredded raw carrot, 3 medium onions, 3 tablespoonfuls minced parsley, 3 tablespoonfuls butter and 4 egg yolks together, put into casserole, arrange 2 or 3 strips of bacon on top. Bake in hot oven until firm. Serve on platter, surround with steamed Frenched green beans, baked small beets and lemon sections.

## CORNED BEEF LOAF

| | |
|---|---|
| 3 cups chopped cooked corned beef | 1 tablespoonful onion juice |
| 4 beaten egg yolks | ½ cup chopped celery |
| 2 tablespoonfuls minced green pepper | ½ cup mashed tiny green peas |
| | 1 tablespoonful lemon juice |

Combine all ingredients and blend well. Form in loaf and bake on glass platter, in moderate oven. Serve with tomato sauce.

## COTTAGE CHEESE

*(from sour or clabber milk)*

Warm sour or clabber milk to body temperature. Stir occasionally, and keep at even temperature until casein begins to coagulate. Let stand a few minutes while curd separates from whey. Pour into double cheesecloth bag and hang up to drain. The drained liquid is whey and makes a palatable and nutritious beverage. If the milk is very sour, cold water may be poured over the separated curd; hang again to drain away all water. Cream may be added to the curd and the mixture beaten until smooth.

## COTTAGE CHEESE PANCAKES

| | |
|---|---|
| 1 cup cottage cheese | ¾ cup buttermilk |
| 3 tablespoonfuls vegetable oil or melted butter | |
| 6 egg yolks | 1 cup protein flour |
| 1 tablespoonful Tupelo honey | |

Beat egg yolks until light; add cottage cheese, buttermilk, honey and shortening. Beat with rotary beater until as light as possible. Beat in flour. Cook on oiled griddle. Serve with butter and Tupelo honey.

## CRAB MEAT IN CREAM

| | |
|---|---|
| 2 cups crab flakes | ½ teaspoonful onion juice |
| 1 tablespoonful minced green pepper | ½ cup cream |
| | ¼ lb. sliced fat bacon |

Combine crab, cream, onion and pepper. Place in casserole and cover with bacon strips. Set in hot oven and cook until bacon is crisp and brown.

## CRAB MEAT ROLLS

Large head green lettuce
1½ cups crab flakes
½ cup chopped celery

2 tablespoonfuls minced onion
1 tablespoonful minced pimiento
2 cups small green peas

2 tablespoonfuls butter

Steam lettuce for a minute or two so that leaves will be slightly wilted and easy to separate. Combine broken crab flakes, celery, onion and pimiento, and distribute on lettuce leaves. Roll each leaf tightly. Place in buttered casserole. Add peas and butter. Bake in moderate oven. Add a little boiling water as needed to prevent browning.

*Note*: Chicken may be used in place of crab flakes.

## CRABS IN TOMATO ASPIC

1 tablespoonful granulated gelatin
¼ cup cold water
¾ cup strained tomato juice
¾ cup boiling water

2 tablespoonfuls lemon juice
¼ cup chopped celery
¼ cup minced green pepper
1½ cups crab flakes

½ teaspoonful vegetable salt

Soften gelatin by soaking in cold water about 5 minutes. Add to hot water and stir until dissolved. Strain into tomato juice. Add lemon juice and salt. Chill until ready to congeal, then stir in crab flakes, celery and green pepper. Chill in mold until firm. Serve on bed of lettuce.

## CRABS IN TOMATO SAUCE

2 cups crab flakes
1 cup button mushrooms
3 tablespoonfuls minced pepper, sauted

½ cup tomato purée
½ cup vegetable broth
2 tablespoonfuls butter
2 egg yolks

Cook mushrooms in butter until lightly browned. Add vegetable broth, pepper and tomato purée. Simmer for a few minutes. Pour into well beaten egg yolks. Set over hot water, and stir until smooth and thickened. Add crab flakes and heat thoroughly.

## CREAMED SEA FOOD

1 cup small oysters, steamed
1 cup scallops, steamed

1 cup shrimp, steamed
1 cup heavy cream

1 tablespoonful lemon juice

Combine sea food. Sprinkle with lemon juice. Heat cream and add to sea food. Serve hot. If fresh shrimp are not available, always use wet pack canned shrimp.

## CREAMED SWEETBREADS

| | |
|---|---|
| 1 pair sweetbreads | ¼ teaspoonful onion juice |
| 1 cup cream | 2 egg yolks |
| 1 teaspoonful vegetable salt | 1 teaspoonful minced parsley |
| ¼ teaspoonful paprika | ½ cup small green peas (steamed) |
| 1 tablespoonful lemon juice | 1 cup sauted mushrooms |
| ½ cup sliced steamed celery | |

Wash sweetbreads, plunge into boiling water with 1 tablespoonful lemon juice. Boil 20 minutes. Rinse in cold water. Chill, remove membranes and cut into cubes. Combine with sauce.

### Sauce:

Heat cream, add salt, paprika and onion juice. Beat egg, add lemon juice, and parsley, and continue beating while adding hot cream. Cook over hot water until slightly thickened. Add sweetbreads, peas, mushrooms and celery. Heat and serve. Garnish with olive rings or pimiento stars.

## CREAMED TERRAPIN

Boil terrapin until meat of feet is tender. Cook and clean carefully removing nails from feet, shell, gall bladder and sandbags. Some cooks use liver and small intestines with meat; but originally only the eggs were saved. Reheat diced meat in a little heavy cream flavored with brandy.

## CROWN ROAST OF LAMB

Wrap ends of bone with slices of bacon to prevent burning. Season with a little vegetable salt. Roast in moderate oven. Remove bacon and dress each bone in paper frill. Center may be filled with steamed vegetables.

## CURRIED OMELETTE

| | |
|---|---|
| 1 plain omelette, cooked firm | 3 egg yolks |
| 1⅓ cups coconut milk | ¼ teaspoonful curry powder |

### Sauce:

Add beaten yolks to scalded coconut milk and cook over hot water until smooth and thickened. Add curry powder and a few drops of lemon juice if desired. Cut omelette into neat cubes and heat in sauce.

## Dressings for Meats

### CHICKEN FORCEMEAT

Chicken giblets
1 cup almond meal
1 teaspoonful vegetable salt
1 cup sauteed mushrooms
1 cup chopped raw chicken or lamb
1 tablespoonful minced parsley
1 egg yolk

Combine the ingredients. Use to stuff chicken or to fill vegetables to be baked.

### DRESSING FOR DUCK OR GOOSE

1½ cups sliced apple
1½ cups sliced celery
½ cup raisins
1 cup finely shredded, dry coconut
1 tablespoonful minced onion
½ teaspoonful vegetable salt

Combine ingredients. Sufficient for 5 pound fowl.

### FORCEMEAT DRESSING

3 cups ground lean lamb
1 tablespoonful minced onion
1 teaspoonful vegetable salt
¼ cup thinly sliced celery
1 tablespoonful minced parsley
1 teaspoonful powdered thyme

Melt 3 tablespoonfuls butter in heavy pan. Add celery and onion. Cook 2 or 3 minutes. Add meat and cook until rather dry and slightly brown. Add seasonings.

### FRUIT DRESSING

3 cups sliced celery
2 cups nutmeal
1 cup raisins
½ cup Tupelo honey
1 cup crushed, drained pineapple
Grated rind of 1 lemon

Combine ingredients until thoroughly mixed.

### MUSHROOM AND OYSTER GARNISH FOR FISH OR ROAST

Select medium sized mushrooms; dip in oil and broil in oven with convex side up. Turn over on broiling pan. Place 1 oyster and a small piece of butter in each mushroom cap. Return to broiler until oysters are curled.

## PROTEIN BREAD DRESSING

3 cups bread crumbs
1 cup thinly sliced celery
½ teaspoonful vegetable salt
¼ teaspoonful paprika

¼ teaspoonful thyme, sage or marjoram
1 tablespoonful minced parsley
2 tablespoonfuls minced onion
¼ cup butter or vegetable fat

Combine crumbs and seasonings. Add melted butter slowly and toss ingredients together to blend. Sufficient filling for 5 pound fowl.

## VEGETABLE DRESSING

1½ cups shredded carrot
1½ cups sliced celery
½ cup minced onion

½ teaspoonful vegetable salt
¼ teaspoonful paprika
½ teaspoonful thyme, sage or marjoram

Combine ingredients. Sufficient filling for 4 pound fowl. Finely shredded, dry coconut or nutmeal may be substituted for 1 cup of carrot.

## VEGETABLE DRESSING FOR VENISON OR GAME

3 cups ground carrots
1 cup sliced celery
1 cup shredded apple

½ cup minced onion
2 cups chopped watercress
1 teaspoonful vegetable salt

6 strips fat bacon

Put bacon through coarse blade of food chopper. Cook in heavy pan until browned. Remove bacon from pan. Pour off all free fat. Place all ingredients for filling in pan and cook, stirring constantly, for 15 minutes. Add bacon broken into small particles.

## VEGETABLE AND MUSHROOM DRESSING

1 cup finely chopped carrots
1 cup finely chopped celery
½ cup finely chopped string beans

1 cup chopped mushrooms
1 large onion, chopped
½ cup chopped pecans

2 egg yolks

Season with marjoram or thyme and vegetable salt to taste. Steam vegetables, then add nuts, egg yolks and seasonings. Mix thoroughly.

## WATERCRESS DRESSING

3 cups chopped celery
1 cup chopped apple

½ cup minced watercress
1 teaspoonful vegetable salt

2 tablespoonfuls minced onion
2 tablespoonfuls butter or bacon drippings

Heat fat in heavy pan. Add celery and onion. Cook for five minutes. Add remaining ingredients. Use any liquid that collects on celery to baste the meat while roasting.

## ENGLISH MUTTON CHOPS

Prepare chops by securing one section of kidney in the fat part of chop by means of skewer. Brush all over with bacon drippings or melted beef suet. Season lightly with vegetable salt and broil using high temperature.

## EGGPLANT STUFFED WITH HAM

| | |
|---|---|
| 1 eggplant | 1 cup mushrooms |
| ½ cup thinly sliced onion | 1 cup chopped cooked ham |
| 2 tablespoonfuls bacon fat (drippings) or vegetable oil | |

Cut eggplant in halves lengthwise. Scoop out flesh leaving walls about ½ inch thick. Chop mushrooms and center of eggplant rather coarsely and cook with onions in the fat for ten minutes. Add ham. Fill eggplant shell. Sprinkle with nutmeal. Bake in hot oven until shell is tender.

## ESCALLOPED CHICKEN

2 cups chopped cooked chicken    2 cups steamed small green peas
1 cup cream

Arrange chicken and peas in layers in casserole. Cover with cream, into which has been stirred ½ teaspoonful vegetable salt and 1 teaspoonful minced parsley. Sprinkle with protein bread crumbs. Bake in moderate oven.

## ESCALLOPED OYSTERS

Oysters    Carrots    Celery    Butter    Egg yolks

Place oysters in buttered baking dish. Alternate shredded carrots and chopped celery with oysters until dish is full. Whip yolks of 4 eggs and pour over top. Bake in moderate oven.

## ESCALLOPED SALMON

| | |
|---|---|
| 2 cups flaked red salmon | 1 cup steamed celery |
| 1 cup steamed green peas (small) | Thin cream |

Sprinkle fish with lemon juice. Place alternate layers of fish and vegetables in buttered casserole. Pour over enough cream to moisten well. Dot with butter and bake in moderate oven. Shrimp may be substituted for salmon.

## FILLET OF FLOUNDER

Serve flounder either broiled or steamed. Follow recipe for broiled or steamed fillet of sole.

## FILLET OF HADDOCK IN SOUR CREAM

Fillet of haddock or any other white fish may be prepared in this manner. Cover fish with sour cream or whey and let stand one hour. Drain, and steam until tender. Serve with melted butter and a dash of grated nutmeg.

## FILLET STEAKS

| | |
|---|---|
| 4 small tenderloin steaks one inch thick | 1 cup balls cut from steamed beets |
| 1 cup tiny green peas, steamed | 1 cup small steamed brussel sprouts |
| | 1 cup sauted button mushrooms |

Rub steaks with olive oil, and broil to desired state. Arrange on hot platter with (hot) vegetables attractively disposed as garnish. Place sauted mushrooms on steaks.

## FISH CASSEROLES

| | |
|---|---|
| 2 cups flaked, cooked fish | ½ teaspoonful vegetable salt |
| 1 cup celery broth plus 2 table-spoonfuls cream | ⅛ teaspoonful paprika |
| 4 well beaten egg yolks | 1 tablespoonful minced parsley |
| | 1 tablespoonful minced green pepper |

Stir all ingredients together until well mixed. Pour into buttered individual casseroles. Set in pan of hot water and poach in moderate oven until firm. Turn out on hot buttered platter. Garnish with parsley and lemon slices.

## FROG LEGS

| | |
|---|---|
| 4 pairs frog legs | 4 tablespoonfuls butter |
| 2 tablespoonfuls chopped chives | 1 cup celery broth |

Simmer chives in butter for a few minutes. Remove with strainer. Cook frog legs in same butter for ten minutes, without browning. Add celery broth and simmer until meat is tender, and liquid partially absorbed. Garnish with crisp cress.

## GRILLED GUINEA HEN

Young guinea hen may be prepared following directions for Broiled Spring Chicken. Serve with jellied fruit purée.

## GRILLED PRAIRIE HEN

Follow instructions for Broiled Spring Chicken. Garnish with cider molds on rounds of pineapple.

## GRILLED SPRING TURKEY

Small young turkey may be grilled. Follow instructions given for Broiled Spring Chicken. Sprinkle with vegetable salt when about half done. Garnish with wild strawberries molded in gelatin and set in cups of lettuce leaves.

## GRILLED SWEETBREADS

Use only sweetbreads from calf for broiling as these should not be par-boiled. Split lengthwise, coat with melted butter and broil under electric unit using medium heat. Sprinkle with vegetable salt, garnish with cress and serve.

## GRILLED WOODCOCK

Small young woodcock may be prepared as Broiled Spring Chicken.

## HALIBUT IN COCONUT MILK

1 lb. halibut steak                1 cup coconut milk
1 tablespoonful minced parsley

Arrange halibut steak on buttered oven platter. Pour coconut milk over. Bake in moderately hot oven. Liquid should be absorbed. Sprinkle with parsley. Garnish with lemon points.
Any firm white fish may be substituted for halibut.

## HALIBUT STEAK, SHRIMP DRESSING

1 lb. halibut steak                1 cup Hollandaise sauce
¾ cup steamed whole shrimp

Brush halibut with melted butter. Place in buttered glass baking dish and cook until tender. Cover with sauce. Distribute shrimp over sauce.

## HAM AND APPLE CASSEROLE

1 slice of ham 2 inches thick

Place ham in baking dish, add 2 cloves, 1 tablespoonful onion juice. Peel, core and quarter 6 large tart apples. Add 2 tablespoonfuls of butter and 2 table-spoonfuls Tupelo honey. Bake in covered dish until tender.

## HAM AND CELERY CASSEROLE

1½ cups chopped cooked ham          3 egg yolks well beaten
1 cup vegetable broth               1 cup sliced steamed celery
1 tablespoonful minced onion

Pour hot broth over egg yolks. Cook until smooth over hot water. Add celery, onion, ham. Mix well together, turn into buttered casserole and bake in moderate oven.

## HAM IN GELATIN

| | |
|---|---|
| 2 cups finely chopped, cooked ham | 1 cup whipped cream |
| 1 cup whipped lemon gelatin | 2 tablespoonfuls tomato purée |
| 1 cup plain lemon gelatin | (Combine above ingredients.) |

Set individual molds in pan of cracked ice. Coat inside of molds thickly with plain lemon gelatin. Chill until firm. Fill with ham mixture to within ½ inch of top. When firm cover with plain gelatin. Chill. Turn out on crisp lettuce.

## HAM LOAF

| | |
|---|---|
| 2 cups chopped raw ham | ¼ cup minced onion |
| 3 egg yolks, beaten | 1 cup sliced celery |
| 1 cup shredded carrots | 1 tablespoonful minced parsley |
| ½ cup shredded apple | |

Combine ingredients. Shape into loaf. Bake in moderate oven.

## HAM AND SALAD SANDWICHES

Slices cooked ham        Fruit or vegetable salad of choice

Cut sliced meat in even-sized, attractive shapes. On one slice of meat arrange salad. Top with second slice. Garnish with crisp watercress and jellied mayonnaise.

## IMPERIAL CRABS

| | |
|---|---|
| 1 pound crab flakes | 2 tablespoonfuls minced ripe olives |
| ¼ cup finely shredded green pepper | Mayonnaise |
| 2 tablespoonfuls minced pimiento | 4 scrubbed crab shells |

Pick over crab flakes carefully to remove any particles of shell, cook green pepper in 2 tablespoonfuls of butter until tender. Combine crab, pepper, pimiento, olives and sufficient mayonnaise to hold other ingredients together. Pile into shell, bake at moderate temperature.

## INDIVIDUAL GRILLED STEAKS

| | |
|---|---|
| 4 filet steaks | 4 steamed onions |
| 1 cup diced steamed turnip | 2 cups steamed baby peas |
| 1 cup steamed carrot rings | 4 large broiled mushroom caps |

Broil steaks (dipped in melted butter) under hot grill. Sprinkle with vegetable salt. Set one broiled mushroom cap on each steak. Remove center from onions and fill with peas. Arrange steak and vegetables on hot platter.

## JELLIED BEEF

4 lbs. beef
½ cup chopped celery
¼ cup sliced carrot

1 cup tomato juice
2 tablespoonfuls minced parsley
1 slice onion

1 bay leaf

Cover meat with cold water and add vegetables. Cook gently until meat falls from bones. Strain broth and reduce to 1 cup by cooking. Dice lean meat and add to reduced broth. Pour into mold and chill. Serve sliced, with mayonnaise to which horseradish has been added.

## JELLIED MEAT PUDDING

1 cup diced chicken (cooked)
1 cup shredded ham (cooked)
½ cup sliced chicken liver (cooked)
½ cup sliced steamed mushrooms
½ cup steamed baby peas
½ cup steamed carrot rings
½ cup shredded tender celery

½ cup small dice crisp cucumber
4 sliced hard boiled eggs
2 tablespoonfuls minced green pepper
1 tablespoonful minced parsley
½ teaspoonful onion juice
3 cups cool lemon gelatin

Combine all ingredients, pour into glass serving dish. Chill. Top with cottage cheese and whipped cream (equal parts) seasoned with shredded marinated steamed beets and minced olives. Sufficient for twelve servings.

## KIDNEY CASSEROLE

1 pound lamb or calf's kidneys
2 cups diced or canned tomatoes
2 tablespoonfuls minced onion

1 tablespoonful minced parsley
1 teaspoonful vegetable salt
2 cups diced carrot

Drop kidneys in boiling acidulated water (2 tablespoonfuls lemon juice to 1 quart water). Boil 2 minutes. Remove kidneys from water. Cut away membranes and strings. Dice. Add to remaining ingredients. Bake in casserole at moderate temperature.

## LAMB CASSEROLE

1½ pounds lamb cut into cubes
1½ cups green peas
1 cup sliced celery

1 cup diced carrots
¼ cup chopped parsley
About 3 mint leaves

Place meat and vegetables in layers in casserole, add a little boiling water to keep moist and a small amount of vegetable salt (about ½ teaspoonful) and paprika. Cover and bake until lamb is tender.

## LAMB CHOPS WITH ORANGE

4 loin lamb chops              4 slices orange

Arrange alternately around baking dish. Bake in moderate oven until meat is tender. Fill center of dish with minted peas.

## LAMB CUTLETS

1½ cups chopped, cooked lamb        1 tablespoonful chopped parsley
1 cup base for protein croquettes       or mint
(See Sauces)

Combine ingredients, spread one inch thick on waxed paper or glass and chill. Cut into shape of chops, dip in beaten egg, then in protein bread crumbs, and broil under hot fire. Serve with tomato sauce or mint flavored gelatin.

## LAMB PATTIES WITH PINEAPPLE

1 lb. finely chopped lamb (raw), pineapple slices, (raw)

Cover pineapple slices with chopped lamb to which has been added one teaspoonful minced mint leaves and ½ teaspoonful vegetable salt. Set on broiling rack, pour small amount melted butter over meat and broil.

## LAMBS' TONGUE, SPANISH

1½ pounds lambs' tongues        3 cups strained tomato
2 tablespoonfuls butter         ½ teaspoonful salt
1 onion sliced                  1 clove of garlic (optional)

Cover lambs' tongues with boiling water, then simmer until tender (about 1 hour). Drain and remove skin and any tough portion. Heat butter, add sliced onion and garlic, if used; cook until a golden brown, then remove garlic and add tomato, seasonings and tongues. Heat thoroughly and serve.

## LIVER LOAF

1 lb. beef liver, chopped          2 teaspoonfuls minced green pepper
1 cup protein breadcrumbs          ½ teaspoonful thyme
2 egg yolks                        2 tablespoonfuls minced onion
4 slices crisp, broiled bacon      ½ teaspoonful vegetable salt

Combine ingredients. Shape into loaf. Bake at moderate temperature.

## LOBSTER IN EGG SAUCE

2 cups steamed lobster meat
2 tablespoonfuls melted butter
2 teaspoonfuls lemon juice
2 beaten egg yolks
½ cup broken hard-boiled egg yolks
1 cup steamed button mushrooms
1 cup cream

Heat lobster with butter and lemon juice, add cooked egg yolks and mushrooms. Cook cream with beaten egg yolks until smooth, over hot water. Add lobster mixture. Serve hot.

## MEAT BALLS WITH TOMATO SAUCE

1 pound round steak finely ground
1 tablespoonful minced onion
1 tablespoonful minced green peppers
1 egg yolk
Vegetable salt, about ½ teaspoonful

Combine the above ingredients, shape into small balls, roll in protein flour, brown in a little bacon drippings. Place in casserole, cover with tomato sauce. Bake for about 45 minutes.

## MEAT LOAF

### With Jellied Tomato Sauce

4 cups ground beef
1 cup sautéd mushrooms
1 tablespoonful onion juice
2 cups chopped celery
¾ teaspoonful vegetable salt
1 tablespoonful minced green pepper
½ cup vegetable broth
4 egg yolks, slightly beaten

Combine ingredients, bake until tender. Do not allow to become brown. Remove from pan, and cool. Pour ½ cup water and 1 cup tomato purée into pan. Remove any fat. Cook for five minutes. Add 1 teaspoonful softened gelatin. Cool in small individual molds. Surround meat loaf with molds of sauce, and roses made of jellied mayonnaise put through pastry tube.

## MOLDED SALMON, CUCUMBER SAUCE

1 can red salmon
½ teaspoonful vegetable salt
2 egg yolks
2 tablespoonfuls cold water
¾ cup cream
¼ cup lemon juice
¾ tablespoonfuls granulated gelatin

Soak gelatin in cold water. Remove salmon from can and separate in flakes. Beat egg yolks, add salt and cream, cook over boiling water, stirring constantly until mixture thickens. Add gelatin, cool, add salmon, pour into molds, chill.

## OYSTER CASSEROLE

2 cups chopped onions          1 cup oyster liquor
¼ cup butter                   2 or 3 cups oysters

Melt butter in heavy frying pan. Add onions and oyster liquor. Cook slowly until onions are clear. Remove to buttered shallow casserole. Cover with oysters. Put lid on tightly, and bake until oysters begin to curl. Serve at once.

## OYSTER OMELETTE

12 oysters                     6 egg yolks
          2 tablespoonfuls butter

Chop oysters finely. Beat egg yolks slightly and add oysters. Melt butter in omelette pan and pour mixture into it. Cook slowly. Fold over and garnish with mounds of hot cubed beets.

## OYSTER STEW WITH EGG YOLKS

1 quart oysters                4 hard boiled egg yolks
1 cup thin cream               4 tablespoonfuls butter
1 cup celery broth             1 tablespoonful lemon juice
          Pinch of celery salt

Scald cream and celery broth. Press egg yolks through fine sieve and beat smooth with a little of the hot cream. Add to remaining liquid. Stir in a few grains of paprika. Keep hot. Brown butter slightly, add oysters and heat until edges curl. Add lemon juice. When ready to serve beat cream until foamy and combine with oysters.

## PANNED OYSTERS

1 pint small oysters (no juice)          ¼ lb. butter

Melt butter in heavy pan. When slightly browned, add oysters and cook until edges begin to curl. Serve at once.

## PIKE OR PICKEREL

Usually only the fillet of pickerel is served. Follow recipe for either broiled or steamed fillet of sole.

## PINEAPPLE AND HAM SOUFFLE

1 cup chopped cooked ham      4 small slices canned or cooked pineapple
        1 cup cream                    3 egg yolks

Beat egg yolks. Combine with cream and ham. Pour into 4 baking cups.

Place pineapple slices on top. Poach for 45 minutes or until set. Place under broiler for a few minutes to brown pineapple. May be turned out to serve.

## PLANKED SHAD

Place shad, skin side down, upon buttered plank. Sprinkle with lemon juice and a little vegetable salt. Bake in hot oven until tender. Pour a little melted butter over fish, garnish with cress and pimiento strips. Serve at once on plank.

## PLANKED STEAK

1 Porterhouse steak, cut 1½ inches thick

Place steak on well-oiled broiler rack and broil about ten or twelve minutes. Turn at least twice. Place in center of hot plank and sprinkle with vegetable salt. Surround with steamed whole onions over which has been poured a little melted butter, and steamed whole carrots, sprinkled with chopped parsley.

## PLANKED WHITEFISH

Follow directions for Planked Shad.

## PLOVER

These birds may be broiled, either whole (following recipe for Broiled Quail) or only the breast dipped in melted butter and broiled. To roast plover, dress and stuff with mushrooms and chopped celery. Baste with white cherry juice or cooking wine. Keep oven temperature moderate.

## POACHED EGG YOLKS WITH ASPARAGUS

4 poached eggs              1 lb. steamed asparagus tips

Trim off whites of eggs and discard. Form nests of asparagus tips. Pour one tablespoonful melted butter over each. Place a poached egg yolk in each nest.

## POT ROAST

3 lbs. lean lamb or center chuck of      8 baby carrots
        beef                             2 cups small onions
2 tablespoonfuls suet                    2 medium turnips cut in quarters
        Tomato juice                     4 hearts of celery

Melt suet and brown meat in it. Add a little tomato juice to prevent hardening of outside of meat and cook over slow heat until tender. One hour before serving add vegetables. Season with vegetable salt.

## PROTEIN BISCUITS

2 cups Protein Flour, sifted
3 tablespoonfuls vegetable shortening or butter
3 teaspoonfuls tartaric baking powder
¾ cup water (approximate measure)
1 tablespoonful Tupelo honey

Sift flour with baking powder, cut in shortening. Add liquid slowly until a soft dough is formed. Roll on slightly floured pastry board to ½-inch thickness and cut with floured biscuit cutter. Bake in hot oven.

## PROTEIN BREAD

2 tablespoonfuls butter or vegetable fat
1½ tablespoonfuls Tupelo honey
½ teaspoonful salt (may be omitted, if desired)
2 cups boiling water
6 to 7 cups protein flour
¾ cup soy bean milk powder
1 yeast cake dissolved in 4 tablespoonfuls warm water

Pour boiling water over shortening, honey and salt and allow to cool until about 100 degrees. Add yeast dissolved in warm water, soy bean milk powder and then flour until stiff enough to knead. Knead until smooth and elastic to the touch. Place in an oiled bowl and allow to double in volume. Knead and set to rise until double in bulk again. Knead lightly, form into loaves, place in oiled pans and let rise until double in size. Bake in moderate oven for about 50 minutes.

## PROTEIN MUFFINS

2 cups sifted protein flour
3 teaspoonfuls tartaric acid baking powder
¼ teaspoonful salt if desired
2 egg yolks
1 cup cream and water mixed
1 tablespoonful vegetable oil
3 tablespoonfuls Tupelo honey

Mix and sift dry ingredients. Combine beaten egg yolks, liquid and oil and add to flour mixture, stirring until combined smoothly. Fill oiled muffin pans two thirds full, bake in moderate oven.

## PROTEIN PANCAKES

2 cups protein flour
3 teaspoonfuls tartaric acid baking powder
1 tablespoonful Tupelo honey
2 egg yolks beaten light
1 cup water
½ cup cream

Mix and sift flour and baking powder. Combine eggs, cream, water and honey, add to flour mixture and beat until smooth. Bake on hot griddle.

## RABBIT STEW

1 dressed rabbit cut in pieces for serving

| | |
|---|---|
| 1 cup green peas | 1 green pepper, shredded |
| 1 cup sliced carrots | ¼ cup sliced onion |

1 cup vegetable broth or tomato juice

Place all ingredients in casserole, add vegetable salt to season. Cover and bake at moderate temperature until meat is tender.

## ROAST CAPON

Prepare capon for roasting. Stuff with chopped celery root, mushrooms and diced carrots; or protein bread dressing. Truss and rub over with softened butter. Roast in moderate oven.

## ROAST DUCK

Stuff prepared duck with vegetable filling or quartered apples. Season with vegetable salt and minced onion. Roast in moderate oven basting frequently with juices in pan, or fruit juice. Prick skin over fatty areas so that excess fat will drain from duck.

## ROAST DUCK WITH SAUERKRAUT

Roast duck in covered casserole to keep meat moist. Bake equal parts of sauerkraut and sliced apple in a separate casserole at moderate temperature to prevent browning. Arrange the sauerkraut in center of a platter and surround with slices from the breast of the duck. Garnish with crisp bacon curls.

## ROAST FILLET OF BEEF WITH PEARS

| | |
|---|---|
| 1½ lbs. fillet of beef | Juice from canned pears, |
| 6 slices bacon | unsweetened |

8 halves, canned pears, unsweetened

Place three rather thick slices of bacon in bottom of roaster; on these lay the meat. Top with remaining bacon. Place in very hot oven for ten minutes. Baste with pear juice to which has been added a few drops lemon juice. Reduce heat and continue cooking until as well done as is desired. Remove meat to hot platter. Lay pears in roaster and set under broiler until slightly browned. Arrange around roast.

## ROAST GOOSE

Prepare, stuff and truss goose. (See vegetable filling for fowl). Prick all over fat deposits to allow excess fat to escape. Season with vegetable salt. Place on rack in roaster and keep heat moderate. Fresh cider is excellent for basting the goose.

## ROAST LEG OF LAMB

Best grade leg of lamb will weigh about six pounds. Have butcher remove all glutinous tissue, as this is cause of strong "mutton taste." Rub all over with soft butter. Sprinkle with vegetable salt. Bake in covered roaster in moderate oven. One hour before serving add a few whole baby carrots, small onions and whole tomatoes. Serve vegetables around roast.

## ROAST OYSTERS

| | |
|---|---|
| 20 large oysters | ¼ cup minced green pepper or |
| 20 half shells | pimiento |
| 4 tablespoonfuls butter | 1 tablespoonful minced onion |
| ½ cup finely minced raw ham | 1 tablespoonful minced parsley |
| About ¾ cup heavy cream | |

Scrub oyster shells, and dry. Use half of shell that has deep curve. Cook ham, pepper and onion in butter until ham is tender,—about four minutes. Add parsley. Distribute on shells. Place an oyster on each, ½ tablespoonful cream on each oyster and roast in quick oven until edges curl. Serve on beds of heated rock salt.

## ROAST TURKEY

Stuff and truss turkey. (See vegetable filling for fowl or protein bread dressing). Set on rack in roaster and cook in moderate oven until tender and well browned. Baste with fat and juices in pan. Season with vegetable salt and paprika when half done. If the fowl is not too fat, cover breast with slices of fat bacon while cooking, or add butter to fat in pan. Garnish with pears colored green and decorated with bits of red cherry, orange rind, etc.

## ROAST WILD DUCK

Fill duck with whole stalks celery. Wild duck is always served rare. Oven must be very hot. Turn frequently and baste each time with equal parts orange juice and butter. Discard celery. Serve duck with orange sauce.

## ROAST WILD TURKEY

Prepare wild turkey the same as domestic variety. If bird is very large it will be old and strong flavored, in which case the usual filling will not be used; fill such a fowl with chopped celery leaves, ground carrot and chopped apple. Roast in moderate oven until tender and well browned. Baste frequently with equal parts white grape juice and melted butter together with juices in pan. Discard filling which will have absorbed strong, wild taste to some degree.

## ROAST WOODCOCK

Stuff with chopped celery and celery tops. Place in covered roaster and cook in moderate oven, basting occasionally with white wine or orange juice flavored with non-alcoholic sherry flavor. When tender and nicely browned, remove celery. Sprinkle with a little vegetable salt; place a small baked apple (colored clear bright red with vegetable color) in each bird. Serve on hot platter garnished with green lettuce leaves which have been dusted with paprika, curry and turmeric to simulate autumn leaves.

## SALMON LOAF

| | |
|---|---|
| 1 can red salmon | ½ cup minced onion |
| 1 cup shredded carrots | 2 egg yolks, beaten |
| ½ cup sliced celery | 1 tablespoonful minced green pepper |

½ teaspoonful vegetable salt

Combine all ingredients. Shape into loaf. Bake at moderate temperature.


## SALMON PATTIES

| | |
|---|---|
| 2 cups red salmon | 2 tablespoonfuls tomato purée |
| 2 tablespoonfuls grated onion | 1 teaspoonful lemon juice |

Bacon strips

Flake salmon and add lemon juice, onion and tomato purée. Let stand for fifteen minutes. Drain off any liquid and press fish lightly into small round cakes. Set on buttered baking sheet, lay one short strip of bacon over each patty and cook under broiler for six or seven minutes.


## SALMON SOUFFLÉ

| | |
|---|---|
| 2 cups red salmon (flaked) | 1 cup thin cream |
| 1 tablespoonful lemon juice | 4 egg yolks, well beaten |

½ tablespoonful onion juice

Pour lemon juice over flaked salmon. Heat cream and beat into egg yolks. Add onion juice, also ½ teaspoonful vegetable salt and ¼ teaspoonful paprika. Fold in salmon and pour into buttered casserole. Poach in moderate oven.


## SAUTED CALF LIVER

| | |
|---|---|
| 1 lb. liver, sliced | 3 egg yolks, beaten |

1 teaspoonful lemon juice

Beat lemon juice into egg yolks. Dip slices of liver in egg and cook until tender in oiled pan, over quick heat.

*Note:* When preparing liver, dip each slice in boiling water. Drain. Remove skin and unedible portions. The boiling water seals the juices within the slices and assures a tender product.


## SCALLOPS IN EGG SAUCE

Follow directions for terrapin in egg sauce.

## SCRAMBLED EGGS WITH MUSHROOMS

6 egg yolks                          ½ teaspoonful vegetable salt
1 tablespoonful thin cream           ½ cup sautéd mushrooms
                    1 oz. butter

Melt butter in heavy pan. Add all ingredients and stir over low heat until set.

## SHRIMP IN MUSHROOM SAUCE

2 cups steamed shrimp                2 hard boiled egg yolks
1 cup sautéd mushrooms               1 cup thin cream
2 tablespoonfuls sautéd green pepper 3 egg yolks (beaten)

Heat cream and beat into egg yolks. Cook over hot water until smooth and thickened. Add chopped egg yolks, shrimp, mushrooms and pepper. Heat thoroughly before serving.

## SLICED BEEF IN TOMATO SAUCE

2 tablespoonfuls butter or olive oil  ½ teaspoonful vegetable salt
3 tablespoonfuls chopped onion        1 cup tomato purée
3 tablespoonfuls chopped green pepper 1 lb. thinly sliced roast beef

Brown onion and green pepper a little in butter. Add salt and tomato. Heat and add sliced beef. When meat is thoroughly heated, it is ready to serve.

## SLICED HAM WITH ORANGE

1 slice ham ¾-inch thick             2 tablespoonfuls butter
1 cup orange juice                   Sections of two oranges

Cook ham in butter without browning for five minutes. Add orange juice and simmer until tender. Take ham from pan and arrange on hot platter. Place orange sections in pan and brown slightly, under broiler. Arrange on ham and serve.

## SOY BEANS BAKED IN TOMATO SAUCE

1 pound soy beans                    1 teaspoonful onion juice
2 tablespoonfuls butter              1 tablespoonful minced parsley
2 cups tomato purée or canned        1 tablespoonful minced green pepper
    tomatoes                         2 tablespoonfuls Tupelo honey
                    Vegetable salt to season

Soak the soy beans over night in enough water to cover. Steam or simmer till tender. Place in casserole. Add remaining ingredients, cutting butter into small pieces to distribute over the top. Bake at moderate temperature for 3 hours.

## SOY BEAN BISCUITS

  1 cup soy bean flour
  1 egg yolk and 1 tablespoonful Tupelo honey in measuring cup,
    fill ½ full with cold water
  3 teaspoonfuls tartaric acid baking powder
  3 tablespoonfuls butter

Sift flour and baking powder together several times. Cut in butter. Add liquids. Shape with fingers. Does not roll well. Bake in hot oven.

## SOY CASSEROLE

  2 cups cooked soy beans
  1 tablespoonful minced onion
  2 tablespoonfuls minced celery
  1 teaspoonful vegetable salt
  1 cup cooked tomatoes

  1 cup cooked soy macaroni
  1 teaspoonful minced parsley
  4 tablespoonfuls olive oil
  ½ teaspoonful paprika
  1 cup chopped cabbage

Simmer onion, parsley and celery in olive oil until lightly browned. Add salt, paprika and cabbage and simmer until cabbage is tender. Add macaroni and beans and simmer all together until well blended and of correct consistency to serve. Place in individual casseroles, put 1 square cream cheese on top of each. Set under broiler until cheese is lightly browned.

## SOY CHILI

  2 cups cooked soy beans
  2 cups cooked or canned tomatoes
  ½ green pepper

  1 pound ground round steak
  ½ cup chopped onion
  4 slices bacon

Cook bacon slowly until crisp. Remove bacon from pan. Drain off all but 2 tablespoonfuls fat. Cook pepper and onion in fat in pan until lightly browned. Add steak and cook until browned. Add remaining ingredients. Simmer or bake in moderate oven until of desired consistency. Season with vegetable salt and paprika. Add crisp bacon just before serving.

## SOY BEAN SPAGHETTI WITH MEAT BALLS

Boil soy bean spaghetti until tender but not broken. Place in collander and rinse with hot water. Place in casserole. Arrange meat balls on top of spaghetti and cover with tomato sauce. Bake at moderate temperature for one hour.

## MEAT BALLS FOR SPAGHETTI

  1 pound ground round steak
  1 teaspoonful vegetable salt

  4 slices fat bacon, chopped
  ½ teaspoonful paprika

Combine all ingredients, mixing thoroughly. Roll in soy bean flour. Brown in butter or bacon drippings.

This dish is very concentrated. Small servings should be the rule.

## SOY BEAN MUFFINS

| | |
|---|---|
| 2 cups soy bean flour | ½ teaspoonful baking soda |
| ¼ cup Tupelo honey | 1 teaspoonful tartaric acid |
| ¾ cup sour cream | baking powder |

2 egg yolks

Sift baking powder into flour; beat egg yolks well, cream butter and egg yolks. Mix cream and soda. Add butter mixture. Fold in flour. Bake in buttered muffin tins in moderate oven.

## SPAGHETTI WITH TOMATO SAUCE

1 quart boiled protein spaghetti

Arrange in casserole with ½ cup minced onion. Add tomato sauce to cover and bake in moderate oven.

## STEAK SMOTHERED IN ONIONS

Rub hot pan with suet. Brown steak quickly on both sides. Remove meat from pan. Add 2 tablespoonfuls chopped suet or butter and brown 3 pints sliced onion in this. Sprinkle with vegetable salt and paprika. Place steak on onions, cover and cook until steak is tender. Porterhouse or Sirloin steak will cook in about 15 minutes, while the less choice cuts such as round or rump or flank steak will require about one hour.

## STEAMED BREAST OF GUINEA HEN

Allow one breast for each serving. Steam until tender. Baste with a little currant juice or white grapejuice while cooking. Season with vegetable salt. Garnish with bunches of crisp grapes and green endive.

## STEAMED CLAMS

Scrub clams in salt water (sea water if possible). Place on damp sea-weed or other greens in roasting pan, cover with greens or dampened paper towels. Bake in moderate oven until shells open a little. If overdone they will be tough. Serve with lemon butter in hot ramekins.

## STEAMED FILLET OF FISH

1 lb. fillet of any white fish        3 tablespoonfuls butter

Wipe fish with damp cloth, rub with oil and steam until tender. Heat butter in small heavy pan until lightly browned. Serve over fish. A few drops of lemon juice will improve flavor.

## STEAMED FRESH COD

Place trimmed slices of cod on rack in steamer and cook until tender. Serve with butter or any tart sauce.

## STEAMED MUSSELS

Scrub mussels in salt water (sea water if possible). Place on damp sea-weed or other greens in roasting pan, cover with greens or dampened paper towels. Bake in hot oven until shells open. Serve with butter or horseradish sauce.

## STEAMED PHEASANT BREASTS

One breast for each serving. Steam until tender. During steaming pour a few drops orange juice over each piece every fifteen minutes. Remove from steamer. Dip in melted butter. Broil until evenly browned. Serve with grape frappé made from wild grape juice.

## STEAMED PROTEIN BROWN BREAD

| | |
|---|---|
| 2 cups protein flour | ½ cup cream |
| 1 teaspoonful cinnamon | ½ cup water |
| ¼ teaspoonful salt | ¾ teaspoonful baking soda |
| 1 cup raisins | 2 egg yolks |
| ½ cup sliced nuts | ¾ cups Tupelo honey |

Sift flour, cinnamon and salt together, add raisins and nuts. Add beaten egg yolks with soda dissolved in cream and water. Add honey. Mix thoroughly. Steam 2½ hours.

## STEAMED SALMON

| | |
|---|---|
| 4 slices fresh salmon (about 1 lb.) | 1 tablespoonful chopped parsley |
| 4 tablespoonfuls butter | 1 tablespoonful lemon juice |

Trim salmon evenly. Steam until tender. Heat butter, lemon juice and parsley together. Pour over fish and serve immediately, garnished with grape-fruit sections.

## STEAMED SMOKED TONGUE

Scrub smoked tongue. Steam on rack in pan of boiling water until tender. Remove skin and membranes. Marinate in French dressing with desired herbs for flavoring; or place in covered dish and keep moist with fruit juices or cooking wine. Slice thinly to serve. May be cut into small dice and used in salad.

## STEWED CHICKEN AND VEGETABLES

| | |
|---|---|
| 3 lb. chicken | 1 teaspoonful vegetable salt |
| 2 cups tomato cubes | 4 tablespoonfuls minced onion |
| 2 cups boiling water | 1 cup turnip balls |
| 1 teaspoonful minced parsley | 1 cup carrot cubes |
| 1 cup sliced mushrooms | |

Clean and cut chicken for serving. Place in casserole, add tomato, water, salt, parsley. Brown mushrooms, carrots, turnips and onion in melted butter and add to casserole. Cook in moderate oven until chicken is tender.

## STEWED OYSTERS

1 pint oysters                    2 cups thin cream

Heat oysters in their own liquor. Heat cream separately. Combine and serve at once. For additional flavor, add one teaspoonful minced parsley or one teaspoonful onion juice.

## STUFFED BAKED HADDOCK

Stuff fish with vegetable filling. Secure with small skewers or sew. Cover fish with sliced bacon and cook in moderate oven until tender. Remove bacon a few minutes before taking from oven. Garnish with a few large broiled mushroom caps filled with parsley butter.

## STUFFED BAKED HAM

10 pound ham                      1 cup seedless raisins
4 cups finely shredded carrots    1 cup Tupelo honey
1 cup crushed, drained pineapple  1 cup chopped walnuts or pecans

Have ham boned. Combine remaining ingredients and stuff into cavity. Sew or truss. Bake in moderate oven. Baste with pineapple juice and Tupelo honey combined.

## STUFFED CALVES HEARTS WITH FRUIT

2 calves hearts                   ½ cup dried apricots, soaked
½ cup dried prunes, soaked and pitted    1 tablespoonful lemon juice

Wash hearts and remove veins. Fill with fruits. Roll in soy bean flour. Brown in butter or oil. Place in covered baking dish and bake in moderate oven until tender.

## STUFFED FLANK STEAK

1 flank steak with pocket         2 tablespoonfuls minced green
1 cup solid tomato dice (no juice)    pepper
½ cup diced onion                 1 cup mushrooms
1 cup diced celery                1 cup cream
            ¾ teaspoonful vegetable salt

Have flank steak lightly scored and pocket cut in it. Rub inside of pocket lightly with salt. Stuff with vegetables (all but mushrooms) and secure sides. Place in buttered baking pan and bake in moderate oven. When done remove to hot platter. Set baking pan over direct heat to brown residue in pan. Add 2 tablespoonfuls butter and mushrooms broken in pieces. When mushrooms are slightly brown, add cream. Cook three minutes and serve in bowl.

### STUFFED LAMB CHOPS

Select loin lamb chops about 1 inch thick. Have pocket cut in each chop. Fill pockets with chopped celery and shredded pineapple (equal parts) or shredded pineapple and raisins. Broil until tender. Sprinkle with vegetable salt when cooked.

### STUFFED ROAST LAMB

Boned leg or shoulder of lamb          Vegetable filling

Stuff lamb with vegetable filling. Secure with skewers or sew openings. Roast in moderate oven, basting with liquid in pan. Vegetable salt may be used for seasoning.

### STUFFED TOMATO WITH COTTAGE CHEESE

Fill tomato cups with cottage cheese mixed with a little minced parsley and pimiento. Bake until tomato is tender. Serve with bacon curls.

### SWEETBREADS AND OYSTERS EN CASSEROLE

2 cups diced steamed sweetbreads          1 cup heavy cream
2 cups small oysters          ½ teaspoonful celery salt

Add salt to cream. Place sweetbread dice and oysters in buttered casserole in layers. Pour cream over. Bake in moderate oven.

### SWISS STEAK

1½ pounds round steak sliced thick

Cut in pieces for serving. Pound soy bean flour into steak, using about 1 cupful. Brown in bacon drippings. Place in covered casserole, pour over tomato sauce. Bake at moderate temperature until tender.

### TERRAPIN IN EGG SAUCE

3 cups steamed terrapin          2 beaten egg yolks
1 cup heavy cream          ½ cup chopped ripe olives

Heat cream, add to egg yolks and cook over hot water until smooth and thickened. Season with grated lemon rind, minced parsley, minced chives, vegetable salt and paprika. Add terrapin and olives. Heat thoroughly.

### TERRAPIN, HOLLANDAISE

2 cups steamed terrapin          1 cup steamed asparagus tips
1 cup steamed button mushrooms

Combine ingredients, sprinkle with vegetable salt. Serve with Hollandaise sauce.

## TERRAPIN IN SHERRY SAUCE

3 cups diced cooked terrapin                    Sherry sauce

Heat terrapin in sauce over boiling water.

## TOMATO AND CHEESE SOUFFLE

1 cup strained tomato juice and pulp
1 cup cottage cheese, forced through finest wire strainer
4 egg yolks                    1 teaspoonful vegetable thickening
2 tablespoonfuls shredded green pepper
1 tablespoonful paprika

Beat egg yolks as light as possible. Combine with all other ingredients, season with vegetable salt. Poach in moderate oven until set.

## TRIPE IN TOMATO SAUCE

1¼ lbs. tripe        1½ cups tomato sauce

Cut tripe into pieces for serving. Cover with cold water and bring to boiling point. Drain. Cover again with boiling salted water and simmer until tender. Drain thoroughly. Serve with tomato sauce.

## TUNA CASSEROLE

1½ cups tuna                              1 cup thick cream, 1 cup water
¾ cup steamed tiny green peas        4 beaten egg yolks
½ teaspoonful vegetable salt

Combine heated cream and water with salt and beaten egg yolks. Pour over tuna and peas arranged in buttered casserole. Poach in moderate oven.

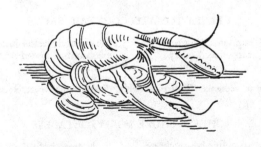

# SAUCES

### ANCHOVY BUTTER

*(for steak)*

2 tablespoonfuls anchovy paste          ¼ cup creamed butter

Beat ingredients together. Spread on hot broiled steak and serve at once.

### APPLESAUCE

Select richly flavored fruit, not over ripe. Wash apples and cut in small pieces. Do not remove skin or seeds. Steam until tender. Press through sieve. Sweeten to taste with Tupelo honey. Serve hot or cold.

### BASE FOR PROTEIN CROQUETTES

4 tablespoonfuls butter or vegetable fat          4 tablespoonfuls protein flour
1 cup liquid (vegetable broth, water or cream and water combined)
½ teaspoonful vegetable salt          ¼ teaspoonful paprika

Melt butter, add flour and stir until smooth. Add liquid and seasonings. Stir and cook until smooth and thick.

### BEET SAUCE

½ cup minced cooked beets          1 tablespoonful lemon juice

Combine ingredients and serve hot with beef.

### CELERY-TOMATO COCKTAIL SAUCE

½ cup tomato purée          3 tablespoonfuls lemon juice
½ cup minced celery          3 tablespoonfuls grated onion
1 teaspoonful grated fresh horseradish (optional)

Combine ingredients. Chill thoroughly. Season with vegetable salt.

### CHEESE SAUCE FOR VEGETABLES

3 tablespoonfuls cream cheese          ½ teaspoonful lemon juice
1 teaspoonful vegetable paste          ½ cup tomato purée

Heat all ingredients in double boiler. Stir and cook until well blended.

## CIDER FRAPPE

2 cups fresh cider
1 cup orange juice

1 cup grated apple
1 cup prepared lemon gelatin

Mix and freeze to mush.  Serve in frappe glasses, with meat course.


## CIDER MOLDS FOR BAKED HAM

½ cup boiling water          1½ cups sweet cider, cold
1 tablespoonful granulated gelatin

Soften gelatin by soaking in a little cider for a few minutes.  Add to boiling water and stir until dissolved.  When cool add remaining cider.  Chill in individual molds.  Turn out on crisp lettuce.


## COCKTAIL SAUCE

½ cup tomato purée
3 tablespoonfuls lemon juice
½ cup minced celery

Grated rind of 1 lemon
2 tablespoonfuls minced green pepper
2 tablespoonfuls onion juice

1 tablespoonful grated fresh horseradish

Combine all ingredients.  Keep cold.


## CUCUMBER SAUCE

1½ cups chopped cucumbers
½ teaspoonful grated lemon rind

2 tablespoonfuls lemon juice
1 teaspoonful Tupelo honey

Serve raw with fish; or simmer until cucumber is clear and pack in sterilized jars.


## CUSTARD SAUCE

1 cup thin cream
2 egg yolks, well beaten

¼ teaspoonful vanilla
2 tablespoonfuls Tupelo honey

Pour hot cream over egg yolks, beating constantly.  Cook over hot water until thick and smooth.  Add honey.  When cool stir in flavoring.


## CUSTARD FOR DECORATING
(for soup or protein salads)

2 egg yolks, beaten well          2 tablespoonfuls cream
Small pinch of salt

Mix ingredients, poach in buttered ramekins in hot water.  When cold, slice thinly and cut into fancy shapes.

## DRESSING FOR BROILED FISH

2 egg yolks
¼ cup heavy cream
2 tablespoonfuls lemon juice
2 tablespoonfuls minced parsley
2 tablespoonfuls minced pimiento

Beat all ingredients together. Spread on steamed fish and broil until brown.

## EGG SAUCE

### (for fish)

½ cup butter
Yolks of 3 eggs
2 tablespoonfuls lemon juice
½ teaspoonful paprika
½ cup boiling water
Pinch of salt

Beat butter to a cream, add egg yolks, one at a time and continue beating; when very light add lemon juice, salt and paprika. When ready to serve, add boiling water and beat constantly over hot water until thick.

## FORCEMEAT

1 cup scraped meat
3 egg yolks
2 tablespoonfuls heavy cream

May be made from lamb or breast of chicken. Use a sharp knife to scrape meat. Pound in mortar and press through coarse sieve. Combine ingredients, form in balls, and simmer in celery broth. Use to garnish plain soup, or (with additional cream) for filling vegetables.

## FROZEN APPLESAUCE

2 cups applesauce          Red cherries

Freeze applesauce in individual molds. Turn out and top with red cherries. Serve with meat course, or with whipped cream or lemon sauce for dessert.

## GARLIC SAUCE

### (for venison or other game)

2 tablespoonfuls olive oil
2 tablespoonfuls scraped onion
4 tablespoonfuls grated carrot
1 clove garlic
3 tablespoonfuls minced ham
4 tablespoonfuls lemon juice
2 whole cloves
4 tablespoonfuls minced green pepper
1 cup celery broth
2 egg yolks

Cook vegetables and ham in oil for five minutes. Add lemon juice and celery broth. Pour over beaten egg yolks and cook over hot water until smooth and thick. Remove cloves and garlic. Serve hot.

## GIBLET AND CELERY SAUCE

*(for fowl)*

2 cups chopped celery       1 cup cream
Giblets of fowl, steamed and minced

Steam celery until soft. Put through sieve. Add cream. Heat and beat slightly with rotary beater. Add hot giblets and serve.

## GOLDEN SAUCE

2 egg yolks       1 tablespoonful lemon juice
½ cup celery broth       Pinch of salt
Paprika

Heat celery broth to boiling point. Pour over well beaten egg yolks, and cook over hot water until smooth. Add lemon juice, and one tablespoonful butter. Season with paprika, onion juice, etc.

## GRAPE SAUCE

Add 2 beaten egg yolks to 1 cup cream. Cook over boiling water until smooth. Add ½ cup seedless grapes, cut in halves and drained. A little grated lemon rind may be added.

## HOLLANDAISE SAUCE

½ cup butter       3 egg yolks
1 tablespoonful lemon juice       ½ cup hot water
Pinch of salt

Cream butter, add egg yolks, one at a time, beating constantly. Add salt and lemon juice. Add hot water and cook in top of double boiler until smooth and thickened, stirring continuously.

## HORSERADISH SAUCE

¼ cup grated celery root       2 tablespoonfuls grated horseradish
¼ cup grated white radish       Lemon juice

Combine grated vegetables and mix with enough lemon juice to give desired consistency.

## JELLIED FRUIT PURÉE

3 cups purée of fruit       1½ teaspoonfuls granulated gelatin

Soften gelatin in one-half cup cold water or fruit juice. Add to purée while warm. Chill in individual molds. Serve with game or any meat.

## LEMON BUTTER

Combine melted butter and lemon juice in proportion of one tablespoonful of lemon juice to each half cup of butter. Add minced parsley or paprika if desired. Shake together. One tablespoonful grated lemon rind may be added to each cup butter.

## LEMON CREAM SAUCE

Combine heavy sweet cream and grated lemon rind in proportion of one cup cream and one tablespoonful lemon rind. Heat over water and serve with vegetables or sea food.

## MAYONNAISE COCKTAIL SAUCE

| | |
|---|---|
| 1 cup mayonnaise | 1 tablespoonful paprika |
| ¼ cup thick tomato purée | Vegetable salt |

Combine ingredients. Chill.

## MINT SAUCE

| | |
|---|---|
| ½ cup lemon juice | 1 cup water |
| ½ cup chopped fresh mint | 2 tablespoonful Tupelo honey |

Simmer lemon juice, 1 cup water and ¼ cup mint until reduced to half the quantity. Strain. Add honey. Chill, then add remaining mint.

## MUSHROOM SAUCE

| | |
|---|---|
| 1 cup thick tomato purée | 1 cup broken mushrooms |
| 2 tablespoonfuls olive oil or bacon fat | |

Cook mushrooms in fat until browned. Add tomato purée and cook a few minutes longer to blend. Chopped parsley or any desired herb may be added for seasoning.

## OLIVE SAUCE

### (for Duck)

| | |
|---|---|
| 1 cup lemon gelatin | 2 tablespoonfuls sherry flavoring |
| 2 tablespoonfuls minced ripe olives | |

Soften lemon gelatin over warm water, add flavor and olive rings.

## ONION PEPPER RELISH

1 pint chopped green and red, sweet peppers

| | |
|---|---|
| 1 pint chopped onions | ½ cup lemon juice |
| ½ cup Tupelo honey | 1 teaspoonful celery seed |

1 tablespoonful vegetable salt

Simmer all ingredients together until thickened.

## ORANGE JELLY

### (for Roasts)

| | |
|---|---|
| 2 tablespoonfuls granulated plain gelatin | 2½ cups orange juice |
| | ½ cup cold water |

Orange sections for garnishing

Soften gelatin in cold water. Stir over boiling water until dissolved. Add to orange juice, and mold. Garnish with sections of orange.

## ORANGE MINT SAUCE FOR LAMB

| | |
|---|---|
| ¼ cup finely chopped mint | ¼ cup lemon juice |
| ¼ cup orange juice | ¾ tablespoonful Tupelo honey |

Combine and serve warm.

## ORANGE SAUCE

| | |
|---|---|
| ½ cup orange juice | 4 egg yolks, beaten |
| 1 tablespoonful lemon juice | 1 cup orange dice |

Heat orange and lemon juice. Pour over beaten eggs and cook over hot water until smooth and thickened. Add orange dice. Serve hot.

## PAPRIKA BUTTER

### (for Fish)

| | |
|---|---|
| ½ cup creamed butter | ½ teaspoonful paprika |

1 teaspoonful lemon juice

Beat ingredients, spread over cooked fish.

## PARSLEY SAUCE

### (for hot vegetables)

| | |
|---|---|
| ¼ cup chopped parsley | 1 tablespoonful butter |

Add parsley and butter to "Golden Sauce."

## PEACH SAUCE

### (for Cold Ham)

1 cup finely diced peaches     3 egg yolks
½ cup peach or pineapple juice     Pinch of salt

Beat egg yolks very light, with salt. Gradually add hot fruit juice. Cook over hot water until thick and smooth. Add diced peaches and one tablespoonful sherry flavoring. Chill.

## PRUNE SAUCE

½ pound prunes     2 cups water
1 lemon     2 whole cloves
1 teaspoonful whole allspice
½ cup Tupelo honey

Soak prunes in water. Remove pits. Slice lemon as thinly as possible, discarding seeds. Tie spices in cheesecloth bag. Simmer prunes (and any remaining water), lemon and spices together for an hour. Remove spices. Add honey, cook until desired consistency is reached.

## QUICK MINT SAUCE

1 cup prepared lemon gelatin     2 tablespoonfuls bruised mint leaves

Break gelatin and stir over warm water with mint leaves, until softened. Strain and serve.

## RAISIN SAUCE

¼ cup Tupelo honey     1 cup boiling water
¼ cup lemon juice     ¼ cup seedless raisins
1 tablespoonful butter

Simmer all ingredients except butter until somewhat thickened. Add butter.

## SAVORY SAUCE

### (for fish)

¼ cup butter     2 tablespoonfuls lemon juice
1 tablespoonful minced parsley     ½ teaspoonful paprika
1 tablespoonful pimiento minced     ¼ teaspoonful vegetable salt

Melt butter, add remaining ingredients and heat.

### SHERRY SAUCE

Combine strained orange juice with cooking sherry in proportion to suit taste. Heat, pour over beaten egg yolks, (three for each cup liquid) and cook over boiling water until thickened.

### TOMATO SAUCE

2 tablespoonfuls butter
1 cup tomato purée
1 teaspoonful minced onion
1 tablespoonful minced parsley
1 tablespoonful minced green pepper
¼ teaspoonful celery salt

Cook onion and pepper in butter. Add tomato, parsley and celery salt. Cook for five minutes.

### TOMATO SAUCE WITH APPLE

1 apple
3 ripe tomatoes
1 teaspoonful onion juice
2 tablespoonfuls chopped celery leaves
¼ of a green pepper
2 tablespoonfuls Tupelo honey

Cook all ingredients together until softened. Rub through strainer. Season with vegetable salt. If not as thick as desired, cook until proper consistency is reached.

# VEGETABLES

### ASPARAGUS MOLDS

1 cup asparagus purée (hot)          2. hard-boiled egg yolks
3 egg yolks beaten light             1 cup asparagus tips
                4 large mushroom caps, broiled

Combined hot purée and egg yolks. Place ½ of a hard-boiled egg yolk in each of four individual buttered molds, cut side down. Pour purée over and poach until firm. Turn out and garnish with hot asparagus tips. Set one broiled mushroom cap on each mold.

### ASPARAGUS SOUFFLÉ

1 cup cream                          1 cup asparagus purée
                4 egg yolks, well beaten

Pour hot cream over egg yolks. Beat well. Stir in asparagus purée. Bake in individual buttered molds until firm. Turn out on warm plates, and surround with steamed asparagus tips.

### BAKED BEETS

Scrub beets. Do not cut tops away until after beets are cooked. Bake in casserole in moderate oven until tender. Small young beets are most satisfactory for baking.

### BAKED CARROTS

Scrub carrots. Discard tops. Bake in casserole in moderate oven until tender.

### BAKED CELERIAC

4 cups sliced celeriac          Cream

Arrange vegetable in casserole. Add cream to keep moist, sprinkle with vegetable salt and bake until tender.

## BAKED EGGPLANT

| | |
|---|---|
| 1 eggplant | ½ cup chopped onion |
| 4 tablespoonfuls butter | 3 tablespoonfuls minced green |
| 1½ cups tomato dice | pepper |

½ cup sautéd mushrooms

Cut slice from top of eggplant, remove enough of center to make room for filling. Pare. Rub outside and inside with bacon fat (drippings). Mix tomato, onion, green pepper, mushrooms and butter (melted) and fill eggplant. Set top on and secure with small skewers if necessary. Place in buttered casserole and bake in moderate oven. Baste occasionally with water or vegetable broth.

## BAKED ENDIVE

4 small heads endive          2 tablespoonfuls melted butter

Set endive in buttered casserole. Pour butter over. Cover and bake until tender. Turn each head over when half done. Oven heat must be moderate.

## BAKED KOHL-RABI

Scrub kohl-rabi. Bake in glass casserole until tender.

## BAKED SALSIFY

3 cups sliced raw salsify          1 cup cream

Arrange salsify in buttered casserole. Pour cream over. Add a little vegetable salt. Bake in moderate oven.

## BAKED SAUERKRAUT

4 cups sauerkraut

Place sauerkraut in casserole and cover top with sliced bacon. Bake in hot oven until bacon is crisp. Use same recipe, substituting two cups sliced apple for half given amount of sauerkraut. Or fill red apples with sauerkraut, cover with chopped bacon.

## BAKED STUFFED MUSHROOMS

| | |
|---|---|
| 1 lb. large firm mushrooms | 1½ tablespoonfuls butter |
| ¾ cup white chicken or crab meat | ½ cup cream |
| 1 tablespoonful lemon juice | 2 tablespoonfuls minced green pepper |

Sliced cooked breast of chicken or ham

Peel mushrooms and remove stems. Reserve two tablespoonfuls chopped stems; steam remainder until tender and put through coarse sieve for purée.

To chopped chicken or crab meat add two tablespoonfuls mushroom stems and lemon juice. Fill caps with this mixture. Bake on buttered glass tray until tender.

*Sauce*

Cook green pepper in butter, add mushroom purée and cream. Simmer until well blended. Set baked mushroom caps on meat slices and serve with sauce.

## BAKED TOMATO

4 large ripe tomatoes                4 teaspoonfuls butter

Select firm, ripe tomatoes. Wash and wipe dry. Rub with olive oil. Remove stem and make cavity large enough to hold one teaspoonful butter. Bake in hot oven.

## BAKED TOMATOES FILLED WITH OKRA AND CORN

4 smooth ripe tomatoes        ¼ cup chopped crisp broiled bacon
2 cups steamed okra and grated fresh corn combined

Combine bacon and okra mixture. Season with minced fresh thyme or parsley. Stuff tomatoes with vegetables and bake.

## BAKED TOMATO, MUSHROOM FILLING

4 smooth ripe tomatoes        2 cups blanched button mushrooms
4 tablespoonfuls melted butter

Remove centers from tomatoes. Fill with mushrooms. Pour over each one tablespoonful melted butter. Bake until tender.

## BAKED TURNIPS

Scrub solid young turnips. Bake in glass casserole in moderate oven until tender.

## BEETS IN ORANGE SAUCE

3 cups diced cooked beets        ½ cup orange juice
1 tablespoonful grated orange rind

Simmer beets in orange juice for ten minutes. Sprinkle with grated orange rind.

## BEET TOPS AND LETTUCE

2 quarts chopped beet tops
2 quarts chopped green lettuce

2 tablespoonfuls butter
2 tablespoonfuls lemon juice

Steam beet tops and lettuce together until tender. Melt butter and add lemon juice. Blend with greens. Serve hot.


## BLANCHED BUTTON MUSHROOMS

3 cups button mushrooms     3 tablespoonfuls melted butter

Cook mushrooms in boiling water until tender. Drain thoroughly. Serve in hot dish with melted butter. Save liquid for flavoring vegetable or meat dishes.


## BOILED CORN ON THE COB

Corn when picked very young and tender in full milk may be used as a vegetable; but should be eaten within twenty-four hours of the time of picking, otherwise it should be treated as a starch. Immerse in boiling water, set over direct heat. When water reaches boiling point again the corn is sufficiently cooked. Serve on cob; or cut off and dress with melted butter or cream.


## BOILED COLLARDS

4 small heads collard          2 ounces bacon in piece

Score bacon and boil in a little water to extract flavor. Add collards. Simmer until tender and water is nearly boiled away. Discard bacon.


## BOILED ESCAROLE

Follow instructions for boiled collards.


## BOILED FETTICUS

Follow instructions for boiled collards.


## BOILED WHITE ONIONS

8 medium size onions
2 cups milk

2 cups water
4 tablespoonfuls butter
½ teaspoonful celery salt

Peel onions. Combine milk and water and heat to boiling point. Drop onions into this and simmer until tender. Drain, add butter and vegetable salt and serve immediately.

## BRAISED BORECOLE (*Kale*)

½ peck borecole          4 tablespoonfuls butter

Melt butter in heavy pan. Add drained small heads of borecole. Steam until tender.

## BRAISED CELERY AND CARROTS

2 cups sliced celery                    2 cups diced carrots
3 tablespoonfuls butter

Cook celery and carrots in butter for five minutes. Remove to casserole, add a bit of onion salt if desired. Cook in moderate oven until tender.

## BRAISED CELERY HEARTS

8 celery hearts          ¼ cup butter
¼ cup vegetable broth

Cook whole celery hearts in butter for ten minutes, or until golden colored. Place in casserole, add vegetable broth. Bake in moderate oven until tender.

## BRAISED CHICORY

Substitute chicory for endive in recipe for Braised Endive.

## BRAISED ENDIVE

2 lbs. endive          2 tablespoonfuls butter or bacon fat
3 tablespoonfuls water

Wash and carefully pick over endive. Cut in two-inch lengths. Melt butter or bacon fat in heavy pan, add endive. Cover and cook slowly for fifteen minutes. Remove cover and continue cooking until liquid is absorbed or evaporated.

## BRAISED LETTUCE

4 small heads iceberg lettuce          ½ cup water or celery broth
2 tablespoonfuls butter                ½ teaspoonful vegetable salt

Melt butter and cook lettuce heads in it for five minutes, turning frequently. Remove to buttered casserole and pour liquid around lettuce. Cook until tender, and liquid is evaporated or absorbed.

## BROILED APPLE RINGS

8 rings cut from large apples (skin not removed)
⅓ cup chopped raw fat bacon

Rub apple rings with oil on one side. Place oiled side down on baking sheet. Distribute chopped bacon over rings and broil.

## BROILED MUSHROOM CAPS

1 lb. large solid mushrooms          4 tablespoonfuls olive oil
1 bead of garlic

Peel mushroom caps. Discard stems. (These may be used for purée.) Rub a small bowl with bruised garlic. Place mushrooms in bowl, add oil. Shake about until each cap is covered with oil. Let stand for half an hour. Drain. Broil under hot flame. Place small piece of butter in each cap.

## BROILED SAVORY TOMATO SLICES

Thick slices ripe, firm tomato          Thin slices sweet large onion
Chopped raw fat bacon

Butter large broiling sheet. Set tomato slices on sheet, one onion slice on each. Top with chopped bacon. Broil under medium heat.

## BRUSSELS SPROUTS

Soak in acidulated or salt water for one hour to remove any insects. Rinse in clear water. Steam until tender. Serve with: (1) Melted butter; (2) Lemon juice; (3) Hollandaise Sauce.

## BUTTERED ASPARAGUS CHICORY SPROUTS

1½ lbs. sprouts

Steam until tender. Serve with butter. A good substitute for fresh asparagus.

## BUTTERED BEEFSTEAK LETTUCE

4 heads tender beefsteak lettuce

Steam until tender. Serve with melted butter.

## BUTTERED BEETS

4 cups baby beets          2 tablespoonfuls butter

Steam beets until tender. Remove skins. Shake in melted butter and serve hot. One tablespoonful of lemon juice may be added.

## BUTTERED CARROTS

3 cups steamed carrots          2 tablespoonfuls green pepper  ⎫ optional
1½ tablespoonfuls butter          1 tablespoonful pimiento       ⎭

Melt butter and pour over carrots. Pimiento and green pepper to be cooked in butter for five minutes before adding to carrots, being careful not to brown.

## BUTTERED CARROTS AND PARSLEY ROOT

2 cups carrot rings          2 cups diced parsley root

Steam together until tender.  Serve with butter or desired sauce.


## BUTTERED FRENCH ASPARAGUS BEANS

1½ lbs. beans

Break or cut the beans into two or three-inch lengths.  Steam until tender


## BUTTERED KOHL-RABI

1½ lbs. kohl-rabi          2 tablespoonfuls melted butter

Pare vegetables (thinly) and cut into dice or wedge-shaped pieces.  Steam until tender.  Pour butter over and serve hot.


## BUTTERED MIXED VEGETABLES

1 cup carrot cubes, steamed          ½ cup turnip balls, steamed
½ cup string beans, steamed,          ½ cup cauliflower, steamed
    (2-inch lengths)          ½ cup peas, steamed

Add ½ teaspoonful melted butter to each vegetable.  Arrange in separate mounds on hot dish.  Any combination of vegetables may be used.


## BUTTERED STRING BEANS

4 cups steamed green beans          2 tablespoonfuls melted butter

Combine and serve hot.


## BUTTERED TURNIPS AND PEAS

2 cups steamed fresh green peas          2 cups steamed diced turnips
2 tablespoonfuls melted butter

Arrange vegetables in layers in serving dish.  Pour butter over.


## CABBAGE AND TOMATO CASSEROLE

3 cups chopped cabbage          2 cups tomato dice
½ teaspoonful vegetable salt

Add salt to tomato dice.  In buttered casserole, arrange alternate layers of cabbage and tomato.  Bake in moderate oven.

## CABBAGE WITH BACON

| | |
|---|---|
| 1 firm head cabbage | 3 tablespoonfuls chopped onion |
| 1½ tablespoonfuls bacon drippings | 3 tablespoonfuls shredded carrot |
| ½ cup vegetable broth | |

Quarter cabbage, remove heart. Set in bacon drippings in small casserole. Add onion, carrot and vegetable broth. Bake in moderate oven until tender.

## CARROT PURÉE WITH PEAS

| | |
|---|---|
| 1½ cups carrot purée | 1½ cups steamed tiny peas |
| 2 tablespoonfuls butter | |

Stir peas into purée. Dot with butter. Cook in buttered casserole in moderate oven for twenty minutes.

## CASSEROLE OF APPLE AND GREEN LIMAS

| | |
|---|---|
| 2 cups steamed baby limas | 2 cups applesauce |
| 3 tablespoonfuls butter | |

Arrange alternate layers of beans and apple sauce in buttered casserole. Dot top with butter. Bake in moderate oven.

## CASSEROLE OF CABBAGE AND ONIONS

| | |
|---|---|
| 2½ cups steamed cabbage | 2 tablespoonfuls melted butter |
| 1½ cups steamed onion rings | plus one teaspoonful parsley |

Arrange cabbage and onions in layers in casserole. Sprinkle a little parsley butter over each layer. Bake in moderate oven.

## CASSEROLE OF RED CABBAGE AND APPLE

| | |
|---|---|
| 3 cups red cabbage, shredded | 1 tablespoonful minced onion |
| 2 tablespoonfuls chopped raw fat bacon | 1 teaspoonful celery salt |
| 4 tart apples | |

Cook bacon and onion for a few minutes. Add to cabbage and sliced apples. Bake in moderate oven until tender.

## CAULIFLOWER WITH HOLLANDAISE

Serve steamed cauliflower flowerettes masked with Hollandaise sauce. Garnish with pimiento stars.

## CAULIFLOWER MOLDS

Using recipe for Asparagus Molds, substitute cauliflower for asparagus.

## CAULIFLOWER, PUNGENT SAUCE

| | |
|---|---|
| 1 head cauliflower, steamed | ½ teaspoonful vegetable salt |
| 1½ tablespoonfuls butter | 2 tablespoonfuls minced pepper |
| 2 tablespoonfuls lemon juice | 2 tablespoonfuls minced pimiento |

Set steamed cauliflower in hot serving dish. Pour sauce over.

### SAUCE:

Melt butter, add lemon juice, salt, pepper and pimiento. Blend well and heat.

## CELERY AND BRUSSELS SPROUTS

| | |
|---|---|
| 1½ cups sliced celery | 1 tablespoonful butter |
| 2½ cups steamed sprouts | ¼ cup cream |

Cook celery in butter for five minutes. Add cream. When tender add sprouts. Heat thoroughly and serve.

## CELERY AND CABBAGE IN CREAM

| | |
|---|---|
| 2 cups celery, sliced and steamed | 2 cups steamed shredded cabbage |
| ¼ cup cream | |

Combine ingredients. Serve hot.

## CELERY BROTH

| | |
|---|---|
| 4 cups chopped celery | 3 cups water |

Simmer until celery is soft. Strain. Add ¼ teaspoonful vegetable salt.

## CELERY WITH PARSLEY BUTTER

| | |
|---|---|
| 8 small celery hearts | 4 tablespoonfuls olive oil |

Heat oil in heavy pan. Place celery in oil. Cook gently until tender. Remove to hot platter. Spread top (side) of each stalk with parsley butter.

## CHINESE CABBAGE

| | |
|---|---|
| 4 cups chopped Chinese cabbage | ½ cup tomato purée |
| 2 tablespoonfuls minced onion | |

Steam cabbage until tender. Add tomato purée, and onion cooked for five minutes in olive oil. Mix thoroughly and simmer for a few minutes, to blend.

## CORN PUDDING

2 cups corn
2 tablespoonfuls butter
1 teaspoonful vegetable salt

4 egg yolks
1 cup cream
1 tablespoonful Tupelo honey

Beat egg yolks as light as possible. Add all other ingredients. Poach in casserole in moderate oven.

## CREAMED ASPARAGUS

1½ lbs. asparagus                    1 cup cream

Cook asparagus in steamer until tender. Heat cream until steaming and pour over asparagus.

## CREAMED CABBAGE

1 solid head white cabbage          ½ cup cream

Cut cabbage in quarters. Remove heart. Steam until tender. Add cream and simmer for five minutes.

## CREAMED CABBAGE AND PEPPERS

3 cups chopped steamed cabbage      ¼ cup sautéd sliced pepper
                 ½ cup cream

Combine ingredients and serve.

## CREAMED CARROTS AND MUSHROOMS

1½ cups blanched button          1½ cups steamed diced carrot
     mushrooms                     ½ cup cream
             ½ teaspoonful vegetable salt

Combine ingredients and serve hot.

## CREAMED CORN AND PEPPERS

3½ cups corn cut from cob        1½ tablespoonfuls butter
½ cup shredded green pepper      ½ cup cream

Melt butter in frying pan. Add corn and peppers, cook slowly until tender, but not browned. Add cream, simmer five minutes, and serve hot.

## CREAMED ONIONS

1 pint steamed onions            ¼ cup cream
       ¼ teaspoonful vegetable salt

Heat onions in cream with celery salt. Serve hot.

## CREAMED ONIONS AND TURNIPS

Cook onions in milk until tender. Drain. Slice 1½ cupfuls.
Simmer turnips in celery broth until well done. Drain. Dice 2 cupfuls.
Combine vegetables with ½ cup cream. Season with vegetable salt. Heat thoroughly.

## CREAMED PEAS

4 cups tiny green peas                ½ cup sweet cream

Steam peas until tender. Add cream. Heat.

## CREAMED STRING BEANS

4 cups steamed green beans            ⅓ cup cream

Combine and serve hot.

## CREAMED TURNIPS

3 cups steamed turnip balls           ⅓ cup cream

Combine turnips and cream, heat together.

## CUCUMBER CHICKS

2 large cucumbers                     1 cup vegetable broth
1½ cups chicken forcemeat             8 tender, small celery tips

Make four cups from cucumbers. Fill with chicken forcemeat. Place in buttered casserole, surround with vegetable broth and bake until tender. When ready to serve, insert celery tips on sides of cucumbers for "wings."

## CURRIED CABBAGE

2 tablespoonfuls butter               1 teaspoonful minced parsley
2 tablespoonfuls onion or chives,     5 cups chopped cabbage
   minced                             1 teaspoonful curry powder
                Coconut milk

Cook onion, parsley, and cabbage in butter over direct heat until browned. Add sufficient coconut milk to moisten. Simmer until tender. Five minutes before serving add curry.

## CUSTARD RING WITH VEGETABLES

6 egg yolks          2 cups veegtable broth (or part cream)

Beat egg yolks very light, add hot broth, and ½ teaspoonful vegetable salt. Poach in ring mold in moderate oven until firm. Turn out on hot platter, fill center with cooked peas or vegetable of choice.

## DOCK

Dock, if gathered when quite tender may be served raw as a salad or cooked as any greens.

## EMERALD CAULIFLOWER

1 head steamed cauliflower      3 tablespoonfuls melted butter
2 tablespoonfuls finely minced parsley

Heat parsley in butter. Pour over hot cauliflower.

## EGGPLANT AND TOMATO CASSEROLE

1 eggplant              ¼ cup cream
3 tomatoes          ¼ cup chopped crisp fat bacon

Peel eggplant and cut into thick slices. Skin tomatoes and slice. In buttered baking dish place a layer of eggplant. Sprinkle over this a little chopped bacon. Add a layer of tomatoes and more bacon. When vegetables are arranged, pour cream over all and bake in moderate oven.

## ESCALLOPED CAULIFLOWER AND MUSHROOMS

2 cups flowerettes of cauliflower    1½ cups broken mushrooms
½ cup cream               ½ teaspoonful vegetable salt

Arrange ingredients in buttered casserole. Bake in moderate oven until vegetables are tender.

## FRENCH SORREL

French or Garden Sorrel may be served in any style suitable for spinach.

## GIANT DANDELION

Cultivated dandelion is tender and may be purchased either green or bleached. Green variety is excellent steamed or as a salad.

## GREEN CURLY CABBAGE (*Savoy Cabbage*)

1 head green curly cabbage    1½ tablespoonfuls melted butter

Place cabbage head in pan with small amount of boiling water. Keep cooking rapidly until water is all absorbed or·evaporated, and vegetable is tender. Add butter and serve hot.

## GREENS

POLK — Cook like asparagus.

NETTLE — (gathered when 3 - 4 inches long) — Steam.

SWISS CHARD; PLANTAIN; MILKWEED; LAMB'S QUARTER; MUSTARD GREENS; DANDELION; SWEET POTATO TOPS; BEET TOPS; RADISH TOPS; TURNIP TOPS; LEAVES FROM KOHL-RABI; FETTICUS; all may be steamed, and served with or without butter or sauce.

MILKWEED, DANDELION, and PLANTAIN should be used raw for salads frequently.

## GRILLED TOMATO SLICES

1½ lbs. firm tomatoes

Do not peel. Cut into one-inch slices, discarding uneven top. Dip each slice in oil and broil under hot flame.

## GROUNDCHERRIES AND OKRA

2 cups yellow or red ground cherries        2 tablespoonfuls butter
3 cups okra pods (sliced if large)

Melt butter. Add groundcherries and okra. Simmer together until well blended. Vegetable salt or any herb may be added for flavor.

## MASHED PARSNIPS

4 cups steamed parsnips        1 tablespoonful butter
4 tablespoonfuls cream

Mash parsnips as soon as tender; beat butter and cream into the vegetables and reheat in baking dish.

## MASHED TURNIPS

4 cups steamed turnips

Put through potato ricer and drain. Serve hot. Two tablespoonfuls butter may be added if desired.

## MOLDED CHARD WITH HOLLANDAISE

3 cups steamed chard        Hollandaise sauce

Form four molds of hot steamed chard. Serve with Hollandaise sauce.

## MUSHROOM TIMBALES

2 cups mushroom purée        4 tablespoonfuls cream
4 egg yolks, well beaten      ½ teaspoonful celery salt

Combine ingredients. Pour into buttered timbale molds and poach until firm. (Moderate oven.) Serve with tomato sauce.

## ONIONS, BAKED WITH TOMATO SAUCE

12 white onions                2 cups tomato purée (thick)
2 tablespoonfuls shredded green    ½ teaspoonful vegetable salt
pepper                         Dash of Paprika

Steam onions until tender. Place in buttered casserole and pour over the tomato purée which has been mixed with green pepper and seasonings. Bake in moderate oven.

## ONIONS IN CREAM

4 large mild onions            ½ cup thin cream
½ teaspoonful vegetable salt

Slice onions thinly, arrange in layers in buttered casserole. Pour cream, mixed with vegetable salt, over onions and bake until tender.

## PARSLEY CARROTS

4 cups steamed carrot balls    1 teaspoonful minced chives
1 tablespoonful minced parsley    (optional)
½ cup cream

Combine ingredients and serve hot.

## PEAS, MINTED

4 cups steamed peas        2 tablespoonfuls minced mint
2 tablespoonfuls butter

Combine and serve hot.

## PEPPERED CORN

3 cups young corn              2 tablespoonfuls minced onion
2 tablespoonfuls shredded green    1 tablespoonful minced pimiento
pepper                         ½ teaspoonful vegetable salt
3 tablespoonfuls butter        ½ teaspoonful paprika
or vegetable oil               ½ cup cream

Cook onion and green pepper in butter until golden color. Add remaining ingredients. Simmer until corn is tender and mixture is thickened.

## POTTED BEANS

4 cups tender green beans cut in 1-inch lengths
1 teaspoonful summer savory

Follow directions for Potted Peas.

## POTTED PEAS

4 cups tiny green peas                    6 lettuce leaves

Place three large lettuce leaves in bottom of casserole. Add peas. Top with lettuce leaves. Cover tightly. Set in pan of boiling water in moderate oven and cook until peas are tender. One teaspoonful chopped mint may be added to peas.

## SAUERKRAUT ROSES

4 smooth ripe tomatoes            1½ cups sauerkraut
4 teaspoonfuls butter

Remove centers from tomatoes. Fill with sauerkraut, top with one teaspoonful butter, and bake in moderate oven.

## SAUTEED OYSTER PLANT

4 cups diced oyster plant          1½ tablespoonfuls butter
2 tablespoonfuls minced parsley

Melt butter, add vegetable and a little vegetable salt if desired. Cook gently until tender. Sprinkle with minced parsley.

## SAVORY CARROTS

4 cups carrot rings or balls         ¼ cup minced onion
¼ cup butter                        1 cup vegetable broth
2 egg yolks

Cook onion and carrot in butter until browned a little. Add vegetable broth and simmer until tender. Remove carrot and beat two egg yolks into liquid. Cook until smooth and pour over carrot. Garnish with chopped parsley.

## SAVORY WAX BEANS

3 cups yellow wax beans             1 cup rings of mild onions
1 cup sliced celery                 2 oz. fat bacon, scored deeply

Cover bacon with boiling water. Add beans, celery and onion rings. Simmer until vegetables are tender, and water absorbed. Discard bacon.

## SHREDDED BEETS

5 cups shredded raw beets          2 tablespoonfuls butter

Melt butter in heavy pan. Add beets and cook quickly until tender, stirring occasionally.

## SOUR CABBAGE

4 cups sliced cabbage              2 tablespoonfuls Tupelo honey
2 cups sour apples, diced          ¼ cup minced onion
4 tablespoonfuls lemon juice       ½ cup purple grape juice

Combine onion and apple. Place in casserole in layers alternately with the cabbage. Combine grape juice, honey and lemon juice, and pour over vegetables. Bake in moderate oven.

## SPINACH CUPS

2 cups chopped, drained, steamed   3 well beaten egg yolks
    spinach                        ½ teaspoonful vegetable salt
½ cup thin cream, hot              4 large broiled mushrooms
            2 tablespoonfuls melted butter

Beat cream and salt into egg yolks. Add spinach and place in buttered individual molds. Set in pan of hot water and poach in moderate oven until firm. Turn out on hot plates. Set a mushroom on each timbale of spinach and distribute butter over mushrooms.

## SPINACH RING WITH BEETS

3 cups steamed chopped spinach     2 tablespoonfuls butter
1 tablespoonful lemon juice        2 cups steamed beet cubes or balls

Add butter and lemon juice to spinach and press into ring mold. Keep hot. Turn out on hot platter and fill center with beets.

## SPINACH RING WITH MUSHROOMS

3 cups steamed, chopped spinach    2 cups sautéd button mushrooms
3 tablespoonfuls lemon juice       ¼ cup heavy cream

Combine spinach with lemon juice. Press into ring mold. Keep hot while preparing mushrooms. When mushrooms are sautéd in butter, add cream. Heat well. Turn spinach out on hot platter. Fill center with creamed mushrooms.

## STEAMED BROCCOLI WITH HOLLANDAISE

4 servings steamed broccoli     8 slices broiled bacon
Hollandaise sauce

Place two strips of bacon over each serving of broccoli. Serve with Hollandaise sauce.

## STEAMED BRUSSELS SPROUTS, ORANGE SAUCE

3 cups steamed Brussels sprouts
*Orange Sauce*:
⅓ cup butter     3 tablespoonfuls water and lemon juice (equal parts)
1 tablespoonful grated orange rind

Cook above ingredients together for two minutes. Add ¼ cup orange juice, pour over one beaten egg yolk and cook over hot water until smooth and thick. Pour over hot Brussels sprouts.

## STEAMED CABBAGE

5 cups shredded cabbage

Steam until tender. Serve hot, with or without butter or sauce.

## STEAMED CARROTS AND TURNIPS

2 cups yellow turnip balls     2 cups carrot rings
2 tablespoonfuls butter

Place vegetables in steamer and cook until tender. Dress with melted butter. (Equal amount of peas may be added.)

## STEAMED CAULIFLOWER WITH TOMATO SAUCE

1 large cauliflower     1 cup tomato sauce

Separate cauliflower into flowerettes. Tie in four even bundles. Steam until tender. Serve with tomato sauce.

## STEAMED CELERY AND PEAS

2 cups celery cut in 1-inch lengths     2 cups small green peas
2 tablespoonfuls butter

Place celery and peas in pan together and steam until tender. Serve with melted butter, or sauce if desired.

## STEAMED CELERY-ASPARAGUS

1½ lbs. celery asparagus

Steam until tender and serve with butter or desired sauce.

## STEAMED CHARD

½ peck chard                    2 tablespoonfuls butter

Young tender chard will be steamed, chopped and served like spinach. Melt butter and pour over chard. Older leaves must be treated differently, the green leaf should be stripped from its thick stem, then treated as the young leaf. Stems may be steamed separately and served in the manner of asparagus.

## STEAMED CHICORY

Steam chicory until tender and serve with butter or sauce of choice.

## STEAMED COLLARDS

½ peck selected collards

Chop and steam until tender. May be served with melted butter or desired dressing.

## STEAMED COS LETTUCE

4 heads cos lettuce                    2 tablespoonfuls butter
½ teaspoonful onion juice

Steam cos lettuce until tender. Serve with melted butter combined with onion juice.

## STEAMED FINOCCHIO

4 cups diced stalks and root of finocchio

Steam until tender. Serve with butter, cream or desired dressing.

## STEAMED JAPANESE TURNIP LEAVES

½ peck leaves from Japanese foliage turnip

Steam until tender. Pack into individual molds and serve with melted butter.

## STEAMED LEEK TIPS

Select small tender leeks. Cut to about five inches in length. Tie in individual bundles. Steam until tender. Serve plain, with butter, or cream as desired.

## STEAMED LETTUCE AND PEAS

3 cups tiny green peas          1 tablespoonful grated onion
2 tablespoonfuls butter         1 large heart of lettuce

Melt butter and combine with onion. Cut lettuce heart into four sections and place in buttered dish. Distribute peas evenly in dish and pour butter over. Steam until vegetables are tender.

## STEAMED MANGEL-WURZEL TOPS

Young tender tops may be steamed as kale or other greens.

## STEAMED PARSLEY ROOT

Roots of turnip-rooted parsley may be sliced or diced and steamed. Serve with butter, or sauce if desired.

## STEAMED PEAS

4 cups small green peas      2 tablespoonfuls melted butter

Steam peas until tender. Serve with melted butter.

## STEAMED ROMAINE

Large head of romaine      3 tablespoonfuls butter
1 small onion sliced thinly

Cut leaves into two inch pieces. Melt butter in small sauce-pan, add onion. Cook for five minutes, being careful not to brown onion. Stir into the romaine and place in steamer. Cook until tender.

## STEAMED SAUERKRAUT

3 cups sauerkraut      ¼ teaspoonful caraway seeds

Place sauerkraut mixed with caraway seed in buttered casserole. Add sufficient sauerkraut juice to keep moist and steam until tender.

## STEAMED SEA KALE GREENS

½ peck sea kale leaves

Steam until tender. Serve with butter or sauce of choice.

## STEAMED TENDERGREEN

Tie tendergreen in bundles and steam until tender. May be served in any manner used for spinach.

## STEAMED WHITE CUCUMBER

1½ lbs. fresh white cucumbers

Cut into thick slices, remove seeds making rings of the vegetable. Steam until tender.

## STEAMED WHITE GUMBO

1 quart white gumbo pods

Slice gumbo pods. Steam until tender. Serve with cream or butter.

## STEWED CABBAGE

| | |
|---|---|
| 1 solid head cabbage | 1 tablespoonful parsley, minced |
| 2 tablespoonfuls butter | 1 tablespoonful minced onion |
| ½ cup celery broth | |

Cut cabbage into quarters, remove hard center. Place in buttered au gratin dish. Pour over hot celery broth with butter, onion and parsley. Cook in moderate oven until tender.

## STEWED CUCUMBERS

4 cups 1½ inch slices of cucumber      2 tablespoonfuls butter

Cut cucumber slices in quarters and remove seeds. Simmer in milk until tender. Drain. Melt butter in flat heavy pan. Shake cucumbers in butter over medium heat to expel moisture. Do not brown.

## STEWED TOMATOES

| | |
|---|---|
| 5 ripe tomatoes, sliced | ¼ teaspoonful vegetable salt |
| 1½ tablespoonfuls butter or olive oil | 1 teaspoonful onion juice |
| 1 tablespoonful minced green pepper | |
| 1 tablespoonful Tupelo honey | |

Melt butter. Add remaining ingredients. Cook until tomatoes are tender.

## STRING BEANS WITH HOLLANDAISE

4 cups steamed string beans      1 cup Hollandaise sauce

Arrange beans to form nest. Sauce in center.

## STUFFED BAKED ONIONS

| | |
|---|---|
| 4 large mild onions | 1 egg yolk, beaten light |
| ½ cup chopped ham (cooked) | ½ cup vegetable broth (boiling) |
| ¼ cup chopped green pepper | 2 tablespoonfuls butter |

Skin onions. Cut a slice from top of each. Steam until tender. Remove centers, leaving firm shell. Add two tablespoonfuls onion from centers to prepared filling, dot tops with butter and bake in moderate oven, surrounded by vegetable broth to prevent drying.

### Filling:

Pour hot vegetable broth over egg yolk. Beat well. Add ham and pepper.

## STUFFED PEPPERS

| | |
|---|---|
| 4 green peppers | ½ cup tomato purée |
| 1½ cups chopped cooked meat | 1 tablespoonful minced parsley |
| ½ cup vegetable broth | |

Prepare peppers by removing stem, seeds and membrane. Rub with olive oil. Fill with meat, tomato and parsley combined with ½ teaspoonful vegetable salt. Set in buttered casserole, surround with vegetable broth and bake in moderate oven.

## SUGAR PEAS

| | |
|---|---|
| 2 tablespoonfuls butter | 1 tablespoonful chopped parsley |
| 2 tablespoonfuls minced onion | Pods from peas |
| 1 tablespoonful chopped mint | 3 cups green peas |

Cook all ingredients except shelled peas together with 1½ cups water, until pods are soft. Put through sieve. Add peas to purée and cook until tender.

## SUMMER HASH

| | |
|---|---|
| 2 tablespoonfuls chopped fat bacon | ¼ cup minced green pepper |
| 1 cup sliced sweet onion | 4 cups summer squash (diced) |
| 1 cup tomato dice | Minced parsley |

Prepare squash by removing seeds and cutting into dice. Do not pare if skin is tender. Saute bacon, remove cooked particles from fat. Add onion to fat and cook until lightly browned. Add tomato, pepper and squash. Season with vegetable salt. Cook gently until squash is tender. Remove from pan leaving fat. Add bacon particles and sprinkle with parsley.

## SUMMER SQUASH

Cut squash in quarters, remove seeds and fibre. Steam until tender. Serve with melted butter.

## SUMMER SQUASH IN CREAM

Steam diced squash until tender. Add a sprinkle of vegetable salt and one tablespoonful cream for each cup of cooked squash.

## TOMATOES AU GRATIN

3 cups diced or sliced tomato     1 tablespoonful minced parsley
1 cup cottage cheese     1 tablespoonful minced chives
½ teaspoonful vegetable salt

Arrange tomato and cheese in layers in buttered casserole. Distribute parsley, chives and salt evenly. Bake in moderate oven.

## TURNIPS IN CREAM

4 cups turnip balls     3 tablespoonfuls minced onion
2 tablespoonfuls butter

Cook onion and turnips in butter until browned lightly. Add ½ cup vegetable broth. Simmer until tender, cooking away all moisture. Add ½ cup thin cream and a little vegetable salt.

## TURNIPS, LEMON SAUCE

3 cups steamed diced turnip

While hot, serve with boiled dressing freshly made, and hot.

## TURNIP OR CARROT CUPS WITH PEAS

Large carrots that appear in the markets during the winter months should be used for cups. Steam the carrots until tender. Shape into cups and fill with hot buttered peas. Steamed turnips may be cut into cups and filled with peas.

## VEGETABLE BROTH

4 cups mixed vegetables     4 cups water

Simmer vegetables in water until soft. Strain.

## VEGETABLE PURÉE

Steam any desired vegetable or combination of vegetables, until tender. Press through sieve. If a thick purée is desired, simmer over moderate heat until desired consistency is reached.

### VEGETABLE RING

2 cups purée of mixed vegetables    6 egg yolks (beaten)
1 cup thin cream

Mix ingredients and poach in buttered ring mold. Turn out on hot platter, fill center with meat cubes in desired sauce; or with coddled egg yolks.

### VEGETABLE SOUFFLÉ

Use any desired vegetable. Follow recipe for spinach cups.

### WINTER STRING BEANS

1 can green beans        2 tablespoonfuls chopped fat bacon
2 tablespoonfuls minced onion

Heat beans in their own liquid. Cook bacon and onion together until light brown and add drained beans. Serve hot. Use liquid from beans in making vegetable broth.

### WILTED DANDELION

Combine chopped dandelion with Bacon Dressing. Stir over moderate heat until dandelion is wilted. Sprinkle broken crisp bacon over top.

### BACON DRESSING

3 strips fat bacon                    1 tablespoonful minced onion
2 tablespoonfuls lemon juice          1 teaspoonful Tupelo honey

Pan-broil bacon until crisp. Remove from pan. Add lemon juice, honey and onion to fat in pan. Stir until blended. Add dandelion.

# DESSERTS

### ALMOND JELLY

2 cups cherry gelatin      ½ cup shredded almonds
½ cup red cherry rings

When gelatin is ready to congeal, add almonds and cherry rings. Chill in molds.

### AMBROSIA

Sliced orange sections      Sliced strawberries
Shredded fresh pineapple      Shredded fresh coconut

Arrange fruits and coconut in layers, using equal parts each fruit and about one-third as much coconut as combined fruit.

### APPLE BETTY

Arrange in layers in baking dish, sliced apples, raisins and shredded coconut. Pour a little Tupelo honey over and bake until the apples are tender.

### APPLE SOUFFLÉ

1 cup diced apple      3 egg yolks
2 cups thin cream      ¼ cup Tupelo honey
Cinnamon

Combine heated cream with honey and egg yolks. Stir apple thru custard. Pour into buttered baking dish. Dust with cinnamon. Poach in moderate oven until firm. Serve cold.

### APPLE SPONGE

1 cup applesauce      1 tablespoonful lime juice
1 teaspoonful gelatin      ¼ cup cold water
1 cup whipped cream
3 tablespoonfuls Tupelo honey

Soften gelatin in cold water. Set over hot water and stir until dissolved. Add honey and lime juice. When cooled add to grated apple and set in cool place until almost ready to congeal. Fold in cream. Chill in frappé glasses.

## APPLE WHIP

4 medium sized apples                  ½ cup chopped raisins
1 cup nut meal                         1 cup whipped cream
                Few grains grated nutmeg

Grate apples and add nut meal and raisins. Combine with cream and nutmeg. Place in individual serving dishes and chill.

## APPLESAUCE CAKE

1½ cups and 2 tablespoonfuls protein flour
1 teaspoonful baking soda              1½ cups chopped raisins
1 teaspoonful cinnamon                 ¼ cup soft butter
¾ teaspoonful cloves                   ¾ cup Tupelo honey
1 cup chopped nuts                     2 egg yolks
                1 cup applesauce

Bake in glass or pottery casserole at moderate temperature.

## APRICOT PUFF

2 cups apricot purée                   1 tablespoonful granulated gelatin
2 tablespoonfuls cold water            1 teaspoonful lemon juice
                ⅓ cup Tupelo honey

Soften gelatin in cold water. Stir over hot water until dissolved. Add to apricot purée with honey and lemon juice. Chill. Beat with wire whisk until very light, chill in mold. Serve with custard sauce.

## AVOCADO ICE

2 medium sized avocados                ¼ cup Tupelo honey
                3 tablespoonfuls lemon juice
                        *or*
2 tablespoonfuls lime juice            1 cup orange ice

Put avocado pulp through sieve. Combine with honey and juice. Place in freezing tray. When frozen to a mush, remove from tray and beat as light as possible. Return to continue freezing.

## BAKED APPLES, LEMON SAUCE

4 large baking apples                  ¾ cup cold lemon gelatin

Prepare apples for baking as usual. Do not fill centers. Bake. When tender, remove from oven and fill with gelatin. Heat from apples will melt the gelatin and make sauce of it. Serve warm or cold with a spoonful of whipped cream.

## BAKED APPLES, ORANGE SAUCE

4 baking apples

1 cup orange juice

2 tablespoonfuls lemon juice

2 tablespoonfuls butter

⅓ cup chopped raisins

4 egg yolks, beaten light

Prepare apple for baking, stuff with raisins and butter, mixed. Pour ½ fruit juices over apples and bake until tender. Remove apples from baking dish. To juice remaining in dish add enough boiling water to make ½ cup. Add to ½ cup orange juice, and remaining lemon juice and heat to boiling point with ⅓ cup Tupelo honey. Combine with egg and stir over hot water until thick. Pour over apples and serve when cold.

## BAKED APPLE DUMPLINGS

4 tart baking apples          Protein Biscuit Dough

Roll biscuit dough ¼ inch thick. Cut into 6 inch squares. Place a pared and cored apple in center of each square, fill cavity of apple with raisins, dust with cinnamon. Fold dough up over apple, moisten edges with water and seal. Prick with fork. Bake in hot oven for 15 minutes, reduce heat to moderate and continue baking for about 25 minutes.

## BAKED CUSTARD

4 egg yolks

2 cups light cream

4 tablespoonfuls Tupelo honey

Vanilla, if desired

Beat egg yolks slightly, add honey and cream, strain and pour into custard cups, and set in a pan of hot water. Place in a moderate oven and bake until firm in the center, which can be determined by plunging a knife through the center. If the knife comes out clean, the custard is baked.

This may be varied by adding nutmeg, cinnamon, raisins or coconut.

## BAKED PEACHES

4 large peaches          4 tablespoonfuls orange juice

4 tablespoonfuls Tupelo honey

Scald and peel peaches. Set in buttered baking dish; add honey and orange juice. Cover and bake until fruit is clear. Chill and serve with whipped cream.

## BAKED PEARS

4 large ripe pears          1 teaspoonful lemon juice

Cut slice from top of pears. Remove cores. Sprinkle with lemon juice and bake slowly until tender. Fruit may be pared if preferred.

## BAKED STUFFED APPLES

4 baking apples                    ½ cup English walnuts
4 tablespoonfuls chopped, dried apricots, soaked until tender

Prepare apples for baking. Fill centers with nuts and apricots mixed. Pour
1 tablespoonful Tupelo honey over each apple. Bake until tender.


## BAKED STUFFED ORANGES

4 large seedless oranges     About ½ cup shredded fresh coconut
½ cup chopped seeded raisins

Cut thick slice from top of oranges. Remove all pulp carefully to prevent
crushing. Discard all membrane, cut pulp into even-sized pieces. Combine
with raisins and coconut and fill orange shells. (Quantity of coconut will
vary with size of oranges.) Set in shallow baking dish; surround with equal
parts Tupelo honey and orange juice, and bake in moderate oven. Keep enough
liquid in dish to prevent browning or drying of orange rind.


## BROILED GRAPEFRUIT

Remove seeds from grapefruit halves, taking care not to break sections. Leave
pithy centers to preserve shape. Add 1 tablespoonful Tupelo honey to each half.
Place in heated oven or broiler. Cook until skin begins to brown and the fruit
is heated through.


## CHERRY COBBLER

2 cups sour cherries, sweetened to taste with Tupelo honey
Protein Muffin Batter

Place cherries in baking dish. Drop muffin batter on top of fruit and bake
in hot oven for 15 minutes, reduce heat and continue baking at moderate temperature about 30 minutes. Peaches, apricots or berries may be substituted for
cherries.


## CHERRY CUSTARD

Follow recipe for Apple Soufflé, substituting 1 cup drained canned cherries
for apple.

## CHILDREN'S EASTER DESSERT

| | |
|---|---|
| 1 cup strawberry gelatin | 1 cup lime gelatin, colored green |
| 1 cup orange gelatin | 8-10 eggs |

Cut small hole in end of egg shells; remove eggs by shaking gently. Rinse shells and remove membrane from inside if possible. Pour cool gelatin into shells. Let stand 24 hours.

*Bowl*: Pour one quart custard in bowl. Let stand 24 hours. Cut out center to form nest. Carefully remove shells from gelatin eggs and place in bowl. Serve with thin cream.

## CIDER SPICED APPLES

Prepare apples for baking. Fill with Tupelo honey or fruit. Stick with whole cloves. Mix 1 cup cider with 3 tablespoonfuls Tupelo honey and use part of this mixture in bottom of baking dish to prevent drying or browning. Baste with remaining cider mixture.

## COCONUT APPLES

| | |
|---|---|
| ½ cup chopped raisins | ½ cup shredded coconut |
| 2 tablespoonfuls coconut milk | 4 baking apples |

Core apples and pare half way to bottom. Dip pared halves in orange juice, and set apples upright in buttered au gratin dish. Fill with raisins mixed with coconut and coconut milk. Bake until tender.

## COCONUT ICE CREAM

| | |
|---|---|
| 2 cups thin cream | 1 cup double cream (whipped) |
| 1 cup grated coconut | 1 oz. Tupelo honey |

Combine ingredients and freeze. If prepared in electric unit, remove from pan when partially frozen, beat thoroughly and return to freeze.

## CURRANT WHIP

| | |
|---|---|
| 2 cups lemon gelatin | 1 cup currant gelatin |

Whip chilled lemon gelatin until light and fluffy. Break red currant gelatin with spoon, and fold into beaten part. Pile into sherbet glasses and chill.

## CUSTARD SAUCE

| | |
|---|---|
| 1 cup 20% cream | 1½ tablespoonfuls Tupelo honey |
| 1 egg yolk | 5 drops vanilla |

Heat cream in top of double boiler. Pour over egg yolk beaten with honey. Return to double boiler and cook until mixture will coat a spoon. Strain and add vanilla.

## EMERGENCY DESSERT

2 cups whipped cream        ½ teaspoonful grated orange rind
2 cups diced chilled fruit

Combine and chill in frappé glasses. Top with cherries or orange cubes.

## FROSTED PINEAPPLE

Cut pineapple in halves lengthwise. Pare and remove eyes. Cut out core. Cut into ½ inch strips then cut these strips in halves crosswise. Place in freezing tray. Freeze lightly.

## FROZEN APRICOT PURÉE

1 can unsweetened apricots        ¼ cup Tupelo honey

Press apricots through colander. Add honey and mix. Freeze and serve with whipped cream or pieces of apricot for garnish.

## FROZEN CUSTARD

1 pint thin cream              ½ pint whipping cream
4 egg yolks, well beaten       1 teaspoonful pure vanilla extract
1½ oz. Tupelo honey

Heat thin cream, pour over beaten egg yolks and cook over hot water until smooth. Add honey. Cool. Add remaining cream and vanilla. Freeze.

## FROZEN FRUIT PUDDING

2 cups cream (20%)             1 cup whipped cream (40%)
2 egg yolks, well beaten       1 cup mixed fresh fruits
1½ oz. Tupelo honey

Heat 20% cream, add to egg yolks, and cook over hot water until thickened. Add honey. Cool. Blend with whipped cream and a few drops pure vanilla extract. Fold in fruit, and freeze.

## FROZEN FRUIT

1 cup sliced strawberries          1 cup shredded orange
1 cup diced canned peaches         1 cup juice from canned peaches
  (unsweetened)                      A little non-alcoholic brandy flavor
1 oz. Tupelo honey

Place all ingredients in freezing tray. Stir two or three times while freezing, always from edge toward center of pan. Do not allow to become too hard.

## FROZEN PUDDING

2 quarts vanilla ice cream
½ cup red sour cherries (cooked
      until candied in honey)
Rum flavoring to taste

½ cup chopped raisins
½ cup sliced almonds
¼ cup shredded citron

Ice cream must be soft enough to stir. Add remaining ingredients, stir until evenly distributed. Freeze in trays.

## FROZEN PUDDING SAUCE

1 cup 40% cream          ¼ cup Tupelo honey
1 teaspoonful vanilla or Sherry flavoring

Whip the cream until as light as possible. Add honey and flavoring. Freeze in tray.

## FRUIT BASKETS

1½ cups strawberry gelatin
1½ cups lemon gelatin

¾ cup mixed chopped fruit
¼ cup whipped cream

Cool gelatin in 4 ramekins. When firm, turn out, then invert. Carefully remove centers and fill with chilled fruit. Top with whipped cream. Arrange orange rind strips for handles.

## FRUIT BOMB

3 cups whipped cream (flavored and sweetened with Tupelo honey)
2 cups thick fruit purée or chopped fruit

Line mold with whipped cream. Set in electric refrigerator and freeze. Fill center with fruit and cover with balance of whipped cream. Freeze thoroughly. Turn out on cold plate and cover with shredded almonds.

## FRUIT COMPOTE

Bake pear halves with a little honey until clear. Place in compote. Cover with stewed red raspberries. Cool.

## FRUIT GELATIN

¼ cup cold water                1¼ cups fruit juice
½ cup boiling water             1 tablespoonful granulated gelatin
3 tablespoonfuls Tupelo honey

Soften gelatin by soaking in cold water for a few minutes. Dissolve in boiling water. Add honey. When cool add fruit juice.

Gelatin made with colorless fruit juices such as cider should be slightly tinted with pure vegetable coloring.

When using fresh pineapple or fresh pineapple juice, always heat to boiling point before adding to gelatin mixture or it will prevent congealing.

## FRUIT MOLD

2 tablespoonfuls cold water     ½ cup pitted red cherries
½ cup boiling water             ½ cup seedless white grapes
1 cup unsweetened fruit juice   ¼ cup diced pineapple
1 tablespoonful granulated gelatin   ¼ cup loganberries or raspberries
¼ cup Tupelo honey

Drain all juice from fruit. Soften gelatin in cold water. Dissolve in boiling water. Cool. Combine all ingredients. Chill in ring mold. Turn out on cold plate. Fill center with whipped cream.

*Note*: Always heat fresh pineapple to scalding point, and cool before adding to any gelatin combination.

## FRUIT MOUSSÉ

2 cups fruit purée
2 cups whipped cream, sweetened with Tupelo honey

If fruit purée is not thick add one teaspoonful plain gelatin (softened and melted over hot water). Fold chilled purée and whipped cream together and freeze, in mold.

## FRUIT PIE

Press freshly grated coconut ¼ inch thick in bottom and around sides of individual baking dishes to form crust. Fill with sliced fresh or canned fruit and chopped raisins. Cover top with coconut. Bake at moderate temperature until fruit is tender.

## FRUIT PURÉE

Press steamed, baked or canned fruit through a sieve. May be sweetened to taste with Tupelo honey.

## FRUIT SOUFFLÉ

1 cup purée of fruit
1 cup cream

3 egg yolks well beaten
1 tablespoonful granulated gelatin

Soften gelatin in ¼ cup cream. Heat remaining cream and pour over egg yolks. Stir and cook over hot water until smooth. Add softened gelatin. Stir until dissolved. When cool, add fruit purée. Chill in molds. Serve with chopped fruit.

## GLACE FRUIT PIE

2 cups drained canned peaches, apricots or cherries
or a combination of these
½ cup Tupelo honey    1 tablespoonful granulated gelatin
1½ cups fruit juice

Soften gelatin in ½ cup of the cold fruit juice. Heat remaining juice to boiling point, add soaked gelatin and stir until dissolved. Add honey, cool mixture until it begins to congeal. Arrange drained fruit in baked protein pie shell, pour gelatin mixture over and chill. Top with whipped cream.

## GRAPE FRAPPÉ

2 cups grape juice
½ cup orange juice
1 tablespoonful lemon juice

1 cup cold water
1 cup boiling water
2 tablespoonfuls granulated gelatin
¼ cup Tupelo honey

Soften gelatin in a little of the cold water. Dissolve in boiling water. Cool. Combine all ingredients and freeze to a mush.

## GRAPE SHERBET

2 cups grape juice
1 tablespoonful granulated gelatin

2 tablespoonfuls cold water
1 pint thin cream
¼ cup Tupelo honey

Soak gelatin in water. Add to ½ cup grape juice and the honey, and heat until gelatin is dissolved. Add to remainder of grape juice and chill. Freeze to a mush in rotary freezer, then add cream and continue freezing.

## HONEY APPLE PIE

Line a pie pan with Protein Pastry. Fill with halved or quartered cooking apples. Bake until apples are tender and crust crisp. Pour ¾ cup Tupelo honey over apples, distributing it evenly. Allow pie to stand until apples have absorbed honey. May be topped with whipped cream sweetened with Tupelo honey and flavored with a little cinnamon or nutmeg.

## HONEY BLANC MANGE

| | |
|---|---|
| 1 tablespoonful granulated gelatin | 3 tablespoonfuls Tupelo honey |
| 1 pint thin cream | ½ teaspoonful vanilla |
| ⅛ teaspoonful nutmeg | |

Soften gelatin by soaking in ¼ cup cream for 5 minutes. Add honey and heat over boiling water until gelatin is dissolved. Strain into remaining cream, adding vanilla and nutmeg. Pour into sherbet glasses and chill.

## HONEY PARFAIT

| | |
|---|---|
| 4 egg yolks | ¾ cup Tupelo honey |
| 2 cups heavy cream (40%) | |

Heat honey in double boiler to scalding. Pour slowly over beaten egg yolks, beating constantly. Cool. Whip cream and combine with honey mixture. Freeze in tray.

## JEWELED JELLY

½ cup green lime gelatin, cut into tiny dice
½ cup red strawberry gelatin cut into tiny dice
½ cup orange gelatin cut into tiny dice
2 cups lemon gelatin

Beat cool lemon gelatin in pan of cracked ice until thickened. When ready to set, stir diced clear colored gelatins through and turn into mold. Chill.

## LADY WASHINGTON FROZEN PUDDING

| | |
|---|---|
| 2 cups mashed red cherries | 1 cup grated coconut |
| 2 cups chopped seeded raisins | 3 cups whipping cream |
| 1 tablespoonful granulated gelatin | 1 teaspoonful vanilla |
| 15 drops almond extract | |

Soak gelatin in ¼ cup juice from cherries. Stir over hot water until dissolved. Add cherries and raisins. Chill. Beat cream until light. Add vanilla, almond extract, and half of the coconut. Beat fruit combination until smooth; combine with cream mixture.

Line mold with remaining coconut, reserving enough to sprinkle over top. Turn pudding into mold; cover top with coconut and freeze. Serves 12.

## LEMON CHIFFON PUDDING OR PIE FILLING

1½ cups orange juice         Grated rind of ½ lemon
¼ cup lemon juice             3 egg yolks
½ cup Tupelo honey         1 tablespoonful granulated gelatin
1 cup whipping cream

Heat lemon and orange juice with honey in double boiler. Beat egg yolks as light as possible. Pour hot juices over egg yolks, stirring constantly. Return to double boiler and cook until smooth and thickened. Stir gelatin (softened by soaking for 5 minutes in 4 tablespoonfuls cold water) into hot mixture. Stir until completely dissolved. Cool until slightly thickened, then beat as light as possible with rotary beater. Whip cream and combine with lemon mixture. Chill in sherbet glasses. Top with whipped cream to serve. This pudding may be used as filling for lemon chiffon pie with protein pastry.

## LEMON ICE

½ cup Tupelo honey        ¼ cup lemon juice
2½ cups orange juice      ¼ cup cold water
1½ teaspoonfuls granulated gelatin

Soften gelatin in cold water. Dissolve over hot water. Add to fruit juice and honey. Freeze to a mush in tray in electric refrigerator. Remove to large chilled bowl and beat with rotary beater for several minutes. Return to freezing unit and continue freezing. Stir from sides to center of tray two or three times during last freezing. The beating process may be repeated to produce a very smooth product.

## LEMON TARTS

1 cup orange juice        6 tablespoonfuls lemon juice
1 cup Tupelo honey       Grated rind of 1 lemon
4 egg yolks               1 tablespoonful granulated gelatin
1 cup whipping cream

Soak gelatin in lemon juice. Heat orange juice and honey to boiling point; add to beaten egg yolks. Cook until mixture will coat spoon. Add soaked gelatin and stir until dissolved. Add lemon rind and cool until mixture begins to thicken. Beat as light as possible. Fold in whipped cream. Pour into baked protein pastry shell. Chill. May be topped with whipped cream.

## MINCE MEAT

2 pounds sour apples, cored
1 pound finely shredded raw
carrot
1½ pounds seedless raisins
2 cups Tupelo honey
Grated rind of 3 oranges
and 2 lemons
½ pint grapejuice
1 teaspoonful cinnamon
½ teaspoonful allspice
½ teaspoonful cloves

Put apples and raisins through food chopper. Combine all ingredients and simmer slowly for about one hour.

## MINCE-MEAT APPLES

4 baking apples      ¾ cup mince-meat

Prepare apples for baking. Fill cavities with mince-meat. Bake in moderate oven until tender. When cold, serve with whipped cream flavored with sherry or rum flavoring.

## MOCHA BAVARIAN

1 tablespoonful granulated gelatin
1½ cups prepared coffee substitute, strong, hot
½ cup cold water      6 tablespoonfuls Tupelo honey
1 cup whipping cream

Soak gelatin in cold water. Dissolve in hot liquid. Add honey. Chill until slightly congealed. Beat as light as possible. Whip cream, add a few drops vanilla extract. Combine gelatin mixture and cream. Chill in mold.

## ORANGE ICE

1 quart orange juice
½ cup lemon juice
⅔ cup Tupelo honey
1 tablespoonful granulated gelatin
Grated rind of one large orange

Soften gelatin by soaking in ½ cup orange juice. Heat over boiling water until completely dissolved. Add remaining ingredients. Freeze in rotary freezer.

## ORANGE JELLY RING

2 cups orange gelatin      2 cups diced fruit
2 tablespoonfuls claret flavoring

Mold gelatin in ring. Pour claret flavoring over fruit and chill. When ready to serve, turn out jelly ring and fill center with drained fruit. Serve with whipped cream to which is added ¼ cup shredded almonds.

## ORANGES WITH CUSTARD

2 oranges (sections)                    1½ cups cream
6 egg yolks, beaten

Heat cream, add to egg stirring constantly. Cook over hot water until smooth and thick. Add 1 oz. Tupelo honey. Arrange orange sections in glass dish. Pour custard over. Chill. Serve with whipped cream.

## PARTY FRUIT ICE

1 cup orange juice                    1 cup whole cherries
¼ cup lemon juice                     ½ cup boiling water
1 cup shredded pineapple              ¼ cup cold water
1 cup crushed peaches                 2 cups cold water
2 tablespoonfuls granulated gelatin
½ cup Tupelo honey

Dissolve gelatin (previously soaked in ½ cup cold water) in boiling water. Add fruits, honey, fruit juices and two cups cold water. Freeze.

*Note*: If fresh pineapple is used, scald and chill before adding to gelatin mixture.

## PEACH CUSTARD

2 cups thin cream                     4 egg yolks, well beaten
1 teaspoonful tartaric acid baking    2 tablespoonfuls melted butter
   powder                             2 cups sliced peaches
⅓ cup Tupelo honey

Arrange sliced peaches, or peach halves in buttered casserole. Pour over these the remaining ingredients beaten together. Bake in moderate oven until custard is firm.

## PEACH GELATIN MOLD

1 tablespoonful granulated gelatin,   ½ cup boiling water
   softened in 2 tablespoonfuls       2 cups crushed peaches
   cold water                         1 cup whipped cream
Fresh peach halves for garnishing
⅓ cup Tupelo honey

Add softened gelatin to boiling water, stir until dissolved. Add honey. Add crushed peaches and a few drops pink vegetable coloring. Cool. When ready to congeal, beat with rotary beater until very light and fluffy. Fold in whipped cream. Chill thoroughly. Turn out on cold plate. Surround with peach halves filled with shredded almonds.

## PEACH GRANITE

1 cup chopped peaches
1 cup orange juice

1 cup white grape juice
⅓ cup Tupelo honey

Freeze combined ingredients in rotary freezer.

## PEACH MELBA

4 balls vanilla ice cream              4 halves fresh peaches
1 cup crushed raspberries sweetened with Tupelo honey
1 cup whole red raspberries

Place ice cream in glasses, set peaches on cream. Cover with crushed berries and top with whole berries.

## PECAN MOUSSÉ

2 cups whipping cream
1 teaspoonful vanilla

1 cup chopped pecans
¼ cup Tupelo honey

Whip cream, add nuts, honey and vanilla. Freeze in electric unit.

## PLUM PUDDING

2 egg yolks
¼ cup orange juice
⅓ cup Tupelo honey
Grated rind of 1 large orange
½ teaspoonful cinnamon
2 teaspoonfuls tartaric acid baking powder

2 cups nutmeal
¼ cup sliced raisins
¼ cup red cherries, drained
¼ teaspoonful nutmeg

Steam 2 hours in mold.

## PROTEIN COOKIES

1 cup butter or vegetable shortening
1 cup Tupelo honey
1 teaspoonful baking soda
½ teaspoonful cinnamon

½ teaspoonful allspice
½ teaspoonful cloves
3¾ cups protein flour

Boil butter and honey together for 2 minutes. Sift flour, spices and soda together. When honey mixture is cool, stir in flour mixture; add a little more flour if necessary to make a soft dough. Chill thoroughly. Roll and cut with cookie cutter. Bake in moderate oven.

## PROTEIN PASTRY

2½ cups sifted protein flour
¾ cup butter or vegetable shortening
Ice water, about ⅓ cup

Cut butter into flour with pastry blender or knives. Add water very slowly, stirring with fork until mass can be worked together; use as little water as possible. Work dough until smooth, handling as little as possible. Chill. Roll out ⅛ inch thick, for top and bottom crust of pies. For tarts, cut rounds large enough to cover the bottom of muffin tins. Bake in hot oven.

## QUINCE MOUSSÉ

1 cup quinces stewed over slow heat until red
2 cups whipped cream
Almond flavor

Press quinces thru colander. Sweeten to taste with Tupelo honey. Add to cream with flavoring. Freeze in electric unit.

## RAISIN SYRUP

1 package seedless raisins (15 oz.)          3 cupfuls water

Cook raisins in water fifteen minutes. There should be 1⅓ cupfuls thin syrup, equal to ⅜ cupful brown sugar for sweetening purposes. This may be condensed by boiling.

The raisins need not be discarded, as they may be used in cooking foods, in salads, as a breakfast dish, or a dessert (with or without cream), for any type lunch or dinner.

## RAISIN AND WALNUT ICE CREAM

1 cup heavy cream                    ¼ cup chopped walnuts
½ cup chopped raisins                1 cup thin cream

Beat heavy cream. Add remaining ingredients and place in electric freezing unit. Stir two or three times while freezing, always from edge to center of tray.

## RASPBERRY ICE

1 cup raisin syrup                   1 tablesponful lemon juice
1½ cups raspberry juice              1 teaspoonful granulated gelatin

Soften gelatin in two tablespoonfuls cold water. Heat raisin juice to boiling point and dissolve gelatin in this. Cool. Combine all ingredients and freeze.

## REFRIGERATOR ICE CREAM

2 cups light cream (20%)
2 teaspoonfuls granulated gelatin
2 teaspoonfuls vanilla

½ cup Tupelo honey
½ cup cold water
¾ cup heavy cream (40%)

Soften gelatin by soaking in cold water. Dissolve over boiling water. Combine with honey and light cream. Place in freezing tray and allow to remain until slightly thickened. Remove from tray and beat until as light as possible. Beat heavy cream, add to gelatin mixture and vanilla. Return to tray to continue freezing.

## RUM BISQUE ICE CREAM

1 quart whipping cream
2 tablespoonfuls rum flavoring
1 cup chopped red cherries

1 cup shredded almonds
½ cup chopped raisins
1 teaspoonful grated orange rind

⅓ cup Tupelo honey

Combine ingredients and freeze in rotary freezer.

## SNOWBALLS

¼ cup cold water
½ cup orange juice
½ cup boiling water

1 cup purée of canned pears
1 tablespoonful granulated gelatin
½ cup shredded coconut

3 tablespoonfuls Tupelo honey

Soften gelatin in cold water. Dissolve in boiling water. Add honey. Add orange juice and chill. Fold into pear purée and beat with rotary beater until light. Chill in round bottom cups. Turn out on individual plates covered with whipped cream. Sprinkle with coconut.

## SOY BEAN CHEESE WAFERS

4 egg yolks
½ cup sliced seeded raisins
6 tablespoonfuls whey

¾ cup soy bean flour
¼ cup fresh cottage cheese
⅓ cup sliced pecans

¼ teaspoonful baking soda
1 teaspoonful tartaric acid baking powder

Beat egg yolks; add remaining ingredients. Chill. Shape into small flat wafers, or slice like ice box cookies. Bake in moderate oven.

## SOY BEAN PASTRY

1¼ cups soy bean flour                    1 egg yolk
Thin cream

Sift flour and add a few grains salt. Add egg yolk mixed with 2 tablespoonfuls cream, mix and add enough cream to hold mixture together. Roll out on pastry board. Bake in moderately hot oven.

## SOY BEAN WAFERS

4 egg yolks                                1 cup soy bean flour
½ cup sliced seedless raisins              ½ cup chopped pecans
6 tablespoonfuls cream                     ¼ teaspoonful baking soda
¼ teaspoon allspice

Combine egg yolks and cream. Add raisins, then all dry ingredients sifted together. Fold in the nuts. Bake at moderate temperature.

## STEAMED RAISINS

Soak seedless raisins in warm water until tender. Steam until puffed.

## STRAWBERRY CREME

2 cups mashed strawberries                 ½ cup cold water
1 tablespoonful granulated gelatin         2 cups whipped cream
⅓ cup Tupelo honey

Soak gelatin in cold water for 5 minutes. Set over hot water and stir until dissolved. Add honey. Mix with slightly crushed strawberries. When cold and ready to congeal, fold in whipped cream. Chill and serve in frappé glass. Garnish with whole strawberries.

## STRAWBERRY ICE

1 quart ripe strawberries                  ⅔ cup Tupelo honey
1 teaspoonful granulated gelatin

Soften gelatin by soaking in ¼ cup cold strawberry juice. Dissolve over boiling water. Crush strawberries and put through sieve. Add gelatin and honey. Freeze in rotary freezer.

## TOMATO SWEET

½ cup sliced raisins                       1 cup whipping cream
1 cup drained diced ripe tomatoes
Grated rind of 1 lemon

Whip the cream, fold in remaining ingredients, place in sherbet glasses and chill thoroughly.

## TROPICAL GELATIN

2 cups orange gelatin                    1 cup shredded drained pineapple
1 cup grated coconut

Add pineapple and coconut to prepared gelatin. Chill in individual molds.
Serve with custard sauce, garnish with grated coconut. Always heat pineapple
to boiling point, then chill before adding to a gelatin mixture.

## TROPICAL GRAPEFRUIT

Remove seeds and pith from center of grapefruit halves. Fill cavity with
crushed pineapple. A little Tupelo honey may be added if desired.

# SECTION THREE
# Starch Foods

$\mathcal{S}$ ECTION THREE brings recipes for carbohydrate foods and compatible dishes to accompany them. Carbohydrate foods supply energy to be used in carrying on all body functions. Along with the fat in the diet these foods furnish all the fuel for maintaining body heat, for physical and mental activity. While this class of food is necessary it must be remembered that it is acid forming; therefore the part of wisdom is to avoid indulging in excess quantities. Too high intake of carbohydrate food is one important cause of overweight.

Potential energy of carbohydrate foods may be measured by scientific tests. But each individual is a laboratory and a rule unto himself, — due partly to the variability of rate of metabolism and partly to amount of energy expended and conditions under which it is expended.

The fallacy of depending upon a certain given amount of food to supply a positive calculated energy value in each and every case has been demonstrated some time since. Serving interesting and tasteful vegetables and compatible salads with the starchy or sweet foods has proven the most satisfactory method of limiting the intake of concentrated carbohydrates to desirable amounts.

Choose all items on the carbohydrate menu from this section.

More than any other class of food the starches and sugars are responsible for human ills. The reason is that they are capable of being refined to such a degree that only fine starch or almost pure carbon in the form of sugar can be obtained from them. These devitalized products have been popularized and now form a large part of the diet of the majority of civilized people. The statement that fifty percent of the food eaten by the Average American belongs to this group, is no doubt true. But if whole grain cereals, honey, natural sugars (maple and unrefined cane) and the starchy vegetables (potatoes, sweet and white; artichokes, yams, pumpkins) with the sweet fruits (dates, figs, raisins and bananas) are incorporated in the dietary replacing the denatured articles usually eaten, — then these foods can and will serve the important purpose of supplying life-giving minerals and vitamins and at the same time yield their full quota of energy value.

# INDEX --- SECTION 3

## BEVERAGES AND COCKTAILS

## RELISHES

## SOUPS

## SALADS

# CARBOHYDRATE SALADS

# SALAD DRESSINGS

# MAIN COURSE

# VEGETABLES

# SAUCES

# DESSERTS

# CAKES AND COOKIES

# BREAD

# SANDWICHES

# BEVERAGES

### ALMOND MILK

2 tablespoonfuls almond butter    1 teaspoonful Tupelo honey

Add 1 cup hot water, a little at a time, to make a smooth mixture.

### CEREAL BEVERAGES

Cereal Beverages are prepared as coffee,—that is by either the drip or the percolator method. Follow directions on package.

### CHILLED HONEY CHOCOLATE

3 tablespoonfuls Tupelo honey          ½ teaspoonful vanilla
1½ cup water                           ½ cup cream
2 tablespoonfuls cocoa or grated chocolate

Heat 1 cup water to boiling point, add cocoa and honey. Stir and cook until well blended. Chill and add remaining water and cream with vanilla. Serve very cold. May be topped with whipped cream.

### COCONUT BISQUE

1 quart coconut milk                   1 pint raw tomato juice

Shake together; serve cold.

### COCONUT MILK (*Natural*)

Puncture fresh coconut and drain off milk from center. Strain.

### COCONUT MILK (*Prepared*)

Grate one fresh coconut very finely. Add to an equal measure of cool water. Let stand two or three hours, press through double cheesecloth or linen. The liquid from the coconut may be substituted for part of the water. Chill before serving. This may be added to any fruit or vegetable beverage.

### HERB TEAS

Fresh or dehydrated herbs such as mint, clover, alfalfa or sage are placed in boiling water and allowed to steep for a few minutes,—or until the infusion is of the desired strength.

## ICED POSTUM

Prepare Instant Postum by dissolving in boiling water. Proportion: one teaspoonful of Postum for each cup of water. Serve with cracked ice. Top with whipped cream, sweetened with Tupelo honey.
*Note*: Co-Veg or other coffee substitutes may be used in place of Postum.

## IRON COCKTAIL

Equal parts watercress and parsley or spinach. Combine the juice of these vegetables with orange juice to taste.

## MALTED MILK

½ pint hot water      1 tablespoonful Tupelo honey
1 heaping tablespoonful malted milk powder
2 tablespoonfuls cream

Combine malt powder with honey, add a little water and stir to a smooth paste. Add remaining water and cream.

## SOY BEAN MILK

½ pint warm water      1 tablespoonful Soy Bean Milk Powder
1 teaspoonful Tupelo honey
2 tablespoonfuls cream or 1 tablespoonful Tupelo honey

Combine milk powder with honey and a little water to make a smooth paste. Add remaining water and cream.

## SPRING COCKTAIL

Equal parts dandelion and parsley juice. Add a few drops of onion juice and a little grated lemon rind.

## TOMATO COCKTAIL

1 cup diced firm tomato      2 tablespoonfuls grated carrot
¼ cup shredded cucumber      1 tablespoonful onion juice

Combine ingredients lightly. Serve in cold cocktail glasses, with or without sauce.

## TOMATO JUICE RAW

Select perfectly ripe red tomatoes. Cut into thin slices and press through sieve. May be seasoned with a little vegetable salt if desired. Should be used while fresh.

## VEGETABLE JUICE, RAW

Juice may be extracted from vegetable by machines especially built for the purpose. The electric type is most satisfactory.

## WHEY

Heat soured milk keeping at very moderate temperature until the milk solids (curd) separate from the liquids. Strain through double cheesecloth or linen and chill. Whey may be combined with any vegetable juice.

# RELISHES

ALMONDS, in balls of minced celery and mayonnaise rolled in paprika.
   paprika.

ASPARAGUS TIPS, raw.

AVOCADO SLICES, marinated, in non-acid dressing and drained.

BABY BEETS, cooked.

BALLS OF FINOCCHIO ROOT, hollowed out and filled with pimiento.

BALLS cut from ripe tomato.

CARROT MATCHES, raw with dots of pimiento for heads.

CARROT SPLINTERS, marinated in non-acid dressing and drained.

CAULIFLOWER flowerettes, raw, marinated in non-acid dressing.

CELERY CURLS, small.

CELERY SPIKES.

CELERY ROOT, slices or rings.

COCONUT wedges.

CREAM CHEESE BALLS.

CRESS, three or four spears tied with thin strips of pimiento.

CUCUMBER CUBES, marinated in non-acid dressing.

CUCUMBER SLICES.

GREEN BEANS, cooked, marinated in non-acid dressing and drained. Tie
   three together with pimiento strips.

HEARTS OF ARTICHOKES.

MUSHROOM BUTTONS, tiny raw, marinated in non-acid French dressing
   containing minced chives.

NUT MEATS.

OLIVES, ripe (green or black).

PEPPER RINGS.

RADISH ROSES.

ROBIN HOODS, tiny bundles of dandelion leaves. Stalk ends dipped in non-
   acid French dressing and slipped thru small rings of carrot, olive and
   radish.

SCALLIONS, (green onions).

TEA BERRIES on celery spikes.

# SOUPS

### ACCOMPANIMENTS FOR SOUP

Barley, croutons, brown rice or small whole wheat crackers may be added to soup to be served at carbohydrate meals, when no tomato has been used in soup. Whole wheat macaroni or spaghetti or spinach noodles may be boiled in water, then added to soup in place of barley or rice.

### ALMOND SOUP

| | |
|---|---|
| ¼ cup minced onion | 2 cups water |
| ½ cup chopped almonds | 1 cup cream |
| 3 tablespoonfuls butter | ½ cup steamed small cubes of cucumber |

Cook onion, almonds and butter until browned slightly. Add water and simmer 15 minutes. Add warmed cream. Garnish with cucumber cubes.

### BARLEY SOUP

| | |
|---|---|
| ½ cup cracked whole grain barley | 4 tablespoonfuls chopped onion |
| 2 cups water | 2 cups vegetable broth |
| 2 tablespoonfuls minced parsley | 1 cup thin cream |

Boil barley in water with onion and parsley for 5 minutes. Add vegetable broth. (This may be made from fresh vegetables or with vegetable paste.) Continue boiling for 5 minutes. Season to taste with vegetable salt and any herb desired. Add warmed cream.

### CARROT SOUP

| | |
|---|---|
| 1 cup carrot balls (very small) | ½ cup chopped celery |
| 2 cups chopped carrot | 2 tablespoonfuls minced chives |
| 1 tablespoonful chopped parsley | 4 cups water |

Cook all ingredients except carrot balls in water until soft. Strain. Season clear broth with vegetable salt and paprika. Add steamed carrot balls.

### CELERY SOUP

| | |
|---|---|
| 2 cups steamed celery | 1 tablespoonful butter |
| 1 tablespoonful onion juice | 1 cup cream |
| 2 cups water | |

Put celery through sieve. Heat cream, add celery pulp, water, butter and onion juice.

## CORN SOUP

2 cups green corn, freshly cut and scraped from cob
4 cups boiling water
2 tablespoonfuls minced root from turnip-rooted parsley

Simmer ingredients together until corn is well cooked. Add one cup cream and vegetable salt to season. Place one-half teaspoonful minced fresh sage leaves in each soup plate before pouring soup.

## CORN, CABBAGE AND RIVEL SOUP

| | |
|---|---|
| 1 cup scraped fresh corn | 2 tablespoonfuls butter |
| 1 cup shredded green cabbage | 4 cups water |
| ½ cup whole wheat noodle mixture | |

Melt butter in pan. Add corn and cabbage. Cook five minutes, stirring frequently. Add water, vegetable salt and a bit of minced garlic-top. Simmer until cabbage is soft. Instead of rolling out noodle dough, put it thru food chopper. Add to cooked soup and simmer for fifteen minutes. Garnish with chopped pimiento.

## CREAM OF MUSHROOM SOUP

| | |
|---|---|
| 1 lb. mushrooms | 3 cups water |
| 2 tablespoonfuls butter | 1 cup thin cream |

Cook mushrooms in butter for five minutes. Add water. Simmer until mushrooms are tender. Rub through coarse sieve and add warmed cream. Season with vegetable salt and paprika.

## CUCUMBER SOUP

| | |
|---|---|
| 3 cups chopped cucumber (no seeds) | 2 tablespoonfuls butter |
| 2 egg yolks | 3 cups water |
| ¼ cup cream | |

Simmer cucumber in butter until slightly browned. Add water and cook until vegetable is soft. Put through fine sieve. Beat cream and egg yolks very light. Add to cucumber purée, cook all over hot water until smooth, stirring constantly. Season very lightly with vegetable salt. Dust over with paprika.

## LETTUCE OR ENDIVE SOUP

| | |
|---|---|
| 6 cups chopped lettuce or endive | 1 cup cream |
| 3 cups water | ½ teaspoonful vegetable salt |

Simmer chopped greens in celery broth until soft. Put through sieve. Reduce to 3 cups by cooking gently. Add salt and warmed cream.

## MINTED VEGETABLE SOUP

| | |
|---|---|
| 2 cups purée of fresh green peas | ¼ cup ground carrot |
| 1½ cups cold water | 1 tablespoonful crushed mint, |
| ½ cup ground celery |    finely chopped |
| ½ cup chopped celery tops | ½ teaspoonful vegetable salt |
| 2 tablespoonfuls minced onion | 1½ cups cream |

Simmer together, for thirty minutes, all ingredients except cream. Add heated cream. Beat for a minute or two with rotary beater before serving.

## ONION SOUP

| | |
|---|---|
| 1 pint shaved onion | 1 pint boiling water |
| 2 tablespoonfuls butter or vegetable oil | |
| 4 rounds whole wheat toast | |

Cook onion in fat until lightly browned. Add water and simmer until onion is tender, gradually adding water to replace any that cooks away. Add 1 tablespoonful vegetable paste to prepared soup. Season with vegetable salt and paprika. Spread toast rounds lightly with cream cheese and brown under broiler. Pour soup into cups. Place a round of toast in each cup.

## OYSTER PLANT SOUP

| | |
|---|---|
| 1 cup mashed, steamed oyster | ½ cup cream |
|    plant | ½ teaspoonful vegetable salt |
| 2 cups water | Paprika |

Heat water and cream, add oyster plant, season with salt and paprika.

## POTATO SOUP

| | |
|---|---|
| 2 cups diced potato | 1 teaspoonful onion juice |
| ½ cup sliced celery | A blade of mace |
| 1 cup cream | 1 small bay leaf |

Boil potato and celery together in four cups water, until well done. Keep hot. Heat cream with onion juice, mace and bay leaf. When scalding hot, remove mace and bay leaf. Combine cream and potato mixture. Season with vegetable salt. Dust with paprika.

## POTATO PUREE

2 cups mashed potato
2 cups water in which potato was
    cooked

1 tablespoonful onion juice
1 tablespoonful minced parsley
1 cup cream

Combine all ingredients, and simmer for about ten minutes to blend flavors.

## PUMPKIN SOUP

2 cups cooked pumpkin
2 or 3 leaves of thyme

4 cups water
1 bay leaf

¼ cup fat bacon, put through fine chopper

Cook bacon and herbs in water about one half hour. Add pumpkin and 1 teaspoonful vegetable salt and continue cooking for 20 minutes longer. Put through fine sieve. A little curry powder may be added if desired.

## VEGETABLE SOUP

½ cup diced carrot
½ cup potato balls
¼ cup diced turnip
⅓ cup sliced celery

2 tablespoonfuls minced onion
4 cups water
4 tablespoonfuls butter
1 teaspoonful minced parsley

Combine ingredients and simmer until all vegetables are tender. Season with vegetable salt.

## VEGETABLE BOUILLON

3 cups vegetable (finely chopped or ground)
3 cups water

Any desired vegetable may be used, or any combination. Cook gently until flavor is extracted. Strain. Season with vegetable salt and any desired herb. Add 1 teaspoonful vegetable paste, and stir until blended.

## VEGETABLE CREAM SOUP

⅓ puréed vegetable
⅓ water

⅓ cream

Add vegetable paste, vegetable salt and paprika for seasoning.

## VEGETABLE SOUP STOCK

| | |
|---|---|
| 2 large carrots | 1 quart fresh green or wax beans |
| ½ lb. spinach | 1 onion |
| 3 stalks celery | 1 parsnip |
| 3 green peppers | 1 small bunch each of parsley, |
| 1 bunch asparagus | radishes, mustard greens, broc- |
| 1 beet | coli and the outside leaves of |
| | any green vegetable. |

Any or all of the above mentioned vegetables may be used. Cover with cold water. Simmer over slow fire until flavor of vegetables is extracted. Strain. Cool. Place in ice box. Reheat as needed.

## WATERCRESS SOUP

| | |
|---|---|
| 2 large bunches watercress | ½ teaspoonful vegetable salt |
| 3 cups water | 1 cup cream |

Combine all ingredients except cream. A slice of onion or a tiny point of garlic may also be used if desired. Cook until cress is soft. Rub through coarse strainer and add cream. Heat until steaming. Sprinkle with paprika and serve.

# VEGETABLE SALADS

### ASPARAGUS SALAD

4 bundles cooked asparagus        4 teaspoonfuls tomato juice
1 cup chilled thick sweet cream

Sprinkle asparagus with tomato juice and chill thoroughly.  Serve with cream.

### ASPARAGUS AND BEET SALAD

Cut steamed asparagus into ½ inch pieces. Combine with an equal amount diced cooked beets. Serve on watercress.

### ASPARAGUS, CABBAGE AND BEET SALAD

2 cups raw asparagus tips        1 cup shredded cabbage
1 cup shredded raw beet

Arrange cabbage on beds of lettuce.  Form a star of asparagus points on cabbage. Pile beet in center.

### BEAN AND ONION SALAD

4 cups steamed green beans        2 tablespoonfuls minced chives
Salad dressing        4 medium size mild onions.
Lettuce

Remove as much of center of onions as possible to leave firm shell.  Fill these with dressing.  Cut beans into one-inch lengths, and marinate in non-acid French dressing for fifteen minutes.  Combine minced chives with drained beans and arrange on lettuce.  Place one onion cup on each salad plate.

### BEET SALAD

8 medium sized cold cooked beets        4 tablespoonfuls chopped olives

Cut beets in halves crosswise and marinate in non-acid French dressing for one hour. Drain and serve on lettuce. Garnish with olives.

### BEET AND CELERY SALAD

2 cups diced cooked beets        2 cups sliced celery

Combine diced beets with celery. Serve on lettuce.

## BEET CUP SALAD

4 large steamed beets          1½ cups diced cooked carrot
Lettuce

Remove centers from cooked beets, leaving cups. Marinate in olive oil. Fill with carrots. Serve on lettuce.


## BRUSSELS SPROUT SALAD

3 cups steamed Brussels sprouts          Lettuce

Marinate Brussels sprouts in olive oil for one hour. Drain. Serve on lettuce.


## CABBAGE BOWL SALAD

1 large red cabbage          ½ cup chopped carrots
1 cup shredded celery          2 tablespoonfuls grated onion

Cut a slice from top of cabbage. Remove center of head, leaving firm outer shell. Chill. Chop enough of the cabbage to make one cup, mix with celery, carrots, onion and dressing and pile into cabbage bowl. Surround with crisp celery tops.


## CABBAGE AND CARROT SALAD

2 cups chopped cabbage          2 tablespoonfuls minced onion
1 cup shredded carrots          ¼ cup diced cucumber
Non-acid French dressing

Combine vegetables and dressing. Serve on lettuce or cress.


## CABBAGE AND CELERY SALAD

1½ cups shredded white cabbage          1½ cups sliced celery
4 ripe olives

Combine cabbage and celery. Arrange on lettuce, and slice olives over salad to garnish.


## CABBAGE, CRESS AND CELERY SALAD

1 cup shredded cabbage          1 cup chopped cress
1 cup sliced celery

Combine salad ingredients and serve on lettuce.

## CABBAGE AND NUT SALAD

2 cups shredded white cabbage
1 cup chopped nuts
½ cup onion rings

1 tablespoonful minced green
    pepper
Romaine

Combine salad ingredients. Serve on Romaine.

## CABBAGE AND ONION SALAD

3 cups shredded cabbage        ½ cup chopped onion
            ¼ cup salad dressing

Combine salad ingredients and dressing. Serve on lettuce.

## CABBAGE AND PECAN SALAD

1 cup chopped pecans        2 cups shredded white cabbage
            Lettuce

Combine cabbage and nuts with dressing. Serve on lettuce.

## CABBAGE, TURNIP AND CARROT SALAD

2 cups chopped cabbage        1 cup shredded raw turnip
            1 cup shredded carrot

Combine ingredients. Serve on lettuce.

## CARROT, CABBAGE AND PEPPER SALAD

1 cup grated carrots
1 cup shredded cabbage

½ cup finely shredded green
    peppers
Romaine

Combine carrots, cabbage and pepper. Serve on beds of Romaine.

## CARROT, CRESS AND WALNUT SALAD

2 cups ground carrots        1½ cups English walnuts
            2 cups chopped cress

Combine ingredients and serve on lettuce.

## CARROT AND LETTUCE SALAD

1 cup chopped raw carrots        2 cups shredded lettuce
            4 cabbage leaves

Combine carrot and lettuce. Serve on endive.

## CARROT AND PEA SALAD

1 cup cold cooked peas            1 cup shredded raw carrot
2 cups shredded lettuce

Combine peas and carrots with dressing. Make nests of shredded lettuce and fill with carrots and peas. Dust with paprika.


## CARROT AND RADISH SALAD

1½ cups grated raw carrots              1 cup sliced tiny red radishes
2 tablespoonfuls minced onion

Combine salad ingredients, and serve on endive.


## CARROT RING SALAD

3 cups cooked carrot rings      1 cup chopped Bermuda onion

To prepare carrot rings, slice cooked carrot ¼ inch thick. Remove centers with apple corer. Make a border of overlapping carrot rings on lettuce. Pile onion in center.


## CAULIFLOWER AND BRUSSELS SPROUT SALAD

2 cups Brussels sprouts      1 cup cauliflower flowerettes

Chill steamed vegetables. Combine and serve on lettuce.


## CAULIFLOWER AND CELERY SALAD

2 cups thinly sliced raw cauliflower
2 cups sliced celery                ¼ cup minced pimiento
2 tablespoonfuls shredded green pepper

Marinate cauliflower in French dressing for ½ hour. Drain and combine with remaining ingredients.


## CELERIAC SALAD

3 cups shredded celeriac                        Lettuce
Pimiento strips

Serve on lettuce. Garnish with pimiento strips.

## CELERY, CUCUMBER AND RADISH SALAD

½ cup diced radishes          ½ cup diced cucumbers
1½ cups sliced celery         ¼ cup minced onion

Combine vegetables, Place on lettuce. Garnish with crossed strips of pimiento.

## CELERY AND PEA SALAD

1 can small peas              1 onion
1½ cups sliced celery         Celery tops for garnishing

Drain liquid from peas. Combine peas, grated onion, celery and dressing. Serve from salad bowl garnished with celery tops.

## CELERY AND TOMATO SALAD

1½ cups diced tomato          1 tablespoonful onion juice
1½ cups sliced celery         Lettuce

Combine celery, tomato and onion juice. Serve on lettuce.

## CELERY AND TOMATO CUP SALAD

4 tomato cups          2 cups sliced celery
¼ cup shredded green pepper

Combine celery and pepper. Fill tomato cups with mixture.

## CHINESE CABBAGE SALAD

Cut Chinese cabbage in 1 inch slices. Arrange on crisp endive. Garnish with coarsely shredded red radishes.

## COMBINATION VEGETABLE SALAD

1½ cups diced tomato          1½ cups diced cucumber
½ cup thinly sliced leeks or scallions
½ cup Julienne strips of green pepper

Combine ingredients lightly and serve on lettuce or other greens.

## CRESS SALAD

4 cups cress          1 onion
Lettuce cups

Break cress into two-inch lengths. Arrange on lettuce. Sprinkle finely chopped onion over each salad.

## CRESS, CABBAGE AND CARROT SALAD

1 cup chopped cress     1 cup chopped or shredded cabbage
1 cup ground carrot (coarse)

Mix each vegetable separately with whipped cream to moisten. Pack in layers in brick mold. · Chill. Slice and serve on endive.

## CRESS, CABBAGE AND CUCUMBER SALAD

1 cup watercress cut in one-inch     1 cup diced cucumber
    lengths                          ½ cup diced radishes
1 cup shredded cabbage               Lettuce

Combine salad ingredients. Serve on crisp lettuce.

## CRESS AND CUCUMBER SALAD

2 cups chopped cress     ¼ cup minced scallions
1 cup diced cucumber     ½ cup shredded radishes
            Non-acid dressing

Combine cucumber, cress, scallions and ¼ cup of dressing. Drain. Place on lettuce. Top with shredded radishes.

## CRESS AND NUT SALAD

2 small firm heads of Iceberg lettuce     1 cup cream dressing
2 cups shredded cress                     1 cup ground nuts

Cut through lettuce heads from top to bottom. Cut out centers, and turn on sides to form cups. Fill with shredded cress and nuts mixed with a little salad dressing.

## CRESS AND TOMATO SALAD

4 tomatoes                    1 cup watercress
        2 cups marinated watercress

Prepare tomatoes by removing hard centers. Chill. Invert on beds of marinated cress. Cut slits evenly in tomatoes and insert sprigs of cress in these.

## CUCUMBER SALAD

2 cups sliced cucumbers                    Lettuce

Slice cucumbers paper thin. Sprinkle with vegetable salt and let stand on ice for ten minutes. Arrange on lettuce. Garnish with onion rings and pimiento strips.

## CUCUMBER BASKET SALAD

1½ cups shredded radish        4 baskets cut from large
1½ tablespoonfuls olive oil          cucumbers
Lettuce

Combine radish and oil. Place in cucumber baskets and serve on lettuce.

## CUCUMBER CUP SALAD

4 cucumber cups        ½ cup diced cucumber
½ cup diced tomato        ¼ cup diced mild onion

Combine salad ingredients and place in cucumber cups. Serve on beds of lettuce.

## CUCUMBER AND TOMATO SALAD

3 cups ½-inch slices cucumber    1 cup balls cut from firm tomato

Remove seeds from cucumbers, place a ball of tomato in center of each ring. Serve on lettuce.

## DANDELION SALAD

4 cups chopped dandelion       1 tablespoonful chopped chives
Non-acid dressing

Combine dandelion with chives and dressing. Drain. Serve on lettuce.

## ENDIVE AND CUCUMBER SALAD

2 cups diced cucumber        2 cups chopped endive

Combine vegetables and dressing. Serve on lettuce.

## GREEN BEAN AND CELERY SALAD

1 cup cooked string beans      ¼ cup non-acid French dressing
1 cup sliced celery          Pimiento strips
½ cup chopped onion        Endive
½ cup diced radishes         Watercress

Combine first four ingredients with non-acid French dressing. Drain. Arrange on endive. Garnish with small bunches of cress tied with pimiento strips.

## GREEN BEAN, PEPPER AND CELERY SALAD

1 cup steamed small green beans,
  2-inch lengths
½ cup shredded green pepper

1 cup sliced celery
2 tablespoonfuls grated onion
Non-acid dressing

Toss together salad ingredients and dressing, and serve on lettuce.


## GREEN LIMA SALAD

2 cups steamed baby limas          ¾ cup sliced celery
        ¼ cup minced green pepper

Combine beans, celery and pepper with salad dressing. Serve on lettuce. Garnish with pimiento strips.


## HEAD LETTUCE SALAD

1 large tender head lettuce          ¼ cup shredded almonds

Select a perfect head of lettuce. Immerse in ice water for half an hour. Hold under water and pull leaves apart (open) without breaking. Drain. When ready to serve set upright in salad bowl. Insert salad dressing between leaves. Garnish with almonds. To serve cut into quarters.


## LETTUCE, CRESS AND ENDIVE SALAD

1 cup chopped cress
1 cup shredded lettuce

1 cup chopped endive
½ cup radish rings

Cut centers from crisp radishes and slice remaining shells to make rings. Combine all ingredients with dressing. Serve on lettuce.


## LETTUCE AND ONION SALAD

2 cups shredded lettuce          2 finely sliced sweet onions

Arrange lettuce and onion in layers on salad plates. Garnish with quarters of tomatoes.


## MIXED GREENS SALAD

1 cup shredded lettuce          1 cup shredded chicory
        1 cup shredded water cress

Toss together with dressing.

## MIXED VEGETABLE SALAD

| | |
|---|---|
| 1 cup diced cucumber | 1 cup diced, drained tomato |
| 1 cup sliced celery | ½ cup sliced onion |

¼ cup shredded pepper

Combine ingredients. Dressing may be added before serving if desired.

## NUT AND CELERY SALAD

1 cup chopped nuts                    1 cup sliced celery
2 cups shredded lettuce

Combine salad ingredients. Serve on lettuce. Garnish with halves of English walnuts.

## ONION SALAD

3 Bermuda or Spanish onions      2 cups shredded lettuce
Paprika

Slice onions wafer thin and arrange on lettuce; dust with paprika.

## ONION AND BEAN SALAD

| | |
|---|---|
| 2 large Bermuda onions | 1 cup string beans 2-inch lengths, |
| 1 green pepper | steamed |
| ½ cup shredded carrot | Shredded lettuce |

Place shredded lettuce on individual salad plates. For each service allow three slices onion, rub with olive oil and pile in center of lettuce. One green pepper ring on each salad filled with carrot. Make a border of green beans.

## PEPPER AND BEET SALAD

| | |
|---|---|
| 2 cups finely shredded sweet green | 2 cups diced cooked beets |
| peppers | 1 tablespoonful minced chives |

1 tablespoonful minced parsley

Combine salad ingredients and serve on lettuce.

## PIMIENTO AND PEA SALAD

| | |
|---|---|
| 4 pimiento cups | Salad dressing |
| 2 cups steamed tiny green peas | 1 teaspoonful minced onion |

Celery hearts

Fill pimiento cups with peas and onions mixed with dressing. Place on lettuce leaves and garnish with small celery hearts.

## POINSETTIA SALAD

4 tomatoes                                Lettuce
Ripe olives

Scald, peel and chill tomatoes. Cut (almost through) tomato into eight sections. Pull back sections to resemble flower petals. Make stamens of pieces of ripe olives. Arrange on green lettuce.

## PORCUPINE SALAD

4 ripe yellow tomatoes          1 cup celery in match-like strips
½ cup shredded almonds

Scald, peel and chill tomatoes. Remove hard center and invert on lettuce. Stick full of celery strips and almonds.

## RADISH AND BEAN SALAD

¾ cup thinly sliced radishes          ¾ cup diced crisp cucumber
¾ cup shredded string beans          4 pepper cups

Marinate vegetables for salad in non-acid French dressing. When ready to serve, drain and place in pepper cups. Dust with paprika.

## RADISH AND PEPPER SALAD

1 cup red radishes, thinly sliced          1 tablespoonful onion juice
1 cup shredded green pepper          Lettuce
4 tomato cups

Prepare and chill tomato cups. Combine radish, pepper and onion juice. Place in tomato cups and serve on lettuce.

## ROMAINE AND ESCAROLE SALAD

1½ cups chopped romaine          1½ cups chopped escarole

Toss greens together and serve on lettuce.

## SALAD SUGGESTIONS

Sliced celery, diced Cucumber and chopped Endive. Serve on Lettuce. Garnish with hard boiled egg yolk.

Alternate sections of Tomato and Avocado.

Dates stuffed with Almonds and Cream Cheese. Serve on Romaine. Garnish with freshly grated coconut.

Diced Artichoke bottoms, sliced Celery, minced Green Pepper and Pimiento.

Shredded Beets, Cabbage and Eggplant.

Tomato sections, mound of sliced Celery in center.

Pear balls on Tomato slice.

Shaved Cabbage, shredded Carrots and chopped Watercress.

Diced Avocado and chopped Walnuts.

Julienne Mushrooms and sliced Celery.

Circle of Beet slices, mound of diced Pears in center.

Diced Cucumber, Julienne Celery and Mushrooms.

Circle of alternate slices Beet and Cucumber, diced Tomato in center.

Sliced Asparagus tips and sliced Celery.

Chopped Lettuce and Cress, top with chopped Mint.

Circle of Avocado slices, fill with sliced Celery and shredded Radish.

Chopped Watercress and Julienne Mushrooms, serve on Endive.

Sliced Celery, diced Cucumber and shredded Beets.

Sliced yellow Tomato topped with minced green Pepper.

Chopped Dandelion and Cress, serve in bowl rubbed with Garlic.

Sliced Celery and chopped Raisins on Tomato slice.

Tomato cup filled with steamed Peas and sliced raw Cauliflower.

Sliced baked Beets, garnish with chopped mint.

Shredded Cabbage, sliced Celery and minced Pimiento.

Diced Celery Root, steamed Green Limas, minced Green Pepper and Pimiento.

Sliced Chinese Cabbage, garnish with shredded Radishes.

Mound of shredded Beets in circle of sliced Asparagus tips.

Sliced Celery and Sauerkraut.

Shredded Beets and sliced Celery.

Circle of sliced cooked Beets, steamed Green Limas in center.

Tomato cup filled with shaved Onion and sliced Celery.

Sliced Red Cabbage and minced Green Pepper.

Diced Avocado, sliced Celery, steamed Green Limas and minced Onion

## SAUERKRAUT AND CARROT SALAD

1½ cups sauerkraut  
1 cup shredded carrot

Non-acid French dressing  
½ cup walnut halves

Combine carrots, sauerkraut and dressing. Drain. Arrange on lettuce. Garnish with walnuts.

## SHREDDED CARROT AND TURNIP SALAD

Combine equal parts shredded carrot and turnip, adding a little grated lemon rind to season. Rub wooden salad spoon with a bud of garlic and use with wooden fork to combine vegetables with dressing. Serve on crisp lettuce, sprinkle with shredded almonds.

## SHREDDED VEGETABLE SALAD

1½ cups each, shredded raw beet, carrot and cucumber. Arrange in small mounds on bed of lettuce or endive.

## SPROUTS AND ASPARAGUS SALAD

2 cups Brussels sprouts            1 cup asparagus tips

Combine and serve on lettuce.

## STEAMED VEGETABLE SALAD

½ cup steamed carrots  
½ cup steamed cauliflower  
   flowerettes

½ cup diced steamed beets  
½ cup steamed asparagus tips  
Lettuce

A few ripe olives

Arrange asparagus tips on lettuce, top with mixed vegetables. Garnish with whole olives.

## STRING BEAN SALAD

1 lb. cooked string beans            Lettuce

Arrange beans on lettuce.

## STUFFED TOMATO SALAD WITH BACON

Remove hard center and seeds from tomatoes. Cut through to form petals. Fill center with cream cheese and small pieces of crisp bacon.

## STUFFED TOMATO SALAD WITH CORN

4 tomato cups                    1 cup cold, steamed corn
1 cup cold, steamed baby lima beans
1 tablespoonful onion juice

Combine corn, beans and onion juice. Season with vegetable salt if desired. Fill tomato cups with vegetable mixture. Top with a spoonful of mayonnaise or other dressing.

## TOMATO, CUCUMBER AND RADISH SALAD

4 medium sized tomatoes          4 radishes
2 cucumbers                      ½ sweet green pepper
                    Lettuce

Scald, peel and chill tomatoes. Slice cucumbers and radishes. Arrange lettuce on salad plates, place vegetables in layers on lettuce; first a slice of tomato, then cucumber and last a slice of radish. Sprinkle with chopped green pepper.

## TOMATO AND PEPPER SALAD

2 tablespoonfuls minced green    3 cups balls cut from firm tomatoes
  peppers                        2 tablespoonfuls olive oil

Combine tomatoes, pepper and oil. Serve on lettuce.

## TURNIP AND CELERY SALAD

2 cups steamed turnip balls      ¼ cup non-acid French dressing
1 cup sliced celery              4 tablespoonfuls finely chopped parsley

Marinate turnip balls in dressing for half an hour. Drain. Combine with celery and parsley. Arrange on lettuce and garnish with pimiento strips.

## VARIETY SALAD

1 cup shredded cabbage           ½ cup sliced celery
½ cup diced, steamed beets       ¼ cup minced pimiento
½ cup steamed carrot rings       1 tablespoonful onion juice

Toss salad ingredients together lightly and serve on endive or lettuce.

# CARBOHYDRATE SALADS

### BANANA NUT SALAD

Cut ripe bananas in quarters, slicing lengthwise then crosswise. Roll each piece in chopped nuts. Serve on bed of lettuce.

### BANANA AND TOMATO SALAD

2 large ripe bananas                2 tomatoes

Dice the bananas. Dice and drain liquid from tomatoes. Serve on bed of salad greens.

### BROCCOLI AND POTATO SALAD

Place large flower of steamed broccoli in center of individual salad plate; surround with diced cooked potatoes sprinkled with minced chives and bacon.

### MACARONI SALAD

2 cups whole wheat macaroni          1 pimiento, minced
1 large green pepper, chopped        3 stalks celery, thinly sliced
4 small raw carrots, shredded        1 medium sized onion, chopped
                 ¼ teaspoonful vegetable salt

Cook the macaroni 20 minutes, drain and cool. Add the other ingredients. Chill and serve with raw tomato juice and olive oil.

### MACARONI AND TOMATO SALAD

3 cups cooked whole wheat macaroni
1 cup diced tomato                   1 cup chopped cress

Combine ingredients with desired dressing. Garnish with pieces of crisp bacon or chopped nuts.

### POTATO SALAD

1 quart diced potato, steamed        ½ cup tiny dice of cucumber
   in skins                          6 strips crisp, fat broiled bacon
1 cup celery, thinly sliced          2 tablespoonfuls chopped pimiento
½ cup thinly sliced radishes         2 tablespoonfuls chopped ripe
¼ cup minced onion                      black olives
                 Vegetable salt to taste

Combine all ingredients except bacon with sauerkraut juice mayonnaise or other compatible dressing. Add bacon just before serving.

## POTATO AND CABBAGE SALAD

3 cups diced cooked potatoes
1 cup shredded cabbage                    ½ cup sliced chives
2 tablespoonfuls broken crisp bacon

Combine potatoes, cabbage and chives with desired dressing. Serve on bed of salad greens. Garnish with bacon.

## RICE AND TOMATO SALAD

Fill tomato cups with steamed brown rice combined with minced green pepper and onion. Top with slice of black olive.

## RICE AND VEGETABLE SALAD

1½ cups cooked brown rice          ½ cup sliced celery
½ cup diced cucumber               2 tablespoonfuls minced pimiento
4 ripe olives, minced              2 teaspoonfuls minced onion

Combine all ingredients. Serve on crisp salad greens. Garnish with quarters of ripe tomato.

## STUFFED DATE SALAD

Pour boiling water over dates. Remove skins and pits. Fill with nuts or cream cheese. Arrange on slice of head lettuce placed on bed of any salad greens.

## TOMATO, BANANA AND CELERY SALAD

1 cup thinly sliced celery                2 ripe bananas
1 cup diced, drained tomatoes

Dice bananas. Combine ingredients lightly. Serve on endive or chicory.

## TOMATO AND FIG SALAD

Fill tomato cups with diced avocado and chopped fresh figs. Serve on cress.

# SALAD DRESSINGS

### ALMOND DRESSING

1 cup whipped cream        ¼ cup ground almonds
1 teaspoonful Tupelo honey

Combine and keep cold.


### AVOCADO CREAM DRESSING

Rub avocado through fine sieve, beat until as light as possible. Combine with an equal amount of whipped cream, either sweet or sour.


### BANANA DRESSING

1 cup mashed ripe banana        ¼ cup whipped cream

Combine and chill.


### BANANA NUT DRESSING

1 mashed banana                2 tablespoonfuls nut butter

Beat ingredients together, adding a little cream if desired.


### BUTTERNUT DRESSING

½ cup butternuts, walnuts or pecans     2 tablespoonfuls olive oil

Grind nuts in food chopper, using finest blade. Pound in mortar to paste. Add oil and beat. For starchy salads thin with cream.


### CREAM CHEESE DRESSING

⅓ cup olive oil                    ½ teaspoonful vegetable salt
2 tablespoonfuls sauerkraut juice   ⅛ teaspoonful paprika
3 tablespoonfuls cream cheese

Combine oil, sauerkraut juice, salt and paprika as for French dressing. Mash cream cheese and add the French dressing.


### HONEY DRESSING

2 tablespoonfuls honey        4 tablespoonfuls chopped nuts
¼ cup heavy cream

Beat cream until light. Add honey and nuts.

## NON-ACID FRENCH DRESSING

Equal parts fresh raw tomato juice and olive oil. May be seasoned with paprika or any desired herb or vegetable salt.

## SAUERKRAUT JUICE MAYONNAISE

| | |
|---|---|
| 2 egg yolks | ¼ teaspoonful vegetable salt |
| 2 cups olive oil | ¼ teaspoonful paprika |

3 tablespoonfuls sauerkraut juice (seasoned)
1 tablespoonful Tupelo honey

Let sauerkraut juice stand over night with a mixture of whole spices and a little onion to season. Proportions: 1 teaspoonful whole spices and ½ onion to ½ cup sauerkraut juice. Strain and it is ready for use.

Follow same method of preparation as suggested for mayonnaise. The same vegetable variations may be used.

## THOUSAND ISLAND DRESSING

| | |
|---|---|
| 1 cup sauerkraut juice mayonnaise | 2 tablespoonfuls chopped pimiento |
| 1 teaspoonful grated onion | 1 tablespoonful chopped green pepper |

¼ cup chopped tomatoes (drained)

Combine ingredients and serve. Suitable for plain salads such as Hearts of Lettuce, Chinese Cabbage, etc.

# MAIN COURSE

### ARTICHOKE AND BANANA CROQUETTES

2 egg yolks          4 medium sized bananas, mashed
1 pound artichokes, steamed and mashed
1 cup onion rings, steamed    1 cup whole wheat bread crumbs

Combine all ingredients. Shape into croquettes. Roll in whole wheat bread crumbs. Bake in moderate oven until lightly browned.

### ARTICHOKE, PEA AND CABBAGE CASSEROLE

Arrange sliced Jerusalem or American artichokes, small green peas and shredded cabbage in layers in buttered or oiled casserole. Sprinkle each layer with a little minced onion. Bake in moderate oven.

### ARTICHOKE TOAST

4 cooked artichoke bottoms      4 tablespoonfuls butter
Crisp whole wheat toast

Mash artichoke bottoms to a smooth paste. Add creamed butter, heat over boiling water. Spread on hot toast and serve immediately.

### ASPARAGUS CAMILLE

Cut asparagus into fine pieces. Place in buttered baking dish over layer of whole wheat bread crumbs. Dot over with butter and repeat until dish is full. Then pour over all the yolks of 4 eggs beaten with 4 tablespoonfuls water. Bake in moderate oven.

### BANANA CUTLETS

Break bananas into small pieces with silver fork; do not mash. Add an equal amount of broken nut meats. Shape very lightly into small cutlets. Coat with nutmeal. Bake until lightly browned.

---

## BANANA AND POTATO CROQUETTES

4 bananas  
1 cup whole wheat flakes  
½ cup chopped onion  
2 cups mashed potato  
1 tablespoonful minced raisins  
2 egg yolks

Cook onion in a little butter or vegetable oil until golden brown. Mash bananas coarsely, combine all ingredients adding a little vegetable salt if desired. Shape into croquettes. Roll in whole wheat flakes. Bake in moderate oven.

## BAKED ASPARAGUS TIPS

1 lb. cold cooked asparagus tips        Heavy cream  
Fine whole wheat bread crumbs

Dip asparagus tips in cream, then roll in crumbs. Place on buttered tray and bake until brown and crisp.

## BAKED BANANAS

6 large bananas        4 tablespoonfuls honey  
2 tablespoonfuls melted butter

Place melted butter in baking dish. Peel and remove coarse fibre from bananas. Shake in butter until coated. Pour honey over bananas and bake in moderate oven, being careful not to burn.

## BAKED BANANAS WITH BACON

4 bananas        Sliced fat bacon

Peel and remove coarse fibres from bananas. Cut into halves. Wrap each piece in sliced bacon. Place on broiling rack and bake in moderate oven until fruit is tender and bacon crisp.

## BAKED BROWN RICE

⅔ cup brown rice        1 cup cream, 3 cups water  
1½ tablespoonfuls butter melted

Combine ingredients, pour into buttered casserole. Sprinkle a bit of grated nutmeg over top, and bake until rice is tender.

## BAKED CABBAGE AND POTATOES

2 cups steamed chopped cabbage        2 cups mashed potatoes

Arrange in layers, or beat together and place in buttered casserole. Bake in moderate oven. Top with a few whole wheat bread crumbs.

## BAKED CUCUMBERS

2 large cucumbers    1 tablespoonful minced onion
1 cup whole wheat bread crumbs    1½ tablespoonful melted butter

Pare cucumbers, cut in halves crosswise. Remove seeds. Combine crumbs, onion and butter. Fill cucumber cups. Set in buttered casserole, add a little vegetable broth and bake until tender.

## BAKED HOMINY

3 cups water    ½ cup hominy
1 cup cream    4 egg yolks (slightly beaten)
½ teaspoonful vegetable salt

Heat cream and water to scalding temperature, stir in hominy and cook for five minutes, stirring constantly over direct heat. Place in double boiler and cook over boiling water for about one hour, or until tender . Add boiling water if more liquid is required. Beat in egg yolks and salt. Pour into buttered casserole and poach until firm. For this recipe only finely cracked hominy may be used.

## BAKED ITALIAN SQUASH

2 lbs. Italian squash    2 cups whole wheat bread dressing

Cut squash into three-inch pieces. Do not pare, but remove centers. Fill with whole wheat bread dressing. Arrange in buttered casserole, add a little vegetable broth and bake until tender.

## BAKED ONIONS AND RICE

2 cups cooked brown rice    2 cups steamed sliced onions
½ cup cream    ½ cup water

Place alternate layers of rice and onions in casserole, adding a little vegetable salt to each layer of rice. Cover with cream and water. Top with coarse whole wheat bread crumbs. Bake in moderate oven.

## BAKED POTATO

### (*White or Sweet*)

#### 4 medium size potatoes

Select potatoes that are smooth and similar in shape, so that all will be cooked in same length of time. Scrub with vegetable brush and rinse in cold water. Before placing in oven cut through skin with sharp knife in shape of cross. Bake until tender. Cut edges will turn back, and potato will be dry and well done. Place a square of butter on each potato and serve at once.

## BAKED PURÉE OF PEAS

½ cup cream
1 cup water or celery broth
1½ cups purée of green peas (thin)
½ teaspoonful onion juice

2 egg yolks
1 cup dry whole wheat bread
    crumbs

Combine ingredients, season with vegetable salt, pour into buttered casserole and bake until firm.

## BAKED RICE AND CREAM CHEESE

2 cups cooked rice
8 tablespoonfuls cream cheese
¾ cup cream

4 teaspoonfuls minced pimiento
½ teaspoonful vegetable salt

Combine rice, pimiento, salt and cream. Place 1 tablespoonful cheese in bottom of each of four individual baking dishes. Fill with rice mixture. Top with remaining cheese. Bake in moderate oven until cheese is browned. Serve a thick slice of ripe, raw tomato on top of each dish.

## BAKED SQUASH

Cut a sweet squash in halves. Remove seeds and fibres. Set on baking sheet and bake in moderate oven until well done. May be served from shell, or removed by spoonfuls, piled into hot dish and covered with melted butter.

## BROILED CEREAL SLICES

2 cups cooked whole rice        4 beaten egg yolks

Mix ingredients and cook over hot water until stiff. Pack into small molds or square dish. When cold, slice, dip in melted butter, cook until brown under broiler.

## BROILED PARSNIPS

1 lb. steamed parsnips (cut in 2-inch pieces)
4 tablespoonfuls melted butter or oil
½ cup sifted whole wheat bread crumbs

While parsnips are hot shake in butter until all butter is absorbed. Roll in fine, sifted crumbs and broil until browned.

## BROILED POTATOES

3 cups thick slices cooked potato        2 teaspoonfuls minced parsley

Dip potato slices in melted butter, roll in bread crumbs and broil under quick heat until brown. Garnish with chopped parsley.

## BROWNED POTATO BALLS

3 cups potato balls                2 tablespoonfuls butter or oil

Steam potato balls until tender. Shake in melted butter over quick heat until lightly browned.

## CABBAGE RAMEKINS

2 cups steamed cabbage    Special filling

Pack layers of cabbage and special filling in buttered ramekins. Bake in moderate oven.

### Special Filling:

2 cups whole wheat bread crumbs    1 tablespoonful minced parsley
2 teaspoonfuls butter              2 egg yolks
1 tablespoonful onion juice        ½ teaspoonful vegetable salt

Combine ingredients.

## CANDIED CARROTS

8 medium sized carrots        ¼ cup brown sugar
2 tablespoonfuls butter       2 tablespoonfuls water

Blend sugar, butter and water. Place carrots in syrup and cook slowly until glazed and syrup is thick.

## CANDIED SWEET POTATOES

1½ lbs. sweet potatoes        ⅓ cup brown sugar
¼ cup butter                  1 cup water
              1 teaspoonful rum flavoring

Cook water, butter and sugar to a thin syrup, add flavoring. Pare (and cut into uniform pieces) the sweet potatoes. Lay potatoes in buttered casserole, pour syrup over and bake until potatoes are tender and slightly glazed.

## CARROT LOAF

2 cups ground raw carrots          ½ teaspoonful vegetable salt
¼ cup chopped, broiled fat bacon   2 tablespoonfuls minced sweet
1 cup steamed brown rice              pepper
2 egg yolks                        3 tablespoonfuls butter
              1 tablespoonful onion juice

Mix ingredients in order listed. Shape in loaf. Bake in buttered casserole.

## CARROT PURÉE WITH PEAS

1½ cups carrot purée          1½ cups steamed peas

Stir peas into purée. Dot with butter. Cook in buttered casserole in moderate oven for twenty minutes. Cover with toasted whole wheat bread crumbs.

## CARROTS IN ORANGE SYRUP

4 cups carrot rings          2 tablespoonfuls butter
½ cup brown sugar or honey          1 tablespoonful grated orange rind
¼ cup water

Make syrup of butter, sugar, water and orange rind. Pour over carrot rings and bake in buttered casserole until tender. Keep heat moderate.

## CASSEROLE OF ARTICHOKES AND CAULIFLOWER

1 cup diced steamed artichoke          1 cup steamed asparagus tips
   bottoms          ¾ cup whole wheat bread crumbs
1 cup steamed cauliflower          ¾ cup thin cream
   flowerettes

Arrange vegetables in alternate layers with bread crumbs in buttered casserole. Add cream, dot top with butter and bake in hot oven.

## CELERY AND CABBAGE CASSEROLE

3 cups chopped cabbage          1 cup sliced celery
1 cup cream          1 tablespoonful minced pimiento
   ¼ cup fine Whole Wheat bread crumbs

Arrange cabbage and celery in layers in casserole. Sprinkle with vegetable salt. Add pimientos to cream, pour over vegetables. Top with crumbs. Bake at moderate temperature until vegetables are tender.

## CELERY RAMEKINS

3 cups steamed celery
Special filling (as for Cabbage Ramekins)

Place alternate layers of celery and filling in buttered casserole. Bake in moderate oven.

## CHEESE AND RICE CROQUETTES

2 cups cook  rice          ½ cup cream cheese
½ teaspoonful paprika          1 tablespoonful minced parsley
   ½ teaspoonful vegetable salt

Combine all ingredients. Shape into small croquettes, roll in bread crumbs. Bake until lightly browned.

364 THE OFFICIAL COOK BOOK OF THE HAY SYSTEM

## CHOWDER OF VEGETABLES

¾ cup onion rings
3 tablespoonfuls butter
4 cups boiling water
2 cups turnip balls

1 cup carrot dice
1 cup shredded cabbage
1 teaspoonful vegetable salt
½ cup brown rice

Cook onion in butter for five minutes. Add water and vegetables. When rapidly cooking add salt and rice. Simmer until vegetables and rice are tender. Add a little paprika or curry.

## CORN CHOWDER

2 cups freshly cut corn
¼ cup green pepper
¼ cup minced onion

1 cup diced celery
2 tablespoonfuls chopped raw fat bacon
1 cup potato balls

1 cup water

Cook bacon in frying pan. When crisp, remove bacon from pan, leaving fat. Drop onion and pepper into fat and brown slightly. Add corn, celery and potato balls with water. Simmer until blended and corn is tender. Remove to hot dish. Sprinkle with bacon particles that have been kept hot.

## CORN CHOWDER WITHOUT BACON

1½ cups corn freshly cut from cob
1 cup potato balls
½ cup diced carrot
½ cup sliced celery
2 tablespoonfuls minced onion

½ teaspoonful celery salt
2 tablespoonfuls minced green pepper
1 tablespoonful minced parsley
1 cup cream

Place all ingredients, except cream, in sauce pan and steam until tender. Add cream and shake over direct heat until cream is partly absorbed by vegetables.

## CORN PUDDING

2 cups grated corn
4 egg yolks, well-beaten
2 tablespoonfuls butter

1 cup thin cream
3 tablespoonfuls minced green pepper

½ teaspoonful celery salt

Cook pepper slowly in butter for five minutes. Do not brown. Add to all other ingredients and poach in buttered casserole until firm.

## COUNTRY POTATOES

3 tablespoonfuls each, shredded pepper, minced pimientos and shaved onion
3 cups diced, steamed potatoes    3 tablespoonfuls drippings or vegetable oil

Cook pepper, pimiento and onion in fat until lightly browned. Add potatoes. Place in hot oven and bake until browned over top and on bottom.

## CREAMED ASPARAGUS WITH RICE

½ pound tender asparagus                    1 cup brown rice

Cook rice in boiling water until tender. Rinse with hot water. Shape in ring mold. Steam asparagus cut in 2 inch pieces. Fill center of mold with asparagus with cream or butter as dressing.

## CREAMED CORN AND PEPPERS

2 cups corn                           2 tablespoonfuls butter or oil
½ cup shredded green pepper           ½ cup cream

Melt butter in frying pan. Add corn and peppers, cook slowly until tender, but not browned. Add cream, simmer five minutes, and serve hot.

## CREAMED LEEKS ON TOAST

1¼ lbs. leek tips                  1 cup cream
1 tablespoonful minced parsley

Steam leek tips. Add cream, parsley and a little vegetable salt. Serve on toast.

## CREAMED PEAS ON TOAST

4 cups green peas                    1 cup cream
Whole wheat toast

Steam peas until tender. Add cream. Heat until steaming. Serve on slices of buttered whole wheat toast.

## CREAMED RICE RING

2 cups hot boiled brown rice         ½ cup heavy cream
½ teaspoonful vegetable salt         4 egg yolks

Beat egg, cream and salt until very light. Fold in rice. Poach in ring mold in moderate oven until firm. Turn out and garnish with olive rings or pimiento strips. Fill with cooked vegetables.

## CRISP VEGETABLE LOAF

Cut all crust from loaf of whole wheat bread. Cut slice ½ inch thick from top and reserve. Hollow out center of loaf leaving wall ¼ inch thick on bottom and sides. Fill with vegetable filling, moisten edges along top with beaten egg yolk; place slice from top for cover. Brush outside of loaf with softened butter. Bake in moderate oven until nicely browned. Serve with creamed mushrooms as sauce.

## FILLING FOR CRISP VEGETABLE LOAF

1½ cups fine breadcrumbs, from center of loaf

| | |
|---|---|
| 1½ cups steamed green peas | ½ cup thinly sliced celery |
| ¼ cup minced onion | 2 egg yolks |

4 tablespoonfuls cream

Cook carrot, onion and celery in a little butter or bacon drippings until softened slightly. Combine with bread crumbs, peas and egg yolks that have been beaten with the cream. When thoroughly mixed, place in loaf.

## CURRIED VEGETABLES WITH RICE

| | |
|---|---|
| 2 cups hot boiled brown rice | 1 cup steamed green beans |
| 1 cup steamed diced carrot | (1-inch lengths) |
| 1 cup steamed peas | ½ cup cream |

1 teaspoonful curry powder

In a low casserole make a ring of rice. Fill center with vegetables mixed with cream and curry. Sprinkle top thickly with buttered whole wheat bread crumbs, and bake in moderate oven.

## EGG YOLKS BENEDICT

Cut slices of whole wheat bread into rounds, toast lightly and spread with softened butter. Cover each round with chopped, crisp, fat bacon. Place a poached egg yolk on each.

## EGG YOLKS MELBA

Cut sliced whole wheat bread into 1 inch strips. Dip in melted butter and place in moderate oven until crisp and lightly browned. Steam green asparagus tips of equal length and keep hot. Poach one egg yolk for each serving, trim evenly. Arrange asparagus (drained on folded cheesecloth) and toast strips alternately in pinwheel fashion on serving plate, ends touching in center. Cover center with poached yolk.

## ESCALLOPED CARROTS

| | |
|---|---|
| 4 cups thinly sliced carrots | 1½ tablespoonfuls vegetable oil |
| 2 tablespoonfuls minced onion | or butter |
| 1½ cups fine bread crumbs | 1½ teaspoonfuls vegetable salt |
| ½ cup cream | |

Combine bread crumbs with oil or butter. Arrange layers of carrot mixed with onion alternately with layers of crumbs. Sprinkle carrots with a little vegetable salt. Add remaining salt and cream to enough water to moisten all ingredients. Bake in moderate oven until carrots are tender.

## ESCALLOPED CORN

| | |
|---|---|
| 2 cups corn | 2 tablespoonfuls butter or oil |
| 1 cup whole wheat bread crumbs | ½ cup thin cream |
| ½ teaspoonful vegetable salt | |

Rub butter into crumbs. Arrange corn and crumbs in alternate layers in buttered casserole. Combine salt and cream. Pour over top and bake in moderate oven.

## ESCALLOPED EGGPLANT

| | |
|---|---|
| 1 eggplant sliced thinly | ¼ cup minced onion |
| 2 cups whole wheat bread crumbs | 2 tablespoonfuls minced parsley |
| 2 tablespoonfuls butter or vegetable shortening | |

Work butter into bread crumbs until evenly distributed. Arrange in layers in casserole with the eggplant, placing the combined onion and parsley between layers. Sprinkle breadcrumbs over top. Bake in moderate oven.

## ESCALLOPED POTATOES

4 cups sliced potatoes (scraped or pared)
1 cup thinly sliced onion
2 tablespoonfuls minced parsley
2 cups of thin cream or cream and water
2 tablespoonfuls unbleached or whole wheat flour
¼ cup cold water
3 tablespoonfuls butter

Heat cream and water. Combine flour and cold water to make thin paste. Stir heated cream into this slowly and cook for 5 minutes. Place potatoes, onions and parsley in casserole, adding sauce throughout. Vegetable salt may be added to taste. Cover with buttered bread crumbs. Bake at moderate temperature.

## ESCALLOPED SPINACH WITH RICE

Chop 1¼ cups spinach. Add 1 cup steamed brown rice, 1 tablespoonful grated onion. Place in buttered dish. Over the top sprinkle layer of whole wheat bread crumbs. Bake in moderate oven.

## ESCALLOPED SWEET POTATOES

Peel and slice steamed sweet potatoes. Place in casserole, sprinkle with a little maple sugar, pour cream over to come to top of potatoes. Cover thickly with whole wheat crumbs and bake in moderate oven.

## GLAZED BAKED BANANAS

Peel bananas and bake in covered dish until clear. Remove cover from dish, sprinkle with raw or brown sugar and place under broiler until lightly browned. May be sprinkled with chopped nuts.

## GLAZED CELERIAC

| | |
|---|---|
| 4 cups balls of celeriac | 2 tablespoonfuls brown sugar |
| 2 cups celery broth | 2 tablespoonfuls olive oil |

Dissolve sugar in celery broth. Add olive oil, and celeriac balls. Simmer until liquid is absorbed and vegetable is lightly glazed.

## GLAZED ONIONS

6 mild onions     2 tablespoonfuls butter
2½ tablespoonfuls brown sugar

Steam onions until tender. Melt butter and sugar together in heavy pan. Set drained onions in syrup and cook gently until golden color.

## GLAZED TURNIPS

| | |
|---|---|
| 1 lb. small, young turnips (steamed) | 4 tablespoonfuls brown sugar |
| 2 tablespoonfuls butter | 2 tablespoonfuls water |

Cook water, sugar and butter for five minutes. Add turnips, simmer until well glazed, turning often.

## GLOBE ARTICHOKE ON TOAST

| | |
|---|---|
| 4 steamed globe artichokes | 4 rounds of whole wheat toast |
| 1 cup asparagus tips | 4 tablespoonful hot cream |

Fill artichokes with asparagus tips, set on rounds of buttered toast. One tablespoonful cream over each.

## GREEN POTATO PUFF

| | |
|---|---|
| 2 cups steamed potatoes | 2 tablespoonfuls butter |
| 2 cups steamed peas | 2 tablespoonfuls cream |

Put potato and peas through ricer together. Beat until light with butter and cream.

## HASHED POTATOES

4 cups chopped cold baked potatoes    2 tablespoonfuls butter or oil
½ cup onion rings

Slice onions and shake in whole wheat flour until rings separate and are coated with flour. Cook in butter until crisp. Remove and drain on brown paper or linen. Place potatoes in pan and pat down evenly with spatula. When bottom is browned evenly, sprinkle onion rings over top, turn over like omelet and serve on hot platter.

## HEALTH CUTLETS

| | |
|---|---|
| 2 cups steamed greens, chopped and drained | 1 tablespoonful onion juice |
| | 2 egg yolks |
| 1 cup whole wheat bread crumbs | 1 teaspoonful celery salt |

Combine all ingredients. Spread one inch thick on platter. Chill. Cut in chop shape, coat with buttered crumbs and bake in moderate oven until browned. Serve with crisp bacon rolls.

## HOMINY

1 cup hominy

Wash hominy in cold water. Drain. Drop into boiling water and cook rapidly for ten minutes. Place in fireless cooker, or insulated electric oven and cook until tender. To serve, heat in cream, sprinkle with minced parsley, or ½ cup sauted onion rings. Often used as a cereal, served with cream and maple sugar.

## JACK HORNER POTATOES

4 cups mashed potato    2 cups creamed peas

In glass oven dish, make a shell of mashed potato and fill with creamed peas. Cover with remainder of mashed potato and bake in quick oven. Creamed carrots may be substituted for peas. Garnish with sprigs of parsley.

## JERUSALEM ARTICHOKE

Jerusalem or root artichokes may be served in any way that is suitable for potatoes.

## JULIENNE CASSEROLE

1½ cups julienne strips of carrot        1½ cups julienne strips of turnip
    2 cups diced potatoes        1 cup sliced onion
1½ cups green peas

Arrange vegetables in layers in casserole. Dot top with butter. Bake at moderate temperature.

## KALE SPROUTS WITH POTATO AND TURNIPS

2 lbs. kale sprouts        1½ cups white potatoes mashed
¼ lb. bacon (one piece)        ⅔ to ¾ cup mashed white turnips

Wash kale sprouts. Break or cut with scissors into short pieces. Boil in tightly covered kettle with bacon, until kale is tender. Requires no water except what clings to greens. Cook slowly. There should be no liquid remaining. Pile kale in center of hot dish. Beat mashed potatoes and mashed turnips together with 1 tablespoonful butter (melted). Put through pastry tube or place in small mounds around the kale. Discard bacon.

## MACARONI AND VEGETABLE PLATTER

In center of platter place creamed macaroni, surrounded with steamed vegetables, using carrot rings, diced beets and small spinach molds. Cook macaroni with a few onion slices until tender, add heavy cream mixed with enough Mar-Vel to make a thick sauce (about ¼ teaspoonful to 1 cup cream) and garnish with crisp broiled bacon broken into small pieces.

## MACARONI WITH WALNUTS

1 quart cooked whole wheat macaroni        1 tablespoonful whole wheat flour
    ¾ cup chopped walnuts        4 tablespoonfuls walnut butter
2 egg yolks, beaten with 1 tablespoonful water
½ cup minced onion

Stir flour into cooked macaroni. Add remaining ingredients. Pack into buttered mold and poach in moderate oven. Turn out on hot platter and surround with steamed vegetables if desired.

## MASHED POTATO

4 cups diced potato        6 tablespoonfuls cream
1½ tablespoonfuls butter

Steam potatoes until tender. Put through ricer. Beat until light with butter and cream.

## MASHED POTATO NESTS WITH VEGETABLES

Form nests, on glass baking platter, of fluffy mashed potatoes. Fill one-third with creamed mushrooms, one-third with buttered peas and one-third with creamed carrots and celery. Place in oven long enough to heat thoroughly. Serve on same platter.

## MASHED POTATOES WITH ONIONS

| | |
|---|---|
| 3 cups mashed potato | 2 egg yolks |
| ½ cup mashed steamed onion | A pinch of mace |
| 3 teaspoonfuls butter | |

Beat all ingredients together until very light.

## MASHED POTATO AND PARSNIPS

| | |
|---|---|
| 2 cups cubed potato | 2 tablespoonfuls crisp chopped |
| 2 cups sliced parsnips | bacon |
| ½ teaspoonful vegetable salt | 2 tablespoonfuls cream |

Steam vegetables until tender. Put through ricer, add salt and cream, beat until light. Pile on hot plate. Top with bacon.

## MASHED SALSIFY

4 cups steamed salsify          4 tablespoonfuls butter

Put salsify through sieve, or mash. Beat with butter.

## MASHED SWEET POTATOES

4 cups steamed sweet potatoes          2 tablespoonfuls butter
½ cup baking molasses

Put potatoes through ricer. Add butter, salt and molasses and beat until very light.

## MUSHROOMS AND EGG YOLKS ON TOAST

Cook mushrooms in oiled or buttered pan until lightly browned; sprinkle with vegetable salt and pile on crisp toast. Place one poached egg yolk on each serving. Dust with paprika or sprinkle with minced parsley.

## MUSHROOM SANDWICH—TOASTED

Chop 1 pound of fresh mushrooms and cook for 4 minutes in 3 tablespoonfuls of butter. Add ¼ cup of whole wheat flour, stir and add ¾ cup of cream and water. Bring to the boiling point, season with onion salt and paprika. Cook until thick and spread between thin slices of whole wheat bread. Toast until nicely browned and serve garnished with parsley.

## NEW POTATOES IN CREAM

| | |
|---|---|
| 4 cups steamed small new potatoes | 1 tablespoonful minced parsley |
| ¼ cup cream | ½ teaspoonful vegetable salt |

Heat cream with parsley and salt, add potatoes.

## NURSERY SPAGHETTI

1 quart boiled spaghetti (thin cream to moisten, about ½ cup)
½ teaspoonful onion juice    1 tablespoonful minced parsley

Place all ingredients in shallow baking dish. Sprinkle with grated whole wheat breadcrumbs. Bake in moderate oven until crumbs are brown.

## NUT LOAF

| | |
|---|---|
| 1 cup nut meal | ½ cup shredded carrot |
| 1 cup finely sliced celery | 2 tablespoonfuls minced parsley |
| 1 cup whole wheat bread crumbs | 1½ teaspoonfuls vegetable salt |
| 1 tablespoonful minced onion | 4 beaten egg yolks |
| ½ cup mashed, green peas | ½ cup 20% cream |
| ½ cup water or vegetable broth | |
| 2 tablespoonfuls melted butter or vegetable oil | |

Combine celery, bread crumbs, nut meal, onion, parsley and vegetable salt. Add egg yolks, peas, carrots, cream, water and butter. Mix thoroughly adding more liquid if necessary. Shape into a loaf. Allow to stand for 15 minutes. Bake at moderate temperature. Serve hot with sauce made with vegetable paste.

## PEA AND OLIVE TIMBALES

| | |
|---|---|
| 2 cups purée of peas | ½ cup whole wheat bread crumbs |
| ½ cup cream | ¼ cup chopped ripe olives |
| 1 tablespoonful minced onion | 3 egg yolks (beaten slightly) |

Scald cream and add to egg yolks. Stir into purée of peas. Add remaining ingredients and pour into buttered timbale molds. Poach in oven until firm.

## PEA ROAST

| | |
|---|---|
| ¾ cup whole wheat bread crumbs | 2 egg yolks |
| ½ cup puréed canned peas | ¾ teaspoonful vegetable salt |
| 1½ teaspoonfuls brown sugar | ¼ cup butter |
| ¼ tablespoonful English walnut meats, finely chopped | ½ cup heavy cream |
| | ½ cup water |

Mix bread crumbs, puréed peas, sugar, nutmeats, egg yolks, (slightly beaten), salt, butter, cream and water. Turn into a baking dish which has been buttered. Let stand 15 minutes. Cover and bake in a slow oven.

## PINK POTATOES WITH PARSLEY ·

1 lb. small pink potatoes          2 tablespoonfuls butter
2 tablespoonfuls minced parsley

Steam potatoes. Add butter and parsley.

## POACHED EGG YOLKS WITH CHEESE SAUCE

Melt cream cheese in double boiler, adding a little cream if desired. Stir in minced parsley and chopped pimiento,—using 1 tablespoonful each to 1 cup sauce. Season with vegetable salt. Toast rounds of whole wheat bread, place a poached egg yolk on each round and cover with cheese sauce.

## POTATO BALLS, BACON DRESSING

3 cups steamed potato balls          2 tablespoonfuls chopped onion
2 tablespoonfuls green pepper,       2 tablespoonfuls chopped raw
    minced                               fat bacon

Cook bacon, pepper and onion together. Distribute over potato balls.

## POTATO CROQUETTES

2 cups mashed white potato          Whole wheat bread crumbs
2 egg yolks, well beaten            Melted butter

Shape potato into small croquettes. Roll in beaten yolks then bread crumbs. Place in baking dish and pour one teaspoonful melted butter over each. Bake in quick oven until evenly browned.

## POTATOES WITH ONION RINGS

3 cups potato balls          2 tablespoonfuls butter
1 cup onion rings

Steam potato balls until tender. Brown the onion rings in butter. Place potato balls in hot serving dish and distribute onion rings over top.

## POTATO PIE

1 quart diced cooked potato          ½ cup grated carrot
½ cup thinly sliced onion            Broth made of vegetable paste
1 tablespoonful minced parsley       Whole wheat biscuit dough

Place potatoes in casserole, distributing onion, parsley and carrot evenly. A little vegetable salt may be added if desired. Pour over enough broth to almost reach top of potatoes. Cover with whole wheat biscuit dough, in which openings must be made to allow escape of steam. Bake in hot oven until crust is light and browned a little.

## POTATO ROSES

2 cups mashed potato        3 egg yolks, well beaten

Mix thoroughly. Put through rose pastry tube. Bake for a few minutes in moderate oven, until very lightly browned.

## POTATOES AND TURNIPS, ONION SAUCE

2 cups steamed potato balls
1 cup small dice of steamed
    turnips
3 tablespoonfuls butter
1 cup chopped onion
1 tablespoonful whole wheat flour
½ cup water

Arrange potatoes and turnips in hot serving dish. Pour sauce over.
*Sauce*: Brown onion in butter, add flour and stir. Add water and cook until clear.

## POTATO AND WALNUT CROQUETTES

2 cups mashed potato
4 egg yolks, beaten
4 tablespoonfuls sweet cream
1 cup broken walnut meats
1 tablespoonful minced parsley

Blend all ingredients. Shape in cones. Set in buttered au gratin dish, top each cone with 1 teaspoonful butter. Bake in moderate oven.

## POT POURRI

¼ cup parsnip dice
¼ cup turnip balls
1 cup sweet potato balls
½ cup pearl onions
¼ cup carrot rings
¼ cup sliced celeriac
4 cups celery broth
2 cups mashed potato

Cook first four vegetables in celery broth until tender. Remove and keep hot. Cook sweet potato balls and onion in same broth. Remove and keep hot. Strain 1 cup broth and thicken with egg yolks, for sauce. Arrange sweet potato and onions in center of platter, surround with root vegetables. Set mashed potato roses in ring for border. Serve sauce from bowl.

## PUMPKIN CASSEROLE

2 cups cubes of pumpkin
1 cup sliced celery
¼ cup chopped onion
1½ tablespoonfuls butter
Pinch of salt
½ cup water

Place all together in buttered casserole and bake until vegetables are tender. Then add:

1 cup steamed brown rice
¼ cup cream
1 teaspoonful butter
½ teaspoonful vegetable salt

Finish baking without cover until cream is absorbed by the vegetables.

## PUMPKIN PATTIES

3 cups cooked, mashed pumpkin (well drained)
1 tablespoonful raw or brown sugar      ½ teaspoonful vegetable salt

Mix seasonings with pumpkin. Form into small patties. Dot with butter and bake in hot oven until lightly browned. Serve with crisp fat bacon.

## RICE CROQUETTES

½ cup brown rice                         ½ teaspoonful powdered sage
¾ cup chopped onion                      ½ cup grated carrot
3 cups broth made of vegetable paste

Put all ingredients into double boiler and cook until rice is tender,—about 1 hour. Add vegetable salt to taste. Cool. Shape into croquettes. Roll in cream, then in whole wheat bread crumbs. Bake in hot oven until lightly browned.

## RICE OMELETTE

6 egg yolks                              ½ cup cooked rice
½ cup cream                              1 teaspoonful minced parsley
3 tablespoonfuls minced, crisp, fat bacon

Beat egg yolks until as light as possible. Add remaining ingredients, pour into buttered omelette pan. Cook over slow heat until set. (May be baked.) Turn out on heated platter. Sprinkle with paprika. Serve immediately.

## RICED POTATO

3 cups steamed potato

When potatoes are tender, set in colander in warm place for two or three minutes. This results in mealy texture. Press through ricer onto hot plate and serve at once.

## RICE RING WITH VEGETABLES

1 cup brown rice        2 cups vegetables in cream

Cook rice in sufficient water until tender. Drain. Rinse with boiling water. Press into a ring mold and stand in hot water until ready to serve. Turn out on hot plate, fill with creamed vegetable of choice.

## RICE WITH CARROTS

2 cups boiled brown rice        2 cups steamed, buttered carrot rings
2 tablespoonfuls butter

Pile hot rice in a mound on hot platter. Surround with carrots. Put butter in depression at top of rice mound.

## RICE WITH ONIONS

2 tablespoonfuls butter
4 tablespoonfuls minced onion

3 cups cooked brown rice
2 hard boiled egg yolks

Cook butter and onion until yellow.  Add hot rice.  Grate egg yolks over and serve at once.

## SCRAMBLED EGG PLATTER

In center of platter arrange scrambled egg yolks garnished with crisp broiled bacon strips and parsley.  Surround with mashed potato cups filled with green peas and corn baked on the cob.

## SPAGHETTI AND MUSHROOMS

½ lb. whole wheat spaghetti
2 tablespoonfuls butter
2 tablespoonfuls minced onion

1 tablespoonful minced pepper
1 cup mushrooms (broken in small pieces)

1 cup cream

Cook spaghetti in rapidly boiling salted water, until tender.  Drain and rinse in cold water.  Drain again.  Place in baking dish and cover with sauce.  Sprinkle with buttered crumbs and bake until lightly browned.

*Sauce*:

Melt butter in frying pan.  Add onion, pepper and mushrooms and cook for five minutes.  Add cream.  When hot, pour over spaghetti.

## SPAGHETTI SAUERKRAUT CASSEROLE

2 cups cooked whole wheat spaghetti
2 cups sauerkraut                    Bacon slices

Arrange spaghetti and sauerkraut in layers in casserole.  Cover top with bacon strips.  Bake in moderate oven until bacon is crisp and lightly browned.

## SPINACH NOODLES

Boil 1 pound of spinach noodles until tender.  Drain, and pack into ring mold.  Keep hot until ready to serve.  Turn out on warm plate, and fill center with creamed carrots.

## SPINACH WITH ONION SAUCE

3 cups steamed chopped spinach
    (hot)
1 cup chopped onion

2 tablespoonfuls butter
1 tablespoonful whole wheat flour
½ cup water or vegetable broth

Brown onions in butter.  Add flour and stir until smooth.  Add water and cook until clear.  Pour over hot molded spinach.

## SQUASH CUPS WITH PEAS

4 cups hot mashed winter squash        4 tablespoonfuls honey
2 teaspoonfuls butter        ½ teaspoonful vegetable salt
½ teaspoonful tartaric acid baking powder

Beat all ingredients together. Shape into cups. Fill with steamed green peas.

## STEAMED BROWN RICE

1 cup brown rice (unpolished)        1 quart boiling water

Drop the rice, a few grains at a time, into water which is actively boiling. Boil 5 minutes, place in steamer and cook until tender.

## STEAMED STEEL-CUT OATS

2 cups steel-cut oats        6 cups cold water

Soak the oats over night in cold water. Heat to boiling point, then place in steamer or double boiler. Steam two hours or longer until tender.

## STEAMED WHOLE WHEAT

2 cups whole wheat        2 quarts cold water

Soak wheat over night in water. Heat to boiling point, then place in steamer or double boiler. Steam two hours or longer until tender.

## STUFFED BEETS

4 large steamed beets        2 teaspoonfuls melted butter
1½ cups whole wheat bread dressing

Remove centers from beets and scallop top edges. Fill with bread dressing, top each with ½ teaspoonful melted butter. Set in buttered au gratin dish and bake in moderate oven.

## STUFFED CABBAGE

Firm head cabbage

*Bread Dressing*:

2 cups whole wheat bread crumbs        1 teaspoonful minced onion
2 tablespoonfuls butter        ½ cup thick vegetable purée

Cut slice from top of cabbage. Remove center. Fill with bread dressing, replace top. Set in buttered casserole and bake until tender.

## STUFFED EGGPLANT

Cut slice from side of eggplant. Scoop out center. Fill with whole wheat bread filling. Replace slice and bake in covered casserole, at moderate temperature for about ½ hour.

## STUFFED GLOBE ARTICHOKES

4 steamed artichokes

Fill and bake, surrounded by one cup juice from any cooked vegetable, except tomato.

*Filling*:

1½ cups whole wheat bread crumbs
1 tablespoonful onion juice
1 tablespoonful minced parsley

3 tablespoonfuls chopped cooked
  fat bacon
4 tablespoonfuls cream

Combine ingredients.

## STUFFED BAKED MUSHROOMS

1 pound large mushrooms
1 teaspoonful minced parsley
3 tablespoonfuls minced celery
  Grated rind of ½ lemon

2 cups whole wheat bread crumbs
3 tablespoonfuls melted butter
  or vegetable oil

Peel mushrooms and remove stems. Place on baking sheet. Chop stems and add to crumbs, fat and seasonings with a little vegetable salt if desired. Fill mushroom tops with crumb mixture, dot with butter. Bake at moderate temperature.

## STUFFED MUSHROOM CAPS

8 large mushroom caps          2 tablespoonfuls butter
½ cup purée of vegetables, peas, carrots, etc.

Heat the butter, add mushroom caps and saute until tender. Fill caps with purée of vegetables which is made by rubbing cooked vegetables through a coarse strainer, and adding a few drops of cream. Put the filled mushroom caps on an oiled baking pan in a moderate oven and serve when hot. Serve on toast.

## STUFFED BAKED PEPPERS

Remove stem from peppers and stand on stem end. Cut slice from small end and remove white membrane and seeds. Fill with whole wheat bread filling. Bake at moderate temperature until peppers are tender. Place a little vegetable broth in baking dish to prevent browning of peppers.

## STUFFED PEPPERS WITH RICE

| | |
|---|---|
| 4 green peppers | 1½ cups cooked brown rice |
| ½ cup sliced celery | 2 tablespoonfuls minced onion |

1 teaspoonful minced parsley

Steam the celery until tender. Combine with rice, onion and parsley. Season with vegetable salt. Cut tops from peppers, remove seeds and white fibre. Fill with rice mixture. Place in casserole, add vegetable broth to keep moist. Bake at moderate temperature until peppers are tender.

## STUFFED BAKED PEPPERS WITH WALNUTS

| | |
|---|---|
| 4 green peppers | ½ teaspoonful vegetable salt |
| ½ cup ground walnuts | 1 teaspoonful vegetable oil |
| 1 cup whole wheat bread crumbs | or melted butter |
| ½ cup minced onion | 1 tablespoonful minced parsley |

Cream, about ¼ cup

Combine all ingredients and stuff into peppers. Bake at moderate temperature.

## STUFFED BAKED POTATO

Pare even sized potatoes. Using an apple corer, make a cavity almost the entire length of the potato. Fill with chopped onion and butter. Roll potato in olive oil. Bake in moderate oven.

## STUFFED BAKED POTATO WITH NUTS

| | |
|---|---|
| 4 baking potatoes | ½ cup 20% cream |

¾ cup chopped pecans

Bake potatoes until soft. Cut tops from potatoes and remove centers. Mash the cooked potato. Add remaining ingredients. Beat until as light as possible. Stuff into potato shell, top with nut meal or chopped nuts, and return to hot oven for a few minutes.

## STUFFED SUMMER SQUASH

Remove seeds from tender squash. Do not pare. Fill with whole wheat filling. Bake at moderate temperature.

## SUGAR PEAS

| | |
|---|---|
| 2 tablespoonfuls butter | 1 tablespoonful chopped parsley |
| 2 tablespoonfuls minced onion | Pods from peas |
| 1 tablespoonful chopped mint | 3 cups shelled green peas |

Cook all ingredients except shelled peas together with 1½ cups water, until pods are soft. Put through sieve. Add peas to purée and cook until tender.

## SUMMER CHOWDER

| | |
|---|---|
| 2 cups diced raw potato | 2 cups corn, freshly cut from the cob |
| 2 tablespoonfuls chopped raw bacon | ¾ cup 20% cream |
| 2 tablespoonfuls minced onion | 1 tablespoonful minced parsley |
| 1 tablespoonful minced celery tops | |

Boil potatoes in 4 cups water until tender. Drain. Add bacon and onion previously cooked together until onion is soft. Add remaining ingredients except cream; simmer until flavor becomes rich and mellow. Add heated cream. Season to taste with vegetable salt.

## SWEET CEREAL

Add ¼ cup of chopped dates or other sweet fruit to each cup of cooked cereal just before serving.

## SWEET CORN AND SWEET POTATOES

2 cups sliced baked or steamed sweet potatoes
2 cups steamed corn

Arrange vegetable in layers in buttered casserole. Dot top with butter. Bake in moderate oven to blend flavors. If potato is dry, use small amount of cream to moisten.

## SWEET POTATO CROQUETTES

3 cups mashed sweet potato      3 tablespoonfuls melted butter
4 teaspoonfuls brown sugar

Combine potato and butter, and form 8 croquettes. Roll in buttered crumbs. Make a small depression in top of each croquette in which place ½ teaspoonful sugar. Bake in hot oven until well browned.

## SWEET POTATO SOUFFLE

| | |
|---|---|
| 2 cups hot mashed sweet potatoes | ½ teaspoonful vegetable salt |
| ½ cup cream | 1½ tablespoonfuls butter |

Beat potatoes, butter, salt and cream until as light as possible. Bake in buttered casserole until nicely browned.

## SWEET POTATOES WITH BACON

| | |
|---|---|
| 4 medium sized cooked sweet potatoes | 2 tablespoonfuls honey |
| 4 slices fat bacon | 1 tablespoonful brown sugar |
| | 1 tablespoonful water |

Make syrup of water, sugar and honey. Place potatoes in syrup with a strip of bacon over each. Bake in moderate oven.

## VEGETABLE CHOW MEIN

Omitting meat, follow recipe for chop suey.  Serve with whole wheat noodles.


## VEGETABLE CROQUETTE BASE

| | |
|---|---|
| 1 cup vegetable broth | 4½ tablespoonfuls potato flour |
| 1½ tablespoonfuls vegetable shortening or butter | |

Combine flour and ½ cup cold vegetable broth; beat until smooth.  Add remaining broth heated to boiling point.  Cook mixture in double boiler, stirring constantly until very thick.  Beat in shortening and add cooked vegetables, as desired, with vegetable salt to taste.  Chill the mixture.  Form into croquette shape.  Roll in fine whole wheat bread crumbs and bake in the oven until lightly browned.


## VEGETABLE-NUT LOAF

| | |
|---|---|
| 1½ cups cooked peas | 1½ cups diced carrots |
| ¾ cups chopped walnuts | ¼ cup minced onion |
| 1½ cups Whole Wheat bread crumbs | 1 cup water |
| ½ cup cream | 1½ tablespoonfuls melted butter |
| 4 egg yolks, beaten | 1 teaspoonful vegetable salt |

Combine ingredients.  Bake in loaf pan.  Moderate temperature for 1 hour.  Serve with creamed mushrooms or other sauce.


## VEGETABLE OMELETTE

| | |
|---|---|
| 4 egg yolks | 4 tablespoonfuls cream |
| ½ cup fine buttered whole wheat bread crumbs, crisped in oven | |
| ½ cup grated carrot | 2 tablespoonfuls minced parsley |

Beat egg yolks as light as possible.  Add remaining ingredients.  Season with vegetable salt.  Pour into oiled pan and cook over slow heat or in moderate oven until set.  Turn out on heated platter, fold over and serve immediately.


## VEGETABLE PIE

| | |
|---|---|
| 3 cups mixed cooked vegetables | 2 tablespoonfuls butter |
| 2 cups mashed potato | |

Melt butter, add mixed vegetables and heat through.  Turn into buttered casserole and cover with fluffy mashed potato.  Bake in hot oven.

## VEGETABLE PASTRIES

Line muffin tins with whole wheat pastry. Fill ¼ full with alternate layers of steamed or sautéed onion, mushrooms, carrot or any desired vegetables. Pour over vegetables, a little of the following mixture and bake in a hot oven.

## TOPPING MIXTURE

3 egg yolks beaten with ¾ cup cream. Season with vegetable salt.

## VEGETABLE SHORTCAKE

Combine cooked vegetables such as peas, diced carrots, sliced mushrooms and any others desired, with vegetable sauce. Serve with whole wheat biscuits, split and buttered.

For Sauce:

1 cup cream        1 cup vegetable broth (double strength)
¾ teasponful vegetable thickening

Dissolve vegetable thickening in hot broth. Add cream. Warm.

## WALNUT LOAF

1 cup finely chopped walnuts        ½ cup boiled brown rice
1 tablespoonful chopped parsley     2 egg yolks
½ cup whole wheat bread crumbs      1 teaspoonful chopped onion

Mix together walnuts, rice, bread crumbs and parsley. Beat the egg and mix with the other ingredients. Mold into a loaf and bake in a moderate oven.

## WHOLE WHEAT FILLING FOR VEGETABLES

2 cups fine whole wheat bread crumbs
2 tablespoonfuls melted butter or vegetable oil
1 tablespoonful minced onion     1 tablespoonful minced parsley
½ cup sliced celery

Combine all ingredients. Use as filling for baked vegetables except tomatoes.

## WHOLE WHEAT MACARONI AND WALNUT MOLDS

4 cups cooked whole wheat
   macaroni
½ cup chopped walnuts
¼ cup walnut butter or almond
   butter

3 egg yolks, beaten with
   1 tablespoonful water
1 tablespoonful whole wheat flour
2 tablespoonfuls minced onion
1 teaspoonful vegetable salt

Sprinkle flour over macaroni. Add remaining ingredients. Poach in individual molds for 30 minutes. Turn out and serve with border of mixed steamed vegetables.


## YELLOW VEGETABLE CUPS

2 cups mashed sweet potatoes    1¼ cups creamed or buttered carrots

Form cups from sweet potato, brush over with cream or beaten egg yolk and brown lightly in oven. Fill with carrots.

# VEGETABLES

## AGAR JELLY, VEGETABLE

1 pint vegetable juice        1 rounding teaspoonful agar-agar
1 teaspoonful grated lemon rind

Dissolve agar in ½ cup of the liquid, heating and simmering for a few minutes until completely dissolved. Any chopped, shredded or diced vegetable may be added when jelly is ready to congeal.

## ARTICHOKES STUFFED WITH SPINACH

### 4 steamed artichokes

*Filling*:

½ cup chopped steamed spinach        ¼ teaspoonful vegetable salt
1 tablespoonful melted butter        ½ cup mixed vegetable purée
½ teaspoonful onion juice                 (thick)
⅓ cup minced ripe olives

To make filling, combine ingredients and cook to smooth paste. Fill artichokes and bake in buttered casserole. Add sufficient celery broth to prevent browning.

## BAKED BEETS

Very small, young beets are baked whole. Others may be sliced or shredded. Bake in casserole in moderate oven until tender.

## BAKED BEETS AND GREENS

Bake medium sized beets until tender. Steam beet tops, chop and season with vegetable salt and butter. Slip skins from baked beets. Scoop out centers and fill with prepared greens.

## BAKED CARROTS

Scrub carrots. Discard tops. Bake in casserole in moderate oven until tender.

## BAKED CELERIAC

4 cups sliced celeriac        Cream

Arrange vegetable in casserole. Add cream to keep moist, sprinkle with vegetable salt and bake until tender.

## BAKED ENDIVE

4 small heads endive      2 tablespoonfuls melted butter

Set endive in buttered casserole. Pour butter over. Cover and bake until tender. Turn each head over when half done. Oven heat must be moderate. Sprinkle with celery salt before serving.

## BAKED KOHL-RABI

Scrub kohl-rabi. May be sliced or shredded if desired. Bake in casserole until tender.

## BAKED ONIONS IN CREAM

4 large mild onions      ½ cup thin cream
½ teaspoonful vegetable salt

Slice onions thinly, arrange in layers in buttered casserole. Pour cream, mixed with salt, over onions and bake until tender.

## BAKED SALSIFY

3 cups sliced raw salsify      1 cup cream

Arrange salsify in buttered casserole. Pour cream over. Add a little vegetable salt. Bake in moderate oven.

## BAKED TURNIPS

Scrub solid young turnips. Bake in glass casserole in moderate oven until tender.

## BEETS STUFFED WITH SAUERKRAUT

4 large steamed beets      1½ cups sauerkraut
4 tablespoonfuls butter

Remove centers from beets. Fill with sauerkraut, top with one tablespoonful butter and bake in moderate oven.

## BOILED CORN ON THE COB

Corn when picked very young and tender in full milk may be used as a vegetable; but should be eaten within twenty-four hours of the time of picking, otherwise it should be treated as a starch. Immerse in boiling water, set over direct heat. When water reaches boiling point again the corn is sufficiently cooked. Serve on cob; or cut off and dress with melted butter or cream.

## BOILED COLLARDS

4 small heads collard              2 oz. bacon in piece

Score bacon and boil in a little water to extract flavor. Add the four heads of collard. Simmer until tender and water is nearly boiled away. Discard bacon.

## BOILED ESCAROLE

Follow instructions for boiled collards.

## BOILED FETTICUS

Follow directions for boiled collards.

## BOILED TENDERGREEN

Tie tendergreen in bundles and boil with fat bacon until tender. May be served in any manner used for spinach.

## BRAISED BORECOLE (*Kale*)

½ peck borecole              4 tablespoonfuls butter

Melt butter in heavy pan. Add drained small heads of borecole. Steam until tender.

## BRAISED CELERY AND CARROTS

2 cups sliced celery              2 cups diced carrots
3 tablespoonfuls butter

Cook celery and carrots in butter for five minutes. Remove to casserole, add a little vegetable salt if desired. Cook in moderate oven until tender.

## BRAISED CELERY HEARTS

8 celery hearts              ¼ cup butter
¼ cup vegetable broth

Cook whole celery hearts in butter for ten minutes. Place in casserole, add vegetable broth. Bake in moderate oven until tender.

## BRAISED CHICORY

Substitute chicory for endive in recipe for Braised Endive.

## BRAISED ENDIVE

1 lb. endive          2 tablespoonfuls butter or bacon fat
                      3 tablespoonfuls water

Cut endive in two-inch lengths. Melt butter or bacon fat in heavy pan, add endive and water. Cover and cook slowly for fifteen minutes. Remove cover and continue cooking until water is absorbed.

## BRAISED LETTUCE

4 small heads Iceberg lettuce          ½ cup water or celery broth
1½ tablespoonfuls butter               ½ teaspoonful vegetable salt

Melt butter and cook lettuce heads in it for five minutes, turning frequently. Remove to small buttered casserole and pour liquid around lettuce. Cook until tender, and liquid is evaporated or absorbed.

## BROILED EGGPLANT WITH ASPARAGUS

1 eggplant                          Sifted whole wheat bread crumbs
1 egg yolk (beaten light)           1 lb. steamed asparagus tips
          Lemon cream sauce

Slice eggplant. If small and tender do not remove skin. Steam until tender. Dip into beaten egg, then into crumbs. Set under broiler until brown on top; turn over and brown. Remove to warm plate. Arrange asparagus tips on slices. Serve with cream sauce.

## BROILED OYSTER PLANT

3 cups steamed, mashed oyster plant          Buttered bread crumbs

Form vegetable into small cakes, roll in buttered crumbs and broil under quick heat until browned.

## BUTTERED ASPARAGUS CHICORY SPROUTS

1½ lbs. sprouts

Steam until tender. Serve with butter. A good substitute for asparagus.

## BUTTERED BEETS

1 lb. baby beets          2 tablespoonfuls butter

Steam beets until tender. Remove skins. Serve with melted butter.

## BUTTERED CARROTS

| | |
|---|---|
| 3 cups steamed carrots | 2 tablespoonfuls green pepper ⎱ |
| 2 tablespoonfuls butter | 1 tablespoonful pimiento      ⎰ optional |

Melt butter and pour over carrots. If using pimiento and green pepper, cook in butter for five minutes before adding to carrots.

## BUTTERED CARROTS AND PARSLEY ROOT

2 cups carrot rings          2 cups diced parsley root

Steam together until tender. Serve with butter or desired sauce.

## BUTTERED FRENCH ASPARAGUS BEANS

1½ lb. beans

Break or cut the beans into three-inch lengths. Steam until tender. Serve with melted butter.

## BUTTERED KOHL-RABI

1 lb. kohl-rabi          2 tablespoonfuls butter

Pare vegetables (thinly) and cut into dice or wedge-shaped pieces. Steam until tender. Serve with melted butter.

## BUTTERED MIXED VEGETABLES

| | |
|---|---|
| ½ cup carrot cubes, steamed | ½ cup turnip balls, steamed |
| ½ cup string beans, steamed, 2-inch lengths | ½ cup cauliflower, steamed |
| | ½ cup peas, steamed |

Combine vegetables. Serve with butter or sauce if desired.

## BUTTERED RADISHES

Steam small red radishes whole or sliced, until tender. Serve with melted butter. For creamed radishes, add a little cream in place of butter.

## BUTTERED STRING BEANS

4 cups steamed green beans          2 tablespoonfuls melted butter

Combine and serve hot.

## BUTTERED TURNIPS AND PEAS

2 cups steamed peas              2 cups steamed diced turnips
2 tablespoonfuls melted butter

Arrange vegetables in layers in serving dish. Pour butter over.

## CABBAGE WITH BACON

1 firm head cabbage              3 tablespoonfuls chopped onion
1½ tablespoonfuls bacon drippings    3 tablespoonfuls shredded carrot
½ cup vegetable broth

Quarter cabbage, remove heart. Set in bacon drippings in small casserole. Add onion, carrot and vegetable broth. Bake in moderate oven until tender.

## CARROT CUPS WITH PEAS

Large carrots that appear in the markets during the winter months should be used for cups. Steam the carrots until tender. Shape into cups and fill with hot buttered peas. Turnips may be substituted for carrots.

## CASSEROLE OF LEEKS AND ASPARAGUS BEANS

Cut French Asparagus Beans into four-inch pieces. Arrange in buttered glass casserole with one-fourth their weight in steamed leek tips. Sprinkle with vegetable salt, add cream to moisten and bake in moderate oven.

## CELERY BROTH

4 cups chopped celery              3 cups water

Simmer until celery is soft. Strain. Add ¼ teaspoonful vegetable salt.

## CELERY AND BRUSSELS SPROUTS

1½ cups sliced celery              1½ tablespoonfuls butter
2½ cups steamed sprouts            ½ cup cream

Cook celery in butter for five minutes. Add cream. When tender add sprouts. Heat thoroughly and serve.

## CELERY AND CABBAGE IN CREAM

2 cups celery, sliced and steamed    2 cups steamed shredded cabbage
¼ cup cream

Combine ingredients. Serve hot.

## CELERY CUSTARD

3 cups sliced celery (steamed)          1½ cups thin cream
½ cup shredded green pepper (sautéd)    6 egg yolks
½ cup blanched button mushrooms         1 tablespoonful chopped pimiento

Beat egg yolks. Add hot cream slowly. Fold into mixture the prepared vegetables. Poach in moderate oven until firm.

## CELERY WITH PARSLEY BUTTER

8 small celery hearts          4 tablespoonfuls olive oil

Heat oil in heavy pan. Place celery in oil. Cook gently until tender. Remove to hot platter. Spread top (side) of each stalk with parsley butter.

## CHARD RING

1½ pound Swiss Chard

Strip leaves from stems. Steam and chop leaves. Season with a little vegetable salt and butter. Pack into ring mold and keep hot. Cut stems into 1½ inch pieces. Steam until tender, add a little cream. Season with vegetable salt if desired. Turn out green ring onto serving plate. Fill center with creamed stalks.

## COMPOTE OF VEGETABLES

6 small carrots          2 cups steamed peas
2 bunches scallions      4 cups new cabbage, steamed

Cut carrots into 1 inch sticks. Slice the scallions, and steam these together. Combine peas and cabbage, place in center of serving dish, arrange a border of carrots and scallions.

## CREAMED ASPARAGUS

1 lb. asparagus          1 cup cream

Cook asparagus in steamer until tender. Heat cream until steaming and pour over asparagus. Serve on buttered toast.

## CREAMED CABBAGE

1 solid head white cabbage          ½ cup cream

Cut cabbage in quarters. Remove heart. Steam until tender. Add cream and simmer for five minutes.

## CREAMED CARROTS AND MUSHROOMS

1½ cups steamed diced carrot          ½ cup cream
1½ cups blanched button mushrooms     ½ teaspoonful vegetable salt
Combine ingredients.

## CREAMED CABBAGE AND PEPPERS

3 cups steamed chopped cabbage        ¼ cup sautéd sliced pepper
½ cup cream

Combine ingredients and serve.

## CREAMED OKRA

4 cups steamed okra pods        ½ cup cream
Parsley or paprika for seasoning

Heat all ingredients together.. Vegetable salt may be added. Large pods should be sliced.

## CREAMED ONIONS

1 pint small steamed onions        ½ cup cream
¼ teaspoonful vegetable salt

Heat onions in cream with salt.

## CREAMED ONIONS AND TURNIPS

Cook onions in milk until tender. Drain. Slice 1½ cupfuls. Simmer turnips in celery broth until well done. Drain. Dice 2 cupfuls. Combine vegetables with ½ cup cream. Season with celery salt.

## CREAMED TURNIPS

3 cups steamed turnip balls        ¼ cup heavy cream

Combine turnips and cream, heat together.

## CURRIED CABBAGE

2 tablespoonfuls butter            1 teaspoonful minced parsley
2 tablespoonfuls onion or chives,   3 cups chopped cabbage
    minced                          1 teaspoonful curry powder
Coconut milk

Cook onion, parsley, and cabbage in butter over direct heat until browned. Add sufficient coconut milk to moisten. Simmer until tender. Five minutes before serving add curry.

## DASHEEN

Young leaves are steamed as any greens. Stems are served as asparagus. Bake, boil, scallop or cream the roots which resemble the potato in texture and composition. Leaves and stems may be served with any type meal. Roots combine only with carbohydrate foods.

## DOCK

Dock, if gathered when quite tender, may be served raw as a salad or cooked as any greens.

## EGGPLANT SLICES WITH BACON

½-inch slices eggplant  
2 egg yolks beaten

Whole wheat bread crumbs  
Crisp fat bacon, broiled

Cut eggplant slices in halves crosswise. Dip each piece in egg yolk, then in buttered crumbs. Broil until tender, under moderate heat. Split each slice open and insert two slices of crisp broiled bacon. Serve at once.

## EMERALD CAULIFLOWER

1 head steamed white cauliflower    3 tablespoonfuls melted butter  
2 tablespoonfuls finely minced parsley

Heat parsley in butter. Pour over hot cauliflower.

## FRIED ONIONS

4 cups sliced onions        1 tablespoonful butter

Melt butter in heavy frying pan. Add onions and cook until clear. Just before removing from pan, dust over with one tablespoon sugar and pinch of vegetable salt, and brown lightly.

## GIANT DANDELION

Cultivated dandelion is tender and may be purchased either green or bleached. Green variety is excellent steamed as spinach or other greens, or as a salad.

## GLOBE ARTICHOKES

To prepare artichokes for cooking, cut stem off close to base. Remove bruised sepals. Cut one inch from top and remove choke. Steam until tender. Drain. Serve with melted butter.

### GREEN CURLY CABBAGE (*Savoy Cabbage*)

1 head green curly cabbage          1½ tablespoonfuls browned butter

Place cabbage head in pan with small amount of boiling water. Keep cooking rapidly until water is all absorbed or evaporated, and vegetable is tender. Add butter and serve hot.

### GREENS

POLK — cook like asparagus.

NETTLE — (gathered when 3-4 inches long).

SWISS CHARD; PLANTAIN; MILKWEED; LAMB'S QUARTER; MUSTARD GREENS; DANDELIONS; SWEET POTATO TOPS; BEET TOPS; RADISH TOPS; TURNIP TOPS; LEAVES FROM KOHL-RABI; all may be steamed and served like spinach.

MILKWEED, DANDELION, and PLANTAIN should frequently be used raw for salads.

### LETTUCE IN CREAM

2 heads lettuce                    1 tablespoonful minced onion
½ teaspoonful vegetable salt       2 tablespoonfuls butter
                    ½ cup cream

Cut each head in two and place cut side up in pan. Sprinkle with onion and salt. Steam for fifteen minutes. Add butter and cream and continue cooking until tender. Serve on hot dishes and sprinkle thickly with buttered whole wheat bread crumbs that have been browned in the oven until crisp.

### MASHED PARSNIPS

4 cups steamed parsnips          1½ tablespoonfuls butter
                4 tablespoonfuls cream

Mash parsnips as soon as tender; beat butter and cream into the vegetable and reheat in baking dish. Butter may be omitted.

## MASHED TURNIPS

4 cups steamed turnips

Put through potato ricer and drain. Add 2 tablespoonfuls butter and beat until light.

## MASKED SPINACH BALLS

Shape steamed spinach into small balls about 1½ inches in diameter. Cover with a layer of mashed potatoes about ½ inch thick, bake in oven until potato is brown—about 15 minutes. Baste with melted butter.

## MUSHROOM TIMBALES

2 cups mushroom purée
4 egg yolks, well beaten
4 tablespoonfuls cream
½ teaspoonful vegetable salt

Combine ingredients. Pour into buttered timbale molds and poach until firm.

## PARSLEY CARROTS

3 cups steamed carrot balls
1 tablespoonful minced parsley
½ cup cream
1 teaspoonful minced chives (optional)

Combine ingredients and serve hot.

## PEAS, MINTED

4 cups steamed peas    2 tablespoonfuls chopped mint
2 tablespoonfuls butter

Combine and serve hot.

## PEPPERED CORN

3 cups young corn
2 tablespoonfuls shredded green pepper
3 tablespoonfuls butter or vegetable oil
2 tablespoonfuls minced onion
1 tablespoonful minced pimiento
½ teaspoonful vegetable salt
½ teaspoonful paprika
½ cup cream

Cook onion and green pepper in butter until golden color. Add remaining ingredients. Simmer until corn is tender and mixture is thickened.

## POTTED BEANS

4 cups tender green beans cut in 1-inch lengths
1 teaspoonful summer savory

Follow directions for Potted Peas.


## POTTED PEAS

3 cups tiny green peas    6 lettuce leaves

Place three large lettuce leaves in bottom of casserole. Add peas. Top with lettuce leaves. Cover tightly. Set in pan of boiling water in moderate oven and cook until peas are tender. One teaspoonful chopped mint may be added to peas.


## SAUTÉD OYSTER PLANT

3 cups sliced oyster plant    1½ tablespoonfuls butter
2 tablespoonfuls minced parsley

Melt butter, add vegetable and a little vegetable salt if desired. Cook gently until tender. Sprinkle with minced parsley.


## SAVORY CARROTS

4 cups carrot rings or balls    ¼ cup minced onion
1½ tablespoonfuls butter    1 cup vegetable broth
2 egg yolks

Cook onion and carrot in butter until browned a little. Add vegetable broth and simmer until tender. Remove carrot and beat two egg yolks into liquid. Cook until smooth and pour over carrot. Garnish with chopped parsley.


## SAVORY WAX BEANS

3 cups wax beans    1 cup rings of mild onions
1 cup sliced celery    2 oz. fat bacon

Cover bacon with boiling water. Add beans, celery and onion rings. Simmer until vegetables are tender and water absorbed. Discard bacon.


## SHREDDED BEETS

4 cups shredded raw beets    1½ tablespoonfuls butter

Melt butter in heavy pan. Add beets and cook quickly until tender, stirring frequently.

## SPINACH CUPS

2 cups chopped, drained, steamed spinach
½ cup thin cream, hot

3 well beaten egg yolks
½ teaspoonful vegetable salt
4 large broiled mushrooms

2 tablespoonfuls melted butter

Beat cream and salt into egg yolks. Add spinach and place in buttered individual molds. Set in pan of hot water and poach in moderate oven until firm. Turn out on hot plates (on rounds of buttered whole wheat toast). Set a mushroom on each timbale of spinach and distribute butter over mushrooms.

## STEAMED CARROTS AND TURNIPS

2 cups yellow turnip balls    2 cups carrot rings
1½ tablespoonfuls butter

Place vegetables in steamer and cook until tender. Dress with melted butter. (Equal amount of peas may be added.)

## STEAMED CAULIFLOWER

1 large cauliflower    Cream Sauce

Separate cauliflower into flowerettes. Tie in four even bundles. Steam until tender. Serve with Sauce.

## STEAMED CELERIAC

4 cups sliced celeriac

Steam until tender. Serve with melted butter.

## STEAMED CELERY-ASPARAGUS

1 lb. celery-asparagus

Steam until tender and serve with butter or desired sauce.

## STEAMED CELERY AND PEAS

2 cups celery cut in 1-inch lengths    2 cups green peas
1½ tablespoonfuls butter

Place celery and peas in pan together and steam until tender. Serve in hot dish with melted butter.

## STEAMED CHARD

½ peck chard

Young tender chard will be steamed, chopped and served like spinach. Older leaves must be treated differently, the green leaf should be stripped from its thick stem, then treated as the young leaf. Stems may be steamed and served in the manner of asparagus.

### STEAMED CHICORY

Steam chicory until tender and serve with butter or sauce of choice.

### STEAMED COLLARDS

½ peck collards

Chop and steam until tender. May be served with butter or desired sauce.

### STEAMED COS LETTUCE

4 heads Cos lettuce                    1½ tablespoonfuls butter
½ teaspoonful onion juice

Steam cos lettuce until tender. Serve with melted butter combined with onion juice.

### STEAMED FINOCCHIO

4 cups diced stalks and root of finocchio

Steam until tender. Serve with butter, cream or desired sauce.

### STEAMED GLOBE ARTICHOKES

4 artichokes                          1 tablespoonful minced onion
2 tablespoonfuls minced parsley

Place artichokes in steamer pan. Sprinkle with onion and parsley. Steam until tender. Serve with melted butter.

### STEAMED JAPANESE TURNIP LEAVES

½ peck leaves from Japanese Foliage Turnip

Steam until tender. Pack into individual molds and serve with melted butter.

### STEAMED LEEK TIPS

Select small tender leeks. Cut to about five inches in length. Tie in individual bundles. Steam until tender. Serve plain, with butter, or cream as desired.

### STEAMED LETTUCE AND PEAS

3 cups tiny green peas               1 tablespoonful grated onion
1 head of lettuce                    2 tablespoonfuls butter

Melt butter and mix with onion. Cut lettuce into four sections and place in buttered dish. Distribute peas evenly in dish. Steam until tender.

## STEAMED MANGEL-WURZEL TOPS

Young tender tops may be steamed or boiled as kale or other greens.

## STEAMED OKRA

1 qt. okra pods

Small green okra pods may be steamed whole. Larger pods should be sliced. Steam until tender and serve with melted butter.

## STEAMED PARSLEY ROOT

Roots of turnip-rooted parsley may be sliced or diced and steamed. Serve with butter.

## STEAMED PEAS

4 cups peas                    1½ tablespoonfuls melted butter

Steam peas until tender. Serve with melted butter.

## STEAMED SAUERKRAUT

3 cups sauerkraut        ¼ teaspoonful caraway seeds

Combine sauerkraut with caraway seed. Steam until tender.

## STEAMED SEA KALE GREENS

½ peck sea kale leaves

Steam until tender. Serve with butter or sauce of choice.

## STEAMED WHITE GUMBO

1 quart white gumbo pods

Slice gumbo pods. Steam until tender. Serve with cream or butter.

## STEWED CABBAGE

1 head cabbage, sliced              1 tablespoonful parsley, minced
1½ tablespoonfuls butter            1 tablespoonful minced onion
                1 cup celery broth or cream

Combine parsley, onion and cabbage. Add liquid. Simmer until cabbage is tender. Add butter.

## STEWED CORN

4 cups corn freshly cut from the cob     1 tablespoonful minced onion
½ cup cream                              ½ tablespoonful minced parsley
                    1 tablespoonful butter

Cook butter and onion together until the onion is soft, add the corn and stir constantly for ten minutes over a moderately hot fire. Add cream a little at a time and cook slowly so as to evaporate moisture. Add a little vegetable salt. Serve in a bowl with minced parsley as garnish.

## STEWED CUCUMBERS

4 cups 1½-inch slices of cucumber     1½ tablespoonfuls butter

Cut cucumber slices in quarters and remove seeds. Simmer in celery broth until tender. Drain. Melt butter in flat heavy pan. Shake cucumbers in butter over medium heat to expel moisture. Do not brown.

## STUFFED COCOZELLE

4 small cocozelles (about 5 inches long)
Whole wheat bread dressing

Vegetable may be pared or not as desired. Remove center and stuff with whole wheat bread filling. Bake in covered casserole until tender. Serve with cream sauce.

## SUMMER SQUASH

Cut squash in quarters, remove seeds and fibre. Pare thinly. Steam until tender. Serve with melted butter.

## SUMMER SQUASH IN CREAM

Steam diced squash until tender. Add a light sprinkle of vegetable salt and one tablespoonful cream for each cup of cooked squash.

## TURNIPS IN CREAM

3 cups turnip balls     3 tablespoonfuls minced onion
                1½ tablespoonfuls butter

Cook onion and turnips in butter until browned lightly. Add ½ cup water. Simmer until tender, cooking away all moisture. Add ¼ cup cream and a little vegetable salt.

## VEGETABLE BROTH

4 cups mixed vegetables        4 cups water

Simmer vegetables in water until soft. Strain. Add vegetable salt if desired.


## VEGETABLE CASSEROLE

Fill casserole with layers of green baby limas and sauted mushrooms, add sufficient vegetable broth to keep moist. Bake in moderate oven.


## VEGETABLE PURÉE

Steam any desired vegetable or combination of vegetables, until tender. Press through sieve. If a thick purée is desired, simmer over moderate heat to reduce moisture.


## VEGETABLE RING

2 cups purée of mixed vegetables        3 egg yolks (beaten)
1 cup cream

Combine ingredients and poach in buttered ring mold. Turn out on hot platter, fill center with sautéd bread cubes.


## VEGETABLE SOUFFLÉ

Use any desired vegetable. Follow recipe for spinach cups.


## WINTER STRING BEANS

1 can green beans        2 tablespoonfuls chopped fat bacon
2 tablespoonfuls minced onion

Heat beans in their own liquid. Cook bacon and onion together until light brown and add drained beans. Serve hot. Use liquid from beans in making vegetable broth.

# SAUCES

### ALMOND SAUCE

½ cup shredded almonds              1½ cups thin cream
              1 cup honey or maple sugar

Cook over moderate heat, stirring constantly, for ten minutes. Remove from heat, add one egg yolk beaten as light as possible. Stir until thoroughly blended. Serve hot with pudding, plain cakes or chocolate waffles; cold with ice cream.

### CHEESE SAUCE

Add ½ cup cream cheese to cream sauce.

### CREAM SAUCE

2 tablespoonfuls butter or          1 cup cream or other liquid
    vegetable fat                   ½ teaspoonful vegetable salt
2 tablespoonfuls unbleached flour   ¼ teaspoonful paprika

Melt butter, add flour and cook until combined. Add liquid and seasonings and stir and cook until smooth and thickened.

### CRUMB DRESSING

Work 2 tablespoonfuls butter into ½ cup dry whole wheat bread crumbs. Toast in oven until crisp and lightly browned. Sprinkle over steamed vegetables with 1 hard-boiled egg yolk.

### CUSTARD GARNISH FOR SOUP

2 egg yolks, beaten                 2 tablespoonfuls cream
              ½ teaspoonful vegetable salt

Combine ingredients, poach in buttered ramekin in hot water. When cold, slice thinly and cut into fancy shapes. Serve with soup.

## CUSTARD SAUCE

| | |
|---|---|
| 1 cup thin cream | 2 egg yolks, well beaten |
| ¼ teaspoonful vanilla | 3 tablespoonfuls brown or raw sugar |

Add sugar to egg yolks. Pour hot cream over egg yolks, beating constantly. Cook over hot water until thick and smooth. When cool stir in flavoring. Chill. Serve with sweet fruits or puddings.


## ECONOMY SAUCE

| | |
|---|---|
| ¼ cup minced onion | ½ cup vegetable broth |
| ¼ cup grated carrot | 1 tablespoonful whole wheat flour |

Blend liquid and flour, stirring until smooth. Cook over boiling water until clear and slightly thickened. Cook onion and carrot in oiled pan; combine with thickened broth. Add vegetable salt to taste.


## EGG SAUCE

| | |
|---|---|
| 1 cup heavy cream | 2 hard-boiled egg yolks |
| ½ teaspoonful grated lemon rind | |


## HONEY WAFFLE DRESSING

| | |
|---|---|
| Heavy cream | Sweet butter |
| Honey | |

Combine equal parts above ingredients. Serve hot on waffles.


## LEMON CREAM SAUCE

| | |
|---|---|
| Heavy sweet cream | Grated lemon rind |

Combine cream and grated rind in proportion of one cup cream and one tablespoonful rind. Heat over water and serve with vegetables or plain pudding.


## MAPLE NUT SAUCE

| | |
|---|---|
| ½ cup chopped nut meats | ½ cup powdered brown sugar |
| ¼ cup butter, beaten | 1 tablespoonful maple syrup |
| 2 tablespoonfuls heavy cream, whipped | |

Combine all ingredients except nuts. Beat as light as possible. Add chopped nuts. Excellent with plain puddings.

## PARSLEY BUTTER

¼ cup butter          1 tablespoonful minced fresh parsley

Beat butter until light.   Add parsley.


## POLONAISE DRESSING FOR VEGETABLES

½ cut toasted, buttered bread crumbs          4 grated, hard-boiled egg yolks
½ teaspoonful minced parsley

Combine ingredients lightly.   Serve hot over vegetables.

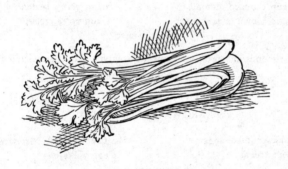

# DESSERTS

## ALMOND CREAM

| | |
|---|---|
| 1 cup whipped cream | 1 cup sliced ripe bananas |
| 1 cup cold custard | ½ cup shredded almonds |

Pile alternate spoonfuls of cream and custard in frappé glasses, with sliced banana distributed through. Top with almonds.

## ALMOND TARTS

Line 6 tart shells with plain pastry. Add filling and bake in hot oven. Serve cold topped with whipped cream or shredded coconut.

### FILLING

| | |
|---|---|
| 1 cup chopped almonds | 2 egg yolks, beaten |
| ¾ cup brown or raw sugar | ⅓ cup 20% cream |
| ⅓ cup water | |

Pound almonds in mortar until smooth; combine with the remaining ingredients.

## ARROWROOT CUSTARD

| | |
|---|---|
| 4 tablespoonfuls sugar | 2 tablespoonfuls arrowroot |
| 2 cups cream | 4 egg yolks |
| Grated orange or lemon rind | |

Heat cream to scalding point in double boiler. Add sugar and arrowroot mixed with a little cold water. Cook until thickened and smooth, stirring constantly. Add beaten egg yolks, flavor, and a few grains salt. Pour into buttered custard cups and poach until firm in center.

## BAKED BANANA DESSERT

Cut bananas in quarters cutting first lengthwise and then crosswise. Roll in grated coconut, bake until clear. Chill. Serve with honey and cream or whipped cream flavored with vanilla and sweetened.

## BAKED CUSTARD

4 egg yolks                                    2 cups cream
4 tablespoonfuls brown sugar

Beat egg yolks slightly, add sugar and cream, strain and pour into custard cups. Set in a pan of hot water and place in moderate oven. Bake until firm in center, determining firmness by inserting a knife through the center. If the knife comes out clean, the custard is baked.

## BANANA CREAM

1 cup banana pulp                    1 tablespoonful cornstarch
1 cup cream                          ¼ cup brown sugar
1 teaspoonful cold water             1 cup whipped cream

Prepare cooked sauce, by mixing cold water and cornstarch with sugar; stir into hot cream. Cook until smooth, stirring constantly. Chill. Add banana pulp. Stir whipped cream into cooked mixture. Serve in frappé glasses.

## BANANA CUSTARD

1½ cups cream                        ½ teaspoonful vanilla
4 egg yolks                          Dash of rose-water
2 tablespoonfuls sugar               1½ cups sliced banana

Scald cream, pour over beaten egg yolks, stir and cook in double boiler until thick and smooth. Add sugar, vanilla and rose-water. Beat for a few minutes with rotary beater. When cool add banana. Chill in sherbet glasses. Garnish with whipped cream put through pastry tube. May be used as filling for individual banana cream pies. Top with whipped cream.

## BANANA PUDDING

1 cup banana pulp                    2 egg yolks, beaten light
¼ cup brown sugar                    ½ teaspoonful cinnamon
2 tablespoonfuls molasses            1 cup cream

Peel and remove coarse fibre from bananas. Press through ricer. Add immediately to other ingredients and poach in buttered individual casseroles. Serve cold.

## BANANA SHORTCAKE

8 graham crackers
2 ripe bananas

2 cups whipped cream
4 figs, canned or preserved

Slice bananas and arrange with whipped cream and graham crackers for individual short cakes. Top each with a fig.

## BANANA AND TOMATO DESSERT

2 bananas
1 cup whipping cream

1 ripe tomato
½ cup sliced raisins

Skin and thinly slice tomato and bananas. Arrange in parfait glasses with raisins and cream, whipped and sweetened with Tupelo honey.

## BANBURY TARTS

Cut 3 inch squares from whole wheat or rye pastry. Brush edges with water. Place 1 tablespoonful filling in center. Fold over into shape of triangle. Press edges together firmly. Brush tops with cream. Bake in hot oven.

### FILLING

1 cup seeded raisins      1 tablespoonful grated orange rind
⅛ teaspoonful each, cinnamon and nutmeg
¼ cup chopped walnut meats      ¼ cup raw or brown sugar

To above ingredients add sufficient water to cover. Cook 10 minutes. Thicken with 1 tablespoonful rye flour mixed with a little cold water. Cook 5 minutes.

## BLACK WALNUT TAFFY

1 cup brown sugar
½ cup molasses

½ teaspoonful cream of tartar
⅓ cup water
⅔ cup black walnuts

Boil without stirring, the sugar, molasses, cream of tartar and water. When thread forms as portion is poured from a spoon, add nuts and pour into buttered pan. When firm, mark into squares and break apart.

## BLUEBERRY PIE

| | |
|---|---|
| 2½ cups blueberries | ½ teaspoonful grated lemon rind |
| ½ cup raw or brown sugar | 2 tablespoonfuls unbleached flour |

Line pie plate with unbleached or whole wheat pastry. Fill with berries combined with sugar and flour; sprinkle grated lemon rind over berries, cover with pastry. Bake in hot oven for 15 minutes. Reduce heat and continue baking.

## BLUEBERRY ROLL

Roll whole wheat biscuit dough ½ inch thick. Spread with blueberries and sprinkle with raw or brown sugar. Roll up like jelly roll, place (seam down) on baking sheet and bake in hot oven for about thirty minutes. Serve with plain or whipped cream or ice cream.

## BLUEBERRY TOAST PUDDING

| | |
|---|---|
| 4 cups blueberries | ¼ cup water |
| ½ cup raw or brown sugar | Whole wheat bread |
| Butter | |

Cook berries, sugar and water together for five minutes. Pour into shallow baking dish, cover with buttered triangles of bread. Bake in hot oven until browned over top. Serve with cream or hard sauce.

## BOILED RAISIN PUDDING

| | |
|---|---|
| ¾ lb. bread dough | 2 egg yolks |
| ½ cup chopped seeded raisins | ½ teaspoonful grated lemon rind |

Work raisins, egg yolks and lemon rind into dough. Set on pudding cloth and allow to rise for a half hour. Tie up cloth, drop into large kettle of boiling water and boil about forty minutes. Serve with almond sauce.

## BOSTON CREAM PIE

| | |
|---|---|
| 2 egg yolks | 2 teaspoonfuls tartaric acid baking |
| 1 cup brown sugar | powder |
| 2 cups unbleached flour | ⅓ cup melted vegetable shortening |
| ½ cup water | |
| 1 teaspoonful vanilla | |

Measure sifted flour and sift again with baking powder. Beat egg yolks, then gradually add the sugar, beating it in with the egg-beater. When creamy, add flour alternately with water, mixing until smooth. Add vanilla and melted shortening, beating until batter is smooth. Pour into 2 oiled layer cake pans and bake in a hot oven. Cool. Spread whipped cream between layers and sprinkle top with powdered brown sugar.

## BREAD AND BUTTER PUDDING

| | |
|---|---|
| 1 cup 20% cream | 6 tablespoonfuls Tupelo honey |
| 1 cup water | 3 egg yolks |

Beat egg yolks until light as possible, combine with remaining ingredients. Pour into buttered custard cups. Place a small round of buttered whole wheat bread on top of each custard. Poach in moderate oven until brown.

## BROILED DATES

Dip dates in boiling water. Drain and remove skins. Remove pits and fill with pecans or English walnuts. Broil at moderate temperature until heated through.

## BUTTERSCOTCH CREAM

| | |
|---|---|
| 1 tablespoonful butter | 3 tablespoonfuls cornstarch or |
| 1 cup brown sugar | arrowroot |
| 3 cups cream | 1 beaten egg yolk |
| ½ cup whipped cream | |

Cook butter and brown sugar in heavy pan until carmelized. Add cream and stir over heat until blended. Add cornstarch mixed with ¼ cup cold water. Set over boiling water and cook, stirring until thickened. Add beaten egg yolk and beat until thoroughly blended. When cold beat as light as possible, add whipped cream. Chill in sherbet or frappé glasses.

## BUTTERSCOTCH PARFAIT

| | |
|---|---|
| ⅔ cup raw or dark brown sugar | 4 egg yolks |
| 2 tablespoonfuls butter | 2 teaspoonfuls vanilla extract |
| ½ cup water | 1 cup whipping cream |

Melt sugar and butter in saucepan, stir constantly to prevent burning. Boil for one minute. Add water and cook slowly until a smooth syrup results. Beat egg yolks, pour syrup over slowly, beating continuously and cook over low heat until light and fluffy. Chill, add cream (beaten stiff) and vanilla. Freeze in tray. Do not stir.

## BUTTERSCOTCH PUDDING

| | |
|---|---|
| ½ cup raw or brown sugar | 3 tablespoonfuls unbleached flour |
| 2 cups 20% cream | 3 egg yolks |
| 1 cup water | ½ teaspoonful vanilla |

Melt half the sugar in an oiled pan, stirring constantly to prevent scorching. When slightly browned, add water. Cook until sugar is dissolved. Pour hot liquid into flour that has been mixed with 1 cup cream. Cook in top of double boiler until thickened and smooth. Add remaining cream; pour mixture over beaten egg yolks. Return to double boiler and cook until thickened and no raw egg taste remains. Strain, add vanilla. Pour into individual serving dishes and cool.

## BUTTERSCOTCH RICE PUDDING

½ cup brown rice
4 cups water (boiling)
2 tablespoonfuls butter

4 tablespoonfuls brown sugar
10 drops vanilla extract
2 egg yolks, well beaten

1 cup cream

Cook rice in boiling water until tender. Melt butter in heavy pan, add sugar and stir until blended. Add to hot rice immediately. Combine egg yolks, vanilla and cream; blend with rice mixture. Poach in moderate oven.

## CANNED FIG PUDDING

2 cups dried whole wheat bread crumbs
1 cup chopped canned figs and juice
2 tablespoonfuls melted butter

Heat figs, juice and butter. Stir into bread crumbs. Pack into four individual molds. Steam for 30 minutes. Turn out and serve with whipped cream.

## CARAMEL FROSTING

2 cups brown sugar          ⅔ cup cream
1 tablespoonful honey

Boil ingredients to soft ball stage. Cool partially. Beat until creamy. Spread quickly on cake.

## CARAMEL PIE FILLING

2 cups thin cream
¾ cup brown sugar
3 tablespoonfuls arrowroot
or cornstarch

3 egg yolks
Pinch of salt
Few drops vanilla

Melt sugar over direct heat, and stir for a moment after it bubbles. Add cream and stir until lumps of sugar are dissolved. Pour into top of double boiler, add arrowroot mixed with a little cold water. Cook until thick, stirring constantly. Add egg yolks beaten light. Cook until raw egg taste is gone. Beat for a few minutes after removing from heat. Add salt and vanilla. Pour into baked crust. When cold spread whipped cream over top and serve.

## CARAMEL PUDDING

| | |
|---|---|
| ¾ cup brown sugar | 1 teaspoonful vanilla |
| ½ cup cream | 3 tablespoonfuls unbleached flour |
| ½ cup water | 3 tablespoonfuls butter |
| | 2 egg yolks |

Mix the flour with the brown sugar and add heated cream and water to this. Cook in a double boiler for 20 minutes. Add the egg yolks and cook until they thicken. Add butter and vanilla. Pour into molds which have been rinsed in cold water. Chill and serve with cream.

## CARROT PIE

| | |
|---|---|
| 1½ cups mashed cooked carrots | ⅛ teaspoonful each, cinnamon |
| 1½ cups 20% cream | and nutmeg |
| ¾ cup raw or brown sugar | 3 egg yolks |

Beat egg yolks until light. Add sugar, salt and spices, then remaining ingredients. Pour into unbaked pie shell. Bake in hot oven for 15 minutes. Reduce heat and continue baking.

## CARROT PUDDING

| | |
|---|---|
| ½ cup butter | 1 cup raisins |
| ½ cup brown sugar | 1¼ cups whole wheat flour |
| 2 egg yolks | ½ teaspoonful soda |
| 1 cup grated raw carrots | 1 tablespoonful water |
| | 1 teaspoonful baking powder |

Beat butter, sugar and eggs to light cream. Add carrots and raisins; add sifted dry ingredients; mix thoroughly; add soda dissolved in water. Beat well. Pour into buttered turks-head mold and steam for three hours. Serve with plain or whipped cream.

## CEREAL JELLY

½ cup crushed whole oats (or steel-cut oats)
Pinch of salt                 3 cups boiling water
½ cup cream

Stir salt and oats into boiling water. Boil and stir for 5 minutes. Place in double boiler and cook for 3 to 4 hours. Strain through fine sieve. Add cream. Turn into individual molds that have been rinsed with cold water. Chill. Serve with sliced figs, raisins or dates and cream if desired.

## CHOCOLATE BUTTER FROSTING

2 tablespoonfuls melted butter        2 squares melted baking chocolate

Combine fats and add sifted powdered brown sugar a little at a time, beating constantly until of the right consistency to spread. Flavor with a few drops vanilla or ¼ teaspoonful cinnamon.

## CHOCOLATE CLUSTERS

1 cup seedless raisins                         1 cup nut meats
                    1 cup softened coating chocolate

Combine nuts, raisins and chocolate. Drop by teaspoonfuls on waxed paper to cool.

## CHOCOLATE CREAM PIE

1 cup 20% cream                    6 tablespoonfuls unbleached flour
2 cups water                       1¼ cups raw or brown sugar
2 ounces chocolate                 1 teaspoonful vanilla
                    3 egg yolks

Heat cream in double boiler. Combine sugar and flour, stir to a paste with a little cold water. Add remaining water, then add this mixture to cream. Cook in double boiler, stirring constantly until smooth and thickened. Add chocolate and beaten egg yolks. Continue cooking until mixture is well blended and no raw taste remains. Cool slightly. Add vanilla. Pour into baked pastry shell May be topped with whipped cream to serve.

## CHOCOLATE DATE PUDDING

2 tablespoonfuls granulated        ¼ cup chopped nuts
   gelatin                         ½ cup cold water
1 cup brown sugar                  1 teaspoonful vanilla
1 cup raisins                      4 tablespoonfuls cocoa
1 cup chopped dates                2 cups thin cream

Soak gelatin in cold water. Put cream, sugar and cocoa in double boiler, and heat until well blended. Remove from fire, dissolve gelatin in this mixture, add vanilla, cool. When ready to congeal, add fruit and nuts. Turn into wet mold, chill until firm. Unmold, serve with whipped cream.

## CHOCOLATE NUTS

Dip nut meats, either plain or toasted, into coating chocolate that is kept soft over warm (never hot) water. Place on waxed paper to cool.

## CHOCOLATE PASTRY

1¾ cups unbleached flour
¼ cup cocoa                    1 tablespoonful raw sugar
⅔ cup butter or vegetable shortening

Sift flour, cocoa and sugar together. Cut in shortening with pastry blender or knives. Add ice water, a few drops at a time, until mixture will hold together. Roll out to ¼ inch thick. May be used as crust for cream pies or baked as wafers.

## CHOCOLATE PUDDING

1 ounce baking chocolate or health chocolate
1½ cups thin cream                    ½ cup water
2 tablespoonfuls cornstarch or arrowroot
6 tablespoonfuls brown or raw sugar        3 egg yolks

Heat cream in double boiler. Stir cornstarch into cold water and add to heated cream gradually, stirring constantly. Add sugar. Cook until thickened. Remove from heat. Add chocolate and stir until well blended. Pour over egg yolks beaten as light as possible. Poach in individual baking cups until set. Serve cold.

## CHOCOLATE RICE PUDDING

2 cups cooked rice                    1 cup water
1 cup cream                          1½ ounces chocolate
½ cup raw or brown sugar              ½ teaspoonful vanilla extract
1 tablespoonful rice flour or cornstarch

Heat cream, water, chocolate and sugar together until well blended. Moisten the flour with 2 tablespoonfuls water and add to chocolate mixture. Add rice and vanilla. Bake at moderate temperature about 25 minutes.

## CHOCOLATE WAFFLES

½ cup brown sugar               ½ cup melted butter
    (pack tightly to secure full     1 teaspoonful vanilla extract
    measure)                       ½ cup cocoa
6 egg yolks beaten with a pinch   2½ cups flour (either unbleached
    of salt                          or part whole wheat)
1½ cups cream                    3 teaspoonfuls tartaric acid
1 cup water                          baking powder

Sift cocoa, flour and baking powder together. Proceed as for any waffle recipe. Serve with vanilla ice cream.

## COCONUT CREAM PIE

| | |
|---|---|
| 1 cup 20% cream | 2 tablespoonfuls unbleached flour |
| ½ cup water | 3 egg yolks |
| ¼ cup raw sugar | ½ cup grated coconut |
| ½ teaspoonful vanilla | |

Heat cream in double boiler. Combine sugar and flour. Add the cold water. Stir until smooth, then pour slowly into heated cream. Cook until smooth and thickened, stirring constantly. Add beaten egg yolks, and continue to cook, stirring the mixture until well combined and no raw taste remains. Add coconut and vanilla. Pour into baked pie shell when slightly cool. Top with whipped cream to serve.

## COCONUT ICE CREAM

| | |
|---|---|
| 2 cups thin cream | 1 cup double cream (whipped) |
| 1 cup grated coconut | ½ cup brown sugar |

Combine ingredients and freeze, stirring often. If prepared in electric unit, remove from pan when partially frozen, beat thoroughly and return to freeze.

## COCONUT PUDDING

| | |
|---|---|
| 1 fresh coconut | 4 egg yolks |
| ½ cup raw or brown sugar | ½ cup cream |
| 1 cup coconut milk | |

Grate coconut, reserving milk. If less than 1 cup milk in coconut, add water to make up amount. Beat egg yolks as light as possible. Combine all ingredients. Poach in oven until set. Chill before serving.

## CORNMEAL CUSTARD

| | |
|---|---|
| 2 cups boiling water | 2 tablespoonfuls brown sugar |
| Pinch of salt | 1 cup chopped dates |
| ½ cup cornmeal | ½ teaspoonful cinnamon |
| 2 teaspoonfuls butter | 4 egg yolks, beaten slightly |
| 2 cups cream | |

Add salt, then cornmeal to boiling water and cook slowly for twenty minutes. Stir frequently. Remove from fire, add butter, sugar, cinnamon and dates, blend well. Combine cream and egg yolks. Stir into cornmeal mixture. Poach in moderate oven. Serve with grated maple sugar and cream.

## COTTAGE PUDDING

½ cup whipping cream     ¾ cup light brown sugar
2 egg yolks     1¾ cups unbleached flour
2 teaspoonfuls tartaric acid baking powder
½ teaspoonful vanilla

Whip the cream, add beaten egg yolks, add sugar, then flour sifted with baking powder. Stir in the vanilla. Bake in muffin tins at moderate temperature until lightly browned on top. When cool, remove center and fill with soft custard or whipped cream. Garnish with whipped cream.

## CREAM FILLING FOR PIE

¾ cup raw or brown sugar     1 cup cream
⅓ cup unbleached flour     1 cup boiling water
4 egg yolks, beaten light     1 teaspoonful vanilla

Sift flour and sugar together, add cream gradually and beat smooth. Add egg yolks. Pour boiling water into mixture slowly, beating constantly to prevent formation of lumps. Place in double boiler and cook until smooth and thickened. Cool. Beat until smooth and light. Add vanilla.

## CREAM PUFFS

1 cup water     ½ cup butter
1 cup unbleached or whole wheat flour
6 egg yolks

Cook water and butter together. When this combination reaches the boiling point, add sifted flour all at once, stirring quickly. Cook, stirring constantly, until dough clings together to form one mass. Cool, then beat in egg yolks one at a time. Beat as light as possible. Drop on baking sheet. Bake at 500 degrees for ten minutes. Reduce heat to 450 degrees, and continue this temperature for 10 minutes. Reduce to 400 degrees. Maintain this temperature until puffs are light, dry, and slightly browned. Entire baking time should be about 45 minutes. Fill with sweetened whipped cream, custard or ice cream. Filling should be added just before serving.

## CRISP BAKED BANANAS

Cut bananas in halves lengthwise, then crosswise. Dip each piece in mixture of equal parts egg yolk and water. Roll in fine dry whole wheat bread crumbs. Bake in hot oven until crisp on the outside. May be served hot or cold.

## DATE CUSTARD

1 cup stoned and chopped dates
2 cups cream

4 beaten egg yolks
Cinnamon or nutmeg

Heat cream. Set over boiling water and add dates. Stir until well blended. Add egg yolks and continue stirring until thickened. Add a little ground cinnamon or nutmeg. Serve cold.

## DATE ICE CREAM

2 cups thin cream
1 quart whipping cream

6 egg yolks
1 pound dates

⅓ cup maple syrup

Beat egg yolks, add maple syrup and cream. Mix and freeze to a mush. Put pitted dates through food chopper, add to frozen mush and continue to freeze. Serves ten.

## DATE PIE

1 lb. stoned dates
1½ cups boiling water

¼ cup brown sugar
1 cup cream

3 egg yolks, beaten until light

Simmer dates in boiling water for fifteen minutes. Put through coarse sieve. Combine egg yolks and sugar, blend thoroughly, add cream. Stir into date purée. Pour into prepared (not baked) crust, and bake in moderate oven until firm. Top with whipped cream.

## DATE PUDDING

3 egg yolks
½ cup brown sugar
½ cup chopped dates

Grated rind of ½ lemon
½ cup chopped walnut meats
1½ tablespoonfuls whole wheat flour

¼ teaspoonful tartaric acid and baking powder

Beat egg yolks and add sugar. Mix dates, grated lemon rind and nut meats, and add to the egg yolks and sugar; then stir in flour sifted with baking powder. Put the mixture in a buttered pan and place the pan in hot water. Bake in moderate oven.

## DATE OR RAISIN PUDDING

¼ cup cream                1 cup whole wheat flour
¼ cup water                ¼ teaspoonful vanilla extract
½ cup brown or raw sugar   1 cup sliced dates or raisins
        1 teaspoonful tartaric acid baking powder
Pour into buttered baking dish and cover with the following sauce:
        2 cups boiling water              ¼ cup butter
                1 cup raw or brown sugar

Combine ingredients and pour over batter in the baking dish. Bake about 45 minutes at moderate temperature. In this method pudding and sauce are cooked together in one dish.

## DATE TORTE

1½ cups chopped dates          1½ cups broken walnut meats
 4 egg yolks, well beaten       ½ teaspoonful vanilla
 ¾ cup raw or brown sugar       1 teaspoonful baking powder
                ¼ cup flour

Sift baking powder with flour. Beat sugar into egg yolks, add vanilla then dates and nuts; combine with flour and baking powder. Bake in shallow pan in very moderate oven about one hour or until mixture will spring back when touched with finger. Cool. Cut into squares to serve. Top with whipped cream.

## EGG CUSTARD

1½ cups cream              6 egg yolks
½ cup water                4 tablespoonfuls sugar

For flavor use a pinch of grated nutmeg, grated orange rind, or a few drops vanilla. Beat egg yolks as light as possible. Add sugar and continue beating for a few minutes. Heat cream and water to scalding point. Add to egg mixture. Add flavor and pour into buttered custard cups. Poach in moderate oven until firm in center.

## FIG CUSTARD

2 cups sliced figs (fresh, canned or steamed dried)
1 cup cream                2 egg yolks
½ teaspoonful grated orange rind

Combine and poach in individual cups. May be served with cream plain or whipped.

## FIG PUDDING

| | |
|---|---|
| 1 cup chopped figs | 2 egg yolks |
| 1 cup molasses | 2¼ cups whole wheat flour |
| 1 cup hot water | 1 teaspoonful soda |

Sift soda and flour together three times. Beat egg yolks slightly, add to these the figs, molasses and hot water. Pour into flour and mix thoroughly. Steam two hours in mold. Serve hot with desired sauce.

## FLOATING ISLAND

| | |
|---|---|
| 1 cup cream | 4 tablespoonfuls raw or brown |
| 3 egg yolks | sugar |
| 1 cup water | 1 teaspoonful vanilla extract |

Beat egg yolks until light. Add sugar and beat smooth. Heat combined cream and water to scalding point and pour over beaten yolks, stirring constantly. Cook in double boiler until mixture coats the spoon. Cool, strain and add vanilla. Pour into serving dish or individual cups. Chill. Just before serving, add "islands" of sweetened and flavored whipped cream.

## FROSTY RICE

| | |
|---|---|
| 3 cups whipped cream | ½ cup brown sugar |
| ½ cup well cooked, unpolished, | 1 teaspoonful vanilla |
| rice—separate grains | 2 tablespoonfuls sherry or rum |
| | flavor |

Mix thoroughly, pack in individual molds and freeze.

## FROZEN CUSTARD

| | |
|---|---|
| 1 pint thin cream | 1 pint whipped cream |
| 4 egg yolks, well-beaten | 1 teaspoonful pure vanilla extract |
| ½ cup sugar | |

Heat thin cream, pour over beaten egg yolks combined with sugar, and cook over hot water until smooth. Cool. Add whipped cream and vanilla. Freeze.

## FROZEN NUT PUDDING

| | |
|---|---|
| 1½ cups light cream (20%) | 2 tablespoonfuls chopped raisins |
| 3 egg yolks, beaten | 2 tablespoonfuls Calimyrna figs |
| ½ cup shredded almonds or pecans | (chopped) |
| ½ cup Tupelo honey | 2 tablespoonfuls chopped dates |
| ¼ cup almond paste | 1 cup heavy cream (40%) |

Scald light cream in double boiler. Pour slowly over egg yolks, beating constantly; return to double boiler and cook until smooth and slightly thickened. Add honey. Cool. Add almond paste. Freeze in trays to a mush. Use half the frozen mixture to line mold. Add whipped heavy cream, fruits and nuts to remaining frozen mixture and fill mold. Freeze.

## FRUIT BALLS

1 cup chopped dates        1 cup chopped figs
1 cup chopped raisins       1 cup chopped nuts
1 cup grated coconut

Mix raisins, dates, figs and nuts. Form into small balls and roll in coconut.

## FRUIT CRUMB PUDDING

½ pint cream      ½ pint water      3 egg yolks
1 pint toasted whole wheat bread crumbs
1½ cups steamed raisins, dates and figs

Warm the cream and water and to this add the bread crumbs. Allow this to stand while cutting the sweet fruit into small pieces. Mix with the bread crumbs and cream. Add the egg yolks and bake in moderate oven. Serve with whipped cream or hard sauce.

## SWEET FRUIT CUP

For individual serving:
½ large ripe banana, sliced     ¼ cup seedless raisins
2 tablespoonfuls fresh grated coconut

Place in layers in sherbet glass. Serve with cream if desired.

## GINGERBREAD WAFFLES

2 cups sifted unbleached or whole wheat flour
¾ teaspoonful baking soda      4 egg yolks
Pinch of salt        1 cup molasses
1½ teaspoonfuls ginger     ½ cup sour cream
¼ cup vegetable oil or melted butter

Sift dry ingredients together. Beat egg yolks as light as possible. Add molasses and beat until combined; add to flour alternately with cream, beating until smooth. Add fat and combine well. Waffles will be very tender. If large iron is used in baking, the waffles should be removed from the iron in quarters to prevent breaking.

## GRAHAM CRACKER ICE BOX CAKE

1 pint whipped cream     20 graham crackers

Spread top of a cracker with whipped cream. Repeat and place one on top of another until all are used. Place lengthwise on an oblong dish or platter and spread entire outside of brick with whipped cream. Cover and set in refrigerator for eight hours. When cold cut diagonally and serve.

## GRAHAM CRACKER PIE CRUST

2 cups crushed, sifted graham
   crackers
1 cup whole wheat flour
½ cup thinly sliced pecans
   (Do not chop or grind nuts)
¾ cup butter
Few drops ice water

Combine flour, cracker dust, nuts, and butter. Proceed as for regular pie crust. Have all ingredients as cold as possible, or this will be difficult to handle. Bake in plate from which it will be served.

## GRAPENUT ICE CREAM

Follow directions for vanilla ice cream adding ½ cup grapenuts, ½ cup chopped raisins and 1 teaspoonful rum flavoring when cream has been frozen to a mush.

## GRAPENUT PUDDING

⅓ cup grapenuts
1 cup water
1 cup cream
4 tablespoonfuls brown
   or raw sugar
2 egg yolks

Beat egg yolks until as light as possible. Combine with remaining ingredients. Poach until set. Serve cold. ¼ cup raisins or sliced dates may be added.

## HALLOW'EEN TAFFY

2 cups raw sugar
¼ cup unsulphured molasses
¼ cup water
¼ cup butter
2 teaspoonfuls vanilla

Boil until when tried in cold water, mixture will become brittle. When nearly done add butter and just before turning into pan, vanilla. When cool enough to handle, pull until the color lightens then cut in sticks with sharp scissors.

## HARD SAUCE

½ cup butter
1 cup powdered brown sugar
1 teaspoonful vanilla
⅛ teaspoonful nutmeg
Heavy cream, about ¼ cup

Cream the butter and beat until light. Add sugar gradually while beating. Add vanilla and nutmeg. Continue beating, adding a few drops of cream at a time until the mixture is soft. Chill in a square mold. Avoid freezing. Slice to serve.

## HOLIDAY PUDDING

2 cups fine whole wheat bread crumbs
⅓ cup whole wheat flour
2 teaspoonfuls tartaric acid baking powder
½ pound dried figs, chopped
1 cup raisins
½ cup chopped dates
¼ teaspoonful mace

1 teaspoonful finely shredded orange peel
1 cup raw or brown sugar
1 cup finely chopped beef suet
½ cup cream and water combined
4 egg yolks
½ teaspoonful cinnamon
½ teaspoonful cloves

Combine crumbs, flour, baking powder and spices. Work into these dry ingredients the suet, until evenly distributed. Combine egg yolks and liquid. Add this with fruits, peel and sugar to dry ingredients. Mix thoroughly. Steam in oiled pudding mold for 3 hours.

## HONEY CUSTARDS

1 cup cream
1 cup water
Pinch of salt

6 egg yolks, well beaten
¼ cup honey

Scald cream and water and add to egg yolks. Add honey and salt and cook over hot water until smooth, and no raw egg taste remains. Pour into frappé glasses and chill. Sprinkle with grated coconut.

## HONEY PUMPKIN PIE

1½ cups cooked, sieved pumpkin
1½ cups cream
3 egg yolks well beaten

1 cup honey
1 teaspoonful cinnamon

Mix ingredients in order given. Pour into unbaked, pastry shell. Place in hot oven for 15 minutes. Reduce heat to moderate and continue baking.

## HUCKLEBERRY PIE

3 cups huckleberries
2 tablespoonfuls unbleached flour
½ teaspoonful grated lemon rind

1 cup raw or brown sugar

Whole wheat or unbleached flour pastry

Line pie pan with pastry rolled about ¼ inch thick. Place berries in pastry shell and cover with mixture of sugar, flour and rind. Moisten edge of crust with cold water. Cover with pastry rolled ¼ inch thick. Bake in hot oven for 15 minutes, then reduce heat to moderate and continue baking.

## ICE CREAM PIES

Bake tart shells of unbleached or whole wheat pastry. Cool. When ready to serve fill with ice cream and top with whipped cream.

## MAPLE CANDY

1 lb. maple sugar          ¾ cup cream
1 tablespoonful butter

Boil slowly to spin a thread — ball stage — remove from fire — beat as for fudge.

## MAPLE FLUFF

4 egg yolks (beaten very light)     1 cup maple syrup (hot)
1 pint whipping cream

Add hot syrup to beaten egg yolks, beating constantly. Cook over hot water for a few minutes, until smooth and creamy. Cool while beating. When cold, add cream (whipped). Freeze in individual molds.

## MAPLE SOUFFLÉ

2 cups thin cream (half water may be used)
6 egg yolks, beaten light
½ cup maple sugar

Beat egg yolks as light as possible. Add scalded cream slowly with maple sugar. Poach in small buttered molds in moderate oven until soufflé is set. Serve cold.

## MAPLE WALNUT ICE CREAM

1 pint whipping cream          ¾ cup maple syrup
2 egg yolks                    1 cup chopped walnuts

Beat egg yolks. Add whipped cream, syrup and nuts that have been crisped in hot oven. Freeze mixture in refrigerator tray or use regular ice cream freezer. If ice cream freezer is used do not whip cream.

## MAPLE PECAN PIE

1 cup maple sugar or brown sugar     3 tablespoonfuls unbleached flour
2 tablespoonfuls butter              1 cup maple syrup
4 egg yolks, beaten light            1½ cups pecans, chopped coarsely

Cream the butter and sugar until very light. Add beaten egg yolks, flour and syrup. Beat until well blended. Stir in nuts. Pour into prepared raw crust, bake in moderately hot oven. Cool, top with whipped cream.

## MAPLE PRALINES

1½ cups sugar (raw or brown)        2 tablespoonfuls butter
1 cup maple syrup        ½ cup cream
1 cup pecans

Boil sugar, syrup, butter and cream until soft ball forms in cold water. Stir frequently while cooking. Let cool 20 minutes. Beat until creamy, add nuts and drop portions from tip of spoon onto buttered dish or waxed paper.


## MAPLE PUFF

1 cup maple syrup        3 egg yolks
½ cup cold water        ½ tablespoonful granulated gelatin
1 cup whipped cream

Heat maple syrup to boiling and pour slowly over the beaten egg yolks. Place over the fire and stir until the mixture is thickened. Add gelatin which has been soaked in cold water. Stir until dissolved. Cool until ready to congeal, then beat as light as possible and fold in whipped cream. Chill in mold.


## MOCHA MOUSSÉ

¾ cup strong prepared coffee or substitute
6 tablespoonfuls Tupelo honey        2 teaspoonfuls vanilla
1½ cups heavy cream (40%)        1 teaspoonful gelatin

Soften gelatin in ¼ cup beverage. Heat ½ cup beverage to boiling point and add softened gelatin. Stir until gelatin is dissolved. Add honey. Cool until mixture begins to congeal then beat as light as possible. Add cream, whipped, and vanilla. Freeze in tray without stirring.


## MOCHA PARFAIT

1 cup raw or brown sugar        ½ cup prepared coffee substitute
3 egg yolks, beaten until light        1 pint 40% cream

Cook sugar and coffee substitute until it thickens and will form a thread when dropped from a fork. Pour over beaten egg yolks; cook in double boiler until the mixture will coat a spoon. Chill, then add 1 teaspoonful of vanilla and beat until as light as possible. Add to cream which has been whipped. Freeze in tray or mold.

## MOCHA SPONGE PIE

1 baked pastry shell or tart shells
1 cup cereal beverage, double
   strength
1 cup whipping cream

1 tablespoonful gelatin
¼ cup cold water
4 egg yolks
1 cup raw or brown sugar

1 teaspoonful vanilla

Soak gelatin in cold water for 5 minutes. Beat egg yolks as light as possible, gradually beat in ½ cup of sugar, add liquid slowly. Place in double boiler and cook until thickened. Add softened gelatin and cook until gelatin is dissolved. Chill until mixture begins to thicken. Whip cream and add remaining sugar. Fold into gelatin mixture. Turn into baked pastry shell. Chill until firm. Garnish with nuts.

## MOLASSES PARFAIT

½ cup molasses heated to boiling point     1 well-beaten egg yolk
2 cups whipped cream

Pour molasses over egg yolk beating constantly. Cook over hot water until thickened. Cool and combine with cream. Freeze in mold.

## MOLASSES PUDDING

½ cup butter
1 cup baking molasses
1 cup cream and cereal beverage
   mixed
1½ cups stoned and chopped dates

2 cups whole wheat flour
1 cup sifted whole wheat or rye
   bread crumbs
1 teaspoonful baking soda
¼ teaspoonful each, cinnamon,
   nutmeg, clove, allspice

Cream butter, add molasses and liquid. Add dates with sifted dry ingredients. Steam in buttered mold. Serve with desired sauce.

## NOUGAT MOUSSE

6 cups cream
1 cup honey
⅔ cup chopped almonds

⅔ cup chopped pecans
⅔ cup chopped raisins
⅛ cup chopped dates

Whip cream. Add remaining ingredients. Freeze in tray or mold.

## NURSERY PUDDING

4 slices whole wheat bread, spread
   with creamed butter
¼ cup brown sugar

2 cups thin cream (half water may
   be used)
2 egg yolks

Arrange bread, sprinkle with sugar, in casserole. Blend egg and cream and pour over bread. Poach in moderate oven until firm. Serve cold.

## NUT BRITTLE

2 cups toasted nut meats      2 cups brown sugar
2 tablespoonfuls butter

Melt butter in heavy pan. Add sugar. Stir over moderate heat until sugar is melted. Pour over nuts that have been spread over a buttered platter. Break into uneven pieces when cold.

## NUT MEAL BREAD PUDDING

1 cup dried whole wheat bread crumbs
1 cup water                    1 cup cream
4 egg yolks                    1 tablespoonful butter
Grated rind of ½ lemon         ½ cup sliced raisins
½ cup nut meal

Combine bread crumbs, water, cream and beaten egg yolks, melted butter, lemon rind, raisins, and nut meal in the order named. Poach until firm and serve with whipped cream.

## PECAN PIE

4 egg yolks                    1 cup maple syrup
½ cup brown sugar              1 cup chopped pecans
2 tablespoonfuls butter

Line a pie plate with whole wheat pastry. Bake slightly and remove from oven. Beat eggs thoroughly and add sugar, butter and syrup. Pour into pie crust and bake in hot oven for 30 minutes. When it begins to set add the nuts and finish baking for 10 or 15 minutes in a moderate oven.

## PECAN MOUSSÉ

2 cups whipping cream          1 teaspoonful vanilla
1 cup chopped pecans
4 tablespoonfuls honey or ⅓ cup sugar

Whip cream, add nuts, honey and vanilla. Freeze in electric unit.

## PENUCHE

1 pound dark brown sugar       1 cup heavy cream
1 cup chopped nuts             ½ cup sliced raisins
¼ teaspoonful vanilla

Cook sugar and cream together till it forms a firm ball when tested in cold water. Cool, beat until creamy, add nuts and raisins. Pour into buttered pan. When firm, cut in squares.

## PERSIMMON PUDDING

1 cup persimmons (rubbed thru coarse sieve)
½ cup light brown sugar
4 tablespoonfuls creamed butter
3 egg yolks

1 cup cream
1 cup unbleached wheat flour
1 teaspoonful tartaric acid baking powder
¼ teaspoonful powdered mace

Beat sugar, butter, egg yolks and persimmon purée until as light as possible. Add cream, then flour sifted with baking powder and mace. Beat to blend thoroughly. Bake in individual buttered cups, or steam in tube mold. Serve with cream or desired sauce.

## PIE CRUST (*Plain Pastry*)

1 cup whole wheat or unbleached flour pastry    ⅓ cup butter
Few drops ice water

Have flour, as well as butter, ice cold. Cut butter into flour with pastry blender, until pieces are size of peas. Add sufficient ice water to combine and form into ball. (The least possible moisture should be added.) Roll to one-eighth inch thickness, place on inverted pie pan. Trim edges evenly. Prick with fork in several places to prevent bubbles. Bake in very hot oven, and watch carefully to prevent burning. Cool before filling. Double quantity for pie with top crust.

## POOR MAN'S PUDDING

¼ cup brown rice
1 cup 20% cream
⅓ cup raw or brown sugar

½ teaspoonful vanilla
Pinch of nutmeg
3 cups water

Combine all ingredients. Bake in slow oven until thickened and rice is tender. Stir frequently.

## POP CORN BALLS

1 cup honey
2 cups brown sugar

2 tablespoonfuls butter
4 quarts freshly popped corn

Cook honey and sugar until it forms crisp taffy when dropped into cold water. Add butter. Pour over corn and form into balls, using large wooden spoons (well buttered) for handling.

## PUMPKIN CUPS

1 pint sieved, cooked pumpkin
½ pint thin cream

¼ cup Tupelo honey
3 egg yolks

Combine all ingredients. Add a little nutmeg or cinnamon if desired. Poach in moderate oven.

## PUMPKIN PIE

2 cups cooked pumpkin, put through sieve
3 egg yolks                    1 cup raw or brown sugar
½ teaspoonful each, cinnamon, nutmeg and ginger (if desired)
2 cups light cream (20%)

Beat egg yolks as light as possible, add sugar, spices, pumpkin and beat to blend. Add cream and pour into pastry lined pie pan. Bake in hot oven for 15 minutes. Reduce heat to moderate and continue baking until filling is set. May be topped with whipped cream.

## RAISIN CARAMELS

2 cupfuls brown sugar                    ½ cupful chopped raisins
⅞ cupful thin cream                      1 teaspoonful vanilla

Combine sugar and cream and cook until the mixture forms a soft ball in cold water. Turn onto large platter, cool slightly and work with a wooden spoon or spatula until creamy. Add raisins and vanilla and spread evenly in a buttered pan. Cool and cut in cubes.

## RAISIN PIE

2 cups seeded raisins                    ⅓ cup brown or raw sugar
2 tablespoonfuls arrowroot or cornstarch

Cook raisins slowly in enough water to cover. Add cornstarch moistened with a little water. Continue cooking for 3 minutes. Remove from heat and add ½ teaspoonful grated orange or lemon rind or ¼ teaspoonful cinnamon. Pour into unbaked pie crust; cover with top crust. Bake in hot oven for 15 minutes, reduce heat to moderate and continue baking until crust is lightly browned.

## RAISIN TARTS

2 cups seeded raisins                    2 tablespoonfuls arrowroot
½ cup brown sugar                        Few drops orange extract or
                                         a pinch of ground cinnamon

Wash raisins, add enough water to cover them. Avoid an excess of water. Let soak one hour. Place over heat, bring to boiling point. Add a little water now if necessary to bring liquid to top of fruit. Mix sugar and arrowroot with a little cold water. Add to raisins, stirring constantly. Boil two minutes. Add flavor. Line muffin tins with pie crust. Fill with raisin mixture. A top crust may be added, or ¼ inch strips may be placed crosswise over top. Bake in hot oven until crust is crisp.

## RAISIN AND WALNUT ICE CREAM

1 cup heavy cream  
½ cup chopped raisins  

¼ cup chopped walnuts  
1 cup thin cream  

Beat heavy cream as light as possible. Add remaining ingredients and place in electric freezing unit. Stir two or three times while freezing, always from edge to center of tray.

## RICE BAVARIAN

½ cup brown rice  
3 cups cold water  
Pinch of nutmeg  

½ cup raw or brown sugar  
1 tablespoonful granulated gelatin  
½ teaspoonful vanilla extract  
1 cup whipping cream  

Cook rice with sugar in water, stirring frequently. Soak gelatin in 4 table-spoonfuls cold water, stir into hot rice mixture, and set aside to cool. When ready to congeal, add whipped cream, vanilla and nutmeg. Chill in individual molds.

## RICE IN COCONUT MILK

1 cup unpolished rice        2 cups coconut milk

Soak rice in coconut milk for several hours or until liquid is absorbed. Steam until tender. Serve with a little grated maple sugar.

## RICE WITH FIGS

Add ¼ cup sliced figs to each cup cooked rice. Steam for 20 minutes. May be served with cream or sauce.

## RICE PUDDING

2 cups steamed brown rice  
2 cups thin cream  
½ cup chopped dates  

½ cup chopped figs  
3 tablespoonfuls brown sugar  
Pinch cinnamon  

Mix all ingredients thoroughly. Bake in buttered casserole until lightly browned over top, and of right consistency.

## RUM BISQUE ICE CREAM

1 quart heavy cream, whipped  
2 tablespoonfuls rum flavoring  
½ cup shredded almonds  

¼ cup shredded candied orange peel  
½ cup powdered brown sugar  
¼ cup chopped raisins  

Combine ingredients, beat until very light and freeze in tray or mold.

## RYE PASTRY

¾ cup rye flour          ¼ cup butter
Ice water

Combine flour and butter with pastry mixer. Add ice water a few drops at a time. Roll out on cold board. Sufficient for one crust.


## SOUTHERN SUGAR PIE

Rub together 2 tablespoonfuls of fine whole wheat flour with 2 tablespoonfuls of softened butter, and stir into ½ pint of thin cream and ½ pint of water over the fire until the mixture boils. Add 1½ cups brown sugar, and when the sugar is dissolved stir in the beaten yolks of 5 eggs. Turn into a pie plate lined with whole wheat pastry and bake until the mixture is firm in the center.


## SOUR CREAM RAISIN PIE

1 cup chopped raisins
½ cup chopped walnuts or pecans
½ teaspoonful grated lemon rind
1 tablespoonful unbleached flour
1 cup sour cream
1 cup raw or brown sugar
4 egg yolks, beaten

Add sugar to egg yolks and beat until smooth. Stir in cream gradually. Combine flour with nuts and raisins. Combine egg mixture with flour mixture. Add lemon rind. Beat until smooth. Pour into unbaked pastry shell. Bake in hot oven for 15 minutes, then reduce heat to moderate, and continue baking until done.


## SQUASH CUPS

¾ cup mashed Hubbard squash
  (drained well)
4 tablespoonfuls maple syrup
1 tablespoonful butter
2 cups thin cream (one cup water
  used in cooking pumpkin may
  replace one cup cream)
4 egg yolks, beaten light
Few grains nutmeg

Add cream and maple syrup to eggs, mix well. Add melted butter, squash and spices. When well blended, pour into buttered ramekins and poach in moderate oven until set. Serve cold with cream or grated maple sugar.

Use this recipe for filling for squash or pumpkin pie. Pour into unbaked pie crust and bake in hot oven for ten minutes. Reduce heat to moderate and bake until firm in center.

## STEAMED DATE PUDDING

| | |
|---|---|
| 2 cups stoned, chopped dates | 2 egg yolks, well beaten |
| 1 cup raisins | 1 teaspoonful soda |
| ¼ cup brown sugar | Dash of cinnamon |
| ½ cup thin cream | Few grains nutmeg |

Enough whole wheat flour to thicken to consistency of loaf cake

Dissolve soda in cream. Add to egg yolks. Beat in sugar. Add spices and fruit. Mix with sufficient flour. Steam in buttered mold for three hours.

## STEAMED GRAHAM PUDDING

| | |
|---|---|
| 2 cups graham flour | 1 cup raisins or figs |
| ½ cup dark brown sugar | 1 teaspoonful cinnamon |
| ½ cup baking molasses | Pinch of salt |
| 1½ teaspoonfuls soda | 1¼ cups water |

3 egg yolks

Mix all ingredients and steam in buttered mold for three hours.

## STEWED DRIED FRUITS

Wash unsulphured, dried figs, pears or raisins. Cover with cold water. Soak until fruit has regained its original shape. Use only as much water as is necessary. Steam until tender. Tupelo honey may be added during steaming if desired. A little lemon rind will add flavor to raisins and pears.

## STUFFED DATES

1 pound dates, skinned and pitted
About 1 cup nut meats

Stuff nutmeats into dates. Roll in coconut.

## SWEET POTATO CUSTARD

| | |
|---|---|
| 1 cup mashed sweet potato | ¾ cup thin cream |
| 4 tablespoonfuls butter | 2 egg yolks, well beaten |

4 tablespoonfuls molasses or sugar

Beat butter into potato. Add molasses and egg yolks. Beat well. Add cream and when well blended pour into buttered baking dish, and poach in moderate oven until firm. This recipe may be used as filling for sweet potato pie. Pour into unbaked shell and bake in hot oven for ten minutes, reduce heat and bake until firm.

## SWEET POTATO ICE CREAM

1 cup thin cream
½ cup cooked sweet potato (put thru fine sieve)

1 cup whipping cream
½ cup honey or sugar
Pinch of mace or nutmeg

Beat potato, thin cream and honey as light as possible. Add double cream (whipped) and spice. Freeze in tray or mold.

## SWEET POTATO PIE

### Ingredients for Sweet Potato Custard

Combine all ingredients, and beat to blend. Pour into unbaked pie shell. Bake at high temperature for 15 minutes, reduce heat to moderate and continue baking.

## WHIPPED CREAM TARTS

Bake tart shells over muffin tins, using whole wheat or unbleached pastry. Cool and remove from pans. When ready to serve, cover bottom of shells with sliced banana and fill with sweetened whipped cream. Top with nut meats.

# CAKES AND COOKIES

### ALMOND UP-SIDE-DOWN CAKE

½ cup blanched almonds          ¾ cups brown sugar
1 tablespoonful butter

Cook butter and sugar until caramelized. Add enough water to reduce to thick syrup. Pour into buttered round cake pan. Add almonds. Pour any plain cake batter over. Bake in moderate oven. Turn out while hot on serving plate. Serve warm with cream, — plain, whipped or frozen.

### BANANA UPSIDEDOWN CAKE

¼ cup butter or vegetable shortening
¾ cup raw or brown sugar
1½ cups banana or potato flour
2 teaspoonfuls tartaric acid baking powder
⅓ cup water
2 egg yolks

Prepare batter from the above ingredients, beating the butter and sugar until light, then adding egg yolks. Add sifted flour and baking powder alternately with water, a little at a time.

2 tablespoonfuls butter          ¼ cup walnut meats
½ cup raw or brown sugar          3 ripe bananas, cut in thick slices

Melt butter in heavy pan. Add sugar, and stir until melted. Pour over nuts and sliced bananas arranged in a glass baking dish. Immediately pour in batter, and bake in moderate oven. Cool cake in dish in which it is baked. Turn out on platter to serve.
1½ cups steamed figs may be substituted for bananas.

### BLUEBERRY CAKE

2 cups sifted, unbleached flour          1 cup brown sugar
3 teaspoonfuls tartaric acid baking      ⅓ cup thin cream
    powder                                ⅓ cup water
⅓ cup butter or vegetable shortening     ¾ teaspoonful vanilla or
2 egg yolks, beaten light                ½ teaspoonful grated lemon rind

Cream shortening, add sugar gradually and continue beating. Add egg yolks. Add flavoring to liquids and add these alternately with sifted flour and baking powder. Put half the batter into small, deep cake pan. Cover with 1½ cups well drained blueberries. Add remaining batter. Bake in moderate oven about 50 minutes. Serve warm or cold, with cream if desired.

## BRAZIL NUT DAINTIES

½ cup butter or other fat
⅓ cup brown sugar
2 egg yolks

6 tablesp. ground Brazil nuts
3 tablespoonfuls honey
1 teaspoonful grated lemon rind

1 cup sifted rye or whole wheat flour

Beat creamed butter, sugar and egg yolks until light. Add ground nuts and all other ingredients except sliced nuts. Drop by teaspoonfuls on oiled baking sheet. Sprinkle with sliced nuts. Bake at moderately hot temperature.

## BROWNIES

4 egg yolks
5 tablespoonfuls vegetable oil
1 cup dark brown sugar
½ cup unbleached flour

½ teaspoonful tartaric acid baking powder
½ teaspoonful vanilla
½ cup chopped walnuts or pecans

2 ounces baking chocolate

Combine egg yolks, sugar and oil. Beat until light. Add melted chocolate and beat to blend. Sift flour and baking powder into chocolate mixture. Add vanilla and nuts. Bake in oiled square cake pan in moderate oven. Turn out on cooling rack and cut into one inch squares.

## BUTTERSCOTCH STRIPS

2 cups brown sugar
1½ cups unbleached, rye or whole wheat flour

8 egg yolks
2 teaspoonfuls baking powder
1 cup chopped nuts

Beat brown sugar and egg yolks together until as light as possible. Cook 20 minutes in top of double boiler, stirring constantly. Cool. Add flour and baking powder sifted together, then nuts. Spread ½ inch thick on oiled paper-lined baking pan. Bake in moderate oven about 20 minutes. Cut into strips. Roll in powdered brown sugar and cool.

## CARAMEL FIG CAKE

2 cups whole wheat flour, sifted
2 teaspoonfuls tartaric acid baking powder
2 egg yolks

1 cup brown sugar
¼ cup thin cream
¾ cup water
¼ cup melted butter

½ teaspoonful vanilla

Measure sifted flour and sift again with baking powder. Beat egg yolk, then add sugar and beat until creamy. Add flour alternately with the liquid, mixing until smooth. Add vanilla and melted butter, beating until the batter is smooth. Pour into oiled layer cake pans. Bake at moderate temperature. Spread fig filling between layers. Cover with caramel icing.

## FIG FILLING

½ pound Black Mission Figs          ⅓ cup brown sugar
1¼ cup boiling water

Mix ingredients in the order given and cook in a double boiler until thick enough to spread. Spread while hot. Figs may be chopped quickly by forcing through a meat chopper.

## CARAMEL ICING

1½ cups brown sugar          ¼ cup heavy cream
½ teaspoonful vanilla

Put sugar in a saucepan, add cream and stir until sugar is dissolved. Place over the fire and when mixture starts to boil, cook three minutes. Take from the fire at once, add butter, place saucepan in cold water and beat until creamy. Then add vanilla and spread on cake. Chopped walnuts may be added.

## CEREAL MACAROONS

1 cup sifted brown sugar          1 cup grated coconut (dried)
2 egg yolks          2 cups whole wheat flakes
½ teaspoonful vanilla extract          ½ cup chopped nuts

Beat egg yolks, adding sugar gradually, until very light. Fold in remaining ingredients. Drop by teaspoonfuls onto oiled baking sheet. Bake in moderate oven until lightly browned.

## CHOCOLATE CAKE

1½ cups brown sugar (pack hard to          4 egg yolks
    secure full measure)          4 squares baking chocolate
½ cup water          1 teaspoonful vanilla
1 cup thin cream          2 cups unbleached flour
½ cup butter          ¼ cup warm water
1 teaspoonful soda

Cook chocolate, 1 cup sugar and ½ cup cream over boiling water until thickened and smooth. Beat egg yolks, ½ cup sugar and butter to a light foam. Add vanilla. Add water and sifted flour a little at a time, beating constantly. Add cooled chocolate mixture, then soda dissolved in warm water. Bake in two buttered layer cake pans, in moderate oven.

## CHOCOLATE WAFERS

⅓ cup butter
1¼ cup brown sugar
4 egg yolks
3 squares chocolate melted
½ cup sour cream
1¾ cups flour (rye, whole wheat or unbleached)

1 teaspoonful tartaric acid baking soda
½ teaspoonful baking soda
½ teaspoonful vanilla
40 blanched almonds or walnut halves

Beat butter to cream, add sugar gradually, add beaten egg yolks. Stir in the melted chocolate. Add sour cream to first mixture alternately with all sifted dry ingredients and vanilla. Beat to combine well. Drop by teaspoonfuls on oiled baking sheet, place nut in center of each. Bake at moderate temperature.

## CINNAMON CAKE

2 cups whole wheat flour, sifted
2 teaspoonfuls tartaric acid baking powder
2 egg yolks
1 cup brown sugar

¼ cup thin cream
¾ cup water
¼ cup melted butter
½ teaspoonful vanilla
1 teaspoonful cinnamon

Measure sifted flour and sift again with baking powder. Beat egg yolk, then add sugar and beat until creamy. Mix flour with cinnamon and add alternately to the liquid, mixing until smooth. Add vanilla and melted butter, beating until the batter is smooth. Bake at moderate temperature.

## COCONUT DROPS

½ lb. butter
1 lb. brown sugar

½ cup baking molasses
1 lb. grated fresh coconut

Whole wheat flour

Combine butter, sugar and molasses. Beat vigorously. Add coconut and enough flour to make batter. Drop from spoon. Bake in moderate oven.

## CREAM CAKES

1 cup whipping cream
4 egg yolks
1½ cups brown sugar

2 cups flour (unbleached)
4 teaspoonfuls tartaric acid baking powder

1 teaspoonful vanilla

Whip the cream and egg yolks together until as light as possible. Add sugar and vanilla then flour sifted with baking powder. Bake in oiled muffin tins in moderate oven.

## DATE OR FIG CAKE

2 cups whole wheat flour, sifted
2 teaspoonfuls tartaric acid baking powder

| | |
|---|---|
| 2 egg yolks | ¾ cup water |
| 1 cup brown sugar | ¼ cup melted butter |
| ¼ cup thin cream | ½ teaspoonful vanilla |

½ to ¾ cup finely chopped dates or figs

Measure sifted flour and sift again with baking powder. Beat egg yolk, then add sugar and beat until creamy. Add flour alternately with the liquid, mixing until smooth. Add vanilla and the melted butter, beating until the batter is smooth, then add dates or figs. Bake at moderate temperature.

## DATE LOAF CAKE

| | |
|---|---|
| 2 cups pitted chopped dates | 4 squares baking chocolate |
| 2 cups dark brown sugar | ½ cup butter |
| (firmly packed) | 2 cups sifted unbleached flour |
| ½ cup thin cream | (half rye may be used) |
| 4 egg yolks (beaten) | 1½ teaspoonfuls baking soda |

½ teaspoonful ground cinnamon

Cover dates with one cup boiling water. Cook together cream, chocolate and one cup of the sugar until thick — about seven minutes. Beat together creamed butter and remaining cup of sugar until very light. Add beaten egg yolks and continue to beat until blended. Add flour and soda sifted with cinnamon. Combine chocolate and date mixture. Add to butter mixture. Beat three minutes. Bake in buttered loaf pan in moderate oven.

## DATE PINWHEELS

| | |
|---|---|
| 1 cup butter or other fat | 2 cups brown sugar |
| 6 egg yolks, beaten | 4 cups unbleached flour |

½ teaspoonful baking soda

Combine fat, sugar and egg yolks, beat until light. Add remaining ingredients. Chill. Divide dough into two parts. Roll each separately until less than ¼ inch in thickness. Spread each with date filling. Roll up like jelly roll. Chill over night or for several hours. Cut into slices ¼ inch thick. Bake on oiled baking sheet at moderate temperature.

## DATE FILLING

| | |
|---|---|
| 1 package dates (stoned) | ½ cup brown sugar |
| ½ cup chopped nuts | ½ cup water |

Cook together until thick.

## DATE SQUARES

¾ cup butter 1½ cups whole wheat flour
1 cup brown sugar 1½ cups oatmeal
4 teaspoonfuls tartaric acid baking powder

### FILLING

1 pound dates 1 cup water
1 cup brown sugar

Cook and have ready to combine with other mixture.

Cream butter, add sugar, add dry ingredients, mix and place half of the mixture on a baking sheet. Spread on the date filling. Crumb on the rest of the mixture and pat with a knife. Bake in moderate oven. Cut in squares or rectangular shapes.

## DATE WAFERS AND FILLING

2 cups whole wheat flour 1 cup brown sugar
2 cups oatmeal 2 teaspoonfuls tartaric acid
1 cup shortening baking powder
¼ cup water

Cream butter, add sugar. Mix and sift dry ingredients. Add flour and water alternately. Chill, then roll and cut with cutter. Place on baking sheet and bake in a moderate oven.

### FILLING

1 pound dates ½ cup sugar ¼ cup water

Boil together until thickened, when cookies are baked put together with filling.

## FRUIT CAKE

½ pound butter 1 cup unbleached or rye flour
½ teaspoonful cloves ½ pound sliced figs
½ pound raw or brown sugar 1 teaspoonful cinnamon
4 teaspoonfuls tartaric acid baking ½ pound dates
    powder ½ teaspoonful nutmeg
12 egg yolks, beaten ½ pound pecans, almonds or walnuts
½ pound raisins 1 tablespoonful grated lemon rind

Prepare fruits, dredge with flour and nutmeal in equal parts. Cream butter, add sugar and egg yolks. Beat until light. Add dry ingredients which have been sifted together. Stir in fruit and grated rind. Steam in casserole for three hours. Remove cover from casserole, cover with unglazed paper and bake in slow oven.

## FRUIT-NUT FILLING FOR COOKIES

⅓ cup chopped dates
⅓ cup chopped raisins
¾ cup raw or brown sugar

1 cup water
1 tablespoonful grated orange rind
½ cup sliced pecans

Combine all ingredients except nuts, and cook until thickened sufficiently to spread. Cool and add nuts.

## FRUIT AND NUT WAFERS

1 pound butter
2½ cups brown sugar
6 egg yolks
1 tablespoonful honey

1 teaspoonful vanilla
1 teaspoonful baking soda
7 cups whole wheat flour
1 cup seeded raisins

1 cup sliced nut meats

Combine butter and sugar. Beat until very light. Add beaten egg yolks, honey and vanilla. Sift flour and soda together and add to butter mixture. Work in raisins and nut meats. Form into rolls about 1½ inches in diameter and place in ice box to chill thoroughly. Slice about ¼ inch in thickness and bake in moderate oven.

## GINGER CUP CAKES

2 egg yolks
½ cup baking molasses
½ cup dark brown sugar
¼ cup butter
½ cup sour cream or whey

1 cup unbleached flour
¼ cup rye flour
1 teaspoonful ground cinnamon
1 teaspoonful ground ginger
1¼ teaspoonfuls baking soda

Beat egg yolks, molasses, sugar and butter together until light. Add sour cream or whey then dry ingredients sifted together. Beat to combine thoroughly. Bake in buttered cake cups.

## GINGER ICE BOX WAFERS

1 cup butter
2 cups brown sugar
4 egg yolks beaten

½ cup baking molasses
4½ cups rye or whole wheat flour
2 teaspoonfuls ginger

1 teaspoonful baking soda

Cream butter, add sugar gradually, add egg yolks and molasses. Beat thoroughly, add sifted dry ingredients. Shape into small rolls and place in refrigerator for several hours. Slice and bake on baking sheet at moderate temperature.

## GINGER LAYER CAKE

Prepare batter for ginger cup cakes. Bake in two layers. When cool put together with sliced ripe banana or caramel frosting between layers.

## GOLDEN BARS

⅔ cups butter or vegetable oil
2 cups brown sugar                    1 teaspoonful vanilla
4 egg yolks, well beaten              ¾ cups sliced English walnuts
1½ cups sifted whole wheat or unbleached flour
2 teaspoonfuls tartaric acid baking powder

Melt butter. Blend fat, sugar and egg yolks. Add remaining ingredients. Beat until thoroughly blended. Spread in shallow pan (12 x 8 inches) that has been lined with wax paper. Bake at moderate temperature. Cool. Cut into bars 1 x 3½ inches.

## GOLD CAKE

1 cup strained egg yolks              1 tablespoonful grated lemon rind
1 cup sifted light brown sugar        1 cup unbleached flour
Pinch of salt

Beat egg yolks as light as possible. Add 2 tablespoonfuls water, and lemon rind with sugar. Add flour and salt sifted together. Bake in tube pan.

## HONEY COOKIES

1 cup vegetable shortening or butter
1 cup honey                           1 teaspoonful baking soda
½ teaspoonful each, cinnamon, cloves and allspice
3¾ cups flour (whole wheat or unbleached)

Cook honey and butter together to boiling point. Cool. Sift flour, spices and soda together; add sufficient flour to make a soft dough (about 3¾ cupfuls). Form into thin rolls and chill thoroughly in ice box. Slice to bake.

## HONEY CREAM CAKES

1 cup honey                           2 cups sifted rye or unbleached flour
½ teaspoonful grated lemon rind       1 teaspoonful tartaric acid baking
1 cup sour heavy cream                   powder
4 egg yolks                           ½ teaspoonful baking soda

Combine flour, soda and baking powder, sift three times. Beat egg yolks until very light, gradually add honey then lemon rind. Add dry ingredients alternately with cream and beat until as light as possible. Bake in loaf pan at moderate temperature or in muffin tins for cup cakes.

## HONEY WAFERS

¼ cup water
2 cups brown sugar (packed)
1½ cups shortening
1 cup honey

⅓ cup egg yolks
1 teaspoonful baking soda
6 cups whole wheat flour
1 teaspoonful cinnamon

Heat sugar, shortening and honey in ¼ cup water, until melted. When cool, add egg yolks and flour mixed with soda and cinnamon. A half nut meat may be added to each cookie before baking. Bake in a moderate oven on oiled cookie sheet.

## HONEY WHEAT GERM COOKIES

¾ cup honey
¼ cup vegetable shortening or
    butter
2 egg yolks
½ teaspoonful baking soda

½ teaspoonful cloves
½ teaspoonful cinnamon
2¼ cups unbleached flour
1 cup wheat germ
1 cup raisins

Warm the honey and combine with shortening. Cool and add beaten egg yolks. Add dry ingredients and raisins. Beat until well blended. Drop from teaspoon onto oiled baking sheet and bake in moderate oven for the first three or four minutes, then reduce heat a little and continue baking.

## ICE BOX WAFERS

1 pound butter
1 pound brown sugar
6 egg yolks
1 tablespoonful honey

1 pinch salt
1 teaspoonful baking soda
7 cups whole wheat flour
1 cup sliced raisins

1 cup sliced nutmeats

Beat butter to cream, add sugar gradually, add beaten egg yolks, beat until very light. Add honey, vanilla, salt. Sift soda with flour and work into first mixture. Add raisins and nuts. Chill in refrigerator 6 to 8 hours before baking. Slice and bake at moderate temperature.

## LADY FINGERS

6 egg yolks                    10 tablespoonfuls powdered brown sugar
½ cup sifted unbleached flour    ½ teaspoonful vanilla extract

Beat egg yolks as light as possible, add sugar gradually, beating constantly. Fold in flour then add vanilla. Press through pastry tube onto oiled paper-lined baking sheet, making narrow strips about 3 inches in length. Dust with powdered brown sugar. Bake in moderate oven about 12 minutes.

## MAPLE CUP CAKES

2 cups maple syrup
¾ cup whipping cream
4 egg yolks

3 teaspoonfuls tartaric acid baking powder
Unbleached flour

Beat cream and egg yolks until very light. Add syrup. Add baking powder with one cup sifted flour. Beat to blend thoroughly, add sufficient flour to make a soft batter. Bake in buttered glass oven cups or muffin tins.

## MOLASSES ICE BOX COOKIES

1 cup butter
2 cups brown sugar
4 egg yolks
½ cup unsulphured molasses

4½ cups flour (whole wheat, unbleached or rye)
1½ teaspoonfuls ginger
1 teaspoonful baking soda

Beat butter and sugar until very light. Add egg yolks and molasses. Add sifted dry ingredients. Shape into small rolls. Place in ice box to chill thoroughly. Slice about ¼ inch thick and bake in moderate oven.

## NORWEGIAN PRESS COOKIES

1 cup butter
⅔ cup light brown sugar

3 egg yolks
2 and ¾ cups unbleached flour

2 teaspoonfuls almond extract

Cream the butter, add sugar gradually, beat in the egg yolks, then extract and flour. Put through cookie press on ungreased baking sheet. Bake at moderate temperature.

## NUT CAKES

2 cups whole wheat flour, sifted
2 teaspoonfuls tartaric acid baking powder
2 egg yolks
1 cup brown sugar
    ¼ cup cream
    ¾ cup water

¼ cup melted butter
½ teaspoonful vanilla

    ½ cup finely chopped walnuts, pecans or almonds

Measure sifted flour and sift again with baking powder. Beat egg yolk, then add sugar and beat until creamy. Add flour alternately with the liquid, mixing until smooth. Add vanilla and melted butter, beating until the batter is smooth, then add the nuts. Bake in oiled muffin tins or individual glass cups.

## NUTMEAL CUP CAKES

6 egg yolks
1 cup water
⅓ cup cream
1½ cups brown sugar

3 cups whole wheat (or unbleached) flour
Pinch of salt
½ teaspoonful soda

1½ cups English walnuts or pecans
6 teaspoonfuls tartaric acid baking powder

When measuring nuts shake down into cup so you will have full measure. Put nuts through fine blade of food chopper with ½ cup of the flour. This will absorb any oil expressed from nuts. Beat egg yolks as light as possible. Add cream, sugar, salt and soda. Continue beating. Add nutmeal, then water, and flour sifted with baking powder. Bake in buttered muffin tins. May be covered with Caramel Frosting.

## NUT MEAL SPICE COOKIES

1½ cups brown or raw sugar
6 egg yolks
½ teaspoonful cinnamon
1 tablespoonful hot water

½ cup butter or vegetable shortening
2 cups whole wheat or unbleached flour
1 teaspoonful baking soda
1 cup sliced dates

1 cup nut meal

Cream sugar and butter, add well beaten egg yolks, then add sifted flour and cinnamon; add soda dissolved in hot water, dates and nut meal. Mix to combine thoroughly. Drop from a teaspoon on buttered baking sheet. Bake at moderate temperature.

## OATMEAL ICE BOX COOKIES

2 cups dry oatmeal
2 cups whole wheat flour
1 teaspoonful soda
1 teaspoonful cinnamon
1 cup chopped nut meats

1 cup chopped dates or raisins
½ cup butter
1 cup brown sugar
4 beaten egg yolks
¼ cup cream

Beat butter and sugar, add egg yolks and cream. Add nuts and fruit with dry ingredients. Form into roll. Chill. Slice and bake in moderate oven.

## PECAN DROP COOKIES

2 cups sifted whole wheat or unbleached flour
2 teaspoonfuls tartaric acid baking powder
¾ cup chopped pecans

½ cup butter or vegetable shortening
1 cup raw or brown sugar
½ teaspoonful vanilla
2 egg yolks
¼ cup thin cream

Sift measured flour with baking powder. Cream shortening, add sugar gradually, beating smooth between each addition. Add beaten egg yolks, then cream. Add flour and nuts, add vanilla last. Drop by small spoonfuls onto buttered baking sheet. Bake in moderate oven.

## PECAN PUFFS

4 egg yolks
1 cup dark brown sugar
2 tablespoonfuls softened butter

1 cup finely chopped pecan meats
½ cup whole wheat flour
1 teaspoonful tartaric acid baking
    powder

Sift sugar, beat with butter and egg yolks until very light. Add nuts with sifted flour and baking powder. Beat until blended thoroughly. Drop from spoon. Bake on buttered cookie sheet in moderate oven.

## PECAN WAFERS

Roll rye pastry ¼ inch thick. Sprinkle with grated maple sugar and ground pecans. Cut into small rounds. Press ½ pecan into center of each round. Bake in moderate oven.

## POUND CAKE

1 pound sifted unbleached flour
1 tablespoonful tartaric acid baking
    powder
1 teaspoonful nutmeg
1 pound sifted light brown sugar

1 teaspoonful grated lemon rind
2 tablespoonfuls water
1 pound egg yolks, beaten as light
    as possible
15 ounces butter

Sift flour, baking powder and nutmeg together three times. Cream butter, add sugar gradually beating until smooth after each addition. Add lemon rind and water, beat to combine. Add beaten egg yolks and beat mixture as light as possible. Beat in flour. Bake in 2 small or 1 large loaf pan lined with heavy waxed paper. Keep temperature moderate. Will require about 1½ hours.

## PRESS COOKIES

1 cup butter
4 egg yolks
4½ cups unbleached flour
1 teaspoonful baking soda

2 cups brown sugar
½ cup baking molasses
2 teaspoonfuls ginger
1 pinch salt

Beat butter to cream, add sugar and beaten egg yolks, add molasses. Sift flour, ginger, salt and baking soda together and work into first mixture. Chill and put through cookie press. Bake at moderate temperature.

## QUICK COFFEE CAKE

2 cups whole wheat flour, sifted
2 teaspoonfuls tartaric acid baking powder

2 egg yolks                         ¾ cup water
1 cup brown sugar                   ¼ cup melted butter
¼ cup thin cream                    ½ teaspoonful vanilla

Measure sifted flour and sift again with baking powder. Beat egg yolk, then add sugar and beat until creamy. Add flour alternately with the liquid, mixing until smooth. Add vanilla and melted butter, beating until the batter is smooth. Pour batter into oiled shallow pan. Sprinkle top with brown sugar and cinnamon. Bake in hot oven. Cut in squares and serve.

## RAISIN CAKES

2 cups whole wheat flour, sifted
2½ teaspoonfuls tartaric acid baking powder

2 egg yolks                         ¾ cup water
1 cup brown sugar                   ¼ cup melted butter
¼ cup thin cream                    ½ teaspoonful vanilla
                1 cup raisins

Measure sifted flour and sift again with baking powder. Add raisins. Beat egg yolk, then add sugar and beat until creamy. Add flour and raisin mixture alternately with the liquid and melted butter, beating until the batter is smooth. Pour into oiled muffin tins (¾ full) and bake at moderate temperature.

## ROLLED SUGAR COOKIES

⅔ cup light brown sugar             2 cups unbleached flour
⅔ cup butter                        1½ teaspoonful tartaric acid
4 egg yolks well beaten                 baking powder
1 teaspoonful vanilla               Grated rind of ½ lemon

Cream butter, add sugar gradually, beat in egg yolks and vanilla then sifted dry ingredients. Chill the dough, roll out to ⅛ inch thickness, cut with cookie cutter, bake in moderate oven. Dust very lightly with cinnamon combined with powdered brown sugar.

## SPICE CRUNCH SQUARES

Bake batter for Ginger Cup Cakes in large flat sheets. Before placing in oven, sprinkle thickly with ground walnuts. Cover nuts thinly with grated maple sugar. Bake in moderate oven. Cut into squares before removing from pan.

## SPONGE CAKE

6 egg yolks
1 cup sifted light brown sugar
½ cup boiling water
1½ cups unbleached flour

2 teaspoonfuls tartaric acid baking
  powder
Grated rind of 1 lemon
½ teaspoonful lemon extract

Beat egg yolks until as light as possible with a rotary beater; add sugar gradually beating continuously. Add hot water slowly. Add flour sifted with baking powder. Combine as quickly as possible. Bake in moderate oven.

## WHIPPED CREAM CAKE

2 cups whole wheat flour, sifted
2 teaspoonfuls tartaric acid baking
  powder
2 egg yolks

1 cup brown sugar
¼ cup cream
¾ cup water
¼ cup melted butter

½ teaspoonful vanilla

Measure sifted flour and sift again with baking powder. Beat egg yolk, then add sugar and beat until creamy. Add flour alternately with the liquid, mixing until smooth. Add vanilla and melted butter, beating until the batter is smooth. Pour into 2 oiled layer cake pans and bake. When cool, spread whipped cream between layers and sprinkle top with brown sugar. For coconut cream cake, prepare same as cream cake adding shredded coconut to filling.

## WHOLE WHEAT COOKIE THINS

1 cup seeded raisins
1 cup dates
2 cups whole wheat flour
3 oz. butter

2 egg yolks
About ¾ cup sour cream and
¼ cup water
½ teaspoonful baking soda (scant)

Pit dates. Cut dates and raisins fine with wet scissors. Sift flour over dates and raisins and mix. Cream butter, then stir in unbeaten egg yolks and mix well. Add sour cream to which the baking soda has been added. Stir in dry ingredients. Drop by teaspoonfuls on a well buttered cookie sheet and do not place too close together. Bake in a moderate oven.

# BREAD

## ALMOND SWIRLS

Biscuit dough          Almond butter

Roll out biscuit dough about one-half inch thick. Keep edges even. Spread with almond butter. Roll up. Slice about one-half inch thick. Bake on floured baking sheet.

## BACON MUFFINS

| | |
|---|---|
| 1½ cups whole wheat flour | 3 tablespoonfuls brown sugar |
| ¼ cup cornmeal | 2 egg yolks, well beaten |
| Pinch of salt | ⅓ cup thin cream |
| 2 teaspoonfuls tartaric acid baking powder | ⅓ cup water |
| | 4 tablespoonfuls chopped, broiled, fat bacon |

Sift dry ingredients together. Add egg yolks, cream and water. Beat. Stir in crisp bacon.

Bake in buttered muffin tins, in moderate oven.

## BACON WAFFLES

Make batter for corn waffles. Have ready 1 cup chopped raw bacon. Sprinkle bacon over batter before closing waffle iron.

## BAKED BANANA TOAST

Butter thin slices of nut bread. Cover half the bread with sliced bananas. Place a buttered slice over bananas. Place in moderate oven or under broiling unit to brown lightly.

## BEATEN BISCUITS

1 quart flour (half whole wheat, half unbleached          ½ cup soft butter
Ice water

Sift flour. Work butter into flour with pastry mixer or knife blades. Add water, a few drops at a time, to make very stiff dough. Lay on biscuit block and beat with wooden mallet for one hour, turning over often. Roll out about one-half inch thick. Cut into small rounds. Prick top with fork. Bake on floured baking sheet. Hot oven for twenty minutes, reduce heat to moderate and continue baking until biscuits are light and well done.

## BISCUIT VARIATIONS

Basic recipe: All ingredients should be cold for best results.

2 cups unbleached, whole wheat or rye flour
4 teaspoonfuls tartaric acid baking powder
4 tablespoonfuls vegetable shortening or butter
¼ cup cream and ½ cup water

Sift together flour and baking powder, cut in shortening with pastry blender or silver knife, add liquids slowly and combine to make a soft dough. Turn out on floured board, knead very lightly until smooth, roll out about one-half inch thick, cut with floured biscuit cutter, bake in hot oven. This recipe makes 15 to 18 small biscuits.

### 1. ALMOND BRAIDS

Roll biscuit dough ¼ inch thick, cut into thin strips, braid closely. Cut into 3 inch pieces, sprinkle with brown sugar and chopped almonds. Bake as usual.

### 2. ORANGE SQUARES

Roll biscuit dough ½ inch thick, cut into small squares, sprinkle liberally with raw sugar combined with grated orange rind. Bake as usual.

### 3. FIG TURNOVERS

Roll biscuit dough ¼ inch thick, cut into rounds about 3 inches in diameter, place one half of a steamed or canned fig at one side of round, moisten edges with cream, turn over. Bake as usual.

### 4. BUTTERSCOTCH ROLL

Roll out dough ½ inch thick, spread with a mixture as follows: ⅓ cup butter, ¾ cup dark brown sugar and one cup of chopped nuts. Roll up like a jelly roll, moisten edges with cream, slice about ¾ inch thick, bake as usual.

### 5. HONEY BISCUITS

Roll dough about ½ inch thick, spread with honey and brown sugar combined in equal parts, sprinkle lightly with cinnamon, roll and slice.

### 6. STUFFED BISCUITS

Roll biscuit dough ¼ inch thick, cut in small rounds, moisten edges with cream. Place a spoonful of creamed chopped mushrooms in center of half the rounds, top with plain rounds, press edges together closely. Bake as usual.
*Note*: Cream sauce on mushrooms must be heavy to prevent sogginess.

## BRAN MUFFINS

1½ cups whole wheat flour
½ cup fine bran
1 tablespoonful tartaric acid
    baking powder
½ teaspoonful soda

4 tablespoonfuls brown sugar
2 egg yolks (beaten)
3 tablespoonfuls melted butter
1 cup whey

Combine egg yolks, sugar, butter. Beat thoroughly. Add whey, then dry ingredients. Bake in buttered muffin tins.

## BROWN RICE MUFFINS

Follow recipe for whole wheat muffins, substituting rice flour for unbleached flour, and 1 cup steamed brown rice for steamed whole wheat.

## CINNAMON BREAKFAST BREAD

1 lb. bread dough
2 tablespoonfuls soft butter

¼ cup sifted brown sugar
Cinnamon

Reserve dough when making bread. Roll about one-half inch thick. Spread with butter, sprinkle with sugar and cinnamon. Bake on buttered pan.

## CINNAMON TOAST

1 slice whole wheat bread    1 teaspoonful brown sugar
⅛ teaspoonful cinnamon

Toast bread. Spread with soft butter. Sprinkle with sugar and cinnamon well mixed. Place under broiler until sugar melts.

## COCONUT WAFFLES

Sprinkle grated coconut over batter before closing waffle iron.

## CORN BREAD MELBA

1 cup corn meal
½ teaspoonful vegetable salt

1 cup boiling water
3 tablespoonfuls melted butter

Mix corn meal and boiling water. Stir till smooth. Add salt and melted butter and stir again. Spread very thinly and evenly on flat pan. Bake in moderate oven. Cut in squares and serve hot.

## CORNMEAL PANCAKES

⅔ cup cornmeal
1¾ cups boiling water
1½ cups thin cream (part water
  may be used)
2 cups whole wheat flour

3 teaspoonfuls tartaric acid
  baking powder
Pinch salt
2 tablespoonfuls brown sugar
¼ cup melted butter

4 well-beaten egg yolks

Stir cornmeal into boiling water and cook rapidly for ten minutes. Stir constantly. Place in large bowl and add cream, mix well. Sift flour, baking powder, salt and sugar, and stir into cornmeal mixture. Add melted butter and egg yolks. Beat thoroughly. Cook on hot griddle. Serve with butter and maple syrup.

## CORN STICKS

Bake corn waffle batter in heated corn stick molds.

## CORN WAFFLES

1 cup corn meal
½ cup whole wheat flour
1 cup unbleached flour
3 tablespoonfuls tartaric acid
  baking powder

4 beaten egg yolks
1 cup thin cream
1½ cups water
¼ cup melted butter
¼ cup brown sugar

Sift dry ingredients together. Combine egg yolks, liquids, butter and sugar, add to dry materials. Beat to blend thoroughly. Bake as any waffle.

## CRACKED WHEAT BREAD

Toast one cupful whole grain wheat in a slow oven until crisp and very lightly browned. Grind in wheat mill or any fine grinder. Add to recipe for whole wheat bread, replacing an equal measure of flour when kneading first time.

## CREAM BISCUITS

4 cups whole wheat flour
Pinch of salt

4 teaspoonfuls tartaric acid baking
  powder

2 cups heavy cream

Sift dry ingredients together several times to blend. Add chilled cream. Roll to desired thickness on floured board. Cut in small rounds. Brush tops with slightly beaten egg yolk. Bake in moderately hot oven.

## DATE BREAD

1½ cups whole wheat flour
¼ cup brown sugar
1 cup chopped dates

1 teaspoonful soda
1 cup hot water
2 tablespoonfuls melted butter

2 egg yolks, well beaten

Mix dates, hot water and soda. Sift flour and sugar together, add to date mixture. Beat in butter and egg yolks. Turn into buttered loaf pan and bake in moderate oven.

## DATE MUFFINS

2 cups whole wheat flour
3 teaspoonfuls tartaric acid baking powder
½ cup water and ¼ cup thin cream
2 egg yolks

4 tablespoonfuls brown sugar
4 tablespoonfuls vegetable oil or melted butter
½ cup sliced dates sprinkled with flour

Beat the egg yolks, add sugar and beat until smooth. Sift the dry ingredients together and add alternately with the liquid, beat in the fat. Fold in the dates and bake in muffin tins or individual glass cups.

## EGG NOODLES

2 egg yolks
2 teaspoonfuls cold water

Pinch of salt
Whole wheat flour

Beat egg yolks and water. Add salt. Put through fine strainer. Add whole wheat flour in small amounts until no more will be taken up. Roll as thin as possible on floured board. Allow to dry for about one hour. Roll up and slice thinly. Shake noodles apart and leave to dry thoroughly. To cook, drop into large quantity boiling salted water and boil until tender. Drain in colander.

## ENGLISH CRUMPETS

1 cup boiling water
1 cup thin cream
½ teaspoonful salt

3 ounces butter, melted
½ yeast cake
2 cups whole wheat flour

1 cup rye flour

Combine cream and water. Soften yeast cake in ¼ cup of this liquid when slightly cooled. Add salt, butter, yeast and flour to cooled liquid. Beat thoroughly. Let rise in a warm place until very light. Place muffin rings on griddle. Pour batter into rings (half full) and bake. Turn frequently to prevent too much browning.

## FRIED NOODLES FOR CHOW MEIN

Brown drained noodles in butter.

## HONEY WHOLE WHEAT BREAD

| | |
|---|---|
| 6½ cups whole wheat flour | 2 tablespoonfuls honey |
| 1½ cups warm water | 2 tablespoonfuls vegetable oil |
| ½ cup thin cream |     or melted butter |

1 cake yeast

Add yeast to warm water and stir until smooth. Add honey and butter then cream which has been scalded and cooled to lukewarm. Add sifted flour until of the right consistency to knead. Knead well for 10 or 15 minutes. Let rise until doubled in bulk. Divide into 2 equal parts. Place in oiled loaf pans and allow to rise in warm place for 30 minutes. Bake in moderate oven.

## ICE BOX ROLLS

| | |
|---|---|
| 1 cake yeast | 1 cup smooth mashed potatoes |
| ½ cup warm water | 1 cup thin cream, warmed |
| ⅔ cup vegetable shortening or butter | 4 egg yolks |

¼ cup raw or brown sugar

6 - 8 cups unbleached or whole wheat flour

Add fat, sugar and egg yolks to mashed potatoes and beat until very light. Dissolve yeast in warm water, add to the warmed cream and combine with potato mixture. Add sifted flour to make a stiff dough. Knead on floured board. Place in large bowl and let rise until double in bulk. Knead slightly. Place in casserole, brush top with melted butter. Cover tightly and place in refrigerator. About 1 hour before baking time shape the dough into rolls as desired, cover and let rise until light (about 45 minutes). Bake in a rather hot oven.

## MAPLE SUGAR BISCUIT

| | |
|---|---|
| 1 cup whole wheat flour | 4 teaspoonfuls tartaric acid baking |
| 1 cup unbleached flour |     powder |
| ⅓ cup butter | ½ cup grated maple sugar |

About ¾ cup thin cream

Sift dry ingredients together with a little salt. Cut butter into flour. Add cold thin cream sufficient to make soft dough. Roll out thin on cold board. Spread one-half with soft butter and grated maple sugar. Turn plain half over and press together lightly. Cut into rounds, fingers or crescents. Bake in hot oven.

## MELBA TOAST

Cut ¼ inch slices from day old bread. Toast in moderate oven until crisp and lightly browned.

## NUT BREAD

3 cups whole wheat flour
3 tablespoonfuls tartaric acid
   baking powder
½ teaspoonful salt
½ cup brown sugar
1 cup thin cream

½ cup water
2 beaten egg yolks
½ cup dates or figs (chopped)
1 cup sliced pecans or
   butternuts

Sift flour, baking powder, salt and sugar together. Add cream, water and egg yolks with fruit and nuts. Bake in small round buttered molds in moderate oven.

## OATMEAL PANCAKES

1½ cups cooked oatmeal
½ cup unbleached flour
¾ cup thin cream
2 egg yolks (beaten)

1 tablespoonful melted butter
1 teaspoonful tartaric acid
   baking powder
2 tablespoonfuls brown sugar

Beat oatmeal and eggs until smooth. Add butter and sugar with cream. Beat in dry ingredients. Bake on hot griddle.

## ORANGE WAFFLES

Add grated rind of 1 orange to recipe for sour cream waffles.

## POPOVERS

1 cup sifted unbleached flour
Pinch of salt
1 cup liquid (half water—half cream)

4 egg yolks

Sift salt with flour. Combine egg yolks and liquid and gradually add flour, beating with rotary beater until well blended. Use heavy iron muffin pans or individual glass baking dishes; place these in oven while preheating to 450 degrees. Coat each cup with cooking oil and pour batter into hot cups,—about ⅓ full. Place immediately in very hot oven and bake for about twenty minutes; reduce heat to 350 degrees and continue baking until popovers are firm. Take care to avoid burning.

## PULLED BREAD

Cut crust from whole wheat bread, break apart in lumps, using fork. Place in moderate oven until crisp all through and lightly browned.

## QUICK NUT BREAD

2 egg yolks        2½ cups unbleached or whole wheat flour
½ cup thin cream and ½ cup water
1 tablespoonful vegetable oil or melted butter
3 teaspoonfuls tartaric acid baking powder
1 cup broken nut meats      4 tablespoonfuls brown or raw sugar

Beat egg yolks until light, add fat and liquid. Sift dry ingredients together, add nuts to the dry ingredients and combine them with the liquid mixture. Turn into an oiled loaf pan, bake about 1 hour.

## RAISIN BISCUITS

2 cups whole wheat flour      About ½ cup water
2 teaspoonfuls tartaric acid baking    ½ cup chopped raisins
    powder               3 tablespoonfuls butter
           Pinch salt

Sift flour baking powder and salt. Add butter by cutting into dry ingredients. Add raisins. Use enough water to make a soft dough. Roll to ½-inch thickness. Cut in small rounds or diamonds. Brush top of biscuits with cream. Bake in hot oven.

## RAISIN RING

1 lb. bread dough         1 tablespoonful lemon rind
1 cup seedless raisins       ½ cup shredded almonds

Roll bread dough into long strip. Spread with butter. Sprinkle with raisins and lemon rind. Fold over lengthwise. Twist and form into a ring. Brush with maple syrup, sprinkle with shredded almonds. Bake in moderate oven.

## RYE BREAD

1½ cups warm water       ½ teaspoonful salt
½ cup thin cream         1 cake yeast
3 tablespoonfuls raw or      3 tablespoonfuls butter
   brown sugar           Rye flour (about 6 cups)

Place liquids, salt, sugar and butter in large mixing bowl. Stir until butter is melted. Add crumbled yeast cake and 3 cups flour, and beat thoroughly. Gradually add enough flour to make a dough that can be handled. Turn out on floured pastry board; knead until smooth and elastic. Place dough in oiled bowl, brush top with oil, cover and let rise until doubled in bulk. Knead again. Place in oiled baking pans, brush tops of loaves with oil. Let stand until doubled in bulk. Bake in hot oven for twenty minutes then reduce heat to moderate and bake about 40 minutes longer. If desired, 1 tablespoonful caraway seeds may be added to dough at second kneading.

## RYE DROP MUFFINS

2 cups sour cream                    ¼ cup brown sugar
3 egg yolks                          1 teaspoonful soda
                    Pinch of salt

Beat cream, egg yolks, sugar and salt together. Add soda with one cup unbleached flour. Stir into batter enough rye flour to make soft dough. Bake in buttered glass oven cups.


## SCONES

2 cups unbleached flour              ¼ cup butter or vegetable
3 teaspoonfuls tartaric acid            shortening
   baking powder                     3 egg yolks
2 tablespoonfuls raw sugar           Cream, about ⅓ cup

Sift flour and baking powder together. Cut in butter as for pastry. Add egg yolks beaten with sugar and enough cream to make a soft dough. Roll out to ½ inch in thickness. Cut in tiny circles. Cook on griddle.


## SOUR CREAM WAFFLES

2 cups sifted unbleached flour, or whole wheat flour
1 teaspoonful baking soda                        Pinch of salt
        1 tablespoonful raw sugar or honey
4 egg yolks                          2 cups sour heavy cream

Sift flour with salt and soda. Combine beaten egg yolks with cream; add to flour and beat until smooth.


## SPICED MUFFINS

1 cup whole wheat flour              ½ teaspoonful ground ginger
½ cup rye flour                      3 egg yolks (beaten)
½ cup unbleached flour               ¼ cup baking molasses
3 teaspoonfuls tartaric acid baking  ¾ cup thin cream (part water may
   powder                               be used)
½ teaspoonful ground cinnamon        ¼ cup melted butter

Sift dry ingredients together. Beat remaining ingredients to blend, then combine mixtures. Beat for two minutes. Bake in buttered muffin pans. Dates or raisins may be added.

## SPINACH NOODLES

Follow formula for egg noodles, substituting 1 cup dehydrated, sifted spinach leaves for part of the flour.

## SPOON BREAD

⅓ cup granulated hominy
3 cups boiling water
Pinch of salt
3 tablespoonfuls butter, melted

¾ cup thin cream
6 egg yolks, well beaten
1½ cups corn flour
2 teaspoonfuls tartaric acid baking powder

Cook hominy in boiling water for thirty minutes, stirring frequently. Add salt, butter, eggs and cream. Sift corn flour with baking powder and add to batter. Beat thoroughly. Bake in buttered casserole in moderate oven. Serve with spoon while hot.

## STEAMED BROWN BREAD

2 cups corn meal
1 cup rye meal or flour
1 cup whole wheat flour
¼ cup molasses

Pinch of salt
½ tablespoonful cream of tartar
⅓ teaspoonful soda, dissolved in 1¼ cups cold water

Mix all ingredients thoroughly. Steam in buttered mold for four hours.

## SWEET POTATO BISCUITS

1 cup whole wheat flour
2 tablespoonfuls baking powder
Pinch of salt

¼ cup butter
1 cup mashed sweet potato
½ cup thin cream

Sift flour, salt and baking powder together. Cut butter into flour. Add potato and cream. Work until smooth. Roll on floured board, cut into very small rounds, press one-half pecan or walnut meat into each biscuit. Bake in hot oven.

## WAFFLE BISCUITS

Add cream to any biscuit recipe in sufficient quantity to produce consistency of waffle batter. Bake as any waffle.

## WALNUT ROLLS

1 lb. bread dough
1 cup chopped walnut meats
2 tablespoonfuls butter

4 tablespoonfuls brown sugar
1 tablespoonful whole wheat flour

Blend sugar and flour, cook smooth with ½ cup water. Add nuts. Roll out bread dough. Spread with nut mixture. Fold together and roll lightly. Cut into rounds or crescents. Spread lightly with butter. Bake in moderate oven.

## WHEAT GERM BISCUIT

2 cups unbleached flour
5 teaspoonfuls tartaric acid
baking powder
1 cup wheat germ

3 tablespoonfuls vegetable
shortening
⅞ cup liquid (half thin cream,
half water)

Roll to ¾ inch thickness. Bake in hot oven.

## WHOLE WHEAT BREAD

1 cup lukewarm water            1 cake yeast
2 cups whole wheat flour

Combine these ingredients and let stand twenty minutes in a warm place.

### *Add*:

1 cup warm water
¼ cup brown sugar
About 6 cups whole wheat flour

Pinch of salt
¼ cup melted butter

Dough should be soft. Knead thoroughly for five minutes. Cover and let rise until doubled in bulk. Knead again, shape into loaves and set in buttered pans to rise again. Bake in moderate oven.

## WHOLE WHEAT DATE MUFFINS

2 cups whole wheat flour
⅓ cup honey
¼ cup butter
¾ cup sour cream

1 teaspoonful soda
1 teaspoonful baking powder
½ lb. dates
2 egg yolks

Pinch of salt

Pit and chop dates. Sift baking powder into flour, beat egg yolks well, cream butter, add honey, salt and egg yolks. Mix cream and soda. Add to butter mixture. Fold in flour and dates. Bake in buttered muffin tins in moderate oven.

## WHOLE WHEAT GRIDDLE CAKES

2½ cups whole wheat flour      ½ cup 20% cream
5 teaspoonfuls tartaric acid      2 cups water
   baking powder      4 egg yolks
2 tablespoonfuls honey

Mix flour and baking powder, then stir in water, honey, and cream. Add egg yolks which have been well beaten. Mix thoroughly and bake on a hot griddle.

*Note*: If sour cream is used instead of sweet, use 2 teaspoonfuls baking powder and ¼ teaspoonful baking soda.

½ cornmeal and ½ whole wheat; or ½ buckwheat and ½ whole wheat may be used for variety.

## WHOLE WHEAT MUFFINS

1 cup steamed whole wheat      ¼ cup melted butter
1½ cups whole wheat flour      1¼ cups thin cream (part water
½ cup unbleached flour         may be used)
3 tablespoonfuls tartaric acid      2 egg yolks (beaten)
   baking powder      ¼ cup brown sugar

Combine sugar, eggs and butter. Add cream, then dry ingredients. Bake in buttered muffin tins.

## WHOLE WHEAT WAFFLES

2 cups whole wheat flour      4 egg yolks, beaten light
4 teaspoonfuls tartaric acid baking      1 cup thin cream
   powder      1 cup water
Pinch of salt      4 tablespoonfuls melted butter

Sift dry ingredients together three times. Combine egg, butter and a little cream. Add dry ingredients, and remaining liquid, a little at a time. Beat vigorously for two minutes. Bake in hot waffle iron.

## VEGETABLE PANCAKES

1½ cups grated raw carrot      ¾ teaspoonful vegetable salt
1 cup grated raw potato      ½ cup potato flour
1 tablespoonful onion juice      1 teaspoonful tartaric acid baking
¼ cup sieved cooked spinach         powder
2 egg yolks

Beat egg yolks until light. Combine with vegetables and salt. Add baking powder and salt sifted together. Bake on hot griddle.

# SANDWICHES

### BUTTERSCOTCH SANDWICHES

Cut bread into desired shapes. Spread with butterscotch filling and toast.

*Filling*:

| | |
|---|---|
| 1 cup brown sugar | ⅓ cup creamed butter |

Beat together until very light.

### CHOCOLATE SANDWICH

*Filling*:

| | |
|---|---|
| 1 cup thin cream | ½ cup brown sugar |
| 2 ounces baking chocolate | 2 egg yolks |

Heat cream to scalding point. Melt chocolate in double boiler. Beat egg yolks until very light, add sugar and beat smooth. Pour hot cream over egg and stir well. Add mixture to chocolate and continue cooking over hot water until smooth and thick, stirring constantly. Add a few drops vainlla. Cool.

Spread on graham crackers and put together for sandwiches.

### CLUB SANDWICH

| | |
|---|---|
| Whole wheat bread | Crisp fat bacon |
| Slices firm ripe tomato | Crisp lettuce |

Bread may be lightly toasted if desired; trim slices evenly. Allow three for each sandwich.

On bottom slice arrange tomato, and sprinkle lightly with vegetable salt. Butter center slice on both sides. Set on tomato. Cover with bacon and a leaf of lettuce. Arrange top slice.

### ROLLED SANDWICHES

Remove all crust from fresh whole wheat loaf. Slice thinly. Spread slices with sweet filling and roll up like jelly roll.

*Sweet Fillings*:

1. Walnuts — dates — whipped cream
2. Nut butter — figs
3. Honey — chopped nuts — minced celery

## SANDWICH FILLINGS

Cream cheese with:

| | | |
|---|---|---|
| olives | parsley | raisins |
| figs | vegetable paste | celery |
| dates | pimiento | green pepper |
| onion | crisp fat bacon | maple sugar |

Chopped hard boiled egg yolk with:

| | |
|---|---|
| sauted mushrooms | olives |
| celery and onion | bacon |

Crisp fat bacon with tomatoes or bananas
Avocado with chopped onion and celery
Almonds, walnuts or pecans with:

| | | |
|---|---|---|
| honey | figs | dates |
| cream cheese | raisins | bananas |

Butter, grated maple sugar
Ground figs, dates or raisins, whipped cream
Dates, celery
Walnuts, celery
Raisins, nuts
Tomato slices
Cucumber slices
Steamed green beans, almond dressing
Onion slices dipped in oil
Raisins, celery
Vegetable salad
Chopped dandelion
Lettuce
Cabbage
Cress
Any combination of raw greens
Hard boiled egg yolk, celery, almond dressing
Minced vegetables
Crisp, fat bacon
Scrambled egg yolks
Lettuce and tomato
Chopped ripe olives and lettuce
Chopped dates and ground coconut
Bananas and crisp fat broiled bacon
Banana, lettuce and nut butter
Dates and chopped pecans

## TEA SANDWICH

Cut crust from whole wheat loaf.  Slice lengthwise into three equal layers.
Spread bottom layer with mixture of ground figs, dates and whipped cream.
Set second slice over filling and spread with a layer of almond dressing.  Arrange
top slice.  Mask entire loaf with slightly sweetened whipped cream.  Sprinkle
with chopped almonds.  Chill thoroughly.  Slice crosswise to serve.

## VEGETABLE CLUB SANDWICH

Toast on one side, 3 thin slices of whole wheat bread.  Spread butter on
untoasted side and lay over each piece one slice onion, cucumber, green pepper
and tomato.

# SECTION FOUR
# Miscellaneous

THE Great American Burden of ill health is unquestionably caused by too much food, improperly chosen.

To keep physically fit, sufficient food must be supplied; but care must be exercised in selection of varieties and combinations of items. It is folly to pretend that even the most modern family submits to the formality of meal time merely to supply the necessary chemicals for body functioning. The homely pleasure derived from palatable food is very important to most people. The task of directing the family tastes and formation of food habits rests with the mother. She cannot be too well informed.

Breakfast is an entirely superfluous meal and could be discarded. If this seems too drastic, limit the breakfast menu to one of the suggestions given here, — page 464.

When an entirely vegetarian diet is being followed, luncheon should consist of a raw vegetable or fruit salad, with choice of one of the following:

1. Hot soup
2. Not more than 4 oz. shelled nuts
3. Cup custard

The evening meal may be any one of the luncheon or dinner menus containing a starchy food.

For the average healthy person, engaged in manual labor, a starch luncheon and protein dinner will be the best choice. Those living more sedentary lives will do much better to choose a light luncheon consisting of fruits and vegetables. Plan to alternate protein and starch menus for dinner service, keeping one day each week to a strictly vegetable diet.

Let moderation be your watchword and scientific combinations your aim.

# INDEX --- SECTION 4

## MELON RECIPES

## MISCELLANEOUS

# BREAKFAST SUGGESTIONS

| *For Alkaline Section* | *For Carbohydrate Section* |
|---|---|
| Acid Fruits | Corn Sticks |
| Baked Apple with Cream | Corn Waffles |
| Buttermilk | Crisp, Buttered Whole Wheat Toast |
| Canned Tomato Juice | Crisp Fat Bacon |
| Chilled Cooked Santa Clara Prunes in Orange Juice | Fresh Tomato Juice |
| Clabber Milk | Oatmeal Pancakes |
| Fresh Tomato Juice | Poached Egg Yolks on Hot Buttered Rice |
| Fruited Milkshake | Prepared Whole Rice Cereal with Sliced Banana and Cream |
| Grapefruit Juice | Sliced Bananas and Figs with Cream |
| Grapejuice | Steamed Raisins and Cream |
| Melons | Sunrise Waffles |
| Milk | Waffle Biscuits |
| Minted Pineapple Juice | Whole Wheat Muffins |
| Orange Juice | Whole Wheat Waffles |
| Steamed Raisins and Cream | |

## ALKALINE DINNER MENUS

### 1

Onion Soup

Strawberry and Grape Salad

Vegetable Timbales

Baked Beets          Sour Cabbage

Junket

### 2

Vegetable Bouillon

Grapefruit, Orange and Avocado Salad

Corn Chowder

Shredded Parsnips     Steamed Chard

Cherry Custard

### 3

Watercress Soup

Apple and Celery Salad

Alkalin Chops

Buttered Radishes     Steamed Spinach

Ambrosia

### 4

Clear Beet Soup

Pineapple and Citrus Fruit Salad

Tomato Cheese Souffle

Carrot and Lima          Steamed

Casserole          Broccoli

Sliced Peaches

### 5

Vegetable Soup

Beet and Apple Salad

Baked Eggplant

Steamed Brussels          Mashed

Sprouts          Salsify

Fruit Gelatin

### 6

Celery          Ripe Olives

Pepperpot Soup

Cress, Cabbage and Carrot Salad

Mushroom Omelette

Stewed Tomatoes          Steamed

and Celery          Okra

Apple Betty

## PROTEIN DINNER MENUS

### 1

Endive Soup
Mixed Greens Salad
Pot Roast of Beef
Steamed Onions    French Green Beans
Jewelled Jelly

### 4

Tomato and Okra Soup
Cabbage and Pineapple Salad
Stuffed Baked Mackerel
Steamed Peas    Steamed Rutabagas
Orange Ice

### 2

Cream of Tomato Soup
Shredded Vegetable Salad
Boned Roast Chicken
Steamed                         Mashed
Green Limas                 Parsnips
Mincemeat Apples

### 5

Vegetable Soup
Cauliflower and Cucumber Salad
Stuffed Shoulder of Lamb
Grilled Tomato        Creamed Carrots
Slices                    and Mushrooms
Peach Melba

### 3

Vegetable Bouillon
Hearts of Lettuce Salad
French Dressing
Chili Con Carne
Steamed Chard        Steamed Carrots
Fruit Cup

### 6

Fruit Cup
Radishes    Celery    Green Ripe Olives
Pepperpot Soup
Poinsetta Salad
Roast Turkey, Protein Bread Dressing
Baked        Steamed        Steamed
Parsnips    Sauerkraut    Asparagus
Plum Pudding
Nuts    Demi Tasse    Raisins
(coffee substitute)
Savories

## CARBOHYDRATE DINNER MENUS

### 1

Corn Soup

Asparagus Salad

Crisp Vegetable Loaf

Braised Celery Hearts    Steamed Kale

Butterscotch Pudding

### 2

Almond Soup

Beet and Celery Salad

Stuffed Baked Potatoes

Escalloped Cauliflower        Steamed

and Mushrooms            Peas

Raisins

### 3

Vegetable Soup

Shredded Vegetable Salad

Candied Carrots    Steamed Spinach

Eggplant Almano

Rice Pudding

### 4

Oyster Plant Soup

Cucumber Cup Salad

Egg Yolks, Melba

Shredded Beets    Steamed Baby Limas

Chocolate Cake

### 5

Celery Soup

Radish and Bean Salad

Nut Loaf

Creamed            Steamed Cabbage

Corn                Sections

Floating Island

### 6

Cream Cheese Balls    Black Olives

Fennel

Corn Soup

Porcupine Salad

Mashed Potato Nests with Vegetables

Creamed            Grilled

Asparagus            Onion Slices

Ice Cream

## ALKALINE LUNCHEON MENUS

### 1

Luncheon Soup

Pear and Cherry Salad

Vegetable Platter:

Steamed Broccoli

Baked Shredded Beets

Steamed Wax Beans

Coconut Cup Custard

### 4

Tomato Juice Cocktail

Cream Pineapple Salad

Baked Parsnips   Steamed Green Beans

Fruit Compote

### 2

Asparagus Soup

Orange and Prune Salad

Steamed Kohlrabi        Steamed Peas

Mocha Gelatin

### 5

Cream of Mushroom Soup

Strawberry and Grapefruit Salad

Steamed                          Baked

Brussels Sprouts        Sliced Carrots

Applesauce

### 3

Cream of Onion Soup

Grapefruit and Avocado Salad

Braised

Steamed Spinach        Celery Hearts

Fruit Cup

### 6

Jellied Vegetable Bouillon

Apple and Celery Salad

Baked Tomatoes                    Corn

filled with Okra            on the Cob

Junket

## PROTEIN LUNCHEON MENUS

### 1

Cream of Pea Soup

Tomato Aspic Salad

Baked Shad Roe

Braised Celery            Steamed

Hearts                    Chard

Strawberries

### 4

Vegetable Soup

Apricot Salad

Individual Omelettes

Steamed Kale            Baked Celeriac

Applesauce Cake

### 2

Onion Soup

Chicken Liver Salad

Steamed Asparagus    Steamed Carrots

Cherries

### 5

Cream of Tomato Soup

Sunnyside Salad

Grilled Sweetbreads

Broiled                    Steamed

Mushroom Caps          Green Beans

Raspberry Ice

### 3

Cucumber Soup

Pineapple Salad

Baked Ham with Fruit

Steamed Broccoli      Baked Parsnips

Fruit Compote

### 6

Almond Soup

Frozen Canned Fruit Salad

Panned Oysters

Steamed                    Steamed

Green Baby Limas          Turnips

Baked Stuffed Pear

## STARCH LUNCHEON MENUS

### 1

Celery Soup

Asparagus Salad

Vegetable Pastries

Braised Endive     Mashed Rutabagas

Broiled Dates

### 4

Cream of Broccoli Soup

Beet and Celery Salad

Stuffed Peppers with Rice

Steamed          Steamed Wax Beans

Leeks               with Parsley

Cup Custard

### 2

Lettuce Soup

Cucumber and Radish Salad

Escalloped Potatoes

Steamed Fennel     Baked Sliced Beets

Raisins

### 5

Cream Vegetable Soup

Shredded Vegetable Salad

Squash Cups with Peas

Steamed                    Steamed

Cauliflower                Asparagus

Figs

### 3

Watercress Soup

Lettuce and Tomato Salad

Macaroni with Walnuts

Steamed                    Baked

Cabbage Sections          Carrots

Fruit Balls

### 6

Malay Purée

Cress Salad

Banana Cutlets

Creamed                   Steamed Globe

Corn                      Artichokes

Ice Cream

## MENUS FOR SCHOOL LUNCHES

### ALKALINE

| 1 | 2 |
|---|---|
| *Cream of Asparagus Soup | Vegetable Bouillon Cubes |
| Apple and Celery Salad in Apple Cup | (to be dissolved in boiling water) |
| 2 ounces Almonds | Pineapple and Cream Cheese Salad |
| Tangerines | Pears        *Milk |

### PROTEIN

| 1 | 2 |
|---|---|
| *Hot Tomato Juice | Sliced Cooked Ham |
| Cold Chicken | Spinach Cup |
| Ripe Olives        Celery | *Strawberry and Pineapple Beverage |
| Fruit Gelatin | Peaches |

### STARCH

| 1 | 2 |
|---|---|
| Whole Wheat Macaroni Salad | *Vegetable Soup |
| Tomato        Celery Hearts | Hard Boiled Egg Yolk and Bacon |
| Cup Custard | Sandwiches |
| | Carrot Sticks        Lettuce |
| | Cookies |

* indicates thermos bottle

# SAVORY SEASONING

Select seasonings from those listed below, use in moderation (particularly spices), and blend carefully to produce delicacy of flavor. Here is the secret that marks the difference between novice and skilled artist in the first and last of all high arts, — cookery.

Almonds,
Anise
Bacon
Bay leaves
Butter
Capers
Caraway seed
Celery broth, *leaves, root, seed*
Chicory, *leaves, root*
Chives
Chocolate
Cinnamon
Cocoa
Coriander
Cress
Curry
Dill
Extracts of fruit flavors
Garlic
Honey — *Carbohydrate*
Horseradish
Kelp
Kimmel
Leeks
Lemon rind
Mace
Mint
Mushrooms
Mustard Greens
Nasturtium Seeds (*green*)
Non-alcoholic liquor and wine
    flavors
Nutmeg
Olives (*ripe*)
Onion

Orange Peel
Paprika
Parsley
Peppermint
Peppers (*sweet*)
Pimiento
Radish
Raisins and Juice
Rose Geranium leaves
Rose leaves
Rosewater
Sage
Shallots
Spearmint
Sugar, *brown, maple, raw*
    (*for Carbohydrate Section only*)
Summer Savory
Sweet basil
Sweet fennel
Sweet Marjoram
Tarragon
Thyme
Truffles
Turmeric
Vanilla, *bean, extract*
Vegetable broth
Vegetable salt
Watercress
Winter Savory

————

*Protein Section*
In addition to those listed above acid fruits and their juices are valuable sources of flavor for protein foods.

# HOME CANNING

Success in canning depends on four elements:

1. Packing as soon as products are gathered;

2. Processing sufficiently to kill bacteria;

3. Perfect sealing to exclude air;

4. Storage in cool, dry, ventilated shelves.

Gather fruits and vegetables when they have reached the perfect degree of ripening. Green or undeveloped products are hard to keep and never have a good flavor. Over-ripe specimens will become mushy and tasteless when canned. If possible have the food in the jar and ready to process within two hours from time it was picked. Pack only perfect products in the jar, reserving spotted pieces. These may be freed from bad parts and used to make boiling juice to cover fruit in jar. Wash thoroughly every food to be canned.

Time and temperature for processing vary according to size of jars used, density of packing, whether product is acid or non-acid. Use only glass jars with glass tops; the wire clamp type is best. For the family of four the quart size container seems most suitable. Enough liquid should be added to keep foods from becoming too tightly packed in the center of the jar, as this makes it difficult to heat sufficiently to destroy micro-organisms. When juice is acid, bacteria is more quickly killed by subjecting to boiling temperature. Non-acid vegetables require six hours at boiling temperature to free them from all bacteria. For this reason, we recommend that such vegetables be canned only by processing in pressure cooker. By this method a much higher temperature can be reached, thus requiring a shorter time for processing.

When processing is completed and each jar perfectly sealed, turn up-side-down for a few minutes to examine seal. Cool in a dry place where air can circulate between jars, but not in a direct draft, for this may cause breakage of jars and shrinkage of canned food. Examine each jar daily for a week before placing in regular storage.

Label all canned goods plainly. The storage shelves should be inspected, cleaned, and aired thoroughly before the new crop of vegetables is added. If the fruit cupboard is in the basement or cellar, be sure there is no dampness or earthy odor about. Storage space must be clean, cool, dry and dark. Inspect the canned food supply weekly. Constant light is an important factor in spoilage, and will cause deterioration in color, texture and finally in flavor of foods.

Examine jars carefully before opening. Rubbers should be in place, liquids clear, pieces whole. There should be no signs of leakage. If there is any unusual odor after can is opened the contents may be spoiled. When any appearance of spoilage is noticeable, discard the food; never taste such foods — serious illness might result.

Use neither salt, sugar, nor any other condiment or preservative. Sufficient heat for proper length of time will destroy all bacteria. Only by this method can the real flavor of foods be retained.

## DIRECTIONS FOR CANNING

The water-bath method of canning is best for home use, where no special equipment is available. Use as large a container for boiling water as can be heated, if a great many jars are to be handled. It is best to can fruits and vegetables as they become ripe, a few jars per day. A wire basket or tray that fits into the boiler is required to keep jars from coming in contact with metal bottom. When jars are in place, keep covered one inch over top with boiling water.

Use glass jars with glass lids, wire clamp fasteners. Always use NEW rubbers. Sterilize jars before filling by boiling in water.

The well-known "cold pack" method is satisfactory for fruits and tomatoes. Non-acid vegetables must be pre-cooked, *i.e.,* heated to boiling point before packing in jars. This shrinks vegetables by removing air and assists in thorough cooking in processing.

## FRUIT AND TOMATOES

Pack prepared foods into sterilized jars. Fill to within half inch of top with boiling juice made from selected parts of imperfect fruit. Add liquid carefully to prevent breaking jar. Boiling water is used with figs; with other fruits always use fruit juice if possible.

## TIME CHART

*(Pint or Quart Jars)*

| Fruit | Preparation | Process time in minutes |
|---|---|---|
| APPLES | Core, quarter, pack. Cover with boiling juice. Half seal. | 15 |
| APPLESAUCE | Pack hot. Fill jars to top. Seal completely. | 5 |
| APRICOTS | Cut in halves. Remove pits. Cover with boiling juice. Add one pit to each jar. Half seal. | 20 |
| BERRIES (except Strawberries) | Pack. Cover with boiling juice. Half seal. | 20 |
| CHERRIES | Pack. Cover with boiling juice. Half seal. | 25 |
| FIGS | Steam until tender. Pack. Cover with boiling water. Fill jars to top. Seal completely. | 30 |
| PEACHES | Follow directions for Apricots. | 25 |
| PEARS | Pare and heat to boiling point. Pack. Cover with boiling juice. Add ½ teaspoonful grated orange rind to each jar. Fill jars to top. Seal completely | 20 |
| PINEAPPLE | Pare, core, remove eyes. Slice. Pack. Cover with boiling juice. Half seal. | 30 |
| PLUMS | Prick skin with fork. Pack. Cover with boiling juice. Half seal. | 20 |
| STRAWBERRIES | Heat to boiling point. Pack. Cover with boiling juice. Fill jars to top. Seal completely. | 10 |
| TOMATOES | Scald, peel. Pack whole or cut, in jars. Cover with boiling juice. Half seal. | 45 |
| TOMATO JUICE | Heat to boiling point. Fill jars to top. Seal completely. | 5 |

*Note*: Time of processing given is sufficient at sea level and up to one thousand feet altitude. Boiling point of water is lower in higher altitudes, therefore 20 percent increase in time should be allowed for each additional 1000 feet. Count process time from moment water begins to boil vigorously.

## NON-ACID VEGETABLES

There is no assurance that bacteria can be destroyed in non-acid vegetables at boiling point unless this temperature is maintained steadily for six hours. These vegetables should, preferably, be processed in steam pressure cooker, in which case, follow the time table planned for the particular cooker used. If you wish, however, to attempt canning these foods by water-bath method, it will be necessary to pre-cook them. (See directions for preparation.)

Use hot, sterile jars. Fill *to top* with water in which vegetable is heated. (The cooking has expelled all air, thus making it unnecessary to allow any space in jar for expansion.) Seal jars completely. Process six hours, counting time from moment when water begins to boil vigorously.

## PREPARATION OF NON-ACID VEGETABLES FOR CANNING
### (*Pint or Quart Jars*)

| | |
|---|---|
| ASPARAGUS | Stand upright in kettle, ¾ cover with boiling water. Boil 3 minutes. Pack. Cover with cooking liquid, filling jars to top. Seal. |
| BABY LIMAS | Bring to boil in water to cover. Pack. Cover with cooking liquid, filling jars to top. Seal. |
| BEETS | Steam until skins will slip off. Pack. Cover with boiling water, filling jars to top. Seal. |
| CORN | Cut from cob. Add half weight of corn in water. Heat to boiling point. Pack, filling jars to top. Seal. |
| GREEN BEANS | Cut into 2-inch length. Cover with water. Boil five minutes. Pack. Fill jars to top with cooking liquid. Seal. |
| GREENS | Steam until wilted. Pack in own juice, filling jars to top. (Use boiling water with juice if necessary to prevent too dense packing.) Seal. |
| MUSHROOMS | Use small mushrooms. Clean, immerse in boiling water, using wire basket. Boil 4 minutes. Pack. Fill jars with *freshly boiled water* to top. Seal. |
| OKRA | Cover young tender okra pods with water. Bring to boil. Pack. Fill jars to top with cooking liquid. Seal. |
| PEAS | Follow directions for Baby Limas. |
| PUMPKIN | Cut pumpkin into 1-inch cubes. Steam until heated through. Pack. Cover with boiling water. Seal. |
| SQUASH | Follow directions for Pumpkin. |
| SWEET POTATOES | Steam until skins will slip off. Peel. Cut in slices. Pack. Cover with boiling water. Seal. |

# MELON RECIPES

Melons alone are good food, but have a somewhat tricky digestion; so that some people cannot safely combine them with other foods.

A good idea is to have a breakfast of all melon desired, and nothing else.

### ALL-MELON SALAD

1 cup watermelon balls
1 cup honey dew melon balls
White lettuce
2 cantaloupes
4 tablespoonfuls French dressing

Cut cantaloupes in halves and remove seeds. Pare carefully with sharp knife. Mix lightly the melon balls and French dressing and pile into cantaloupe cups. Serve on lettuce.

### AVOCADO AND CANTALOUPE SALAD

1½ cups marinated avocado balls        1½ cups cantaloupe balls

Combine and serve on endive with French dressing.

### CANTALOUPE CUPS

4 cantaloupe halves
1 cup grapefruit dice
1 cup cantaloupe balls
1 cup raspberries

Combine last three ingredients and pile into cantaloupe cups. Serve on beds of cracked ice.

### CANTALOUPE SALAD

2 cups cantaloupe balls
½ cup orange dice
½ cup sliced kumquats
Almond dressing

Combine salad ingredients with dressing and serve on lettuce. Garnish with strips of pimiento.

### CANTALOUPE SUNDAE

Fill halves of small cantaloupes with vanilla ice cream.

### CANTALOUPE WITH PEACH BALLS

2 cantaloups        1 cup balls cut from peaches

Fill cantaloupe halves with peach balls. Set in dish of cracked ice to serve.

## GRAPE AND CANTALOUPE SALAD

1 cup seeded white grapes     2 cups cantaloupe cubes
4 tablespoonfuls French dressing

Combine fruit with French dressing. Drain. Serve on lettuce.

## LEMON CANTALOUPE DESSERT

Prepare lemon gelatin as usual. When firm, break into uneven pieces with spoon, and pile high in center of halves of iced cantaloupe.

## MELON CUPS

1 heart of large watermelon     1 ripe cantaloupe

Cut four cubes, about three inches square, from watermelon heart. Hollow out to form boxes. Fill with balls cut from cantaloupe. Sprinkle with lemon juice.

## ORANGE AND MELON COCKTAIL

1 cup diced orange     1 cup melon balls

Arrange chilled fruit in iced cocktail glasses.

## TOMATO AND CANTALOUPE SALAD

4 thick slices tomato          2 tablespoonfuls chopped sweet
1 cup cantaloupe balls           green pepper

Place tomato slices on lettuce. Arrange cantaloupe balls on tomato. Sprinkle with olive oil. Garnish with chopped pepper.

## WATERMELON AND LIME DESSERT

2 cups lime gelatin          Watermelon

Prepare lime gelatin. When cold and firm, cut into cubes, and serve in baskets cut from iced watermelon.

# ALCOHOLIC AND OTHER STIMULATING BEVERAGES

The use of alcoholic or other stimulating beverages is not recommended, inasmuch as any stimulant drives the body at an accelerated speed that must result in a degree of enervation proportionate to intensity of energy expended. Less damage will be done, however, if the rules of compatability are followed carefully.

Malt beverages such as beer, porter and ale, may be served with carbohydrate or natural foods.

Dry wines should accompany only protein or alkalin menus.

Whiskies, gin and rum combine with one type of food as well as another.

Tea and coffee, while acid-forming, may be taken with any type of meal when served plain or with cream. Sugar may be added at carbohydrate or neutral meal. Tea may be accompanied by lemon if included in alkalin or protein menu.

Charged waters combine equally well with all classes of food.

Chocolate may be made with honey when served with alkalin meals.

## SUGGESTED BEVERAGES

### (Alkaline)

All fruit juices.
Cider.
Cooked or canned tomato juice.
Cooked or canned pineapple juice.
Cooked vegetable juice.
Coconut milk.
Herb teas.
Milk.
Pomegranate juice.
Raw pineapple juice.
Raw tomato juice.
Raw vegetable juice.
Soy bean milk.
Vegetable broth.

### (Carbyhydrate Section)

Cereal beverages.
Cooked vegetable juice
  (except tomato).

Coconut milk.
Herb teas.
Soy bean milk.
Raw tomato juice.
Raw vegetable juice.
Vegetable broth.

### (Protein Section)

All acid fruit juices (raw or canned).
Cider.
Clam juice.
Cooked or canned tomato juice.
Cooked vegetable juice.
Coconut milk.
Herb teas served without sugar.
Raw tomato juice.
Raw vegetable juice.
Soy bean milk.
Vegetable broth.

# VITAMIN CHART

| Name | Relative Designation | Solubility | Reaction to heat | Storage Qualifications |
|---|---|---|---|---|
| A* ........ | anti-infective | fat soluble | thermostable | Can be stored to an unusual extent |
| B ........ | This "vitamin complex" has been split into two separate classifications — B and G | | | |
| B 1 ........ | anti-neuritic | water soluble | thermolabile | Cannot be stored to any great extent |
| C ........ | anti-scorbutic | water soluble | thermolabile | Cannot be stored to any great extent |
| D* ........ | anti-rachitic | fat soluble | thermostable | Can be stored to an important extent |
| E ........ | anti-sterility | fat soluble | comparatively thermostable | Can be stored to a certain extent |
| G ........ | anti-pellagric | water soluble | comparatively thermostable | Cannot be stored to any great extent |

* Vitamins A and D are listed as thermostable. No vitamin is entirely resistant to heat. These classifications are necessarily relative.

# VITAMIN CHART (continued)

| Good Sources | Functions in Body | Deficiency Results in | Unclassified Characteristics |
|---|---|---|---|
| Cod liver oil, milk, dairy products, fruits, leafy vegetables. | Essential for growth, well-being and successful reproduction. | Physical weakness, lowered resistance and sterility. | Destruction due to oxidation (development of rancid condition) rather than to heat alone. |
| Yeast, whole grains, milk, fruits and vegetables. | Promotes appetite, digestion and lactation, protects body from nervous disorders. | Nervousness, fatigue, impairment of digestion, constipation, colitis. | Not much affected by low temperature, but deteriorates rapidly at high temperature. |
| Fruits (especially citrus varieties) & vegetables, sprouted grains. | Essential for growth, sound teeth, proper metabolism of bones. | Tooth decay, scurvy, loss of weight, pains and swelling in joints & limbs. | Heating in presence of air more destructive than when air is excluded. |
| Sunshine, cod liver oil, milk, egg yolks, irradiated foods. | Prevents rickets, regulates mineral metabolism of bones and teeth. | Rickets, tooth defects, general weakness. | The first vitamin to be synthesized, i.e., manufactured from a definite chemical compound. |
| Wheat-germ oil, lettuce, watercress, whole grains. | Essential for normal reproduction. | Sterility. | Both vitamins A and E are essential to reproduction. Lack of A causes failure in ovulation, lack of E results in failure of placental function. |
| Yeast, vegetables, glandular organs, lean meat, milk. | Prevents pellagra. | Pellagra. | Once thought to be identical with B, this vitamin is distinguished from it by having greater resistance to heat, and differs somewhat as to sources. |

# GENERAL INDEX

# GENERAL INDEX (*continued*)

# GENERAL INDEX (*continued*)

| RECIPE | PAGE |
|---|---|
| Corned Beef Hash | 246 |
| Corned Beef Loaf | 247 |
| Cornmeal Custard | 413 |
| Cornmeal Pancakes | 448 |
| Corn Pudding | 95, 289, 364 |
| Corn Soup | 45, 167, 337 |
| Corn Sticks | 448 |
| Corn Waffles | 448 |
| Cottage Cheese | 247 |
| Cottage Cheese Pancakes | 247 |
| Cottage Cheese Salad, Molded | 190 |
| Cottage Pudding | 414 |
| Country Club Salad | 176 |
| Country Potatoes | 365 |
| Crab Flake Cocktail | 153 |
| Crab Flake Salad | 191 |
| Crab Meat and Grapefruit Salad | 191 |
| Crab Meat in Cream | 247 |
| Crab Meat Rolls | 248 |
| Crab Salad | 191 |
| Crabs in Tomato Aspic | 248 |
| Crabs in Tomato Sauce | 248 |
| Crab Soup | 167 |
| Crabmeat-Shrimps | 160 |
| Cracked Wheat Bread | 448 |
| Cream Biscuits | 448 |
| Cream Cakes | 434 |
| Cream Cheese Balls | 160, 335 |
| Cream Cheese Dressing | 356 |
| Cream Cheese Salad | 190 |
| Creamed Asparagus | 110, 289, 390 |
| Creamed Asparagus with Rice | 365 |
| Creamed Cabbage | 110, 289, 390 |
| Creamed Cabbage and Peppers | 110, 289, 391 |
| Creamed Cabbage, Carrots and Mushrooms | 390 |
| Creamed Carrots and Mushrooms | 95, 289 |
| Creamed Corn and Peppers | 289, 365 |
| Creamed Leeks on Toast | 365 |
| Creamed Okra | 111, 391 |
| Creamed Onions | 111, 289, 391 |
| Creamed Onions and Turnips | 111, 290, 391 |
| Creamed Peas | 111, 290 |
| Creamed Peas on Toast | 365 |
| Creamed Rice Ring | 365 |
| Creamed Sea Food | 248 |
| Creamed Spinach | 111 |
| Creamed String Beans | 111, 290 |
| Creamed Sweetbreads | 249 |
| Creamed Terrapin | 249 |
| Creamed Turnips | 111, 290, 391 |
| Cream Filling for Pie | 414 |
| Cream Fruit Dressing | 85, 226 |
| Cream Mayonnaise Dressing | 85, 226 |
| Cream of Mushroom Soup | 46, 337 |
| Cream of Tomato Dressing | 86, 226 |
| Cream of Tomato Salad | 211 |
| Cream of Tomato Soup | 46, 167 |
| Cream Puffs | 414 |
| Cream Sauce | 401 |
| Cress | 335 |
| Cress and Cucumber Salad | 71, 212, 346 |
| Cress and Nut Salad | 70, 212, 346 |
| Cress and Tomato Salad | 70, 212, 346 |
| Cress, Cabbage and Carrot Salad | 70, 346 |
| Cress, Cabbage and Cucumber Salad | 71, 212, 346 |
| Cress Salad | 70, 212, 345 |
| Crisp Baked Bananas | 414 |
| Crisp Vegetable Loaf | 366 |
| Crown Roast of Lamb | 249 |
| Crumb Dressing | 401 |
| Cucumber and Apple Salad | 71, 213 |
| Cucumber and Tomato Salad | 71, 213, 347 |
| Cucumber Basket Salad | 71, 213, 347 |
| Cucumber Chicks | 290 |
| Cucumber Cocktail | 33, 153 |
| Cucumber Cubes | 160, 335 |
| Cucumber Cup Salad | 347 |
| Cucumber Jelly Salad | 213 |
| Cucumber Roll Salad | 213 |
| Cucumber Salad | 71, 212, 346 |
| Cucumber Sauce | 273 |
| Cucumber Slices | 160, 335 |
| Cucumber Soup | 46, 168, 337 |
| Curlique Salad | 191 |
| Currant Whip | 307 |
| Curried Cabbage | 95, 290, 391 |
| Curried Omelette | 249 |
| Curried Vegetables with Rice | 366 |
| Custard for Decorating | 120, 273 |
| Custard Garnish | 401 |
| Custard Ring with Vegetables | 290 |
| Custard Sauce | 120, 273, 307, 402 |
| Dandelion | 391 |
| Dandelion Salad | 72, 213, 347 |
| Dasheen | 392 |
| Date Bread | 449 |
| Date Custard | 415 |
| Date Filling | 435 |
| Date Ice Cream | 415 |
| Date Loaf Cake | 435 |
| Date Muffins | 449 |
| Date or Fig Cake | 435 |
| Date or Raisin Pudding | 416 |

[488]

# GENERAL INDEX (*continued*)